Beyond Punishment: Achieving International Criminal Justice

Also by Mark Findlay and Ralph Henham

TRANSFORMING INTERNATIONAL CRIMINAL JUSTICE: Retributive and Restorative Justice in the Trial Process

Beyond Punishment: Achieving International Criminal Justice

Mark Findlay
University of Sydney, Australia

and

Ralph Henham
Nottingham Trent University, UK

palgrave
macmillan

First published 2010 by
PALGRAVE MACMILLAN

Palgrave Macmillan in the UK is an imprint of Macmillan Publishers Limited, registered in England, company number 785998, of Houndmills, Basingstoke, Hampshire RG21 6XS.

Palgrave Macmillan in the US is a division of St Martin's Press LLC, 175 Fifth Avenue, New York, NY 10010.

Palgrave Macmillan is the global academic imprint of the above companies and has companies and representatives throughout the world.

Palgrave® and Macmillan® are registered trademarks in the United States, the United Kingdom, Europe and other countries

ISBN 978–0–230–22268–7 hardback

This book is printed on paper suitable for recycling and made from fully managed and sustained forest sources. Logging, pulping and manufacturing processes are expected to conform to the environmental regulations of the country of origin.

A catalogue record for this book is available from the British Library.

A catalog record for this book is available from the Library of Congress.

10 9 8 7 6 5 4 3 2 1
19 18 17 16 15 14 13 12 11 10

Printed and bound in Great Britain by
CPI Antony Rowe, Chippenham and Eastbourne

Contents

List of Figures

List of Abbreviations

ECHR	European Convention on Human Rights and Fundamental Freedoms
IACHR	Inter-American Commission on Human Rights
ICC	International Criminal Court (the Court)
ICCPR	International Covenant on Civil and Political Rights
ICJ	international criminal justice
ICTR	International Criminal Tribunal for Rwanda
ICTY	International Criminal Tribunal for the Former Yugoslavia
IHRL	international human rights legislation
INGO	international non-governmental organisation
NGO	non-governmental organisation
OAS	Organisation of American States
OECD	Organisation for Economic Cooperation and Development
OTP	Outreach Programme
RPE	Rules of Procedure and Evidence
UN	United Nations
VIS	victim impact statement
VOM	victim/offender mediation

Introduction

The purpose

With *Transforming International Criminal Justice* (Findlay and Henham, 2005) we were breaking new ground. The novel central assertion was that international criminal trial decision-making should be transformed to incorporate retributive and restorative justice processes and outcomes. Since then press commentary and scholarly analysis (Lipscomb, 2006) have challenged the International Criminal Court (ICC) to go beyond its conventional judicial enterprise and advance transitional justice. What was then a radical synthesis and future-seeking recognition for 'the ambition and scope of its intellectual gaze' (Mallinder, 2006: 157) is now being recognised as the inevitable option for the institutions of international criminal justice (ICJ), if their legitimacy and impact are to be confirmed.

The ICC has advanced its role in incorporating the prosecution and punishment of select and significant offenders who endanger humanity, and thereby promoting the peace and security of humankind. The Court's mandate emerges from the United Nation's (UN) Security Council and its standing from the laws and authority of member states. The ICC Statute claims for the Court a 'distinct nature',[1] determined by its expansive aims and differentiation from national courts.

Aligned with this distinction, the constituencies of international criminal law, as symbolically represented by the ICC, are victim communities of genocide and aggression in the most vulnerable states. This is why, in 2005, we nailed our colours to the mast in favour of victim community-centred justice by:

- impugning the relevance of retribution as the sole, or even primary, focus for international criminal justice;
- challenging the international trial process to be transformed in a way that recognises and ensures restorative justice paradigms with at least equal commitment;

- requiring ICJ to focus its attention on legitimate victim interests by enhancing access, inclusivity and integration of these interests within the protective framework of the trial process;
- seeking the reconciliation of victim community interests which are restorative and retributive as a responsibility of the juridical professionals who run international criminal trials;
- and thereby repositioning the role of international criminal justice away from sectarian political dominion, towards accountable and pluralist order maintenance and justice delivery (Findlay, 2008b).

Since then, what had been anticipated as a long-haul argument, engaging legal sceptics, individualist rights advocates, transitional justice marketers and restorative justice separatists has come to be accepted as a legitimate terrain for the progress of ICJ (Drumbl, 2005). Nevertheless, few if any fellow travellers or reluctant sympathisers have yet grappled with the metamorphosis of justice paradigms within a transformed international criminal trial. The materialisation of the synthesis of retributive and restorative justice within the transformed trial is no small test of the merit of the analysis that follows.

It is not just the communitarian constituency which is unique and therefore demanding in the development of ICJ. As the collective reality of global victimisation suggests, the jurisprudence of international criminal law must confront and confer new notions and determinations of criminal liability. Identifying generic crimes for prosecution is not enough. Liability itself needs to be creatively collectivised.

The treatment of joint criminal enterprise, command responsibility and superior orders by the war crimes tribunals and by the legal scholarship that supports their deliberations (Ambos, 2007) has been distinctly unimaginative in addressing this (see chapter 4). The inability to break free of the confines of individual liability when exercising even the retributive arm of ICJ, we suggest, stands in the way of the transformation we envisage.

The same will be said for restrictive interpretations of individualised rights as a responsibility for international criminal law (see chapter 4) (Daamgard, 2008). The Rome Statute,[2] when determining *individual responsibility*, states that the Court shall have jurisdiction 'over *natural persons* pursuant to this Statute'.[3] However, during an address to the second assembly of State Parties (Ocampo, 2006), the first Chief Prosecutor of the ICC, Louis Moreno Ocampo, declared the intention to locate responsibility for crimes of genocide, war crimes and crimes against humanity in Ituri (Democratic Republic of Congo) in a wider arc.

> Different armed groups have taken advantage of the situation of generalised violence and have engaged in the illegal exploitation of key mineral resources ... according to information received crimes reportedly committed in Ituri appear to be directly linked to the control of resource

extraction sites. Those who direct mining operations, sell diamonds or gold extracted in these conditions, launder the dirty money, or provide weapons could be authors of the crime, even if they are based in other countries.

No indictments have yet been laid by the ICC against corporations. Indeed, it has been argued (Eser, 2002: 77) that due to the significant evidentiary difficulties involved, and on the principle of complementarity (if corporate criminal liability is not recognised in many national legal orders), it would be inappropriate for the ICC to claim this jurisdiction.[4] Even as a mechanism for state reconstruction, the tendency to blame many for the crimes that are now sheeted back to the few may not simply or incrementally produce wider reconciliation and satisfaction among the affected populace. The causal by-products of individual and collective liability are as problematic at an international level as they are for state-based criminal justice.

The conflict resolution and peacemaking aims of the ICC, criticised by some as adventurous and inappropriate (see chapter 8), exert pressure for a transformed consideration of liability and responsibility within ICJ. The ICC Prosecutor has signalled an interest to investigate beyond the immediate territory of local and regional armed conflict, and to extend narrower notions of criminal responsibility which have been accepted by the ad hoc tribunals. These courts have preferred to debate the nature of joint criminal enterprise,[5] common purpose and accessorial liability in international criminal law rather than embracing more collective concepts of responsibility which are at the heart of vicarious and corporate liability.

The UN Special Court for Sierra Leone (SCSL) has also identified the illegal international trade in diamonds as central to the funding and motivation for conflict. In response, the UN Security Council[6] expressed 'its concern at the role played by the illicit trade in diamonds in fuelling the conflict in Sierra Leone' and directed that steps be taken by certain states to control the trade. Even so, the SCSL has not indicted any individual or organisation for trading in diamonds, which then financed further military conflict.

The nature of liability is just one challenge for transformation in practice. The recognition of collective liability for communitarian victimisation is also there. There is a need, rather than adapting and straining pre-existing concepts of liability and sanction, to develop a new jurisprudence for ICJ. A new normative framework for ICJ (chapter 1) leading to a reconceptualisation of victimisation as justice constituency (chapter 3) and a new engagement with truth and responsibility is at the heart of the exploration of justice transformation which follows.

This book takes up the challenge of:

- imagining new notions of liability for international criminal prosecutions in the context of truth and responsibility;

- identifying victim communities as a proper focus for international trial justice, with all the problems this may pose;
- constructing new roles for the juridical professional[7] in international criminal trials, to manage and monitor trial transformation and justice synthesis;
- suggesting how enhanced discretion and accountability in trial decision-making will achieve transformation, despite the trend in domestic justice environments to limit and diminish judicial discretion in particular;
- ensuring that the victim's voice is a significant influence over the selection and activation of trial resolution options;
- reconstructing the adversarial trial environment and wresting truth from fact and responsibility from liability in certain process formats;
- thus ensuring the place of ICJ in a regime of global governance which works for the restoration of victim communities as much as the reconstruction of state and political hegemony.

The analytic transition

This book builds on the methodology, theorising, arguments and outcomes of our earlier work (Findlay and Henham, 2005). It needs to be read against this background, although through grappling with the procedural requirements of a transformed international trial process, we have manipulated some of the broader themes explored in our earlier work, and for which the lack of definition was criticised. Further, our more detailed engagement with crime and global governance (Findlay, 2008b) and the internationalisation of sentencing and punishment (Henham, forthcoming) mean that these areas are not fully interrogated.

As already indicated, two themes central to our argument in *Transforming International Criminal Justice* have emerged as significant drivers for the debate about new forms of international court process. The identification of complex victim communities as the first constituencies for the ICC[8] has required recognition of various legitimate expectations for judicial intervention which go well beyond the determination of individual liability and the meting out of retributive justice. Also, the clear invocation for the ICC to adopt governance jurisdictions[9] and employ its functions for peacekeeping and state restoration makes a narrow interpretation of the purposes of international trial justice neither possible nor appropriate.

The case has been made for restorative international criminal justice (Roche, 2005). To this we advance the argument that for truth and reconciliation to move beyond the realm of alternative justice paradigms, and for its 'communities' (victims and perpetrators) to enjoy the rights and protections of more formal trial decision-making,[10] a synthesis of retributive and restorative trial options should be developed (Findlay and Henham, 2005: chapter 7). The 'sites' for transformation within the trial have been identified and the juridical personality proposed as the key to achieving change (chapters 6 and 8). Now the challenge is to bring about the transformation process.

Moving from theorising transformation to materialising the new justice form, it becomes apparent that the competing and complex legitimate expectations of victim communities (Albrecht et al., 2006) necessitated a fresh consideration of the normative framework for international criminal justice. Without this, some of the structural and procedural impediments to integration and synthesis within the current trial model would make transformation unlikely and even unattainable.

New normative framework

The argument that follows commences by linking normative and actual realities of ICJ, governed by *new moralities* that advance the legitimate interests of victim communities. These interests, particularly in conflict and post-conflict contexts, require a 'rights protection' focus if justice processes are to enable their realisation. Yet *rights to justice* are largely meaningless unless they can be enforced, and access to the institutional frameworks and decision-making they protect is crucial to the actuality of rights to justice. In an effort to provide a mechanism that better ensures the rights of victim communities within ICJ, this book is a manual for access, inclusivity and integration within trial decision-making, governed by interventionist and accountable judicial discretion. The primary determinants of when and how this discretion is directed will be a concern for *humanity* (rather than political dominion) and *coexistent rights protection* (individual and collective).

While never perfect, the enunciated and developing rights parameters within which the ICC will operate commend it as an appropriate institution for the major ICJ determinations.[11] At present the institutional protections of international criminal trials are reserved for the few and only meted out within a retributive context. The limited victim focus provides a wedge for reorienting the trial commitments of the ICC. The constitutional foundations of the ICC, released from the UN Security Council's power bloc, which mandates the international criminal tribunals, offer the possibility that the governance aspirations for ICJ will no longer advance political dominance. Instead, through trial transformation, the following rights will govern the instrumental capacity of ICJ:

- *Access to justice*, in the context of the international criminal trial, becomes both a right in itself and an assurance that trial rights will be activated. In the transformed trial it is access to a justice process that accommodates the sometimes paradoxical expectations of victim communities for protection and punishment, restoration and retribution.
- *Inclusivity* will dominate the operation of the transformed trial process. Legitimate victim interests – both individual and communitarian – will

become the driver for the exercise of judicial discretion and the measure of trial fairness.
- *Integration* will govern the manner in which professionalised justice is administered in order to ensure that the victim's voice will resound through trial deliberations and conflict resolution. Access, inclusivity and integration will be the measures against which the exercise of judicial discretion will be determined as protecting rights and humanity.

The features of the *new morality* will underpin the transformed trial, informing the delivery of ICJ through the protective rights environment of synthesised trial decision-making.[12] It includes:

- *The moral focus on the justice process as a 'good'.* Conceiving ICJ in these terms emanates from the acceptance that conflict, and its resolution, are intrinsic to the human condition. That said, ICJ, and the trial process in particular, has a distinct governance function, which, when exercised intrinsically and inclusively, brings peace out of conflict. Justice structures for conflict resolution are therefore concerned with restoring the relationships of community essential for human life, particularly in victim communities with a clear investment in justice outcomes, or, at the very least, enabling that potential in humanity to be realised. The emphasis on communitarian as well as individual rights protection will require that governance is for the many and not just the few. Humanity will replace dominant political hegemonies as the sponsor of governance. Conflict resolution will promote civil society rather than the exclusion that political dominion and criminalisation alone require.
- *This new morality returns to our concerns with relationships (pathways of influence) as they inform justice decision-making* (Findlay and Henham, 2005: chapter 7). The context of international community[13] relationships governed by morality requires the normative framework to be dynamic, inclusive and representative of the legitimate interests at work across a relationship. International justice resolutions find the parties to a decision relationship rarely limited to individual players. Communities of victims and offenders are drawn together within the justice enterprise. Therefore, the negotiation of liability, and the restoration from harm caused involve collective behaviours and mutual obligation. This paradigm we have identified as *communities of justice* (Findlay and Henham, 2005: chapters 3 and 8).
- *The new morality is focused on 'humanitarianism' (commensurate with the legislative 'crimes against humanity').* Humanity involves people and purpose. Humanity is citizens and excluded communities. Humanity is an invocation to be humane. Humanity is essentially innocent in the context of conflict. Humanity is essentially victimised (in the widest sense) in terms of crimes against humanity. In employing the word humanity here we

are not talking about 'images' of humanity, such as the *global community*, which predominate in the language of retributive ICJ. The new morality is not satisfied by symbolic rights delivery. Rights are a real service available to protect and promote humanity. The relationships which govern and manage *communities of justice* are in essence humanitarian, within this new morality; if not, they are not justice.

- *The normative framework for the new morality is concerned to elaborate on the principles of 'humanity'*, and what sets these apart from the inhumanity of crime and conflict, as the *justice* essence of international criminal justice. The framework espouses *engagement with (and within) humanity* rather than being limited by the scope of jurisdiction or legal dominion, which makes ICJ 'international'.
- *Communities of justice, therefore, are concerned with collective liability and communitarian reintegration more than the individualised rights and responsibilities of conventional criminal justice models.* This is not to suggest that the individuality of crime and justice must be sacrificed within a communitarian morality. In reality, individual criminal justice will not break free from traditions of individual liability (Norrie, 2001). Individualism, however, is subsidiary to, or coexistent with, the focus on humanity for crimes which justify international criminal law. The justice which supports this legality must also prioritise the word humanity over the individual.
- *Humanitarian justice links to an important victim focus for justice.* Victim communities are the 'communities of innocence' which necessitate justice intervention. They provide the structures of citizenship and sovereignty which legitimate ICJ.[14] In advancing justice as the protector of humanity we make no judgement about human actions outside criminal responsibility or otherwise. Yet in order to distinguish ICJ from determining liability alone, we suggest that the peaceful resolution of conflicting actions is good and that our vision of the international criminal process takes this forward by reconciling the interests of innocent communities.
- *Both in determining liability on behalf of humanity and the peacemaking which should flow from this, the importance of 'truth' within new moralities of ICJ cannot be understated.* While a punishment focus is recognised in prevailing retributive justice paradigms,[15] transformed ICJ is liberated from it for the purposes of conflict resolution. Retributive justice works with questions of evidence and fact, whereas transformed trial decision-making needs to determine truth as a foundation for responsibility and resolution. Truth and morality are conflated by virtue of our conceptualisation of criminal process as a *good*.
- *Therefore, legitimate outcomes for transformed ICJ (through new moralities) are both within and beyond punishment paradigms.* Punishment need not lose its presence but will not remain the only or predominant justice outcome. Restoration and conflict resolution through the determination of truth and responsibility will be on a par with punishment as indicia of justice.

- Along with victim focus for ICJ is the recognition that 'humanitarian' justice is inclusive and not just retributive justice which can be exclusive and imposed. The new morality is a recognition that all forms of justice are open to abuse if they do not allow for truth to emerge rather than merely the case to be proved.
- *The new moralities of justice determine the nature and coexistence of current alternative ICJ paradigms for the benefit of legitimate victim community interests.* On the strength of our earlier arguments, if ICJ is to satisfy legitimate victim interests, it must be tolerant (in its transformed state) of restorative and retributive justice processes and determinations. This will mean that legitimate victim interests can have the widest range of opportunities for resolution and attainment.[16]
- *Humanitarian justice, as a 'good', is directed towards restoring and strengthening those relationships essential for resolving conflict.* Therefore, such justice is inclusive rather than symbolic and declaratory. ICJ, based on a new morality, can exhibit both retribution and restoration when either is determined as the appropriate outcome of a finding as to 'truth'.
- *The outcomes of 'humanitarian' justice are multipurpose in order to reflect competing legitimate victim interests.* These complex interests need to be essentially addressed and mediated through judicial discretion if justice is to be effective in dispute resolution. If humanity is the focus of international criminal law, then legitimate victim interests will be the driver for ICJ.
- *How do we recognise the legitimacy of interests?* Our argument is that transformed international criminal process provides the rationale and the structure for the determination of 'truth' which objectifies the legitimacy of particular interests. By being moral rather than essentially legal, 'truth' is legitimised as justice and provides the key to the peaceful resolution of conflict. The transformed trial may provide the forum for making victim interests accountable to the determination of truth and the awarding of responsibility.
- *'Humanitarian' justice, while apolitical, recognises the 'governance' imperatives of ICJ as they presently operate, particularly in the production of hybrid institutions and processes, as well as the relegation of a vast array of disputes to lower-order alternative justice paradigms.* Consistent with the victim as humanity and the advancing of humanitarian interests, dispute resolution and peacemaking will emerge as natural by-products of restorative justice outcomes for ICJ. In addition, peacemaking will be an aim in itself and a legitimator for ICJ without necessarily advancing political dominion.
- *Humanitarian justice, while countering the overt and excessive utilitarian purposes for retributive justice, is interested in connecting realities which identify and create disputes for innocent victim communities.* Where retributive justice tends to 'patch up' disputes through symbolic overlay, the moralities of

humanitarian justice require engagement and inclusion along the way to dispute resolution.

Transformed ICJ rejects consensus achieved or imposed through a dominance (and dependency) model of governance (Findlay, 2008b). The 'new moralities' for ICJ detailed in this book envisage strategic interventions whereby 'truth' is established and its consequences negotiated in order to satisfy as many *legitimate expectations* of victim communities that the trial process in particular can accommodate. In this way legitimacy is enhanced and governance strengthened through the reconciliatory potentials of ICJ.

Having enunciated a new morality for international criminal justice, which will complement the constituency of victim communities, it is now necessary to give life to these entities.

Imagining victim communities

The Chief Prosecutor for the ICC recognises the importance of the victim voice in ICJ. In so doing, Moreno Ocampo has declared that victim communities, with which the Court has a crucial interest, may deserve justice and compensation. How this is to be achieved within the formalist institutions of the ICC as presently constituted, and in the environment of retributive justice, is a challenge, which the Prosecutor openly acknowledges (Ocampo, 2007). Therefore, *victim's justice* will provoke tensions within the delivery of ICJ services and on to global governance. Since the late 1800s in western justice processes, the state has gradually assumed a monopoly over the prosecution of criminal offences. This monopoly has been transferred with little question through victorious military alliances, and representative international organisation, to ICJ, despite the ambiguity of state authority in global governance. Victim interests, in a community context in particular, face the danger of marginalisation within the wider play of retributive justice. At a symbolic level, the prosecution of global criminals has taken centre-stage, with victims assuming a minor role as witnesses or an audience to which the trial decisions are broadcast. These movements make it easy to forget that victims' interests grounded in commonly held communitarian values were the foundation for prosecuting criminalised behaviour in all western liberal systems of criminal justice.

Under *neoliberal* versions of justice which concentrate on autonomy and individual liability, the place of the victim in trial and punishment recently has been rehabilitated to some extent. This has led to critical reflections on the purpose of retributive justice and the extent to which harm should drive the determination of sanction (Erez and Rogers, 1999). The victim's voice, through victim impact statements, is given at least normative presence in the sentencing process. How this injection of victim discourse sits with the protected interests of the accused persons remains unsettled in adversarial trials, and is not much more clearly resolved in the legislative instruments of ICJ.

Some criminal justice traditions, such as in Italy and Russia, provide the victim the right of separate representation and thereby an active role in eliciting and testing evidence that may be crucial to questions of liability and sentence. In England and Wales, too, these possibilities are now being seriously studied for a common law context.[17] Of the international criminal institutions, the ICC in particular has accommodations for victim interest within and outside the trial (see further chapter 6).There is a special bureau of the court administration dedicated to victim concerns. Although the victim's voice in ICC trials is limited to very few contexts of advocacy, concerns to communicate the Court's deliberations to the victim community are highlighted in ICC procedural provisions (Mekjian and Varughese, 2005).

The UN war crimes tribunals have a varied engagement record with victims. As such the legitimacy accorded to tribunal justice, where it is grounded in community consensus and acceptance, is dislocated and specific. One of the reasons that the Rwanda Tribunal, for example, has held its hearings almost entirely outside Rwanda is concern that the people of that conflict-ridden state would not welcome its presence. The International Criminal Tribunal for the Former Yugoslavia (ICTY) prides itself on its victim outreach. However, Milanovic (2007) doubts whether any move from this tribunal to a transitional justice-style outreach has or will be effective in connecting with communities. He is concerned, as was demonstrated by ICJ action between Bosnia and Serbia, to determine who had committed genocide and when, that these central questions of responsibility lose touch with victim communities. Milanovic suggests that it is time for mediation rather than persisting with *show trials* and resultant superficial outreach endeavours.

Even where there have been genuine attempts at victim engagement by the formal institutions and processes of ICJ, this is made more difficult by limitations in *imagining* the victims of genocide and crimes against humanity. Where the crimes in question are generic and encompassing, their victims will be communities, and the community of victims will be comprised by a variety of victimisation contexts.

Tribunal justice focuses on the individual liability of one or several accused. Collective liability is narrowly interpreted in tribunal jurisprudence (Ohlin, 2007). In turn, this has led to a confined construction of victimisation. Victim communities, communities of victims and individual victims within communities are all vitally connected in the horror of genocide. Criminal law – both domestic and international – has traditionally worried over viable notions of collective victimisation and how they can and should be recognised. This is now a much more significant consideration in the delivery and resolution of the International Court of Justice.

Then there is the concern for providing adequate legitimate benefits to victims through a trial voice. The UN has detailed this need and associated rights in its *Declaration of Basic Principles of Justice for Victims of Crime and Abuse of Power.* Fletcher describes the declaration as 'noting less than a major victory for the victims' rights movement' (1995: 554). While rarely if ever allowing direct participation of victims' voices in the trial process, the international criminal tribunals and the ICC recognise as appropriate this influence in determining punishment.

However, if the more formal victim impact statement trend is to expand internationally, the question of who a victim is needs sharper relief. The ICC is struggling to recognise the *victimisation of third parties.*[18] If ICJ is unable to manage collective liability successfully, what hope does it have in recognising the reality of victim communities? According to Drumbl:

> The international community is prosecuting crimes of mass violence without first having developed a thorough criminology of mass violence, penology for perpetrators, or victimology for those aggrieved.
>
> (2005: 576)

This being so, is there a risk for ICJ in victim-centredness? The problems of this direction have been rehearsed in detail when considering victim impact statements in homicides. In such cases, there us no victim voice other than the voices of second parties closely connected to the deceased. This is exacerbated when there is more than one voice to comprise a connected victim community. In the international context, the normative frameworks around harm and victim location may not be as consolidated as they are in the domestic setting.

Then there is the issue of legitimate interests. ICJ is predetermined, at least in its formal manifestations, by competing rights considerations. Conventionally, the rights of the accused persons are the first measure of trial fairness. However, in a neoliberal age, *balance* competes with the presumption of innocence to measure the public acceptability of criminal justice.[19] Not every victim interest is as legitimate as justice. In many situations, victim interests may compete, and victim communities can divide over which justice interests they prioritise. We link this to the problem of how best to represent competing interests *within* victim communities.

Another important theme is the contextual relativity of victimisation. Many violent groups and organisations presently identified as terrorist threats have themselves been victims of harsh repression and counterinsurgency violence. In transitional state conflicts certain sides of the violence hold a privileged identity as both victors and victims, and as such claim considerable domestic legitimacy (Bikundo, forthcoming).

Sovereign decisions on who is a friend and who an enemy are not grounded by force or violence alone, or the authority for their exercise, and against whom they might be directed. More importantly, this distinction depends specifically on the authority of the sovereignty and legitimacy of the distinction among respondent communities. If either is challenged, the valorisation of victims over others beyond questions of innocence may be challenged, and the determination of legitimate victim interests will be contested as a consequence. How is ICJ to resolve this where military and political discrimination has exacerbated the confusion?

The valorisation of victims has an essential bearing on which individuals and communities can claim legitimacy in justice resolutions, thereby having a voice and demanding a dominant place for their interests above those of marginalised or *illegitimate* victim communities. As mentioned above, and to confound conventional considerations of justice, innocence alone may not be the crucial driver for victim valorisation. The same holds for risks and responses: it is the nature of the authority claiming and exercising the power to distinguish between victims and collateral or resistant communities that confers this legitimacy. The issues of who receives citizenship and standing as legitimate victims within ICJ are central concerns for the transformed trial process.

New crime forms and novel determinations of liability

As suggested previously, it is not necessarily the case that with global crime a central concern for ICJ, the seriousness, scope and harm of crime will determine the impact of any international crime type on risk, security and control. Were this so, then illegal arms trade, people trafficking, child pornography, illicit drug marketing and money laundering, to name a few important global crime types, would be the focus of the international criminal tribunals. They are not. The explanation for this contradiction lies in the present risk/security focus of globalisation.

We have indicated (Findlay, 2008b) that today the risk posed by crime, and the security potential of crime control, are important constituents of globalisation and global governance. There are essential qualifications that must be recognised within these relationships, evidenced as they are in the current *war on terror* politics. The ICC, for instance, has its mandate largely restricted to crimes against humanity and genocide. These offence types are determined as arising from illegitimate national and transnational conflict. The inclusion of enterprises and collectives within this criminality is in large measure prohibited from the considerations of the ICC (Findlay, 2008b: chapter 7). Thus, unless other important transnational and international crime types result in crimes against humanity or genocide, they will not be the concern of tribunal-based international criminal justice.

Certain preconditions for international crimes are evidenced in all these crime types:

- They are not bound by geography or jurisdiction.
- They defy traditional notions of legal sovereignty.
- They selectively experience government regulation against legitimate and illegitimate market forces.

- They pit domestic control bureaucracies against international enterprise networks.
- They have the capacity to victimise whole communities.

Yet some international crimes and not others are designated in the present phase of globalisation as the real and present risk to security, and as such a priority for international criminal justice resolution. In addition, the *global order* outcomes of ICJ are prioritised above other crime control concerns as ensuring security.

An explanation for the prioritisation of international crime types and control outcomes may be found in the challenge posed by particular crimes to the nation-state, its authority and its reflection of dominant economic and political values. International terrorism, ethnic cleansing, treasonous military uprisings and crimes against state integrity are branded by the UN Security Council and the dominant political alliance as the principal dangers to global governance. The indictments before international criminal tribunals and special criminal courts under the authority of the UN Security Council confirm this concentration. Decades ago drug trafficking was accorded a similar status, although not offered a similar global response (Chambliss, Michalowski and Kramer, forthcoming) Yet with the onset of the war on terror, risk/security globalisation has justified the shift from the more conventional and sustained global criminal enterprise as the focus for ICJ.

A natural consequence of this narrow *terror risk* focus is to equate security with global order. As defined by western religious and secular interests? Terrorism as the global crime of highest risk poses a direct threat to that order. Economic sanctions and military intervention have featured in the regulatory responses of the dominant political alliance directed at bringing down political orders which challenge global hegemony. Disorder and regime change come first, followed by reordering through the trial of key figures in the regime and the imposition of external justice regimes to resolve conflict and make peace. Even the alternative ICJ paradigms are promoted for their state reconstruction and community reordering capacities.

Assuming that, as with crimes of aggression, the formal jurisdiction of the ICC will expand over time, along with the expectations for its restorative capacity. As a result, there is a need for advocates of a new international criminal trial to assist this progression by discussing the key practical problems for trial transformation. Throughout this book, our consideration of transition in practice will adopt this 'hot-spot' analytical approach.

The nuts and bolts of transformed trial justice

Analysis of the central mechanics of trial transformation has until now been absent from the argument concerning a repositioning of formal ICJ. These are the crucial materialisations of that transformation discussed in detail as the text evolves.

Developments in the juridical professional

The Prosecutor and other trial professionals through their decision-making are given greater power to shape the normative contours of trial decisions. The responsibilities of the Prosecutor will extend beyond the findings and outcome stages of the trial to facilitate the trial's contribution to the broader transitional justice objectives set for the process. A programme will be established for each trial (see chapter 7) and managed by the judge, Prosecutor, Defence and victims' representatives. These proposals will herald fundamental changes in how trial professionals interact and their role in contributing to the trial outcome.

New voice for victims

We argue that the purposeful channelling of discretionary power can provide a crucial vehicle for achieving a greater degree of 'real' inclusion for victim communities seeking trial justice in post-conflict societies. We describe the rationale and normative framework which should allow the ICC Prosecutor to identify and establish meaningful contact with those parties, such as victims and others who may be regarded as stakeholders in the community. Juridical professionals will be proactive in ensuring that those who are identified as having a relevant interest have effective rights of participation and that the trial itself becomes a forum better equipped to satisfy the aspirations of stakeholders in communities of justice.

Truth vs. fact as evidence

The concept of probative value will take on a broader significance. We advocate changed rules for the admission of testimony during any mediatory phases of the trial. The probity of 'facts' will be tested against a more inclusive, non-adversarial context, thus expanding its potential for establishing a broader agreement about the 'truth' of alleged events. Such evidence will have a significant bearing on broader issues of collective responsibility and so play a major role in expanding the reach of ICJ as a more effective contributor to transitional justice strategies. Truth will emerge from the recognition and indulgence of 'story-telling', even if contested within the process of enunciation and representation. Truth will allow for apportioning responsibility when the fact/liability nexus is inappropriate or unsatisfactorily restrictive.

Discretion to transform from adversarial to mediation processes

Although a mediated outcome may become possible at any stage in the process, the trial programme will anticipate advancing to other determination and resolution options. Therefore, the significance of the findings will lie in their contribution to achieving desired outcomes rather than signifying a stage in an adversarial contest. Juridical professionals considering legitimate stakeholder interests and the relative claims of victim communities will make decisions as to which justice paradigm should be engaged and at what stage.

What this will do for trial outcomes (sanction vs. reconciliation)

The adversarial focus on establishing individual responsibility will dissolve into a search for a collective form of accountability. The trial programme will aim to make a specific contribution to achieving a transition to peace and reconciliation by facilitating the reconciliation of the competing justice claims of relevant stakeholders. The trial will recognise and repatriate legitimate interests in humanitarian justice while simultaneously ensuring that its resolutions reach a common objective. That binding motivation is the enduring purpose of post-conflict reconstruction and the transition from conflict to civil society.

These mechanical transformations of the trial process, we argue, will enhance the legitimacy of ICJ in strategies for global governance as a consequence of greater accountability to victim constituencies. As the formal ICJ currently sits within global governance it is substantially and procedurally accountable primarily to instruments derived from the UN Security Council. This is not a representative body beyond its significant reflection of the dominant political alliance. It is true that the membership of Russia and China and rotational states may mean that the views of the UN Security Council in total are not necessarily a reflection of western culture. However, as the second invasion of Iraq clearly demonstrates, when the UN Security Council is not seen by the dominant alliance as reflecting its views, it is bypassed and vilified. This course of action progresses at considerable cost to those involved, polarising prejudice and power, while both amplifying and validating 'threat', 'risk' and 'response' on both sides. Paradoxically, such political privateering strengthens the case for a powerful and interventionist global forum which at least has the potential to influence, and perhaps diffuse, what would otherwise automatically produce conflict.

The war crimes tribunals have always been a feature of victor's justice. In form they reflect the laws and procedures of western military justice (Cockayne, 2005). The selection of who is to be prosecuted and the manner in which these individuals are compelled to appear before the Court, reflect and rely on the victor's considerations of victimisation and resultant liability.

Accountability as a feature of ICJ is not even a significant characteristic of the less formal and alternative justice paradigm. We suggest (Findlay, 2008b: chapter 5) that the debate around amnesty as a trade-off for truth-telling has left many victim communities questioning whether criminals can ever be brought to justice if the truth is to be told. Victims are forced into a *Sophie's Choice* decision, where retributive justice outcomes are off the agenda if they participate in mediation or reconciliation enterprises for the purpose of conflict resolution and truth-telling. As we have argued (Findlay and Henham, 2005), for international trial justice to be transformed, embracing responsibility for a wider range of legitimate victim community interests, stratified justice should not be the inevitable lot of those excluded from the tribunal experience.

The other attraction of drawing victim communities into the international trial structure is that those who have been exposed to witness in community court settings would be expected to receive greater protection through due process. Aligned to this is the reality that higher-profile trial justice, publicly portrayed and managed through independent professionals, may offer victim communities a more transparent and accountable engagement in justice decision-making.

Accountability within ICJ should also encompass how justice can better hold governance responsible to the community over which it holds sway. That ICJ can take on a role in effectively delivering accountability frameworks (something approaching a separation of powers paradigm) for global governance necessitates the reduction of its political patronage. A move away from the service of the dominant political alliance towards communities of justice will help here. Preceding this repositioning, and for it to take hold in the long term, the normative location of ICJ within the service of humanity needs to be practically declared. Our vision for the delivery of trial outcomes that engage directly with communitarian aspirations for reconciliation and peace is testimony to this.

Communities of justice

The communitarian location of ICJ is crucial to its legitimacy. In chapter 1 we indicate the essential synthesis of a new morality for ICJ, focusing on humanity as its essential consistency and invoking communities of justice as the crucial context for international trial resolutions.

More than with domestic criminal justice, the challenge is for all forms of ICJ to engage both with victim communities and communities of resistance as a central mandate and more equitable and universal jurisdiction (Findlay, 2008b: chapter 5) because the crime focus for ICJ is genocide and its protective function is for 'humanity'. The collective and communitarian direction of ICJ is clearly set through the crimes it must prioritise. If, in addition to its restorative role, ICJ is to promote peacekeeping and conflict resolution,[20] then access, inclusion and interaction considerations must rate highly in its service delivery. Victim communities thereby become the first concern. If these victim communities are to reflect humanity, then those communities that resist criminalisation or give comfort to perpetrators may not be excised from justice on offer. For the prosecution of crimes against humanity it is justice for all.

The main challenge for ICJ as it presently operates (formally or less formally) is to establish and maintain a wide and lasting foundation for legitimacy. The importance of respect and consensus above force and compulsion for any system of criminal justice means that legitimacy which generates consensus is a valuable if fragile prize.

The legitimacy of ICJ is selective and currently contested because of the:

- politicisation of ICJ authority and practice;
- restricted engagement with victim and resistant communities;
- professionalisation of formal justice delivery and the tensions inherent in its varied procedural traditions;
- lack of satisfaction for legitimate victim interests beyond retribution and truth-telling;
- selective availability and application of rights protections to stakeholders, depending on which level of ICJ they engage with;
- and overall, the confusion prevailing around who ICJ is meant to serve.

In an earlier analysis (Findlay and Henham, 2005), we suggested that transforming ICJ into a more communitarian governance arena is crucial to its own legitimacy and the legitimacy it offers to global governance at large. The communitarian foundation might better be conceived as communities of justice.This harks back to the new normative framework for ICJ (chapter 1), a framework committed to humanity.

Communities of justice as both the essential constituency and the operational domain for ICJ will depend on access, inclusivity and integration, at all levels of criminal justice service delivery. This injunction is not limited to victim communities and their rights or to the protection of perpetrators. It should, by the nature of communities of justice, be open to exiles, non-citizens and the community, which might otherwise resist determinations of liability. This is the wider challenge for ICJ to engage with victim communities across the divide of individual criminal liability.

It could be argued that this aspiration is impossible to ground in a system where adversarial determinations predominate, at least in the formal institutions and processes of justice. This is true. However, the transformation of ICJ which we have argued for, and now detail, moves on from the adversarial model. The importance of truth-telling, mediation, reconciliation and dispute resolution (chapter 6) holds out possibilities wherein oppositional communities can work through a justice dialogue. The adversarial division and the pressure to allocate liability in retributive justice may present a benefit for innocent victim communities, but it tends to segregate further resistant communities that also have legitimate claims in just and fair conflict resolution.

The relationships which bind communities of justice need to be reflected (and adequately represented?) in the pathways of influence (Findlay and Henham, 2005: chapter 3) which operationalise the crucial sites of decision-making within the trial. We indicate in what follows how this can be achieved and what needs to change that it may be so.

New pathways for ICJ?

This is the question we pose at the conclusion of our analysis (see chapter 8). The new morality for ICJ is crucial in its satisfactory answering. A possible redirection in the *moral* foundations of global governance, as mentioned above, is premised on a tolerance of community identity. Even the most homogeneous communities demonstrate pluralism and diversity. Communities of justice, and their victim community constituents, require the type of governance (and criminal justice) that respects cultural diversity beyond political dominion and criminalised opposition.

The moral dilemma of justice for some in the name of governance for all seems to be overlooked when formal ICJ is responsible to a dominant culture.[21] While broadcasting a commitment to the security of humanity, retributive justice institutions and individual liability processes are failing to engage with legitimate victim community interests. This is a normative and an active stimulus to the development of communities of justice.

The task for governance, including ICJ, remains one of asserting acceptable forms of moral dominion over resistant as well as compliant communities. If there is ever to be an achievable world order more consensual than compelled, then an integrated, inclusive and accessible criminal justice will be essential for its maintenance.

'Communities of justice' is not much more than a syllogism without a complementary normative framework governing formal ICJ. Communities of justice will fail to be a constructive influence over global governance if they are confined to the alternative and informal realms of ICJ. Communitarian justice in theory and in practice can infiltrate the structures and formal procedures of ICJ (Findlay 2008b: chapter 9) through an encounter with procedural traditions which have to date largely remained outside international trial practice. Were this to become a feature of formal ICJ, then a more pluralist community engagement would follow. As a result, the influence of the dominant political culture over the development of ICJ will be lessened.

With the US and several other key UN Security Council players prevaricating over recognising the ICC, the Court has some breathing space in which to experiment with legal pluralism and cultural diversity not available to the war crimes tribunals and the special courts. The ICC will also need to reflect a more communitarian normative commitment if it is to work as an agent of humanity rather than as an offshoot of the UN Security Council.

Partial and politically partisan global governance is the reality of international relations in the foreseeable future. Even so, the transformation of ICJ, and its foundational morality, towards a real engagement with communities of justice can start now.

Thematic issues on which our analysis rests

This book is bound by essential themes of trial transformation. The embryonic notions of victim-centred justice and a new trial process to ensure these, presented in our earlier work, are now actualised within a process where competing claims for *truth* are determined in the interest of victim communities.

This book advances what has gone before by using comparative contextual analysis, and the preferred direction for trial transformation which results, to construct a manual on how this can be achieved. For instance, we wrestle with the consequences of inviting international trial decision-makers to utilise evidence in the quest for liability and truth down the path of restoration. To achieve this requires pragmatic considerations of the nature of facts emerging from adversarial argument as opposed to truth out of conciliation and compromise. What comparative weight will either narrative possess as the trial seeks to achieve the preferred justice paradigm? How will victims have access to the justice which transacts fact and truth in order to achieve their legitimate interests? These and other issues are answered in the book's empirical dimensions.

A crucial and initial question for this work is: why is the victim community the focus for ICJ? The conviction behind this essential constituency comes from an appreciation that international criminal law is essentially concerned with generic crimes against identified 'humanities' (victim communities). The institutions of ICJ, however, seem to have developed with a perpetrator focus that tends to substitute the voice of the justice professional for that of the *violated community* (Findlay, 2008b: chapter 5). This may go some way to explaining the qualified legitimacy of the formal ICJ in the experience of many conflict and post-conflict communities (Albrecht et al., 2006). If ICJ is to achieve a powerful presence in peacemaking and global governance (beyond the symbolic), then the satisfaction of legitimate victim interests is both pressing and pervasive (Braithwaite, 2002). Then comes the need to reconcile contesting interests. Chapter 3 addresses this challenge and projects techniques where justice professionals can appropriately determine and advance legitimate victim interests through transformed trial resolutions.

Another practical concern for the prosecution of international criminal law are the constraints which arise from conventional individual liability paradigms. Victim communities seek the restoration of their communities, as well as the conviction of the guilty and their punishment, often with the communities which fostered their victimisation. As victims are commonly whole communities, then the accused will be associations, groups and enterprises in which the individual may be a contributor to varying degrees. Individual liability conversions, such as joint criminal enterprise, common purpose, complicity and accessorial involvement, are not sufficient, we argue, to manage the collective responsibility of international criminality. We are challenged to devise and apply some novel notions of collective responsibility to better influence the development of international criminal jurisprudence. In so doing, the book looks to the experience of other transitional cultures with hybrid criminal justice traditions, to seek a new jurisprudence for international criminal liability (Findlay, 2008b: chapter 8).

The *truth/fact, responsibility/liability dichotomy* is a central problem underlying the achievement of transformed trial process in particular (see chapter 4). It goes beyond the philosophical challenge of reconciling restorative and retributive expectations for ICJ (argued for in Findlay and Henham, 2005). In fact, understanding the nature of the dichotomy and devising normative frameworks and process strategies for its management, underpins and enlivens transformed ICJ. This book details new approaches to trial decision-making that give recognition to truth and responsibility, while allowing fact and liability their place as victim interests determine. Chapter 8 in *Transforming International Criminal Justice* lays out the main decision sites requiring transformation, but does not elaborate on their new mechanisms and consequences. The re-envisaging of 'evidence' for the dual purposes of fact-finding and truth demonstrates the complexity of a process that recognises the appropriateness, rather than sacrificing the significance, one for the other.

Trial transformation is to be built on enhanced *judicial discretion*.[22] Victim interests from the point of access to justice, and through the various decision sites which negotiate these interests, require the *oversight of judicial discretion* if a *rights protection focus* is to be maintained.[23] The capabilities of ICJ to accommodate legitimate but contesting victim community interests will be a measure of the *new moralities* and their potential for justice.

We have earlier argued for the transformed trial as a preferred and universal arena for justice with rights and dignity (developed in chapter 1). However, trials focused on limited retributive outcomes, professionalised, with limited access for victim communities, will not meet this aspiration. Genuine access and productive integration are preconditions for the transformed trial to recognise restorative and retributive interests, but within a procedural framework where rights and fairness are respected. Such rights may also feature in other institutional forms of justice resolution, but not without accountable and transparent procedures and practices, where impartial adjudicators can require and assure responsibility for decision outcomes.

Enhanced professional discretion within the trial can be a recipe for injustice as much as it might facilitate legitimate victim community interests. In an effort to defuse the power of judicial professionalism to service its own interests and legitimate its authority as a primary concern first, *accountability is to develop in tandem* with the enhancement of judicial discretion in justice transformation. Accountability here is first to legitimate victim community interests and thereby requires an openness of application in order to confront and reconcile where possible competition and contest.

An important by-product, particularly when analysing the potential of ICJ as an agency for global governance, is wider *legitimacy*, particularly within victim communities. This legitimacy is to be determined in domestic, regional and international contexts. The legitimating potential of the *new moralities* of ICJ provides a normative and theoretical framework to enhance individual and collective interventions through ICJ, for the just and fair priority of *conflict resolution*. The contesting interests of victim communities will act as critical empirical contexts for transformed justice resolutions.

Resolving these divergent interests pre-trial and within trial decision-making will provide a crucial measure for the actuality of access and integration, along with the application of accountability, professional or otherwise. These interests need to be empirically identified and critically analysed to reveal the weaknesses in the mechanics of justice transformation, along with new social and cultural requirements for justice at work within particular victim communities. Political responses to particular normative conflicts have too often been the focus of ICJ case analysis (Findlay, 2008b: chapter 1). In the transformed trial as the litmus test for ICJ, however, there should be constant opportunities to reconstruct, reposition and reconcile legitimate justice aspirations from victim communities. The mechanics for, and results from, victim interest resolution within the trial will then lead on to a more applied critique of the conflict resolution potential of ICJ. The final section examines in particular the *instrumental capacity of judicial discretion to recognise and integrate victim community interests within ICJ*. The irresistible consequence of justice so formed and delivered will be good governance and peacemaking.

Chapter summary

Chapter 1 New moralities for international criminal justice

The interests of victims and communities of justice will only be served if they are effectively represented at each stage of the criminal process. Consequently, the ideological rationale for international criminal trial needs to be carefully redefined to reflect the aspirations of such pluralistic demands for legitimacy.

In this chapter we advocate a redirection of the normative paradigm underpinning international trials, providing a consideration of new moralities for ICJ. We argue that such new moralities, once identified, should activate process change supportive of legitimate victim interests and their resolution. By restoring victim interests in conflict and post-conflict injustice, these new moralities will, in a very real sense, come to reflect the justice demands of all participants in the trial and provide a pathway for their synthesis within wider concerns for the perpetuation of a more humanitarian form of global justice.

We suggest that the resolution of 'truth' through process must go further than this and implicate process itself as an integral determinant of 'legitimate' strategies for intervention. Intervention must incorporate and go beyond punishment, recognising retribution and reconciliation as legitimate, compatible and not inconsistent aims for transformed trial justice.

Crucially, we take the view that criminal process, whether global or local, has intrinsic moral worth and does not exist merely to serve the ends of retributive justice. We suggest that criminal process is more than facilitative, as giving normative effect to whatever ideology informs it. We argue that it should be conceived as intrinsically beneficial, not simply because it has an instrumental capacity to serve ends that may be perceived as morally good.

Our conceptualisation of humanity, which provides the moral foundations of trial transformation, is presented in the form of a moral paradigm for ICJ which underpins our arguments about ideological change and gives ethical direction to the practical suggestions for trial transformation that we make in this book.

The problem-solving capacity we develop for ICJ through trial transformation has beneficial implications far beyond the trial itself. Accordingly, we envisage a moral link between the ideology of the trial and its perceived legitimacy as a structure whose outcomes can contribute in a meaningful way to the attainment of post-conflict and transitional justice objectives. In addition, the capacity of transformation to draw the trial and its context together through mediated outcomes suggests that it has an important governance role to play.

Chapter 2 A framework for trial transformation

In this chapter we inject a structural framework into the applied connection between normative aspirations and process mechanisms, and return to an interrogation of the trial 'decision site' model explored in *Transforming International Criminal Justice*. To give this form, we introduce a problem scenario which is analysed against crucial decision sites we later identify as lying at the heart of trial transformation. The pathways of influence that influence these decision sites are elaborated in our discussions of victim communities, communities of justice and the trial professionals whom we charge with the carriage of the transformation project. The judge in particular will assume a central role in making victim access a reality and enabling the wider capacity of ICJ to ensure the accountability of global governance (foreshadowed in Findlay, 2008b: chapters 7 and 9).

More broadly, for governance, we foresee a fundamental transformation of the nature of justice delivery as a positive opportunity to move beyond the (limited) conceptualisations of penality currently prevalent towards a more holistic vision of ICJ capable of reconciling the conflicting demands modern pluralistic societies are likely to make on the structures it sets in place to resolve conflict among human beings.

Chapter 3 Activating victim constituency in international criminal justice

The normative framework suggested in chapter 1 pushes forward victim communities within transformed trial justice. New moralities are designed to support the ethical and procedural changes needed to give effect to the legitimate interests of victims and communities in post-conflict and transitional justice scenarios. Therefore, in a very real sense, new moralities reflect the justice demands of all stakeholders in the trial, and provide a pathway for their synthesis against an ethical framework which derives its moral authority directly from humanitarian principles. Correspondingly, the reciprocal effect is to change the perceived morality of ICJ in terms of the legitimacy attached to the outcomes of international criminal trials.

This chapter is the first of several which introduce and examine key players in the pathways of influence which demand and determine the transformation of trial decision-making. We have declared victim communities to be the essential constituency for ICJ with humanity at its heart. Victim communities therefore have the capacity, if given access, inclusion and integration in the transformed trial, to offer a new and powerful level of legitimacy for ICJ.

However, it is not a simple task to conceptualise victim communities in a manner which counteracts the narrow representation of victims as valorised or excluded within contemporary global governance (Findlay, 2008b: chapter 7). Nor is it practically apparent how or where legitimate victim interests can be distilled from revenge and indeterminate violence of itself. And what will the transformed trial offer to the resolution of contested legitimate victim interests if they are to provide a clear way forward for transformed trial resolutions?

Why victim communities? Crimes against humanity and genocide envisage communities. Here again, the individual is not overlooked in a rush to community orientation. This is a question of balance, one that recognises collective victimisation (along with collective perpetration) as a unique feature of international crime.

The chapter interrogates the idealised victim and the manner in which global political dominance tends to award 'heroic' status to some victims and not others. Why are citizenship and standing awarded to victim communities and denied others, with little regard to the nature of the violence visited on either? This discriminatory backdrop requires critical deconstruction prior to any appealing and 'just' argument in favour of access, inclusion and integration.

As restorative justice traditions have become established, the cohesion and moral location of these communities relative to any justice intervention will have a crucial influence on its perceived, and contested, legitimacy. This then will essentially feed into potentials for governance.

If we are to construct the transformed trial away from more conventional equations of fairness through defence protection or prosecutorial balance, we need to identify the legitimate victim and their interests. Contemplating this we are not anticipating the sacrifice of the accused to victim vengeance. That is why we reiterate the qualification of legitimacy for victim interests as a justice driver. Rather, we recognise and require that ICJ has a particular focus in the protection of humanity. Victims and perpetrators come under this umbrella to be equitably exposed to a more reconciliatory and mediatory domain. The notion of fair and equitable access for humanity to the rights embodied in transformed trial decision-making is a key context for the creation and operation of 'communities of justice' explored in this chapter. Communitarian justice gives:

- form to the legitimate interests of victim communities;
- foundation to the wider conceptualisation of rights on offer in the transformed trial;
- a future to the expanded governance potential of ICJ; and
- frequency to the different justice paradigms on offer in the transformed trial.

Communities of justice are where lay and profession interests and capacities are blended in an atmosphere of enhanced judicial discretion to increase the potential for transformed trial justice to satisfy legitimate victim community interests. The wider application of 'communities' to justice anticipates the resolution of competing interests, recognising the crucial importance of conventional, more individualised trial protections. Restorative justice has developed informed by this model and we have no reason to doubt that transformed trial decision-making cannot replicate this sensitivity and equity. In any liberal democratic notion of civil society, this will lead to positive governance outcomes.

Chapter 4 Truth and responsibility vs. fact and liability

Chapter 3 argues that contested victim community interests will need to be distilled and mediated through the exercise of professional discretion. In chapter 4 we put forward the crucial need to manage truth and fact for restorative or adversarial pathways.

One of the indicia of trial transformation will be the 'harmonisation' of fact/liability and truth/responsibility. We have indicated that evidence as both a facilitator of and outcome from trial transformation will need to be re-envisaged within the new international criminal trial, and the way to achieve this is discussed here.

To support shifts in trial resolution processes and outcomes, we shall introduce an expanded discussion of trial decision sites and plot where we see the most significant procedural and mechanical challenges that will emerge for trial transformation. In addition, some obstacles to the achievement of trial transformation will be elaborated against suggestions that truth and responsibility may present a more flexible and convincing paradigm for harm management.

Outside its practical applications, the analysis will resemble to some extent germane fact/value debates which have long fuelled socio-legal critique. We take this further in a discussion of the purposes of 'evidence' within a new trial structure where the normative driver is 'humanity' and the deliberative outcomes can be either or both retributive and restorative.

The current divide in ICJ is between liability-focused trials and restorative, truth-centred commissions. This is an unhelpful institutional and process divide. Building on the case we have put for integrating restorative and retributive justice within the international criminal trial, it is logical here to open up the manner in which facts and truth can be established and applied for different but not inconsistent trial purposes. This necessitates unlocking the trial from liability and its retributive outcomes, without diminishing or dismissing these as legitimate victim interests. Parallel to this within the domain of judicial discretion, there should exist the possibility in the trial to explore the stories which need to be told and to negotiate truth and responsibility at the expense of liability.

The consequences of the truth/fact alternatives within a more inclusive trial process will be discussed and these will link forward to the enhanced role of judicial professionals. It will be suggested that truth, as much as fact, has a vital place in the discourse and narrative of international trial justice. This will mean that the adversarial model of trial fact-finding will come under the influence of mediation processes that are more common in the truth and reconciliation environment. The conditions in which mediation may be the preferred approach will obviously depend on where truth in place of contested fact is deemed through judicial discretion to best determine prevailing victim interests at that time in the process. The shift from fact to truth, and from adversarial to mediation styles, will evidence the dynamic process of transformed trial justice. Examples of where similar trial practice operates at jurisdictional levels will be explored through the problem scenario technique.

In concluding the chapter, we introduce a dilemma regarding the determination of international criminal liability. We do this to reveal the limitations associated with transforming domestic criminal jurisprudence from the dominant traditions into a context where collective perpetration and victimisation are a more significant reality. In addition, this critical consideration of new liability paradigms should reveal where truth and fact converge when trying to understand the complexity of international criminal responsibility, and more adequately to resolve its consequences.

Chapter 5 Transformed process through enhanced discretionary power

The question flowing unsurprisingly from fact/truth reconciliation is who or what will be responsible for managing this seismic shift from current international trial decision-making. Enter judicial discretion and the significance of professional accountability.

Moving on from the considerations in chapter 3, the nature and role of evidence and fact-finding in trial transformation are key themes of this book. Chapter 5 explores as a specific example how the factual basis for sentencing in international criminal trials might be reconceptualised as part of an agenda for trial transformation. Its focus is on understanding relevant trial procedures within their broader contextual influences and making suggestions for transforming specific aspects of international criminal procedure as part of the wider agenda for trial transformation.

This chapter develops the thesis elaborated in *Transforming International Criminal Justice*, which suggests that discretionary decision-making in international trials should be seen as the appropriate context for developing more integrated and inclusive forms of ICJ. It is suggested that the perceived legitimacy of international punishment will be enhanced by making trial justice more inclusive to victims and the relative demands for justice of post-conflict societies. Within this context the gathering of evidence and fact-finding are identified as key areas for procedural transformation. The chapter explores as a specific example how the factual basis for sentencing in international criminal trials might be reconceptualised as part of an agenda for trial transformation.

The chapter's argument is developed in three section. The first emphasises the need to appreciate the significance of sentencing norms and practice within different jurisdictional contexts and trial traditions, exploring the broader context in which information is attributed as fact for the purposes of sentence. It critiques conventional approaches to describing the process of sentencing and deconstructing punishment rationales in a comparative context and assesses the implications for ICJ.

The second section examines particular procedural questions in greater depth. It focuses on:

- problems associated with conventional approaches to establishing the factual basis for sentence and considers differences between adversarial, inquisitorial and hybridised forms;
- issues of procedural expediency and procedural fairness;
- substantive law issues and their impact on sentence determination;
- the significance of the verdict in excluding evidence relevant to sentence;
- the problem of previous convictions;
- mechanisms for resolving disputes; and
- the role of victims and trial professionals.

The chapter's final section seeks to elaborate the case for change from three interconnected perspectives:

- *Reconceptualising* – changing trial ideology and norms; retaining the balance between retributive and restorative goals for transformation; clarifying the role of facts in establishing truth, liability and community responsibility rather than individual guilt; elaborating notions of integration and inclusive sentencing.

- *Repositioning* – changing the rules for admissibility; providing different levels of probative value to reflect the sources, nature and possible utility of trial evidence; collapsing the two-stage (verdict/sentence) distinction; consideration of intermediate stages and outcomes; changing trial decision relationships; ensuring victim involvement and protection; merging criminal and civil process and its evidential implications for sentencing; recasting rights in relation to evidence; expanding and circumscribing discretion; mixing lay and professional adjudication and establishing the role of information in sentence decision-making.
- *Operationalising* – developing new techniques for rationalising law and legal knowledge; using discretion as a force for developing transformative outcomes and dealing with inconsistency, appeal and enforcement.

In summary, the first section critiques conventional approaches to deconstructing sentencing from a comparative contextual perspective and assesses the implications of this for understanding how the factual basis for sentencing in ICJ is currently conceived. The second section examines particular procedural questions in greater depth, highlighting areas of difficulty and those points of tension and ambiguity which currently frustrate the task of trial transformation. The final section illustrates what is required to give effect to trial transformation through the exercise of discretionary power from the perspectives of changes in ideology, practice and accountability, providing concrete examples.

Chapter 6 Accountability frameworks

It would certainly fly in the face of contemporary domestic criminal justice policy-making to suggest an expansion and enhancement of professional discretion within the trial process, unless it was to be balanced against clear and comprehensible frameworks of accountability. In this chapter we argue this connection between discretion and accountability particularly as it must exist for the achievement of legitimate victim interests to accord with a 'humanitarian' justice focus for ICJ.

The analysis of accountability is at two levels. Internal accountability considerations focus on access to justice for victim communities; While a rights protection outcome as evidence of accountability in its internal dimension will be measured against access, inclusivity and integration for the key stakeholders in communities of justice.

Outside ensuring the interests of trial participants, the trial as a key endorsement of ICJ should be capable of advancing the accountability of global governance. In other work (Findlay, 2008b) we have suggested a reinvigoration of the justice component in a 'separation of powers' model for global governance. Problematic as this may be, it would move the motivation for current global governance away from satisfying the obligations of sectarian political hegemony. Consistent with a wider concern for humanity, ICJ may then require of global governance a more pluralist regulation strategy which complements the cultural diversity implicit in communities of justice.

The governance for ICJ provided by judicial discretion in its broader sense must be tempered by frameworks of accountability developed in tandem with its enhancement for justice transformation. However, this is not simply about the specific accountability of individuals for decisions made about the scope of procedural norms, or the conformity of procedural norms to particular systems or paradigms of rights protection. Our conceptualisation of accountability reflects something more fundamental which we regard as integral to determining the legitimacy of ICJ; a broader notion of accountability which relates directly to the institutions of ICJ themselves.

Consequently, in this chapter we argue that the institutions of international penality should conform to the principles of humanitarian justice elaborated in chapters 1 and 2, especially the importance of inclusivity as extending beyond the individual to the collective, and the significance of this for establishing the legitimacy of ICJ. Hence, this is not a mere provincial issue of whether or not the practice of international trials offers access to justice; it extends to the global question regarding the meaning and significance of accountability for the institutions charged to deliver ICJ. We therefore focus on establishing connections, dialogues and representations of justice from within victim communities, so that the idea of access to justice is unequivocally associated with the more holistic and representative justice which we have described as the essence of the transformed trial. Consequently, we suggest how the notion of rights should be broadened and interpreted within a democratised framework for accountability, so that rights themselves are conceived as an essential component in maintaining the dialogue of justice with victim communities.

In this way accountability moves beyond its conventional role of ensuring the principled enforcement of penal norms by enabling rights to become something which is more socially responsive, acting as a regulator of social justice whose purpose is to ensure that the pluralistic demands of transitional justice in post-conflict societies are met through sensitive interpretation and dialogue.

Chapter 7 Justice as decision-making: the principal pathways of influence

This chapter argues that the mobilisation of judicial discretion for the purposes of transforming ICJ will depend on a cooperative project to reposition the international criminal trial and reflect a more restorative and inclusive influence. As discussed earlier, the trial model ripe for transformation through the empowerment of justicial discretion is a series of crucial decision sites. Our analysis of this model for the purpose of plotting the transformation process will focus on decision sites which are problematic for change.

In so doing we analyse both what needs to be reconstructed in the decision site and the impediments to transformation.

Professional actors in the trial will be instrumental in recognising and protecting the interests of victims and communities, thereby reducing formalism and promoting inclusion. The move will necessarily be away from an adversarial commitment towards a collaborative one. This does not mean that the legitimate aspirations for retribution will be rejected. Rather, these will be required to coexist with other important aspirations of victims and communities, which the judge and the legal professionals will be called on to balance and recognise.

The location of trial transformation and its mechanics is a crucial exercise. The purpose of this chapter is to consider how judicial discretionary power can be mobilised most effectively in order to achieve the more inclusive and restorative form of justice for international trials demanded by trial transformation. Consequently, the chapter suggests particular pathways of influence within the trial where the discretionary power of international judges and their ability to identify and address the interests of victims and communities of justice have the maximum potential for their realisation.

The chapter proposes a new procedural approach designed to realise the objectives of trial transformation by developing a trial programme for each trial, and suggests how this might function for the ICC by implementing particular procedural changes. The chapter then elaborates how trial relationships might be reconfigured in order to deliver transformed justice most effectively for victims, again making suggestions for procedural changes to ICC rules and practice. Finally, this new approach is illustrated through a case study and the chapter concludes with a defence of possible criticisms of the use of mediated resolutions within the framework of transformed justice we have outlined.

Chapter 8 Conclusion: legitimacy, justice and governance

It is now widely accepted that ICJ is a crucial tool in post-conflict global governance (Findlay, 2008b). However, the governance aspirations for ICJ have led to institutional and process distortions that compromise claims to justice or at best create parallel para-justice paradigms, which foster domination and can deny rather than complement democracy and civil society. We recognise these dangers and explain how trial transformation addresses them. Furthermore, in advancing our governance vision for ICJ, we defend it against those who foresee an emasculated role for international trial justice (Damaska, 2008). In particular, we stress how transformed trial justice will contribute to a more meaningful form of collective accountability in post-conflict and transitional states through its enhanced legitimacy. Since the foundations for greater legitimacy will be established from the outset, this will help to avoid confrontation and the kind of procedural breakdown which has recently faced the ICC in dealing with the situation in Sudan and in the Democratic Republic of the Congo.

The transformed trial process which we have proposed in the preceding chapters offers a way forward for the place of ICJ within global governance. The achievement of communities of justice through new trial decision-making paradigms holds out a real possibility without necessitating a new legislative framework for the ICC in particular. As with governing through crime in a jurisdictional setting, the dangers to legitimacy both for ICJ and the governance aspirations to which it is directed are exposed (more fully discussed in Simon, 2007; Findlay, 2008b).

In exploring the preferred nexus between ICJ and global governance, the chapter returns to the 'new moralities' for justice advanced in the book's early arguments. Humanity as a focus for the injection of international criminal law into global conflict begets a strong recognition of legitimate victim interests. For the legitimacy of the justice/governance network to be long-lasting, therefore, its aspirations must shift from conflict resolution compatible with hegemonic dominance, to a much wider commitment to peacemaking for the benefit of civil society.

Here we return to the distinction between heroic victim citizens and the alienated resistant community. Governance which services only the interests of the heroic victim (community) will deepen the divide between resistance and citizenship. In the long term, if ICJ is reserved for heroic victim communities, as defined by a dominant global political hegemony, then the governance potential of ICJ will be compromised.

Justice does not always align with political dominance. ICJ has had little say in its inclusion in the global governance project. The international criminal tribunals, arising as they have out of the security blocs in the UN Security Council, have rarely demonstrated resolutions which challenge the post-conflict political order of dominant global hegemonies. At least from the point of view of its constitutional foundations, the ICC cannot administer such 'lop-sided' justice or be so closely connected to military victory in the manner it selects and executes it mandate.

The book concludes with a critical evaluation of ICJ/global governance network. It employs the transformed criminal trial as the procedural framework from which the 'new moralities' it promotes should feed into a repositioning of ICJ as a governance medium. This will no doubt lead to occasions where ICJ may challenge the dominance of global political alliances. But this, as we see it, accords with the honourable traditions of justice as executed jurisdictionally and regionally.

In conclusion we advance a model of ICJ within global governance concerned more for peace than punishment. The new building blocks advanced for trial transformation will be directed to the consequences of governance with conflict resolution and global order as central concerns, achieved for the benefit of humanity rather than hegemony.

Our final reflections are on how ICJ for global conflict resolution may disentangle governance from political domination. The search for true stories as well as sharp punishment will enable ICJ to help heal community divisions, in preference to denying their relevance through political dominion. The book presents the practical building blocks for a new international trial at the heart of ICJ and global governance.

Notes

1. Rome Statute of the International Criminal Court, 37 ILM 1002 (1998).
2. Article 25:1, Rome Statute for the International Criminal Court (the Rome Statute). This is the empowering legislation for the International Criminal Court (ICC) settled by the UN Diplomatic Conference of Plenipotentiaries on the Establishment of an International Criminal Court (17 July 1998).
3. In commenting on this article, Albin Eser observes that 'there can be no doubt that by limiting criminal responsibility to individual natural persons, the Rome Statute implicitly negates – at least for its own jurisdiction – the punishability of corporations and other legal entities (Eser, 2002: 778). The same is the case for the International Criminal Tribunal for the Former Yugoslavia (ICTY) and the International Tribunal for Rwanda (ICTR) (ICTY Statute, Article 6; ICTR Statute, Articles 1 and 5).
4. The success rate for prosecutions at the Nuremberg Tribunal and cases following of persons playing an economic role in crime was poor (Eser, 2002: 307–10).
5. For instance, before the ICTY, see *Prosecutor v Tadic* Case No. IT-94-1-T, TC Judgment, 7 May 1997; *Prosecutor v Tadic* Case No. IT-94-1-A, Appeal Court Judgment, 17 July 1999.
6. UN Security Council Resolution 1306, 2000.
7. The juridical professionals – judges, Prosecutors and Defence – in transformed justice have the responsibility to inject fidelity into the accountability framework of ICJ. For a detailed examination of the importance of fidelity, see Ashworth (2000).
8. In the Democratic Republic of the Congo it might be child soldiers, and in the Sudan, women rape victims. Critics of the early ICC prosecution have commented on the singling out of geopolitically marginal African victim communities in the creation of what is sarcastically known as the African International Criminal Court.
9. By this we mean functions and frontiers which go beyond the conventions of judicial decision-making and see the prosecution of international crimes as a mechanism for dispute resolution and thereby state reconstruction.
10. In identifying this expectation we recognise some of the counter-concerns raised by Amann (2000) that the international criminal tribunals may not uniformly protect the rights of every participant.
11. It is anticipated that transformed trial decision-making, if achieved at the ICC level, will have positive impacts on regional, national and local trial institutions and processes.
12. For a discussion of this in terms of procedural traditions, see Findlay (2001).
13. We employ concepts of community in an actual rather than symbolic sense more commonly suggested in the amorphous notion of 'international community'.

Particularly in the victim framework, communities may either be united or divided through the harm caused by crime and the justice or injustice which flows from it.

14. For a discussion of 'standing' in these terms, see Findlay (2008b: chapter 7).
15. Even in the transformed trial process we do not suggest that retribution will recede as a legitimate victim interest even with the inclusion of restorative alternatives.
16. The extent to which a victim focus is the appropriate driver for ICJ – in its formal manifestations at least – is recognised in the legislative instruments of the ICC and the international criminal tribunals.
17. A Victim Advocates Scheme in homicide cases has recently been piloted in England and Wales. However, it is clear that the tensions caused by trying to accommodate victims' 'interests' in criminal trials, particularly in sentencing, are unlikely to be eased unless there is greater clarity about what the purposes for victim engagement are and what it is meant to achieve. As we argue in the case of the ICC, the key lies in ensuring that the rights given to victims are real in the sense that their 'interests' are actually factored into discretionary decision-making and that judges are given the normative flexibility to achieve this. See Sweeting et al. (2008); Rock (2009).
18. ICC, Rules of Procedure and Evidence 85(a) defining a victim as a natural person suffering harm.
19. As we argue, the relative balancing of 'rights' for each context flows from the fact that we inject new moral foundations for the practice of ICJ (see chapter 1).
20. While the Chief Prosecutor of the ICC is cautious to identify peacemaking as a central aspiration for 'his' court, the prosecutorial commitment to victim communities and to neutralising violent threats against them means that restorative justice is directed to conflict resolution outcomes.
21. In suggesting this we recognise that the ICC and the war crimes tribunals in particular are accountable to the UN Security Council and to UN member states. At this level it might be said that there is an accountability framework beyond that dominant political alliance. However, as previously argued, the influence of the dominant political alliance, militarily and diplomatically, over the UN and its member states through bilateral arrangements, diminishes the representativeness and independence of this framework.
22. In this, 'judicial' covers judicial professionalism which incorporates the prosecutorial and adjudicatory functions. For a discussion of the challenge of international judicial professionalism, see Amann (2006).
23. Notions of rights require sensitive extrapolation beyond limited, individualised representations if they are to be responsive and relevant to victim communities.

1
New Moralities for International Criminal Justice

Introduction

This purpose of this chapter is to provide a clear statement of the new morality we advocate as the foundation for transformative justice and a summary of how this informs the methodology required for trial transformation which we elaborate throughout the book. It includes an introduction to those trial decision sites we identify as crucial to the transformative enterprise (see Findlay and Henham, 2005: chapter 3) and introduces the reader to a number of important themes that feed into our methodology and analysis of decision-making in later chapters. We draw attention to the pivotal role of discretionary decision-making and set the scene for later consideration of the normative changes we regard as necessary for pathways of influence from victims, communities of justice and trial professionals to channel this discretion into transformative trial outcomes. The judge in particular is identified as crucial to making victim access a reality, and in developing the instrumental potential we see for trial justice and ICJ more generally, in changing the focus of accountability in global governance away from hegemony towards pluralism. However, we first turn to the task of explaining the moral foundations for this work; how this builds on our previous writing, and crucially, how we come to regard the international trial as capable of translating our aspirations for transformative justice into reality.

Arguments for a new morality

In *Transforming International Criminal Justice* (Findlay and Henham, 2005: chapters 6–8), *Governing through Globalised Crime* (Findlay, 2008b) and *Punishment and Process in International Criminal Trials* (Henham, 2005: chapter 3) we argue the case for transforming the rationale, purpose and process of ICJ. This is not only to give it increased legitimacy and to make its governance capacity more accountable, but to reposition its focus for the betterment of those now largely served by alternative justice paradigms. Our argument is based principally on a belief that, for ICJ to move beyond the symbolism of retributive punishment, it has become necessary for it to engage more fully with the legitimate interests of *victim communities* (see chapter 3). Such responsiveness will fashion *communities of justice*[1] in post-conflict and transitional cultures and new governance contexts.

Our interpretation of ICJ and aspirations for it have developed from the realisation that many crucial contexts for justice resolutions are at present poorly served by institutional and formal justice processes. The recent pre-trial conflict of interests between the Office of the Prosecutor in the ICC and victims with standing before the Court emphasises this. Access to these justice forms is limited, if available at all, for many important victim interests, and the voice of victim communities is not being identified and protected by the rights frameworks claimed within ICJ. Rather than precipitating a rapid descent into relativity and conjecture about these dilemmas and their contexts, we have tested the broader legitimacy for ICJ through rejecting the strictures and narrowness of existing comparative methodologies and their epistemological foundations. We are committed to interrogating the contextual realities of ICJ against a radically reimagined trial decision-making model (see Findlay and Henham, 2005: chapter 3). Accordingly, we argue in *Transforming International Criminal Justice* for an approach to analysing justice process and outcomes based on comparative contextual analysis, which provides theoretical rationality and methodological coherence to the comparative analysis of transformed justice resolutions, and from there a repositioned international penality[2] in all its forms (Findlay and Henham, 2005: chapters 1 and 2). However, establishing a capacity for comparative understanding and meaningful generalisation, although crucial, is merely facilitative; it does not invest the research mission itself with any moral justification, nor does it imbue its findings with particular moral claims for achieving justice. We have come to believe that a new and inclusive moral discourse for ICJ needs to be identified if process transformation is to materialise as earlier suggested.

We can, therefore, make the case for questioning the legitimacy of ICJ purely on the grounds of moral principle or more pragmatic sectarian governance demands (see Findlay, 2008b: chapter 7) namely, for ICJ to mean something beyond a partial form of retributivism requires a profound re-examination of the rationales underpinning international penality. Tending to examine the outcomes of ICJ as well as the process, we anticipate developments beyond punishment that encompass a range of resolutions currently the province of alternative justice paradigms to that operating the international tribunals.

Accepting as we do the case for change through the merging of retributive and restorative forms of justice in international trials,[3] we make processual recommendations for bringing change about. Accommodating the contextual dependence of justice by recognising the rights of victims and communities to access and participate fully in decisions affecting justice outcomes may produce paradox, conjecture and compromise. Even so, we suggest that the moral validity of ICJ depends on confronting this challenge. Better this than to continue with the misleading symbolism of retributive justice and the distorted 'truth' it produces through its repressive process which excludes alternative voices of justice from high-profile, formal paradigms (see chapter 4). Perpetuating the distortion and disconnectedness of ICJ can only militate against peace and reconciliation, globally and locally, and provide further sustenance to the dominance model of governance which has come to typify ICJ and international relations since the Second World War (Findlay, 2008b: chapter 1).

A paradigm for new moralities

The interests of victims (individual and collective) and communities of justice will be served if such concerns are effectively represented at each decision site influencing the trial process. Consequently, as the current exemplar of ICJ, the ideological rationale for international criminal trial needs to be carefully redefined in order to reflect these aspirations and pluralistic demands for legitimacy.

The contemporary justification for trial justice is to provide a procedural context where the overriding objective is to facilitate the reconciliation of competing perceptions of 'fact'. Those participants with claims to truth, and the determination of whose version of the truth counts (and the reasons for this), will therefore become implicated in the criminal process as a consequence of trial transformation. This, as we go on to describe, relies on discretionary power being exercised against a normative framework which gives equal preference to individual and collective demands for justice, and where access is guaranteed through rights firmly grounded in humanitarian principles.

This determination of truth and fact provides an interesting example of the need for normative transformation. In conventional trial deliberations, contested 'truth' only obtains trial significance when accorded the status of best evidence, or the preferred 'facts' on which proof stands or is denied. In transformed ICJ, the emphasis on distilling a truth which derives its credibility through adversarial contest is replaced by the emergence of a truth generated through an inclusive process effecting these core values we identify for humanitarian justice. Such a novel foundation for trial justice resolutions will recursively sustain the existence and structure of the trial within transformed ICJ and so promote outcomes that are more appropriate for all parties. In suggesting this we explain how competing interests are identified and reconciled within a protective rights framework (see chapters 5–7).

A redirection of the normative framework underpinning international trial justice requires a consideration of 'new moralities' for ICJ. Obviously, the existing normative foundations for international trials can only partly withstand the transformation recommended. These new moralities, once identified, should activate process change that supports legitimate victim interests and their resolution. These new moralities in practice should be directed at restoring victim interests in conflict and post-conflict injustice. Hence, 'new moralities' will, in a very real sense, come to reflect the justice demands of all participants in the trial and provide a pathway for their synthesis within wider concerns for the perpetuation of humanity (see chapter 3). Correspondingly, the reciprocal effect will be to change the perceived morality of ICJ in terms of the legitimacy attached to the outcomes of international criminal trials.

Once the new moralities have been declared, it is important to provide conceptual linkages between normative and actual reality in satisfying the needs of victims and communities of justice in post-conflict societies, particularly in scenarios of non-international armed conflict when regulatory imperatives may be weaker. More particularly, the paradox between the ideology of universal human rights protection (or 'humanity') and the inadequacies of strategic intervention should be approached from a perspective that envisages rights protection as an imperative in practice, such a focus being necessary if justice processes are to enable their realisation.

Significantly, requiring 'humaneness' of *humanity* declares it as a communitarian entity affected by conflict (and its resolution). Humanity at the heart of ICJ necessitates the conceptualisation of collective rights within humanity and their protection. This is encapsulated in our notion of 'communities of justice' as critical contexts of collective humanity seeking justice through conflict resolution, and the interaction between victims and justice professionals for rights protection.

In this sense, our conceptualisation of rights is derived directly from what we identify as necessary to protect the essence of humanity in terms of its liberty, freedom of expression and bodily integrity.[4] We thereby conceive of individual and collective rights in justice delivery as coextensive, so that our notion of communitarianism is one that situates the victim firmly *in* the community. This foundation for rights counters the notion of trial justice as a hegemonic paradigm promoting sectarian political order (Findlay, 2008b) because rights are set against exclusivity and domination by our adoption of new moralities for justice that are inclusive and representative of humanitarian values.

Justice for humanity through model trial decision-making

The paradox between the rhetoric and the reality of rights is reflected in the failure of contemporary ICJ process *rationality* to accommodate the inherent conflict between punishing violators and protecting the violated. It is clearly demonstrated in parallel processes concerned with truth and amnesty, fact and punishment. More than accommodating these interests, the exploration of trial transformation seeks ways to enable legitimate victim interests to have access to either resolution as a consequence of the truth distillation process and at any appropriate stage.

This conceptual disjunction is portrayed in Figure 1.1.

> *Ideology*: Rationales for the punishment of gross breaches of international humanitarian law, as well as intoning wider communitarian interests for victims.
>
> *Process*: Structures for negotiating ideologies of punishment through adversarialism or mediation (along with repatriation) and legitimising conflicting interpretations of truth as foundations for both.
>
> *Methodology*: Strategies for operationalising the ideology of human rights (individual and communitarian) for those affected by breaches of international humanitarian law.

Figure 1.1 Conflict resolution as a methodological imperative.

Figure 1.1 envisages the trial process as a mediator of 'truth' tasked to determine appropriate strategies for the implementation of solutions that support the legitimate expectations of those who have been most directly affected by armed conflict and social disintegration. At present, for sentencing in particular, the methodological imperative for peace and reconstruction in conflict societies is divorced conceptually and practically from the process of punishment in international criminal trials. There is a clear political imperative in this (Findlay, 2008b: chapter 9). We suggest that the resolution of 'truth' through process must go further and implicate process itself as an integral determinant of legitimate strategies for intervention. The intervention must incorporate and go beyond punishment, recognising retribution and reconciliation as legitimate, compatible and not inconsistent aims for transformed trial justice. In this respect the fascination with sentencing and punishment can be relieved through a purpose for ICJ which looks for truth and enables a choice of consequent resolutions including and beyond punishment.

As in the domestic context, international criminal trials represent but one facet in a range of possible political responses to a particular form of normative conflict. The trial within ICJ at present, however, encompasses a powerful symbolism in post-conflict restoration. Whether the deviant response is individual or collective, political action is shaped by the perceived social and cultural requirements of the powerful elite. The liability of the individual is preferred and collective victimisation relegated to the post-trial mop-up. Where trial justice and penality are predicated on reasoning and structures that promote exclusion, as is currently the case with formal ICJ, the prospects for promoting peace through reconstruction and reconciliation will inevitably remain peripheral and localised. This failing is exacerbated if victims and their communities are subservient to the focus on perpetrators and as such largely excluded from the process of trial justice.

Figure 1.2 suggests modelling for international criminal trials that identifies how the concept of access and inclusivity can be utilised thematically to reposition the ideology and method of international penality in order to better serve humanity. Access to formal justice, as we conceive it, derives from our humanitarian focus on inclusivity, especially its holistic appreciation of the merging of individual and collective interests in 'community', reflecting the relational and dependant nature of human existence. The key to *integration* is through developing the instrumental capacity of *justicial* discretion (see chapter 5).

In addition to our emphasis on judicial instrumentality,[5] we utilise the term 'justicial' to acknowledge the crucial importance of other trial relationships, such as between Prosecutor and judge, or between trial professionals and lay participants in their influence on discretionary decision-making. Positioning humanity at the centre of international trial justice takes several routes.

Integrated and inclusive trial decision-making

The integrated decision-making model proposed in Figure 1.2 is, therefore, one that recognises how inclusivity exists at the ideological level through legal and political context, and at the level of process through the rhetoric of symbolic reconstruction. However, its most important feature is that it acknowledges the constructive potential of judicial discretionary power. This is instrumental power – judicial discretion is envisaged as a methodology for integrating crucial strategies and resolutions as much mindful of reconstruction and peace as priorities for trial justice. Discretion further negotiates justice legitimacy levels of ideology, process and intervention.[6] The perpetuation of this legitimacy beyond the symbolic will rely on networks of accountability to be elaborated outside this model (see chapter 3).

- *Structural inclusivity*: the legal and political contexts in which judicial discretion is exercised.
- *Symbolic inclusivity*: the judicial reconciliation of restorative justice themes within the framework imposed by constrained retributivism.
- *Instrumental inclusivity*: the instrumentality of judicial discretion – this is the autonomous and purposeful channelling of discretionary power for perceived legitimate ends. It is achieved through balancing public/universal interests against individual rights. It is within this discretionary framework that the judiciary is empowered to negotiate legitimacy.

Figure 1.2 Inclusivity as a paradigm for international penality

The adoption of an integrated modelling approach to discretionary decision-making suggests a need to construct and connect trial decision sites (see chapter 2) in terms of the following variables:

- an inclusive and integrative purpose for victim community access;
- rules about meaningful participation;
- how evidence becomes truth, when and with what consequences;
- how truth and fact are utilised for best reflecting legitimate victim interests (determined as these are in chapter 3);
- how truth supports the determination of responsibility, while fact determines liability for their own appropriate outcomes (see chapter 4);
- how value is attributed to fact, as it is with truth;
- how fact and value merge when truth and fact are balanced;
- how a choice and selection of outcomes derive from definitive truth (fact being a secondary technology for liability and punishment);
- how judges are specifically invited through new rules and practice conventions to apply a range of alternative resolution strategies and their outcomes; and
- how legitimate victim/community interests should be recognised to drive the choice of alternative resolutions and their outcomes.

New justice resolution options

This choice of what decision best recognises legitimate victim interests will be determined by whether the revelation of truth or the determination of fact predominates at any decision-making stage. Discretion will enable resolution processes employing alternative concerns for responsibility/reconciliation or liability/retribution.

Currently the essence of the trial as such is fact. Value needs governed inclusion in trial decision-making for contested fact to assume the status of truth. The role of the judge in any such transition is crucial if the trial is to provide enhanced resolution contexts.

These imperatives for transformed trial decision-making envisage a paradigm where the attribution of value to fact through the exercise of discretion provides the power for change and so supports the idea of using the instrumental power and authority implicit in judicial discretion to facilitate victim-sensitive processual outcomes. In other words, judicial discretionary decision-making provides the interactive context for negotiation between moral values and normative behaviour.[7]

This suggestion gives rise to a number of further propositions:

- Law's moral power [8] can be realised through trial justice by developing the capacity for judicial discretionary decision-making to shape social reality and its presence as both fact and truth.

- The capacity for developing the instrumental power of judicial discretion depends on allowing maximum flexibility for decision-makers in the protection of legitimate interests,[9] and their negotiation.
- This means that discretion determines the morally appropriate linkage between value and fact, within a responsible process of accountability to legitimate victim community interests at the very least.
- This correspondingly implies a conceptualisation of trial justice as a process which recognises that:
  - judicial decision-making promotes images of what the law (and justice) signify and produces accounts of how the law impacts;
  - the objectification of trial norms through recursively organised practice simultaneously engages with subjective interpretations of moral legitimacy, enhanced through the search for truth rather than the prevalence of adversarial fact.

Hence, we argue that the ability of judicial discretionary power to engage with morally legitimate conceptions of fact/value depends on the extent to which an identifiable common morality (essential to wider representations of universal humanity as victim) can be said to influence the exercise of discretion. This common morality is tempered by a fundamental concern for truth in a context where it is instrumental in the protection of humanity and not simply its governance. The notion of a common morality has two important dimensions in this context:

1. It refers to the morality of justice as it may be perceived by victim communities seeking justice in post-conflict societies.
2. It is a shared and residual (not contested) morality, because the notion of inclusiveness has been adopted as a key element of trial ideology. This inclusivity makes up the humanitarian focus of ICJ. Hence, the normative framework becomes the vehicle for identifying competing moral claims for justice. Judges are empowered to negotiate these demands through the use of their discretionary power.

Whether ideology and process are comfortable with the notion of judges as a mechanism for flexibility and creativity can, therefore, be envisaged as pivotal to the recursivity of process. In this sense, human agency provides both the means and the ends for enforcing morality and justice and legitimating the structures of ICJ across time and space.

Conceptualising the exercise of judicial discretion as a methodology for operationalising the transformative potential of the criminal process gives it substantive force to achieve justice for victims and communities of justice in post-conflict societies. As we shall argue, this approach suggests a moral imperative for ICJ which underpins judicial discretion as a positive force for change, rather than discretion being regarded as essentially a matter of process, relevant only to the social mechanics of decision-making.

International justice process as a 'good'

We have argued that the processes of discretionary decision-making within the trial are best conceived as socially structured interactions around decision sites and pathways of influence. Hence trial actors continually negotiate the relative realities of their subjective experiences, resulting in outcomes that are objectified by judges through rhetoric and symbolism. Procedural norms, therefore, provide a legal context for the reconciliation and reconstruction of subjective experience into objectively verifiable events. The extent to which judicial discretion may be conceived as an instrumental force for trial transformation depends on whether such a process may be theorised and observed empirically[10] and contextualised and compared as a sociologically relevant phenomenon. Our trial model as a series of decision sites measurably affected by pathways of influence enables this analysis. However, in this book we are dealing with what should be, beyond what is. The notion of trial transformation *per se* implies that there is something about criminal process which is capable of transforming positive law into norms which impact on individual and social life as a matter of perceived reality. The possibility that criminal process may instrumentally serve particular moral ends immediately raises questions about the moral validity of the ends its serves.

Before moving on to elaborate the normative foundations for transformation, it is important to pause and remind readers that the purpose of this chapter is also to explain the link between our new justice morality and its practical application in the transformed trial discussed in chapter 2. To assist the reader in seeing transformation at work we shall introduce and sequentially apply a problem scenario for contextual analysis. The scenario will operationalise new decision sites and the impetus for their transformation. This context will also reveal crucial pathways of influence which negotiate legitimate victim community interests, or presently deny these. Prior to this, however, it is essential to confirm the normative foundations for transformation.

Justice as the revelation of truth and the protection of humanity becomes an essential 'good' in terms of that humanity and its perpetuation. Crucially, we take the view[11] that criminal process, whether global or local, has intrinsic moral worth and does not exist merely to serve the ends of retributive justice. We suggest that criminal process is more than just facilitative, as giving normative effect to whatever ideology informs it. Instead, we take the view that it should be conceived as intrinsically good, and not simply good because it has an instrumental capacity to serve ends that may be perceived as morally good. In this, it is important to emphasise that we mean good for *all*, in the sense of good as inclusive and non-sectarian.[12]

Our argument asserting the inherent goodness of criminal process is based on the proposition that the social activity which it represents embodies essential aspects of the human condition, namely, the propensity to conflict and its resolution. Hence, our conceptualisation of trial justice necessarily entails a refocusing and reconsideration of the essence of conflict resolution as a form of social interaction. Such essentialism is a precondition to any meaningful consideration of structure. Our transformation of the trial operationalises 'new moralities' we regard as crucial for engaging with the demands of victims and communities seeking justice. Its humanitarian focus gives expression to the essence of this particular aspect of human life. It recognises the intrinsic goodness of conflict resolution as integral to the existence of social life, whatever form that may take.

Therefore, whilst sanctioning is necessary to sustain civil society, and as such can be claimed as an inherent good, the resolution of conflict *per se* can equally be envisaged as an intrinsic and valuable good, since it sustains harmony in social relations, and therefore contributes to the maintenance of social life and community. This dimension of justice has been claimed for ICJ. The individualised focus of international trial justice here must incorporate justice as a communitarian endeavour. These are not exclusive but prioritised concerns.

The assertion of the intrinsic moral worth of international criminal process elevates it beyond the level of object or instrumentality, a view that accords with Lacey (1988: 173), who argues that its moral boundaries should extend beyond the 'individuals never being used as means to social ends argument' because of the essential and intrinsic goodness for humans of a peaceful and just society. This notion of social cohesion is vital for a fully developed notion of humanity. As such, repairing the damage caused by deviance[13] is bound up with the conditions necessary for peaceful and productive human life, predominantly a social experience. Consequently, the virtue of reducing damage to relationships (and of social structures designed to achieve this effect) has both individual and social functions, these being reciprocal and symbiotic in nature.

The recognition and restoration of relationships is a definitive feature of communities of justice, as we see them. Communities of justice will evolve as a consequence of the transformed trial, the mechanics of which are described in the chapters to follow. At its heart, international trial decision-making resulting from victim-centred 'pathways of influence' will naturally complement more communitarian justice.

The concept of social value is, of course, ultimately a matter of moral judgment, as is the distinction between something being intrinsically constitutive of the good and something (merely) being an instrument to good ends (Roberts, 2006: 48). Certainly, arguing that the resolution of conflict is intrinsically good implicitly recognises peace and (possibly) solidarity as moral goods. Yet, there remains the difficulty of how we know these are good.

A Durkheimian explanation may suggest that certain kinds of social complexity make it socially appropriate and, therefore, morally desirable that values of universal respect and peaceful cooperation flourish. Even so, it remains difficult to specify exactly what sociological conditions might make these values best suited to society or, indeed, what is meant by 'best' in this context.

However, we would argue that the answer is beyond social ideology and lies within our understanding of what constitutes a particular society's conception of the moral.[14] Since we assert that the intrinsic goodness of criminal process resides in something which is an essential aspect of the human condition; namely, conflict and its resolution, it is important to explore and understand what this means in terms of how humanity is perceived in the context of any particular society. Essentially, this involves scrutiny of what it is to be 'human' within a particular cultural context, and specific understanding of what this means in moral terms. In other words, it is necessary to appreciate the moral bases of what constitutes a fully 'social' being (see chapter 3).

Although understandings of the 'moral' and the 'social' are relative and not necessarily coextensive, our acceptance of the possibility of intrinsic goodness is similar to Finnis's (1980) contention that the intrinsic goodness of something is self-evident and, therefore, by definition normative in its effect. The attraction of such a position is, of course, that it avoids the naturalistic fallacy of deriving 'ought' from 'is' cautioned by Hulme, a criticism frequently levelled at the link made by some writers between their observations of socio-legal processes and their moral arguments for reform (see Cotterrell, 1989). Our argument is that the 'legitimacy' of such processes can only be judged in terms of the moral value attaching to their normativity.

Towards humanitarian justice

We argue that considerations of society and social defence within ICJ are rejuvenated through the humanitarian focus. The international criminal trial in this context is about perpetrators and victims communities insofar as they have relevance for the humanitarian enterprise. In elaborating this assertion, we argue that conceptualisations such as the Zulu concept of *ubuntu* may provide useful insights (Louw, 1998; Wilson, 2001: 9; Andersen, 2003).As Louw suggests, *ubuntu* provides a spiritual foundation for African societies based on a deep understanding of humanity and its potential. It is exemplified in the maxim *umuntu ngumuntu ngabantu* ('a person is a person through other persons'), being the nature of the moral balance between individual and group. Louw argues that *ubuntu* provides a distinctly African rationale for values such as compassion, warmth, understanding, caring, sharing and humanness. While we would not wish to detract from this, we make the broader point that *ubuntu*, along with other similar indigenous foundations for social morality, is rooted in the notion that it is only through others[15] that one becomes a whole person.

Such notions of compassion and respect for others thus represent essential features of humanity which vary according to the emphasis placed on group solidarity as a necessary condition for the existence of social life (Findlay, 1999). We regard it as the task of ICJ to recognise and give effect to the ways in which this humanitarian potential is realised in different social groups and societies by accommodating moral plurality through its ideology and processual activity, yet always promoting a holistic vision of community, giving equal access and rights protection against narrow political sectarian hegemony.

Because the moral value of criminal process, of whatever degree of structural sophistication, is intrinsic to the need to resolve social conflict, this imbues its rationality with a communitarian purpose. Hence, what judicial discretionary power can achieve within such a context is to pursue outcomes which can restore the autonomy of individuals within social groups by recognising and working towards their collective aspirations for justice, collective in the sense that trial outcomes will represent moral and, therefore, legitimately perceived forms of justice for individuals within victimised social groups.

Obviously, the impact of the judge in advancing trial justice could depend on the cultural status and legitimacy of judges and of the constitutional legality they are said to enforce. In transitional cultures such as China, this may not amount to what is taken for granted in western justice traditions. At the international level we will work from the basis of a uniform acceptance of judge-made justice as powerful for regulatory coherence.

Our conceptualisation of humanity, which provides the moral foundations and imperatives for trial transformation, places emphasis on those values that promote peace and social solidarity, such as respect for human dignity, compassion and adherence to social norms. We present it here in the form of a moral paradigm for ICJ that underpins our arguments for ideological change and gives ethical direction to the practical suggestions for trial transformation that we make in this book.

Emphasis on relationships within the trial

In *Transforming International Criminal Justice* we stressed the importance of understanding how relationships of influence within the context of the trial operate through particular pathways, functioning recursively and autonomously from legal and processual norms (Findlay and Henham, 2005: chapter 4). These are especially significant in establishing the social reality of participation in the trial and determining the degree of inclusivity for victims and others in terms of their participation in discretionary decisions impacting on adjudication and accountability.

The moral significance of trial relationships is crucial to our arguments for transformation and the notion of humanitarian justice within international criminal trials. As presently conceived within the context of the prevailing retributive justice paradigm, trial relationships represent something of a moral paradox in terms of the ideology of the trial. This is because, while the ideology of retributive justice focuses on individual accountability, it purports at the same time to be an inclusive form of justice – inclusive in the sense that it provides some form of participatory rights for victims.[16] More broadly based is the access to justice argument internationally in suggesting that trial outcomes resonate with the demand for justice of its two main constituencies: the 'international community' and the communities in post-conflict states where international crimes have been perpetrated.

Paradoxically, the processes and outcomes of international trials claim that individual justice and collective justice are equally satisfied, when the reality is something quite different.[17] In terms of trial ideology, this tendency suggests an ambivalent role for the individual. The rhetoric of individuality prevalent in international trials emphasises individual autonomy, whilst the reality of the process and the outcomes themselves present a more postmodern conception of individual accountability. Individuality is presented in a form that is more compatible with the collective nature of the crimes which have been perpetrated due to the nature of those crimes and the harm they cause.

This disjunction between rhetoric and reality is crucially damaging to trial relationships since it impedes the potential for instrumental development of ICJ for humanity. We would suggest that a moral basis which effectively supports the merging of retributive and restorative forms of justice for ICJ should reflect inclusivity and collectivity; in other words, it should be based on a model of individuality which recognises the interdependence of individuality and community. This does not imply the subordination of individuality to some unspecified, and potentially oppressive, form of collectivism. Rather, it recognises, as Louw (1998: 5) suggests, an acknowledgement that the subjectivity of the individual develops in a relational setting through social interaction, so that individuality reflects a balance between individual and collective humanity. The importance of this conceptualisation for changing the penality of ICJ cannot be understated because it acknowledges the dignity and autonomy of the individual, whilst also recognising the relational context of subjectivity.[18]

Our conception of criminal process as a good depends on seeing structures for conflict resolution as concerned with restoring those relationships of community essential for human life, or, at the very least, enabling that potential in humanity to be fully realised by challenging political dominion. Participation and discourse are seen as vital to the ideology and process of the transformed trial through which relationships are grounded in a morality focused on humanitarian justice.

Principles of humanitarian justice

In this section we elaborate the core principles which underpin our conception of humanitarian justice and constitute the essence of the new moralities for ICJ. We wish to emphasise that our engagement with the notion of humanity is not in any jurisdictional sense, but rather characterises those core values which we regard as essential aspects of human dignity and as necessary ingredients for the promotion of global justice and peace. These provide the moral foundations for our conception of humanitarian justice. This conceptualisation recognises that:

- What comes to be defined as international crime is contextually dependent on humanitarian values.
- The ideology and process of ICJ is contextually dependent.
- ICJ will be driven by an ideology (however imperfect), and a process informed thereby, which seeks to accommodate individual as well as communitarian[19] demands for justice.
- The core values of ICJ should be humanitarian in their justice focus, its context recognising the interdependence of the individual and the collective.
- The overarching objective of ICJ is to address crimes against humanity. From this, appreciating that the primary constituency of ICJ should be the victims and victim communities against which such crimes are perpetrated, thereby accepting for ICJ a responsibility in identifying, distilling, accessing and enunciating the victim's voice.
- The core function of ICJ is to facilitate justice so conceived to promote holistic solutions that transcend conventional interpretations of 'penality'.[20]
- Retributive and restorative forms of justice are contextually dependent, but not essentially incompatible concepts.
- Notions that justice outcomes must satisfy particular demands (international, regional, local) are misplaced if demands for justice are seen purely in those partial terms. Consequently, justice outcomes depend for their legitimacy on satisfying more than individual/partial interests. With 'humanity' as victim, and victim interests measuring justice outcomes, these need to be addressed at the individual and community levels, contested or otherwise.
- The humanitarian approach must be driven by a theory of justice resolution which acknowledges that the ideology and outcome of process are essentially connected. This synthesis is achieved by ensuring judicial and prosecutorial discretionary power is exercised in a holistic justice context, which allows contextual dependency to be heard, understood and respected through the exercise of such discretion, requiring its accountability to legitimate justice constituencies.

- ICJ is important for international governance, and such governance requires regulation in situations involving a plurality of moral views and regulatory alternatives (Findlay, 2008b: chapter 9) which transcend domestic concerns, such as breaches of international humanitarian law.
- The most significant justice demands from the perspective of humanity are truth, responsibility, inclusivity, social justice (welfare and security), accountability (transparency) and reconciliation, in each case recognising contextual dependence. These form the core values we characterise as the ideology of humanitarian justice.
- Humanitarian justice is particularised through a utilitarian ethic whose purpose is to reconcile contextual dependence by promoting solutions having the greatest chance of achieving peace and reconciliation through satisfying the most significant justice demands. These include (in no preferential order):
  - *enunciation* – truth-telling from the perspective of victims and perpetrators;
  - *mediation* of legitimate contested interests;
  - *reconciliation* of those interests for the benefit of 'humanity';
  - *international welfare* through victim protection – a driving force for humanitarianism';
  - *retribution* for the majority of those involved in the conflict situation, whether international players or not;
  - *reaffirmation* of the sanctity of humanity.

It is important to emphasise that retributivism is not seen as capable of reconciling these interests; rather, we regard a utilitarian approach as providing the key to reconciling conflicting demands for justice, whether retributive or restorative, in sympathy with the principles of humanitarian justice. Hence, this is not utilitarianism in the conventional, consequentialist sense of opposing retributive punishment, but rather in the sense of providing a conceptual ethical device for reconciling potentially competing demands for justice. So, a utilitarian ethic imbues the ICJ process to reach whatever outcome tends to favour peace and reconciliation by utilising discretionary power instrumentally.

Conceptually, the utilitarian calculus is not constrained by particular justice paradigms, retributive or restorative, because it is informed by the overriding humanitarian concerns of promoting peace and reconciliation. The exercise of discretionary power is consequently guided by the maximising principle of utility, this being equated with the achievement of justice solutions which promote peace and reconciliation. Effectively, therefore, the values of humanitarianism inform the ideological foundation for justice delivery and the distributive principles we have outlined for trial transformation, including those of retributive and restorative justice.

Taking the notion of justice beyond that of individual autonomy, free will and rights, our conception of humanitarian justice relies on a view of humanity that is relational and communitarian, individual and collective. As a result, justice is conceived as a shared status, while respecting integrated claims for individual autonomy. We therefore interpret the maximising principle of utilitarian ethics in terms that envisage ICJ as promoting shared values for peace and reconciliation (see Beccaria, 1764, trans. 1995).

Our argument so far can be summarised as follows:

- Individuals have autonomy and free will, but essentially within claims for justice operate within social groups.
- The values we recognise as integral to this view of humanity include the need for peace and harmony – relationships of community (communities of justice).
- These we identify as humanitarian values which form the foundations of justice.
- Hence, absence of conflict is seen as morally good, because peace is an essential aspect of social life.
- Processes for resolving conflict are therefore intrinsically good if they serve moral goals – the values of humanitarian justice. In other words, it is the morality of humanitarianism intrinsic to conflict resolution which underpins its normativity.
- Processes for resolving conflict are transformative – sites where, informed by the ideology of humanitarian justice, competing versions of truth can be reconciled – the outcome may include retributive and restorative justice.
- Discretionary and accountable power is the technology for instrumental outcomes based on implementing the ideology of humanitarian justice within an appropriate normative structure.
- Decision-making in ICJ is informed by a utilitarian ethic – maximising the potential for peace and reconciliation through flexible, victim-centred outcomes.
- This is not using individuals as a means to serve the ends of partial accounts of what might produce peace and reconciliation, because justice is based on upholding humanitarian values, like human rights theory, humanitarian justice recognises certain basic rights as attributable to the humankind. This is a concept of humanity where individual and social rights are viewed as reciprocal and symbiotic. Therefore, the basis for intervention is justified by the need to promote social life.
- Individual rights are protected to the extent that to do so would not threaten the prospects for peace and reconciliation. Whilst this offers no guarantee that the rights of specific individuals would never be sacrificed

in the interests of promoting peace and reconciliation, a considerable limitation could be placed on possible abuse by insisting that the degree of threat posed is 'severe'.[21]

- Closer and clearer notions of the pre-eminence of social harmony (as it is a primary notion for the collectivisation of rights in Chinese culture – Findlay, 2008b: chapter 7).

The principle for maximising utility as outlined is not partial in the sense that it favours competing paradigms or particular demands for justice. On the contrary, since the calculus is based on humanitarian criteria, the possible abuses of retributivism and consequentialism are minimised (Hudson, 2003). Instead, utilitarian rationality is adopted to maximise the virtues of truth, responsibility, inclusivity, social justice, accountability and reconciliation, appreciating that the achievement of these ideals is contextually dependent.

Legitimate expectations for resolving conflict within the humanitarian project therefore provide parameters for utilitarian decision-making, based on the criteria for achieving humanitarian justice we have outlined. A descent into eclecticism is avoided because the ideology and normative structure we propose is geared towards discretion being used to promote solutions which favour humanitarian justice. Eclectic judicial decision-making in conventional criminal justice processes has tended to occur where, despite the underlying ideology, the normative structure is insufficiently developed to prevent a collapse of rational decision-making.[22]

It is important to emphasise the paradigmatic nature of what we propose. Transformative justice, and its concrete manifestation in this book, rests on a distinct conceptualisation of the intrinsic goodness of conflict resolution and its utilitarian promotion through principles of humanitarian justice. If a normative structure is clearly elaborated within the framework of the ideological values we have identified as humanitarian justice (the task of this book), then, imperfect as this may be, it will provide a moral and rational basis for discriminating in favour of certain justice demands and rejecting others. This does not, of course, mean that the decisions of ICJ will be moral in any universal sense, merely that they will have been reached on the basis that the criteria for achieving humanitarian justice have been fully considered in each particular case, and that the maximising principle used to guide instrumental decision-making within the trial will have ensured that all claims for legitimacy have been argued effectively.

We would counter any criticism that our ideological framework of humanitarian justice is naïve because it does not recognise the realities of international power and global imperialism. Indeed, facing the reality of the link between ICJ, global governance and sectarian political hegemony (Findlay, 2008b), social structures are essentially self-serving of the interests of the powerful. However, we counterbalance these tendencies by providing the victim perspective and validating justice outcomes through the currency of legitimacy socially located. In so doing trial justice is infused with a morality to counter the pressure for conflict resolution through further political domination. Consequently, we offer something better than that which already pertains, namely, retributive justice against a background of international power politics, because we are offering a new constituency of legitimacy and a new perspective for political accountability which goes on to entrench this. This may be seen as a shift of the politic back to the notion of the *polis*. The moral authority for the legal norms and structures of international law may be seen to rest on the power of the *polis*, if access and voice are ensured.

Relocating the source for the moral authority of ICJ against political authority within a concept of legitimacy based on humanitarian values raises a number of further issues which go to the root of the relationship between justice and political power. These arise because of the need to articulate the relationships implicit in our broader reading of legitimacy for ICJ. Essentially, a more inclusive understanding of what constitutes legitimacy must mean that there is a degree of international consensus underpinning the outcomes of international trials as possessing moral integrity. Instead of the scope of justice being delineated by the moral concerns of nation-states, our conceptualisation of humanitarian justice places the preservation of human dignity as its core governance concern and therefore regards this principle as the fundamental basis of universal political obligations. However, this kind of moral universalism, as Freeman (1999) recognises, transcends the justice moralities of nation-states and gives equal moral prominence to the validity of individual, collectively and universally held views as to the legitimacy of justice (see also Held, 1997). The prioritising of claims to legitimacy can only be justified if it tends to promote the moral virtues of universally held moral obligations,[23] so that the task of a cosmopolitan theory of justice is to ensure that its institutionalised forms seek to uphold and clarify these moral principles.[24]

Universalised moral values which underpin the moral authority of ICJ may also reflect the changing global constituency of criminal justice. The contexts of governance and social control within nation-states, as Garland (1996)suggests, have been gradually recast during the period of late modernity. Relationships between citizen and state have been reconfigured through the process of 'responsibilisation', reflecting significant changes in the state's accountability for crucial areas of penal policy such as crime control. Pratt (1998)has similarly documented the ways in which relationships of trust and mutual dependence between state and citizen established in western democracies during the nineteenth century were gradually diminished through the centralisation of penal authority in the state and the diminution of individual autonomy over the core elements of penality. This reconceptualisation has reduced the moral authority of the state's penality and, correspondingly, the legitimacy of punishment beyond mere rhetoric and symbolism. Further,

Shearing (2003), in considering the reconfiguration of state and inter-state governance in relation to security during postmodernity, has described how tensions within retributive ideology have conditioned the moral framework for developing risk strategies.

These changes in the contexts of global and local penality are highly significant, not simply because they represent breakdowns and shifts in conventional understandings of the relations between penal ideologies, the institutions of punishment and individual citizens, but, more fundamentally, because they signal the further secularisation of penality, the ideas, structures, norms and processes of punishment at all levels have gradually diminished in moral authority. This fragmentation of justice, therefore, reflects more generalised tensions of late modernity between moral pluralism and individual autonomy, so that the institutions of criminal justice become remote and self-serving of political ideologies which drive agendas and paradigms for justice that are starved of context and the demands for legitimacy they engender.

The injection of the humanitarian derivations for justice which we advocate addresses those moral and social issues that should form the basis for an inclusive universe of penality for ICJ. Humanitarian values provide a moral foundation for reconciling the diverging realities of context and their differing justice demands. We suggest that humanitarianism as a basis for justice transcends those conventional conceptions of social contractarianism that continue to underpin present understandings of justice delivery in western liberal democracies. This is not simply to universalise the relationships of justice to correspond to some vague notion of its globalisation, advocating adherence to a ubiquitous humanitarian ideology that can have no concrete existence as ICJ process. On the contrary, we have argued for the need to transcend the moralities of retributive justice which currently debilitate ICJ and to replace them with an ideological conception of justice grounded in the moral virtues of humanity. In particular, we would view the promotion of relationships of individual and collective social life as crucial determinants of what should constitute ICJ, since it is through this that the key to inclusive solutions which favour peace and reconciliation in post conflict states lies.[25]

Engaging humanitarian principles

Humanity as victim: integration against aggregation

It is not our purpose to externalise a juridical concept of the victim or to objectify the notion of victim as 'other'. On the contrary, we deliberately conceptualise the notion of victim, not as a status ascribed to those who suffer the ravages of war and social conflict, but as an exemplar of humanity, so that we regard humanity itself as victimised in terms of crimes against humanity. It follows that, in the context of humanitarian justice, we each have an equal claim to justice whose priority is not determined by the rationality of retributivism. Our appeal to justice therefore goes beyond any neo-Rawlsian vision of retributive fairness, because we recognise that it is only through reconciling ideology and reality that we can move towards a vision of justice which engages with the plurality of human values. If we fail in this endeavour, then, as Foucault (1977) suggests, each of us is in effect victimised by justice itself as, through a spiral of ever-decreasing individual autonomy, humanity becomes increasingly powerless in the face of aggression.

Nor do we relate justice to the symbolic 'images' of humanity, such as the global community, which predominate in the language of retributive ICJ, or the rhetorical assertions of rights and their purported significance for justice in post-conflict states. Instead, in dealing with the humanity which these new moralities define and project, we emphasise the link between victims, communities and cultures in terms of the outcomes of international criminal trials and their relationship to the pain of destruction, human and physical resulting from war and social conflict. Consequently, our consideration of crimes against humanity as harms against human integrity and rights (individual and collective), embraces the right to cultural integrity in the broadest sense.

Victim and community as innocent: if resistant

We adhere strongly to the notion that retributive ICJ can fragment cultures and exacerbate pain by reinforcing social divisions, rather than healing them. Sectarian ICJ (Findlay, 2008b) has potentially enormous destructive effect which may penetrate deep into the cultural psyche. It also tends to distinguish those elements of community/cultural context which are deemed by the victors to be worthy of protection and also worthy of destruction. By endorsing particular 'truths', retributive ICJ can exacerbate existing conflicts and precipitate fresh ones (Findlay, 2008b: chapter 5).

More broadly, the pronouncement of punishment is not simply to do with censure; it can symbolise contempt for humanity through its denial of being, the culture and history of a people. ICJ should instead endorse humanity in all its cultural diversity, since the humanity of each one of us is innocent in the context of unprovoked conflict. We need to transgress the narrow legalistic concepts of innocence or guilt, recognising that humanity has the capacity to act morally or otherwise. ICJ should not, therefore, be morally judgmental. Rather, we suggest that the moral virtue of ICJ lies in its capacity to make a more reconstructive contribution to the resolution of conflict. Our vision for the international criminal trial takes this forward through its emphasis on reconciling the interests of the innocent.

Discourses of humanitarian justice

Morality and truth

We assert the importance of 'truth' within the new moralities of ICJ. In recognising the inevitable punishment focus of the trial, we envisage transformed ICJ as liberated from it for the purposes of conflict resolution. Such liberation extends beyond the purview of retributive justice, since the morality of truth-finding must reach to restorative and other foundations for distributive justice within our conception of trial transformation. This follows from our notion of 'truth' and morality equated within our conceptualisation of criminal process as a good.

Paradigms of humanitarian penality

We argue that legitimate outcomes for transformed ICJ through new moralities are both within and beyond existing paradigms of punishment as the eventuality of trial justice. Along with the victim focus for transformed trials is recognition that 'humanitarian' justice is inclusive. A singular focus on retributive justice, on the other hand, can be both exclusive and imposed, acknowledging that all forms of justice delivery are open to abuse.

The new moralities of justice (humanitarian) determine the nature and coexistence of current alternative ICJ paradigms for the benefit of legitimate victim community interests. For ICJ to best satisfy legitimate victim interests, it is tolerant (in its transformed state) of restorative and retributive justice processes and determinations in order that legitimate victim interests can have the widest range of satisfaction. Humanitarian justice as a good is directed towards restoring and strengthening those relationships essential for resolving conflict. The humanitarian constituency for international trial justice is inclusive rather than symbolic and declaratory, both retribution and restoration being called on if that is the appropriate outcome of a finding as to 'truth'.

The outcomes of humanitarian justice are multi-purpose in order to reflect competing legitimate victim interests. These complex interests need to be essentially addressed if justice is to be effective in dispute resolution. 'Humanitarian' justice, while countering the overt and excessive utilitarian purposes for retributive justice, is interested in connecting realities which identify and create disputes for innocent or contesting victim communities (Findlay, 2008b: chapter 4). It is more holistic in this regard. Whereas retributive justice tends to 'patch up' disputes through symbolic overlay, the moralities of humanitarian justice require engagement and inclusion along the way to dispute resolution.

Nevertheless, humanitarian justice, while being apolitical, recognises the political imperatives of ICJ as they presently operate (Findlay, 2008b: chapters 7 and 9). This is particularly so in the production of hybrid institutions and processes, as well as the relegation of a vast array of disputes to lower-order alternative justice paradigms. Our intention is to challenge this by exposing the potential for synthesis in transformed trial decision-making. We suggest that the transformative rationale enables trial structures for determining a holistic moral 'truth' which is legitimised as justice. By this we are suggesting that the 'truth' of humanitarian justice is literally a discourse of legitimacy – legitimacy objectified through a structure that is sensitive to pluralistic values and their conflicting demands for justice (Findlay, 2008b: chapter 9). It is moral in the sense that we envisage human conflict as capable of resolution through engaging humanitarian principles for justice within the setting of a transformed trial. It is realistic in recognising partiality, which is countered by placing the promotion of outcomes favouring the reconciliation of competing claims for justice at the heart of ICJ.

Changing the face of penal governance – new outcomes for ICJ

We counter the negativity of those who continue to envisage ICJ as somehow incapable of transcending the straitjacket of adversarial and retributive justice (see Roche, 2005). The limited capability for formal ICJ to satisfy the legitimate – and contesting – needs of victim communities impacted by war and social conflict is reason enough to grapple with the challenge of holistic and humanitarian trial decision-making. If the contextual analysis of trial procedures moves outside the two major traditions, trial sites exist where adversarial determinations can give way to mediated justice and the direction of the judge and the wishes of victims (Findlay, 2008b: chapter 8). The scenario which we lay out at the conclusion of this chapter presents the challenge for a diversification and harmonisation of restorative and retributive justice within the protective framework of a transformed trial. The procedures of the ICC envisage the possibility for such synthesis.

What we are suggesting through trial transformation envisages a fundamental rethinking of the rationale for the trial itself and the nature of justice delivery. We would disagree with the broader implications of Roche's observation: 'many insist that a trial, even in some modified state, remains an inherently unsuitable forum for pursuing reparation' (Roche, 2005: 572). If this is so, then it is the trial framework rather than an expansion of its objectives that requires review. What we propose through trial transformation is altogether more radical, and potentially significant for ICJ, because it is *literally* transformative of the trial in terms of its ideology, normative structure and potential outcomes, above all, its moral foundations.

We see a fundamental transformation of the nature of justice delivery as a positive opportunity to move beyond the (limited) conceptualisations of penality currently prevalent towards a vision of ICJ which is truly holistic in its capacity to reconcile the conflicting demands modern pluralistic societies are likely to make on the structures it puts in place to resolve conflict among human beings. We do not naively suggest that a transformed trial is the only answer to satisfying all the complexities of post-conflict justice. However, we do insist that it can make a significant contribution to effecting peace and reconciliation by addressing the legitimacy of ICJ.

The humanitarian foundations of the transformed trial infuse it with distinct values for achieving coexistence and peace which counter the tendency for international penality to be used merely as a technology of power. Hegemonically defined responsibility means that individuals may not attach any moral value to those rationales attributing responsibility or to the power base from which they emanate (Findlay, 2008b: chapter 1). Consequently, the significance of penality for ICJ governance requires a profound reassessment of the complex relationships that exist between the ideologies which inform institutionalised punishment and what is perceived as 'justice' as a matter of subjective perception, commonly shared. In other words, the question is not so much one of asserting that ICJ *is* a technology of power, but rather of extending the question by positing whether it can become a *constructive* technology, not in the sense of being supportive of secular hegemonic aspirations, but rather as a force for positive change and social justice, perceived as such by individuals sharing common values of humanity.

This book explains how new moralities for ICJ can make a positive contribution to the maintenance of global peace, helping to protect communities of justice and the integrity of individuals everywhere because of its humanitarian focus. Our emphasis on the sociological significance of moral values highlights the crucial fact that the capacity for human beings to assert their identity as individuals extends beyond mere physical control, so although physical subjugation and persecution may crush the physical body it does not extinguish the shared value of survival and the desire to promote this by all possible means. Consequently, the significance of ICJ as governance must be addressed in terms that reflect contemporary understandings of that sharing through commonly held values, however expressed. This moral commonality is given flesh through structures of community, but always emphasising the integrative relationship of the individual and the social; this value being mutually reinforced through the outcomes of ICJ.

Notes

1. We elaborate this notion more fully in chapter 3. It is crucial to our essential requirement that transformed ICJ and its new moralities be more inclusive of victim interests in all appropriate contexts.
2. As explained later in this chapter, the broader interpretation of penality adopted in this book extends beyond punishment.
3. By implication, we do not accept the argument that international trial justice is inappropriate and should be replaced by forms of local justice. Nor do we regard restorative forms of justice as incompatible with retributive forms.
4. Characteristics of humanity requiring rights protection may be physical and/or mental, and include dignity, happiness, confidence, security, personal power and a sense of self-worth.

5. The case for utilising judicial discretionary power as the primary vehicle for effecting trial transformation is argued in Findlay and Henham (2005: chapter 6).
6. Trial transformation will require, not just at pre-trial determinations, some capacity through judicial discretion to move from an adversarial to a mediatory environment depending on the development and exposure of legitimate victim interests as the trial progresses.
7. These may be seen as situational or 'pragmatic' contexts (Casanovas, 1999).
8. Internationally, the notion of moral power can be conceptualised in terms of those values operationalised in the foundational aims for international humanitarian law, as embodied in the Preamble to those instruments which establish the *ad hoc* tribunals and the ICC. However, this is not the meaning attributed in this book. Instead, we regard moral power in the sense just referred to as simply hegemonic, more particularly of retributive justice. Our conceptualisation of moral power is key to understanding trial transformation since it refers to the *actual* transformative power of the trial; it is not aspirational or symbolic. Consequently, we refer to a moral power implicitly grounded in humanitarian values and operationalised primarily through judicial discretionary decision-making.
9. Subject, of course, to adequate rights protection and accountability measured in terms of due process conventions and the obligations carried by legal professionals.
10. This could be achieved through the analysis of ICC discretionary decision-making in a specific case-study. At the local level, parallels illustrating the instrumental capacity of judicial discretionary power might be drawn with the English judiciary's repeated attempts to sabotage the underlying rationale of the Criminal Justice Act 1991, whilst the objectification of subjective experience through trial decision-making is well illustrated by Erez and Rogers (1999).
11. For arguments to the contrary, see Roberts (2006).
12. Note the discussion of 'victor's justice' in Findlay (2008b: chapter 5).
13. Here the notion of 'deviance' is not used in a pejorative sense, but simply to indicate the presence of behaviour which fails to correspond to accepted social norms.
14. The cultural relativity of morality is explored in Findlay (1999). It is a strong justification for pluralist regulatory strategies for global governance (Findlay, 2008b).
15. This, of course, includes one's ancestors.
16. As evidenced by the prominence given to victims' rights and access to justice in the Rome Statute.
17. For example, this may consist of judges rationalising procedural mechanisms such as plea agreements as rhetorical devices; emphasising their contribution to reconciliation through 'truth-telling', when the 'reality' is that victim and community participation in the negotiation and formulation of such agreements is limited, and they are concluded within a retributive dominance paradigm for justice delivery.
18. Norrie (2001) similarly suggests that a relational model of justice should be concerned to examine the connections between responsible individuals and communities so that punishment is envisaged as part of a shared experience.
19. This identification of 'crucial contexts' within 'communities of justice' where new moralities should take root is an essential part of this endeavour.
20. Thereby recognising that solutions designed to promote peace and reconciliation, and which may reconcile retributive and restorative demands for justice, are not

adequately characterised within conventional understandings of 'penality', since these are commonly associated with paradigms of retributive justice.

21. Analogous to the concept of 'vivid danger' employed by Bottoms and Brownsword (1982) in the dangerousness debate.
22. For example, non-tariff sentencing in England and Wales following the collapse of the rehabilitative ideal in the early 1970s.
23. Such as Article 1 of the Universal Declaration of Human Rights, which asserts that 'All human beings are born free and equal in dignity and rights'.
24. Held (2004) envisages clear areas of demarcation between those spheres of political activity having transnational or international consequences and those requiring regional or local initiatives. More recently, Drumbl (2007) invokes cosmopolitan theory to sustain the idea of pluralism in ICJ subsidiary to the acceptance of flexible and alternative paradigms such as tort, contract and restitution so that the universal norms of accountability are rendered relational. See chapter 8 for further comment.
25. Our vision for humanitarian justice also mirrors the concerns of Durkheim's notion of individualism in sustaining a shared moral culture which transcends moral boundaries.

2
A Framework for Trial Transformation

Introduction

In this chapter we progress to a more detailed elaboration of trial transformation in order to achieve humanitarian justice. Prior to interrogating the essential victim constituency for humanitarian justice (chapter 3) and its essential communitarian context, it makes sense to reiterate the decision site model which we shall employ to plot transformation.[1] We conclude our consideration of what will underpin trial transformation by introducing the problem scenario which forms a binding analytical technique through the chapters to come.

Trial decision site modelling and analysis

This aim of this first section is to provide a summary of the various sites for decision-making which will:

- Identify the trial sites to be transformed.
- What needs to be transformed.
- What the impact there will be.
- What features of each site will be amenable or resistant to change.

More particularly, it serves as an introduction to the way in which we apply transformative principles to the particular sites or pathways we examine in each chapter, and the major transformation themes these address.

In *Transforming International Criminal Justice* (Findlay and Henham, 2005) we identified the following as crucial sites for decision-making requiring transformation:

- pre-trial decisions;
- prosecutorial decisions;

- defence decisions;
- witness decisions;
- judicial decisions;
- sentencing decisions;
- post-trial decisions.

Our present consideration of these sites employs a number of major themes which we regard as crucial to trial transformation;

- notions of liability (individual and collective);
- the nature and role of evidence;
- the standing of legal professionals and the discretion they employ;
- the significance of the sentence against restorative outcomes.

In the analysis that follows we outline the relevance of these core themes for deconstructing each decision site and provide a summary of the key factors which emerge from our consideration of these sites later. Further, we identify the challenges posed as key stakeholders in the new 'humanitarian justice' take on new roles in the 'pathways of influence' which determine trial decision outcomes. We pose this process at this stage as challenges to transformation, which the unfolding analysis in the chapters to come will address and resolve. First, the scenario.

Analytical tools – the role of the scenario

For the purposes of clarity, and because of its enormous potential as a force for the future development of international criminal justice, our discussion makes frequent reference to the ICC as the international criminal trial exemplar. In doing so we also recognise the need for a locus in which trial transformation can and will work to powerful effect. However, we also make extensive use of other examples, real and imagined, as appropriate, especially those drawn from the jurisprudence of the International Criminal Tribunal for the former Yugoslavia (ICTY) and International Criminal Tribunal for Rwanda (ICTR).

In addition, we have developed a case-study, or scenario, to assist the reader in understanding how our proposals might be applied to a particular (albeit imagined) set of facts. This scenario has been designed specifically to typify the kind of factual situation with which the ICC may be confronted at any time. Our purpose here is to introduce the scenario and discuss briefly the problems it creates for each of the decision sites we summarise. We later take up these challenges, referring to more detailed discussion of each problem, and how we respond to it, where it occurs in the text.

The scenario is as follows.

A small island state, Cornucopia, recently gained independence after years of European colonial rule. The colonial power introduced a common law criminal justice system which largely remained in place after independence. However, the island state is mainly rural, with only two large urban centres, and the formal institutions of domestic criminal justice have little influence outside the towns. The police force is corrupt and inefficient. The courts are overworked and compromised through political influence. Domestic criminal justice and the legislative foundations which support it are dysfunctional. Despite the fact that the Constitution also recognises customary law, the village court system is unable to manage much beyond the most recurrent rural disputes.

Cornucopia is a member state of the Rome Statute and has accepted the jurisdiction of the ICC. It has enacted into its domestic laws the necessary provisions to allow for referral to the ICC and to cooperate where the UN Security Council transfers a reference concerning crimes committed by its nationals or within its domestic jurisdiction.

The rural population is organised in a clan structure and lives in agrarian villages. Cash economies are a very recent introduction and have little impact on rural life. The clans are divided into two tribal groupings, which have a history of violent hostility. Politics in the island has been riven by tribal rivalry and in recent years the UN Security Council sent a peacekeeping force to oversee democratic elections and to prevent tribal killings which would otherwise have resulted.

Several years ago significant mineral resources were discovered in a region largely owned and controlled by the Ubu tribal group, which then did not have dominant political influence nationally. The government awarded the mining rights to a multinational corporation (ComCon) which invested significantly in the mining venture but, due to local resistance, was forced to cede the concession.

Following their departure General Lutobu, a senior military commander from the the Tubu, the tribal group with political power, organised paramilitary forces to attack the communities surrounding the mine in order to reduce their resistance to the venture. It is not clear whether Lutobu was acting on his own initiative or with the agreement of the government. However, his activities were certainly known to the government which did nothing to intervene.

Two of the most notorious events in this 'reign of terror' were:

1. The destruction of an entire Ubu village involving the burning of buildings and crops, the killing of all adult males, the kidnapping of women and girls, and the forced recruiting of boys into paramilitary service. This was initially concealed by the national media and the police. As

a consequence of an international human rights investigation, the government was forced to concede that some violence had occurred at the time and in the area. However, the Minister for Information played down the extent of the horror and categorically denied that genocide had taken place. Indeed, he accorded responsibility for the violence to a group of disgruntled villagers who had been in dispute with village elders over landownership. Some of the women from the village who have been repatriated after the violence refuted this account, but are too fearful of reprisals to give testimony to the events as they saw them. The government has offered no compensation to the surviving villagers.

2. Assistance provided by General Lutobu and his men to a force of mercenaries employed by the mine owners in order to regain control of the mining concession. The mercenaries (Fource5) were given permission to enter and operate in the country by the national government. In doing so the Minister for Information and the local media portrayed them as 'peacekeepers' engaged to protect the private property of the mining company. There is considerable evidence that the mercenaries and General Lutobu's troops committed acts of violence against Ubu villagers and their property. Specifically, Lutobu was said to have enlisted and armed Tubu men to attack and kill local Ubus and ravage the villages in order to grab their land and livestock. Consequently, it is said that local Ubu villagers mounted reprisals against neighbouring Tubu settlements. Most disturbing were instances of rape designed to dishonour the Tubu clan and to disrupt 'bride-price' traditions. The national government and the local media reported these reprisals in detail and domestic prosecutions have been instigated against the perpetrators of the rapes.

The global community has exerted significant pressure on the island's government to prosecute General Lutobu for genocide. No international reference has been directed against the leaders of the Ubu reprisal raids. The Prime Minister has indicated that in the face of the public unrest genocide charges against Lutobu would generate, the local criminal courts do not have the capacity to process any such prosecutions. The Chief Justice of the island, on the other hand, has told the international media that the courts are willing and able to handle the matter.

As a compromise the government has established a truth and reconciliation commission to investigate the events. However, the victim communities on both sides have expressed no confidence in the commission and have refused to cooperate with it. In an effort to establish the victims' legitimate interests, an international non-governmental organisation (INGO) has interviewed victims from both sides. In common they want offenders brought to justice before an international criminal tribunal, and have demanded compensation and reconciliation. Above all, they want their stories to be known as truth, and they want to challenge what they see as systematic misinformation from the media and the government, or from their clan opponents.

The UN Security Council has given the ICC a mandate to issue warrants for crimes committed by Lutobu and the Minister for Information. The island government has offered to cooperate by complying with a warrant for Lutobu's arrest if any proceedings against the minister are suspended. Lutobu, on the other hand, has offered to cooperate with the ICC Prosecutor by giving information concerning the government's and the mining company's involvement. He suggests that he was doing no more than following orders.

The ICC Prosecutor has commenced investigations in Cornucopia. Agents from his office have been offering potential witnesses 'protection and eventual compensation' in return for evidence against the general in particular:

- evidence of the recruitment of child soldiers;
- information on the collaboration between ConCom and the general's troops in the massacre of Ubu villagers;
- information concerning 'ethnic cleansing' of Ubu villagers by Tubu tribesmen incited by the general.

The neighbouring nation-state of Neglectistan, which has a sizeable Tubu ethnic minority, has petitioned the UN Security Council to refer the Ubu reprisals to the ICC, but as yet nothing has happened in this regard.

On a recent visit to Neglectistan, Lutobu was arrested and extradited to The Hague. Indictments have been settled by the ICC Prosecutor against him. Victim witnesses from the Ubu villages involved (and child soldiers in particular) have been taken to The Hague for interview and eventual inclusion in the prosecution case.

Lutobu's Dutch Defence originally applied to have the cases struck out due to lack of evidence and delay of process. The ICC pre-Trial Chamber initially conceded the defence applications and ordered the release of Lutobu, much to the dismay of the victim witnesses. Appeals from the Prosecutor have been successful and the trial is now set to proceed.

In the meantime, the truth and reconciliation commission has found Lutobu responsible for atrocities but has recommended that matters be resolved through traditional tribal justice methods, which include shaming, banishment and material compensation.

It is easy to see where the interests of those most in need of ICJ in this situation require a conscious connection to the trial process if it is to develop as the legitimate justice resolution model. Contemporary international criminal trial practice would fail to satisfy many of these interests. They would in turn find their way into some avenues of alternative justice resolution or remain unresolved. It is in their unrecognised or unaddressed situation where legitimate and contested interests form a powerful challenge to the legitimacy of formal ICJ in particular.

We argue that the challenge posed in resolving the justice interests identified in the scenario gives theoretical and practical location to the dynamics of trial transformation, as each trial decision site evolves.

Pre-trial decisions

Pre-trial decision-making is likely to prove the most significant decision site in terms of delivering a successful transformative outcome for the trial. The reason for this is that it is at this point that the consequences of decisions taken by key players in a particular scenario will crystallise in the form of indictments and begin to play themselves out (chapter 3). The complex nature of these decisions is vital to appreciate in planning a transformative outcome for the trial itself and, more particularly, in elaborating a trial programme, as discussed in chapter 7.

The basis for intervention

However, even before this process can begin, the ICC Prosecutor will need to make a preliminary identification and determination of relevant stakeholder interests and judge the consequences of implicating them in a trial process. Many potential difficulties may arise at this stage. One example is the jurisdictional problem created by the notion of complementarity; namely, that the ICC can only act where national jurisdictions are unable or unwilling to prosecute crimes. One difficulty that may arise in this context is that of determining the legitimacy of locally based processes, for example, local forms of reconciliation, as in Uganda. It is extremely problematic for the ICC to ignore local politics in these kinds of situations. If it pursues an interventionist stance, its claims to provide justice are likely to be discredited, as happened in Uganda and Sudan. The issue then becomes one of how to reach a decision about the legitimacy of competing justice claims and deciding what will be necessary for ICC justice to contribute to reconciliation and peace without undermining the complementarity principle and thereby compromising the impartiality of the Court.

Challenge 1 – how to get matters that need to be there, before a transformed trial. Equally problematic is a scenario where one of the interested parties initially cooperates (as did Uganda's President Museveni) and then changes its mind by offering amnesties to opponents, in the belief that such a course stands a better chance of advancing peace, or with a view to securing other advantages. Other scenarios may arise where one of the main protagonists is in the government itself (as in Sudan) and the current administration completely rejects the ICC. In such a case, it may well be questioned whether the prosecution of low-level suspects in The Hague (as in the case of the Congo) enhances the prospects for peace when more serious perpetrators enjoy immunity and privileges at home.

Challenge 2 – addressing the domestic politicisation of prosecution and the ceding of jurisdiction. Similar difficulties are mooted in our scenario. For example, the government is offering to cooperate by complying with an ICC warrant against an alleged perpetrator of genocide if proceedings against a government minister are suspended. For his part, the alleged perpetrator offers to cooperate with the ICC Prosecutor by providing information on the government and the mining company's involvement. Although Cornucopia is a signatory to the Rome Treaty, there is some doubt about the capacity of its domestic justice system to cope with the prosecution of international crimes. Furthermore, the government's compromise position of a truth and reconciliation commission is rejected by victim communities on both sides.

Challenge 3 – reconciling alternative institutional frameworks and their political origins. On this issue, to what extent should both the customary and formal regulatory paradigms be considered in assessing domestic capacity? Particularly when addressing issues of compensation and reparation which arise as crucial for the eventual legitimacy of prosecutions, how can local systems ensure witness cooperation with whatever trial process eventuates?

Challenge 4 – enhancing the crucial legitimating potential of victim-community participation. These questions raise fundamental issues of governance for ICJ which go beyond questions about the capacity of the ICC to contribute to peace through justice. In essence, it is about deciding what the role of ICJ should be. This role might be envisaged simply in terms of carrying out its mandate of retributive and deterrent punishment and ensuring that perpetrators of international crimes receive their just deserts by undermining the culture of impunity. However, the role of ICJ is also often portrayed as linking justice with peace and reconciliation. It is obvious that decisions made by the ICC to intervene in particular conflict situations, and the manner of any such intervention, are likely to have a significant impact on the capacity of the justice it delivers to contribute to peace and reconciliation. This is exactly what has happened with the ICC's recent interventions in African states, and it is a problem for any intervention the ICC will faced in the future.

Challenge 5 – enabling the best conflict resolution and peacekeeping potential for ICJ. Our approach to this dilemma is dictated by our vision of ICJ as a major force in global governance; a position we elaborate in chapter 8. Essentially, we argue for a separation of powers global governance model wherein ICJ plays a pivotal role. Rather than its interventions being seen as representative of sectarian political hegemony and so discriminatory, we regard ICJ as central in making other structures of global governance accountable through adherence to the principles of humanitarianism described in chapter 1. This more tolerant and culturally sensitive notion of regulation will therefore inform ICC decision-making in the critical initial phases of intervention and those following which dictate its strategy prior to entering the more formal processual phase.

Challenge 6 – redirecting ICJ away from sectarian political hegemony towards a wider accountability capacity in global governance. In practical terms, this should mean that the ICC will no longer be driven by the partial concerns of retributive justice and deterrence, informed by an ill-articulated strategy which symbolically links the justice this delivers to reconciliation and peace. Instead, the decision to intervene will be motivated by communitarian concerns from the outset. This will influence all decision-making, from the identification of legitimate interests to considerations of how the justice aspirations of those interests can be realised through the trial. Crucially, however, the governance concerns we argue for will also be instrumental in setting the broader agenda of transformative justice for the trial, which, as explained below (and in chapter 6), we regard as essential for achieving full accountability.

Challenge 7 – the incorporation of restorative justice paradigms. Clearly, neither the ICC nor any other structure designed to serve the interests of humankind can prevent or deter those who might wish to manipulate the process, whether for political or personal ends. There will always be such individuals and interests in any situation the ICC is likely to face. However, the difference between what we advocate and what has gone before is that the ICC will be engaged from the outset in fact-finding, which will involve much closer cooperation between the Prosecutor's Office, representatives of victims and indigenous communities, INGOs and human rights organisations, and other international and transitional justice analysts.[2] The agenda for this multi-agency initiative will be fourfold in that it will enable the ICC to make a preliminary assessment on:

- identifying legitimate interests;
- possible grounds for intervention;
- likely objectives for the trial;
- broader transitional justice objectives.

Challenge 8 – adjudicating and advancing contested legitimate interests of justice stakeholders. In this, it is essential not to see reparation as a bargaining chip enabling otherwise dangerous and problematic victim participation in eventual prosecutions, domestically or before the ICC.

Establishing trial objectives

One of the most significant proposals we elaborate in chapter 7 is the concept of the trial programme. In facilitating an outcome for the 'trial' which makes a specific contribution to peace and reconciliation, we propose that the Prosecutor produces a programme for the trial which aims to reconcile the competing justice claims of relevant stakeholders. As discussed in chapter 7, to achieve this, the Prosecutor will be involved in pre-trial discussions about charging levels and possible sentence discounts, including the possibility of negotiating a plea agreement bargain. We elaborate this in the context of proposed *differentiated outcomes* for the trial, recognising the capacity of the trial to deliver specific justice outcomes for stakeholders, and relating these to broader identified objectives for achieving transitional justice of which the trial outcome will form part. Such outcomes will be differentiated, not through partial political evaluation, but against the values of humanitarian justice we describe in chapter 1 and prioritised in decision-making by utilitarian considerations for realistic achievement.

Challenge 9 – the need to expand access, inclusivity and integration within key decision sites. This is particularly important, as is evidenced in the procedural wranglings at the commencement of the Lubanga trial before the ICC, in recognising what form the victim voice will take (see chapter 8). Victims also represent the role of crucial prosecution and defence witnesses and the challenge is for the trial process not to exacerbate their victimisation unnecessarily.

Issues for the trial programme

If we consider our scenario in terms of developing a trial programme, this raises a number of difficult issues, which we explore at various stages in later chapters. We might begin by thinking about what general approach should be adopted and what to prioritise at the outset. In chapter 7, we suggest that the pre-trial status conference charged with developing the trial programme should concentrate first on identifying the relevant participants and consider objective and subjective accounts of their apparent role in the conflict and their reasons for participating in it. In terms of victim communities this is also examined in chapter 3.

Challenge 10 – resolving and advancing victim community interests as a central measure for humanitarian justice. The second stage is more specifically concerned with directing the preferred outcome for the trial, so the emphasis is on harm and its impact, especially on victims and communities (see chapter 3). It should be particularly focused on expected outcomes and how these expectations might fit in to broader aspirations for transitional justice. It is important to begin by identifying the interests themselves and to reflect on how each interest might fit into a broader picture of the way forward for a return to civil society. In our scenario, the interests of the government, opposition and the mining company are broadly identifiable, but it is necessary to delve deeply into the social, political and legal history of Cornucopia to gain some appreciation of the reality of what these so-called interests represent. This is more than just being able to describe these contexts, because it requires a subjective understanding of context – how those individuals and groups who comprise the relevant interests actually experience the reality that you have purported to describe. It is for this reason that we have long advocated the use of comparative contextual analysis as a methodology for penetrating this difficult terrain. No matter how difficult, we regard this kind of methodology as indispensable for the development of the trial programme.

Further, there is need here to balance competing interests where they stand as legitimate if contested aspirations for trial justice. Most commonly, as in our scenario, there will be victim communities which have different stories to tell concerning harm, responsibility and reconciliation. Here, the 'pathway of influence' will be where the trial professionals can, where possible, mediate differences in order to produce manageable and achievable outcomes for restorative or retributive justice further into the process.

Another concern is how responsibility and, where appropriate, criminal liability can be established in the claims or charges which may be bargained in order to move forward. We spend time later in our analysis developing a new notion of international criminal liability which is capable of confronting the criminal 'cultures' apparently demonstrated by the mining company and the government in this scenario.

Challenge 11 – the creation of a new jurisprudence on responsibility and liability. In order to determine which interests are legitimate and should prevail, and what amounts to responsibility or liability, the transformed trial will need methods to identify the true account. In composing this account, 'truth' may emerge from the stories of victims, the representations of witnesses (reluctant or otherwise), the official account, media reporting, observations from interest groups, etc. In the conventional trial setting these sources may imbue the resultant understandings with different status as fact or truth, and the procedural consequences will impact on the resolutions which they support.

In our scenario, we have evidence from an earlier UN peacekeeping mission, an international human rights investigation and an INGO survey which can help us to understand the background to the conflict, the kinds of atrocities that took place, the impact of the violence on individuals, communities and the state as a whole, and the aspirations for justice held by different interests and how these might be achieved. However, the kind of evidence we are advocating as necessary goes far beyond what can be gleaned by 'expert' reports, partial or not, or relatively brief surveys of victims' attitudes and opinions on post-conflict justice. Despite contemporary trial conventions that *evidence* be as objective as possible, it must, above all, provide a coherent and penetrating appreciation of each context in the comprehensive terms we have described. Evidence or stories as the substance of truth gain much from their subjective roots and these need to be recognised in the process decisions which the emergent 'truths' suggest.

Challenge 12 – distilling admissible and persuasive 'truths'. Our claim for contextual relativity immediately confronts the adversarial/legalist requirement that evidence should emerge as convincing against the testing and discrimination of contested cases. The argument that trial fact takes on the status of evidence as it emerges triumphant from the adversarial contest must not forget that the foundations of opposing cases are deeply contextual and relative. In addition, as much as the adversarial trial imagines contest over facts, the experience of most trials is that much 'evidence' can become uncontested if the procedural environment favours and supports an 'agreed fact' approach. Whether it is through mediation or adversarial contest, the transformed trial process favours agreement above argument wherever that can be achieved in a humanitarian and accountable framework.

In addition, ICJ must harmonise, where appropriate, with the justice environment of the host culture. With regard to the legal context in our scenario, we need to know and understand much more about the origins and forms of indigenous justice that exist, why the domestic justice system has become so dysfunctional, and why there is such widespread suspicion about the proposal for a truth and reconciliation commission to establish the facts of what took place. So, although the ICC will be directly concerned to identify and prosecute individual perpetrators, the mission of the transformed trial will be to situate these crimes as contexts of criminality to be understood in terms of collective liability. This is so, not just because specific communities or groups have been harmed, or have caused harm, but in recognition of a broader constituency of common interest.

Challenge 13 – for ICJ to recognise the cultural context of justice within the society in conflict beyond narrow considerations of domestic jurisdictional capacity to prosecute. This should accord with a re-determination of international criminal liability and wider social responsibility for harm caused. This broader constituency identified in the diverse justice stakeholders within the scenario challenges the conventional authority of the nation-state to monopolise and manage criminal justice, and from there the very existence of the state itself. How the disparate parties to the conflict and the interests they represent can become reconciled to the harm each has caused and, more importantly, to the reasons why it took place, requires mediation outside the domain of the dysfunctional and compromised state. For this reason, we see comparative contextual analysis as an essential precursor to understanding what it is that will bring interests closer together, through mediation, by allowing victims and communities the opportunity to hear each other and accept responsibility collectively, in the hope of moving forward to begin healing and reconstruction. Therefore, the final phase of the pre-trial status programme will be looking to establish possible grounds for compromise through mediation and thinking about where this might occur most profitably at various points within the trial. This phase will be particularly concerned with:

- the relationship between individual actions and collective liability; and
- identifying the role of the trial in terms of satisfying the justice demands of relevant interests against the broader objectives set for transitional justice – in our scenario, for example, this might include establishing the best way to exploit the mining resources for the benefit of the state as a whole and all its peoples.

Challenge 14 – for the transformed trial to identify and redirect regulation and peace-making possibilities, beyond and ongoing from the limits of even the transformed trial process. Our scenario contains several facts which should focus our attention on the significance of the relationship between individual and collective liability. For example:

- The general indicted by the ICC came from the tribe in political power.
- The government acquiesced in the general's activities, although it is unclear whether or not he acted on his own initiative.
- A senior government official (the Minister of Information) assisted the general to recruit mercenaries to expedite the latter's activities.
- The ICC is mandated to issue a warrant against the Minister for Information.
- The government indicates that it will cooperate with the ICC in proceeding against the general if the court suspends the warrant against the minister.

In terms of the proceedings under international criminal law there is nothing unusual in this scenario and there is no doubt that, as in many cases tried by the ICTY and ICTR, the defence of acting under superior orders and those facts deemed pertinent to its immediate context would be explored by the ICC in reaching its decision should such proceedings move to trial. The defence touches on those fundamental principles of criminal law which establish how individual responsibility for actions is determined in both the common law and civil law world. The essence of criminal liability is therefore individual responsibility, and despite the fact that international criminal law has often invoked the concept of collective enterprise, albeit with considerable difficulty, the primary motivator for proceedings against perpetrators of alleged atrocities is to find them individually responsible (see Fletcher and Ohlin, 2005).

However, as elaborated in chapters 5 and 6, within the context of trial transformation, we envisage individual responsibility in terms of its relationship to the notion of collective liability. This is because we see establishing the responsibility of the individual and the community as a holistic exercise when it comes to delivering this kind of accountability. The emphasis is on seeking to repair the damage done, rather than focusing entirely on issues relating to the allocation of blame and consequential punishment.

Challenge 15 – suggesting an new imagination for collective liability which focuses on organisational or group cultures and interconnections rather than agreements between individuals. For our scenario, then, a significant trial objective will be that of establishing the dynamics of the dealings between the government, the minister and the general against a broader canvass of the history of tribal rivalry and political power. In other words, it will try to get as close as possible to understanding how the criminality of the actions which took place is perceived by the relevant communities of interest, and how these perceptions are constructed and experienced in daily life.[3] This new view will look at the 'criminal cultures' of groups and organisations, particularly those that have power and authority over victim communities and are uniquely placed to collude in criminal outcomes. This does not imply that there is to be some kind of 'watering down' of accountability. Rather, it means that individual and collective accountability are conceived as one, so that it is the task of the trial, through the trial programme, to explain the social reality of the relationship between the two, and why this manifested itself in the conflict in the way it did. This objective will be achieved by facilitating the movement from adversarial to mediatory phases of the trial process.

To summarise, we can identify trial outcome objectives as being concerned with delivering, as far as possible, the justice expectations of the interested parties. These may involve retributive and/or restorative and reparative forms of justice, as in our scenario, but whatever the final outcome, the findings of the trial will reflect the 'context' of the criminality, especially the concept that responsibility for individual actions should be seen within a framework of collective liability. We elaborate this latter concept in chapter 4.

However, these objectives must also fit into the broader *transitional justice objectives* set for the trial. These objectives incorporate governance concerns, especially through the way trial outcomes can contribute to the goals of humanitarian rather than hegemonic justice (Findlay, 2008b: chapter 9), the scale of the role it has to play being very much dependent on each scenario. Our perspective here is to view the trial outcome as doing something (through concession and conciliation) which helps the contesting parties in a conflict to come together *and* puts them firmly on track to achieving transitional objectives about which they can be helped to agree. We see it as a significant role of the trial (especially through mediation) to bring this about.

Of course, agreement as to the communitarian objectives themselves presents a significant challenge beyond the capacity of any trial or other justice paradigm. In reality, this will involve identifying values and objectives for a common society based on mutual respect and tolerance, depending on social and structural (including institutional) renewal, as appropriate. Our scenario, in common with many others, envisages the kind of substantial compensation, and consequent aid, necessary to begin reconstruction, but this cannot begin unless and until there is a commonality of purpose for the new society. This can only come about through compromise, by helping to put the citizens of a state in a position where they feel able to move forward together towards attaining a common end. We believe strongly that transformed trial justice can contribute to this.

Challenge 16 – crucially positioning the trial to stimulate wide communitarian reconstruction, conflict resolution and peacemaking. The adversarial phase of the trial may therefore be seen as a context for establishing responsibility within a transformative context, with the mediatory phase providing opportunities to bring reconciliation closer by suggesting ways to compromise the justice demands of competing interests within a framework of transitional objectives set for the trial. The degree to which punishment should reflect the gravity of what has taken place will thus be balanced against the extent to which a responsible individual's community bears liability collectively for that person's actions. However, the significance of that finding in relation to collective liability for any particular community or social group will be judged by the extent to which it helps contribute to the reconstruction of the whole society or state.

Prosecutorial decisions

In addition to settling charges and plea bargaining, prosecutorial decisions relating to witness testimony, disclosure of evidence and sentence will all be informed by the trial programme. Each of these components of the trial is currently heavily influenced by the retributive dynamic and the adversarial nature of the process. Consequently, sentencing for international crimes, for example, is characterised by a lack of coherent principle coupled, paradoxically, with a significant emphasis on proportionality against which it is presumed the fairness, or otherwise, of the outcome can be assessed. Adversarialism confronts and distances the parties so that disclosure requirements and testimony are driven by the need to vindicate a finding of guilt or innocence, producing a factual account according to which the 'truth' of what took place will be judged. In reality, this is a highly selective and partial view of events designed to satisfy the rules of the adversarial contest.

Challenge 17 – reformulating and repositioning the rules of trial practice to complement restorative justice paradigms. We have already indicated how we envisage a key role for the Prosecutor in transforming the nature of international trials before the ICC. As we explain in chapter 7, the Prosecutor's Office will be proactive in identifying legitimate interests and developing the trial programme. However, the responsibility of the Prosecutor will also extend far beyond the processual stages of the trial by ensuring that the Prosecutor's Office has done everything it can to facilitate the trial's contribution to the broader transitional justice objectives set for the process. This means a commitment to full accountability, one that begins with developing aims, seeing those aims achieved in terms of specific objectives for the trial and, finally, beyond the trial itself, so that the Prosecutor's Office is fully engaged in achieving those targets set for the community, as it was in developing them *ab initio*. This will involve working with indigenous and/or alternative justice mechanisms and other structures of institutional renewal to integrate the consequences of the trial outcome into the wider objectives and processes driving the return to peace and civil society. This process might involve:

- Exploring the history and forms of indigenous justice to establish why and how they developed.
- Seeking commonality between competing interests in terms of rights protected and methods of protection.
- Exploring whether common values are supported by disparate forms of indigenous justice.
- Exploring how trial outcomes can build on existing justice mechanisms without increasing division and precipitating conflict.

Ultimately, of course, success in achieving any or all of the above will depend on agreement being reached about the wider objectives for transition and the perceived role of international criminal justice.

Challenge 18 – empowering prosecutorial discretion to advance restorative justice outcomes. The pivotal role of the Prosecutor in promoting a broader and more inclusive form of accountability for international crimes is emphasised by the fact that we advocate specific responsibility for facilitating rights, participative or otherwise. As we elaborate in chapters 6 and 7, this will be enforced as a duty to the ICC, whether or not the Court is acting in an adversarial or mediatory mode. This does not, of course, imply that the Prosecutor's duty is absolute in this respect. Rather, it gives the Prosecutor *de jure* responsibility for ensuring that the transformative process, whether in its adversarial or mediatory mode, facilitates the achievement of the justice objectives set for the trial by the trial programme, by bringing to the attention of the judge any matter which it is felt might prevent a party from placing their legitimate interests before the Court. This role should therefore be seen as one designed to facilitate access to the trial at key decision sites. This in turn will permit participation where the transformed process prescribes and thereby ensure that those basic rights which underpin our vision of humanitarian justice are given effect, subject to the principled exercise of judicial discretion.

Defence decisions

The corollary of prosecutorial decisions made in the context of an adversarial trial framework are by convention the province of the Defence. These usually include decisions about plea and defences, the nature and ordering of witnesses, nature and disclosure of evidence, and evidence relating to sentence. The ICC is no different in respect of the role envisaged for the Defence. In common with that of the Prosecutor, the Defence role is currently heavily influenced by the dictates of adversarial trial and the dynamics of retributive and deterrent punishment.

Our transformed role for the Defence is discussed at various stages throughout the book. However, the one overriding factor which informs it is the changed nature and role of evidence we foresee for the transformed trial, as elaborated in the trial programme. The ethos of transformation and the objectives set for each trial will circumscribe the role of the Defence. Together with the Prosecutor, the Defence will be tasked to work towards the achievement of these overriding objectives. This will involve a commitment to ensuring that the interests of those parties they represent are protected in such a way that they contribute to the broader objectives of the trial outcome to transitional justice, as elaborated in the trial programme.

This implies a coordinated approach, even during the adversarial phases of the trial, because the role of each legal professional will focus on establishing the part played by the interested party they represent in terms of collective liability for the events that took place and the implications of this, rather than contesting issues bearing on individual responsibility as in a conventional trial. Not only will this mean developing new trial relationships – both lay and professional – based on role and expectation; it will transform the role of evidence and the way in which it is adduced. It will mean that evidence is no longer constrained by strategy and contest, but admitted for the contribution it is judged capable of making to the achievement of trial objectives, as set out in the trial programme.

Challenge 19 – creating new pathways of interest where the Defence responsibility to accused persons is incorporated into the wider restorative mission. The defence role will still be seen as one designed primarily to protect interests, but this will be governed by a duty reciprocal to that of the Prosecutor: to ensure that it does everything in its power to advance the interests it represents through achieving the broader objectives set by the programme for the transformed trial. The transformative context in which this is done will ensure that attempts to misrepresent or manipulate the process to promote interests which work against the establishment of a mediated account of liability and the collective purposes set for the trial will fail, more particularly during the mediatory phases of the process. The degree of liability and the implications of this for achieving transformative objectives will be differentiated through the outcomes agreed for the process as a whole, as well as for each of the participant interests represented.

Witness decisions

Our main focus here is the issue of victim participation and the involvement of victims in the trial. In this we make the conventional distinction between service and participatory rights for victims (Edwards, 2003; Ashworth, 2005: 352), as reflected in the jurisprudence of the ICTY and ICTR, and the procedural norms of the ICC (Henham, 2004a). More particularly, in chapter 7 we argue that even so-called participatory rights for victims are in reality largely symbolic since they do not give victims, or indeed any party with a legitimate interest in seeking justice through the trial, rights participate in *actual* decision-making.

Challenge 20 – constructing crucial frameworks of trial rights as accessible to all legitimate stakeholders within communities of justice. The need for this derives directly from the transformative ethos we suggest for the trial in chapter 3, which stems from its victim focus and concomitant mandate of inclusivity. The nature of this inclusivity extends not only to the identification of legitimate interests, but much further through the imposition of a legal, as well as a moral, duty to ensure that inclusion means real participation in decision-making. The common interest of all included parties in working towards the common goals set out in the trial programme is thus reflected in the differentiated objectives set for each participant. These different objectives therefore not only reflect those set for individual trial participants, but also suggest how the realisation of the latter might fit into the collective account of liability that should result from the trial. Correspondingly, it is envisaged that the collective 'truth' produced by the transformed trial as reflected in its outcome will contribute to transitional justice. We go on to suggest how the normative framework of the ICC could be modified in order to bring about the kind of victim participation we advocate for the transformed trial.

In chapter 7 we describe how a differentiated outcomes model will be developed for each trial. This will elaborate trial outcomes in terms of:

1. objectives for the trial (specific to the trial and including broader transitional justice objectives);
2. objectives for the participants in terms of:
   - outcomes to be achieved,
   - desirable outcomes,
   - subsidiary outcomes,

   and how each of these relates to the objectives in 1;

3. objectives for participants *in* the trial in terms of input (for example, relating to testimony; possible contribution to diverse mediatory phases).

There will also be a *plenary* post-trial phase, in addition to post-trial evaluation.

Our discussion of witness decisions also touches on a number of other issues which have a direct bearing on trial transformation. Some of these relate to the way in which evidential material is admitted for the purposes of establishing the 'truth' of the trial. For example, in chapter 3 we consider the position of the victim as a provider of factual information relating to the circumstances of the alleged events and how that evidence should be treated as against that provided by other kinds of witness. Currently, in adversarial forms of trial, the victim's contribution is limited to testimony that assists in establishing the facts against which the guilt or innocence of the accused can be judged according to the onus of proof which the Prosecutor must discharge in a criminal case, namely, beyond all reasonable doubt. In addition, certain types of witness (for example, children and rape victims) may be protected by special measures, and witnesses generally subject to protection against particular forms of questioning, for example, under Article 6.1 of the European Convention on Human Rights (ECHR), or the ethical codes of legal participants in the trial (Ashworth, 2000a).

Challenge 21 – opening up the trial to 'stories' that are untold and inaccessible in current trail practice. Story telling then becomes a legitimate outcome of transformed trial practice. In chapter 7, we consider the changed nature of the relationship between judge and victim in the context of the transformed trial. One of the most difficult issues for the judge will be the perception of a victim *qua* victim, and also as someone representing a broader constituency of victim that may be seeking compensatory outcomes linked to transitional justice. This broader link between the trial as producing an outcome relevant to both liability and reconstruction places increased importance on the neutrality of the judge and their capacity to view the broader instrumentality of the victim status.

Challenge 22 – returning the role of the judge to a central concern for victim access, inclusion and integration – moderator of the victim voice at all key decision sites. As we discuss in chapter 5, another significant issue which impacts on the quality and extent of witness decisions in the conventional form of trial concerns the relationship between substantive criminal law and sentencing principles. Broadly, there is no necessary symmetry between the elements required to be proved to establish the commission of a substantive offence and the factual basis for sentence. For example, as regards aggravating circumstances, whilst these may be germane to establishing the objective quality of the substantive offence, their relevance to sentence is determined by different considerations related to penalty. We regard such divisions between substantive and sentencing law as reinforced and exacerbated by the distinct verdict and sentencing phases of the international trial process. Consequently, we advocate merging these two phases of the transformed trial, primarily to ensure that no artificial distinctions are drawn between the purposes for which factual information is admitted. An expansion of these purposes and the judicial discretion to facilitate their selection will bring with it a more flexible appreciation of how trial stories can and should best be employed. The stories of witnesses will determine responsibility and/or liability and the sentence might flow on as any other determination of these considerations.

Challenge 23 – when responsibility and/or liability are determined in the transformed trial, to enable a more seamless shift to the outcome whichever resolution supports; verdict and sentence will be one such, but not the only progression. The current debate about victim participation in international trial justice is trapped between advocates of proportionality and those promoting principles of restorative or reparative justice. This dichotomy is fundamental in that retributivists generally regard victims as marginal because they threaten commensurability and the achievement of 'just deserts', whilst restorative advocates see victims as the central focus for sentencing and instrumental in achieving wider reintegrative purposes. We argue for a more radical conceptualisation of participation under the aegis of integration, one that gives the victim a pivotal role in shaping the decision-making processes occurring throughout the trial and pre-trial phases that impact on the eventual outcome. This is consistent with our view that transformative justice must address victim participation and its relationship to trial outcomes as something that is significant throughout the trial process. Hence, our focus is on how trial participants, especially the judge, relate to different conceptions of the victim during the trial, and the implications of this for decision-making.

Challenge 24 – to reformulate the victim voice through access, integration and inclusion beyond the limited role of witness of fact or contributor to sentencing determination. Legitimate victim interests will take a central place in the rights protection framework offered through the transformed trial. Restorative influences are likely to prove challenging to advance in terms of their impact on conventional trial relationships. For example, the following propositions do not sit easily with the dynamics of adversarial trial:

- the idea that victims as well as offenders are accountable for their actions;
- that a main purpose for the trial is for victims to redress the balance of advantage and assert their full rights as citizens;
- that the trial process should be instrumental in helping victims to achieve some kind of closure;

- that the victim concept extends to community; and
- that the trial outcome can be a significant response to community harm.

For these dynamics to become fully integrated into the decision-making processes of the transformed trial requires a concerted programme of training judges and legal professionals, supplemented by detailed practical guidance. These issues are explored in depth in chapter 7. Suffice to say that the reconceptualisation of relationships needed to facilitate the kind of transformative justice we envisage will be a precursor to the successful implementation of any trial programme.

Challenge 25 – facilitated through the notion of 'communities of justice', trial professionals will need to reposition their roles so that in the adversarial phase legitimate victim interests are advanced in a wider trial rights framework. In particular juridical trial professionals have a key stakeholding in the community of justice approach to the adversarial phase. Beyond the mediatory phases of the trial where restorative dynamics will predominate, the way in which trial professionals conduct themselves in the adversarial phases, and in deciding when it is appropriate to move into mediation, will reflect the new transformative ethic we propose to inject into the international criminal trial. Consequently, contested facts in the adversarial phase will be judged against notions of collective liability. This will change the perceived role of the victim and community interests in the trial and its outcome from that of subverting retributive aims to that of seeing the possible relevance of achieving retributive and restorative objectives as part of this wider goal.

Judicial decisions

The conventional role of the judge in adversarial trials is more passive than that normally attributed to inquisitorial forms of justice. It is confined to interventions, rulings, providing explanations, summarising the facts and passing sentence. Even so there are unique occasions, as with the protection of the unrepresented accused, where the trial judge assumes a more interventionist and partial role in rights protection. The inquisitorial judge is much more proactive, controlling, questioning and generally directing the process, including legal and lay participants; doing whatever is necessary to draw out the 'truth' of what is alleged in the dossier. Such caricatures provide an important clue as to the likely behaviour of international judges, especially how they might exercise their discretion in decision-making.[4] Further, if the experience of some hybrid and transitional criminal justice traditions is sought (see Findlay, 2008b: chapter 8), it is left open to the judge to direct the progress of the case and make the move from adversarial detachment to mediatory involvement.

Challenge 26 – judges will need to embrace a new interventionist role in the transformed trial process. Legal culture and social background characteristics are doubtless important variables to consider when analysing the way in which international judges use their discretion (Pakes, 2004). However, it is important to remember that ICC judges have been faced with new challenges and decisions within a new jurisdiction – trying crimes with which they may previously have been unfamiliar and charged with developing a jurisprudence and utilising procedures *de novo* – all this within a context where the boundaries and objectives for justice are far from clear, except as embodied in the rhetoric and symbolism of international treaty documents, or the foundation instruments of the trial structure they inhabit. Small wonder, therefore, that the dynamics of control expressed through retribution and deterrence have driven the decision-making capacity of the international judiciary (Henham, 2003a).

Fortunately, the procedural framework governing the ICC does not impede most of the central elements of transformed trial decision-making and the pathways of influence on which it relies. We have consistently argued that the potential exists for ICC judges to individualise sentences which reach beyond the justificatory rhetoric, symbolism and procedural imperatives of retribution and deterrence to engage with alternative justice paradigms (Findlay and Henham, 2005). In chapter 5, we elaborate this argument, suggesting how the transformative context for judicial decision-making can be realised and describing the normative framework necessary to give this effect. We explain why ICC judges are pivotal in the development of the new normative framework, especially in bringing about changes in lay and professional interaction, effecting victim participation and defining the contexts for admitting evidence within the trial. We go on to suggest how the capacity for ICC judges to achieve a more inclusive form of decision-making can be realised, providing there is a commitment by relevant state parties to facilitate trial transformation.

In chapter 7 we describe how all trial professionals will have designated roles in facilitating a transformative outcome for the trial. This process will be initiated through the development of a trial programme for each trial, directed by the judge. Judges will also be given the power to order a change in the direction of the trial from one phase to another, adversarial to mediation, to facilitate the achievement of restorative and/or retributive outcomes. Judges will be given primary responsibility for ensuring access and inclusion, and ensuring transparency and accountability for discretionary decision-making. Consequently, through using their discretionary power, ICC judges will be able to facilitate the representation of victim and community interests, and be instrumental in directing a more integrated and relevant contribution to meeting their demands for justice.

The trial programme will be case-managed by the judge, with both the Prosecutor and the Defence being consulted before any decision is taken to transform the process to mediation. Consequently, although judge-directed mediation will be with prior consent of the parties given at the pre-trial status conference, the possibility of introducing further mediatory phases of the trial will be at the discretion of the judge, consulting with the Prosecutor, Defence and others representing legitimate interests.

Sentencing decisions

As regards the decision site of sentencing, we identified the following as critical points of debate for trial transformation in *Transforming International Criminal Justice*:

- the role of judicial discretion;
- evidence relevant to sentence;
- the dichotomy between verdict delivery and sentence;
- relationships between judge and legal professionals;
- the relevance of victim and community;
- transparency;
- the impact of legal principle and normative guidance (Findlay and Henham, 2005: 213).

We explore these issues in greater depth in chapter 5, elaborating the changes in sentencing necessary for delivering transformative justice. In particular, we analyse why and how the factual basis for sentencing can be reconceptualised within the context of a transformed process for the ICC, focusing on:

- existing concepts of innocence/guilt and responsibility/liability and their appropriateness for producing the kind of truth needed to underpin transformative outcomes;
- the relevance and probative value of trial evidence, especially how it needs to be reconceptualised when moving from adversarial to mediatory phases of the trial;
- the importance of maintaining a distinction between the verdict and sentencing phases of the trial in the context of delivering transformative justice;
- the role of aggravating and mitigating factors and their reconceptualisation to accommodate trial transformation;
- reconceptualising and changing the procedural context of victim participation and evaluating its impact on the delivery of transformative outcomes;
- considering how relationships between legal and lay participants should be reconceptualised within a more inclusive transformative sentencing framework.

Challenge 27 – expand the resource foundations of the sentencing exercise in ways compatible with restorative outcomes where co-aligned.

Post-trial decisions

Post-trial decision-making in conventional trial settings usually refers to appeal on matters of law and sentence and various issues relating to the enforcement of sentences, depending on the type involved. Our interest in post-trial decisions is much broader than this. As discussed in chapter 6, accountability is the most important concept for the kind of transformative justice we envisage for the international trial. Our conception of accountability is not restricted to matters of appeal and enforcement, crucial as they are, because we see the issues as integral to the wider notion of transformation we espouse. This suggests a reciprocal link between the ideology of transformation which informs the process and the capacity of the trial outcome to satisfy the demands for justice of victims and communities of interests. We regard discretionary decision-making in the transformed trial as the route to fulfilling this link (Findlay and Henham, 2005).

Consequently, post-trial decision-making is fundamental to delivering this form of accountability. We regard to judicial discretion as a key variable for changing the currently narrow notion of accountability to one that engages with legitimate justice demands and supports rights which are consistent with their achievement. This is evidenced by our equation of access to justice with a distinct conceptualisation of victim participation, which suggests that victims and communities of justice should participate fully and have a significant input into discretionary decision-making processes occurring throughout the criminal trial.

In chapter 7 we argue how increasing community control over justice delivery will ensure that it responds to local demands, thus precipitating the demise of purely or predominantly retributive solutions. Since particular outcomes will be sanctioned only if victims and communities of justice deem it appropriate, accountability will be predominantly localised and contextual, so encouraging a profound understanding of the relationship between harm and victimisation. However, as we mention above, we also envisage accountability as something which locates the outcomes of trial transformation in terms of their wider peacemaking role and fundamental significance for international criminal justice as a form of global governance. These issues are explored fully in the final chapter.

Challenge 27 – while the trial professionals need to exercise their enhanced discretion in the most accountable fashion, the service delivery to communities of justice will make all stages of the trial accountable through access, inclusivity and integration. This then will follow on to a more accountable capacity for ICJ in global governance. This chapter has outlined a framework for achieving the structural changes we regard as necessary for trial transformation. The precise content of these changes and their interrelationship will become apparent as our discussion progresses. Nevertheless, it is important here to reiterate the fact the foundational 'new morality' which underpins trial transformation discussed in chapter 1 is essentially driven by our view that international trials should reflect humanitarian values more effectively in fulfilling expectations for justice than in the past. The core constituency for achieving this is that of the victim. In the next chapter we consider the difficulties that need to be overcome if we are to engage fully with notions of victim status and their contextual significance, before moving on to detail the mechanics of trial transformation in the chapters that follow.

Notes

1. This model was devised and detailed in Findlay and Henham (2005: chapter 3). Here we actualise the crucial sites for decision-making and their 'pathways of influence' in order to actualise the practical challenges for trial transformation.
2. It is worth recalling here the dissatisfaction expressed by victim communities with the limited outreach programmes operated particularly by the ICTY.
3. The relevant evidence will be analysed and factored into the trial programme (see chapter 7).
4. What we advocate through transformative decision-making goes far beyond Pakes' (2004: 162) suggestion that a more inquisitorial approach by international judges would benefit the process and outcome of the trial.

3

Activating Victim Constituency in International Criminal Justice

Introduction

This chapter develops from the earlier discussion of a new normative framework on which the transformation of the international criminal trial rests (see also Findlay and Henham, 2005: chapters 7 and 8). It is a position with which no doubt many of our critics will disagree. However, we invite consideration of the essential victim constituency for ICJ being arguably as legitimate and persuasive as any more distant commitment to a global constitutional legality.

Those who would like to see the international criminal trial remain a retributive endeavour reflecting the conventional features and characteristics of domestic trials are concerned that to introduce other expectations for the international trial process will endanger its limited success (Judah and Bryant, 2003). Some critics declare that the ICTY in particular has achieved legitimacy through the effective prosecution of significant offenders important to many victim communities (see Findlay and McLean, 2007). In this it is argued lies justification alone for the expansion of a retributive international trial process in the form of the ICC.[1]

Despite these narrower legalist assertions the ICC, and its Prosecutor, also have claimed more universalist justifications in the form of the Court's potential to assisting in state reconstruction and peacemaking. Further, the ICC, and the international tribunals which precede it, have within their authorising legislation recognition of victim interests, even if this remains largely outside the processes of trial decision-making.[2]

Today in many domestic criminal jurisdictions, the position and voice of the victim are receiving increasing attention and recognition (Schunemann, 1999). Slowly, it seems that the prosecution of criminal trials is moving full circle. Historically, in common law jurisdictions in particular, the prosecution of crimes was the responsibility of the victim. However with the development of the nation-state and the institutionalisation and professionalisation of the criminal courts, as well as the establishment and monopoly of police investigation, it became more realistic for state instrumentalities to take on the prosecution role. This trend has recognised the interest of the state and the communities it protects in crime and punishment as governance tools (Simon, 2007), while tending to see the marginalisation of the victim voice to a place wherein comparable civil trials this exclusion would not be tolerated.

More recently, first with victim impact statements, and then a range of initiatives up to victim advocacy within the trial, the necessity to recognise, consider and enunciate these victim interests in more and more formal trial scenarios has become a feature of neo-conservative justice reforms (Aldana-Pindell, 2002). The imperative for victim inclusion has progressed into the procedures governing institutional international criminal justice.

Besides an emergent political utility in balancing victim interests against the protection of offenders' rights in national courts, this chapter argues that the nature of global crime and the purposes of international criminal justice require a more victim-centred transformed trial process (chapter 5). In saying this we recognise the reservations about the domestic trends to vociferate victim interests and thereby to move away from the consequences of the presumption of innocence towards a more civil jurisdictional consideration of 'balance'. There is good reason for law reformers and criminal justice professionals to be suspicious of the victims lobby when it comes to ensuring even a balanced adversarial contest. The chapter's argument that the nature of ICJ and the global crimes it confronts presents a uniquely persuasive position for a victim constituency despite the challenging partiality of victim interests.

All this must be measured against the crucial importance of accountability as a measure of trial fairness and the protections of the accused which this requires (chapters 4 and 5). Along with accountability to a victim constituency follows the pragmatic persuasion that with a heightened victim purchase over international criminal justice will flow greater legitimacy for this process across a wider range of communities it is said to serve. The legitimacy that the satisfaction of victim interests offers should not be underestimated. It has already been recognised in the United States with the prosecution of those involved in the 9/11 atrocities and other mass killings (Logan, 2008). Prospects for broader systemic legitimation clearly influenced the recent reform of criminal procedure laws in jurisdictions such as Italy, Russia, Japan and China where victim advocacy is provided for and greater community participation in criminal justice advanced. It is not coincidental that the provisions within the ICC Rules identifying the roles of victims in its proceedings extend much further than the conventional trial limitations surrounding the victim witness.[3] The nature and direction of victim legitimation will be examined specifically in this chapter against a range of challenges which might tend to compromise that legitimating process.

In other work (Findlay, 2008b) we have suggested that an incapacity to confront appropriately the victimisation consequences of global crime has tended to mean that ICJ and the governance that flows from it are unsatisfactorily entwined with sectarian international relations and narrow cultural inclusion (Findlay, 2007). Therefore, in governance terms alone, it is compelling that the conceptualisation of global crime victims be expanded and emancipated. As a consequence, the citizenship and standing necessary to enjoy ICJ are more fairly realised.

There is no doubt that an ideologically-driven campaign to prioritise victim interests in criminal justice is at risk of distorting some of the central values that criminal justice traditions have developed over the centuries (Logan 2008). To avoid this, the chapter concludes with an examination of 'communities of justice'. It is argued that victim interests alone should not be overvalued. Communities of justice recognise in their operation that in any criminal justice resolution there may be several victims or victim communities with different stories exercising different interests and values. A distillation of legitimate victim interests in such a contested environment will be a challenge for the transformed criminal trial (as discussed more fully below).[4] Even so, the identification and harmonisation of legitimate victim interest remains a challenge as the trial process advances. Until now most of the expectations, beyond retributive justice and vengeance, that victims enunciate (Albrecht et al., 2006; Weitekamp et al., 2006; Kiza and Rohne, 2008) do not find satisfaction within the formal trial process and are hived off into alternative justice reconciliations (Aertsen et al., 2008). This chapter suggests how such a division of responsibility has tended to deny victims access to the rights protections that formal trial procedure, at least in theory, can afford (Findlay and Henham, 2005).

Communities of justice are presented as the crucial context wherein lay and professional players will interact so that a more communitarian form of justice benefits from the application of the rule of law. As such, communities of justice become a dynamic environment where negotiation is essential and where actionable questions will be transferred into the trial decision-making framework minimising the burden of partial adversarial argument. It is assumed that, if operated with a common aspiration for justice outcomes, these communities of justice will make more reasonable the victim position prior to exposure through trial interrogation (Findlay and Henham, 2005: chapter 7).

The chapter begins by confronting prevailing circumspection about why victims should be prioritised as the constituency for ICJ. The argument moves from the demands of legitimacy to the anticipation that, through communities of justice, a sharper victim focus will require that ICJ be more accountable. This is a theme that prevails throughout and will link our case for transformed criminal trial process to a new age of global governance (Findlay, 2008b: chapter 9). But first it is necessary to locate the chapter's theoretical mission against the perennial struggle between subjective and universalised analysis.

Socio-cultural theorising victimisation

Providing contextual appreciations of socio-legal phenomena like victimisation within different cultures and jurisdictional boundaries is problematic (see Albrecht et al. 2006; Aertson et al., 2008). The difficulties encountered in such research are multiplied when we seek to develop understandings both within and across jurisdictional boundaries, and particularly for the comparative analysis of victim communities.

The research balance between phenomenology and social reality (i.e. what counts as an epistemologically valid explanation) lies in the extent to which there is agreement as to what constitutes the 'objectivity' of victimisation. As we say later, with the conditionality of victim legitimacy, even the status of victim communities can be politically and culturally contingent (Findlay 2008b: chapter 7). Although the reality of victimisation is epistemologically conjectural, we can nevertheless postulate (depending on our theoretical persuasion) some a priori principles by which to measure or evaluate whether such a phenomenon exists 'objectively'. The 'politics' of victim legitimacy, we later argue, is constantly engaged in claiming such objectivity. These principles connect to:

- the nature of the harm inflicted;
- the 'non-combatant' role; and
- the standing of victim communities against measures of political and cultural authority.

Also, if victims or victim communities are deemed resistant to these authorities, then the consequences of victimisation can be markedly different (Findlay, 2007).

The subjectivity of the victim phenomenon is largely determined by measures of 'innocence' and hence concerned with such issues as:

- the perceived legitimacy of the causes and consequences of 'war';
- what it subjectively feels like to be a victim, rather than simply having been ascribed that status; and
- how these intimate influences have shaped the individual attitudes of those claiming victimisation.

Thus the social reality of victimisation is a conflation of subjective and objective measures. Victimisation, particularly in its communitarian sense, is a representation of both what 'victims' claim and what they have ascribed to their status. Communitarian victimisation especially depends for its legitimacy and credibility on the consequences that flow from the community's status and behaviour.

Any social theory which seeks to address the nature and significance of victimisation must necessarily address its legal, socio-historical, economic and political dimensions. The challenge for comparative analysis, and one largely not met in many post-conflict empirical studies, involves appreciating the multi-layered nature of the relationships between the values and actions which produce victimisation within particular cultures and being able to make epistemologically acceptable generalisations about them. This chapter suggests a complex framework of indicators around which such comparative contextual analysis might be mounted.

Certain war victim experience studies offering vital insights into individual perception go beyond conventional empirical victim analysis in the sense that they seek to hypothesise about observed and quantifiable 'facts' such as sentencing patterns (Fletcher, 2005). In so doing, the 'victim experience and aspiration' approach applies quantitative techniques to the analysis of what is essentially an account of the subjective perception of 'facts'; describing what it is like to be a victim in a particular post-conflict society and how this impacts on the perception of what constitutes justice for war crimes. The 'objectivity' of these accounts in such a subjective methodology can only be evaluated to the extent that we are able to understand their meaning within particular contexts. That is why this chapter resorts to the 'communitarian' location of global victimisation as the crucial contextual framework for evaluating justice aspirations and responses in a process sense. The comparative potential is therefore objectified by employing community structures and functions to ground the subjective appreciation and ascription of victimisation.

The repercussions of this tension between subjective methodologies and objective speculation are considerable because, both theoretically and methodologically, there is a clear distinction to be drawn between exploring the aspirational and the empirical dimensions of social experience. The objectivity of any social phenomenon mirrors its subjectivity, and vice versa; the relationship is reciprocal. We can attempt to explain how definitions of 'objectivity' are produced through the analysis of subjective experience, which is a recursive and constantly changing process. Hence, this approach tries to fix the meaning or contextualise social life by deconstructing the subjectivity of individual experience and making generalisations about the extent to which such experiences and understandings are held collectively. Where the collective experience is given objective form through 'community', it follows that the comparative enterprise – community to community and aspiration to justice option – is greatly enhanced. Evidently, such methodologies will be culturally contextual in suggesting ways in which the objectivity of process is constructed subjectively.

War victimisation should, therefore, be conceived as a social construct that involves the interplay between the causes and effects of war and the perceived appropriateness of particular forms of legal and institutional redress.

The analysis of post-conflict victimisation as a comparative endeavour should benefit from community location so that the individualised and collective representation of victimisation, and its selectivity, can be critiqued and materialised in justice outcomes.

Why victim focus?

The first answer is simply that ICJ has no choice but to move towards victim constituency if its legitimacy and functional relevance are to be confirmed beyond the authority of legislative instruments and sponsor agencies. It is a functional and operational shift now required by legitimate victim interests and aspirations for pluralist justice outcomes. In its first trial, the ICC recognised, in a limited fashion through access and representation, this imperative of decisions in favour of victims.

The research carried out in victim communities affected by genocide and crimes against humanity (Albrecht et al., 2006; Weitekamp et al., 2006; Kiza and Rohne, 2008) clearly establishes that victims are not satisfied by the retributive justice alone offered through current international criminal tribunals. This is not a blanket denial that retributive justice is on the list of victim community expectations. Nor could it be said, from the victim community perspectives surveyed, that retribution should be marginalised in any process of trial transformation. Quite the contrary. Along with most victim communities so far studied, we endorse the importance of retributive justice (Findlay and Henham, 2005: chapter 7) in terms of current political resonance for criminal trials and against the dissatisfaction of victims of mass harm in alternative truth and reconciliation options alone. Even the ICC's capacity for restitution and compensation may not satisfy broad restorative concerns. Without a capacity for the international criminal trial to offer more than retributive justice through international penality (see Henham, forthcoming) the potential for victims to justify and legitimate formal international criminal justice may be squandered.

It has become essential for the legitimacy of ICJ that a victim constituency be centrally recognised. The unavoidable justification for this rests in the nature of the international criminal jurisdiction (Zahar and Sluiter, 2007: chapters 1, 3 and Part 2). The types of crimes that international criminal tribunals and courts confront are all inextricably linked to victim communities. War crimes occur within jurisdictional and communitarian limits. The communities at risk and the individuals, communities and cultures that suffer harm can be clearly identified. The crimes which compose war crimes rely on the scope of victimisation for their definition. The same could be said of genocide. With genocide, however, the notion of harm extends beyond communities to cultures and races. In fact, in the case of ethnic cleansing, the purpose of military intervention and violent confrontation may be to victimise and destroy opposing cultural or racial elements. Finally, when dealing with crimes against humanity, it is the global community that is at risk. This community, however defined, is at least in part a community of potential victims and one for which ICJ is clearly constructed.

Essential normative shift

Appreciating the intentions for communities of justice, and having read our arguments in the preceding chapter, it will come as no surprise that we expect ICJ to be both humanitarian and collaborative. Humanity as the focus for both crime victimisation and criminal justice protection globally should provide an identified location for the retributive and restorative energies of ICJ. Humanity, it is suggested, also operationalises the scope and compass of the global community and justifies international governance concerns to maintain peace and good order.

As mentioned above, domestic criminal justice traditions have moved, along with the growth of the nation-state, to situations where the victim is less likely to stand as the initiator of a criminal prosecution. The state and its instrumentalities have replaced victim interests where criminal justice and punishment are concerned, and it is the state and a generalised notion of the community it maintains towards which retribution is directed rather than to the vengeance of individual interests of victims under their communities.

In the context of ICJ the role of the nation-state has not been simply or directly replaced by an international governance collectivity. Depending on one's interpretation of international political relations, there are several ways of interpreting the current global governance condition (Findlay, 2008b: chapter 1). Even the strongest advocates of international diplomatic and political institutions would be hard-pressed to argue that entities such as the UN have duplicated the position of the nation-state as far as ICJ service delivery is authorised. In fact, large INGOs could be said to have as much capacity when it comes to regulating essential elements of world order (such as human rights, commercial probity and now even territorial sovereignty) as could be claimed by international diplomatic and political organisations. There hardly exists a common style and framework for ICJ, let alone a universally accepted governance style like that which would be alleged by domestic government institutions.

Simply because there is no clear institutional replacement for the domestic state to authorise and manage global governance we are not arguing for the dominant place of the victim as a default position. Even if the institutional and process frameworks of global governance were more concrete, the position of the victim in a justice system with crimes against humanity at its heart is impossible to ignore.

As we have argued in chapter 1, a new morality driving ICJ offers both support and stimulus for a victim constituency. Through communities of justice the attainment of ICJ is essentially communitarian and as such the conceptualisation of a victim constituency is collective. The transformed trial which becomes a mechanism for recognising victim constituency accepts the importance of access, inclusivity and integration wherein the place of victims is active at both the pre-trial and trial stages. In this way the normative commitment to humanity as a focus for ICJ is translated into action (see chapters 5, 6 and 7).

Humanity as the constituency for international criminal justice

A new moral foundation for ICJ with humanity at its centre (chapter 1 above) distinguishes the victim focus for ICJ from current trends to inject a higher victim profile into domestic criminal justice processes. It is different for the following reasons:

- Global crimes are crimes against humanity, against communities and against culturalism.
- ICJ agencies have declared an interest in peacemaking and conflict resolution for the benefit of communities and cultures under attack.
- The harms against which ICJ is directed (war, genocide, ethnic cleansing) are collectivised in their impact.
- The extent of liability for global crimes is also collectivised beyond considerations of joint criminal enterprise and superior orders, and humanity is a democratic and inclusive determinant of the global community.

To accept humanity as the natural constituency for ICJ does not require a rejection of 'the rule of law', 'constitutional legality' or 'the global state' as important terms of reference for the exercise of ICJ. It is obvious that the UN and its Security Council, for instance, will play a crucial role in the interventions and priorities of the ICC. In addition, important NGOs will continue to exercise influence in the maintenance of global order. And this is as it should be. The legal professionals in the transformed trial process (chapter 5 below) will play a crucial role in dividing the rights and protections that the adversarial process can advance. With all this in mind, there may be natural and appropriate constraints on the inclusion of the victim's voice in the trial process, but this does not deny the importance of humanity as a constituency for ICJ.

Collectivisation of the victim dimension

We have argued (Findlay and Henham, 2005: chapters 7 and 8; Findlay, 2008b: chapter 1) that international crime victimisation is a collective phenomenon. The terms 'the victim community' recur throughout this text to emphasise the manner in which this collectivisation takes shape. Victim communities can be seen as a challenging concept to distil:

- How can victimisation be removed from individual harm?
- How are communities (in their diversity) to be conceived so that some convincing notion of victimisation can emerge?

- If it does, what are legitimate interests in a community context?
- How are these interests to be revealed, and how is a community to be given access to and voice within criminal justice determinations?
- What particular impact should the voice of victim communities be accorded against the conventional protections for the accused in due process?

All these questions lead on to the requirement of identifying victim communities in action.

The notion of victim engages:

- the communities of these victims which share their harm;
- where wider communities or groups of victims which suffer harm;
- where the crime is directed at community cohesion or cultural integrity; and
- when violence is motivated by the destruction of what makes communities or cultures (language, art, religion, family structure, etc.).

The victim dimension is collectivised because of the nature of global victimisation and also in the legislative sense through the way the global crimes which form the jurisdiction of the ICC are currently conceived.[5] The collectivisation of victims in a global sense from this legislative and jurisdictional foundation invites our later discussion of collective liability (see chapter 8).

Failure of the international criminal trial on access, inclusivity and integration

As mentioned earlier, the empirical studies which investigated the expectations and aspirations of victim communities in post-conflict and transitional states have highlighted that the international criminal tribunals and their trials are not enough to satisfy these concerns. This has meant that many victim aspirations such as truth-telling, restoration, reconciliation and compensation have been moved – if at all – into the alternative justice paradigm. Therefore, it is not surprising the constituency of victim communities and the mandate for conflict resolution are more acceptable and less controversial within these alternative frameworks. Truth and Reconciliation Commissions for interest were constructed where it was thought by post-conflict states and peacekeeping agencies that retributive justice and its institutions could not achieve a legitimate interest of victims within transitional cultures. It is becoming clearer as ICJ develops and gains more significant purchase in global governance that justice for conflict resolution cannot only be relegated to a second tier of truth-telling.

An important justification for transforming the international criminal trial is to enable victims otherwise relegated to alternative justice contexts to benefit from the procedural protections offered within the trial. Recognising that these protections are sometimes problematic in practice, it remains clear that the rights of victims are often ignored or mediated in local justice situations. The transformed trial as we describe it (see chapters 4 and 5) should be premised on commitments to expanded victim access, deeper and more genuine opportunities for inclusion, and a more natural and productive integration of victim aspirations through a greater variety of resolution opportunities.

The transformed trial as we envisage it (Findlay and Henham, 2005) addresses the current failure of formal ICJ at three levels:

1. By emphasising from the victim perspective access, inclusivity and integration to key pre-trial and trial decision sites[6] and, as a result:
2. Enhancing the legitimate role of victims in creating and maintaining pathways of influence out of these crucial trial decision sites. Added to which:
3. Restorative as well as retributive processes will be available within the 'rights-protected' procedures of the trial, enabling victims to better achieve their legitimate aspirations in the trial context.

Besides the necessary procedural and legislative enhancement of the trial to enable structural transformation, there will be a need to reposition the normative foundations of the trial along the way. Essential for the success of trial transformation will be an enlivening of juridical discretion to manage the smooth achievement of greater victim constituency.[7]

Need for conflict resolution as part of ICJ

Our discussion of an enhanced governance potential for ICJ (Findlay, 2008b; also chapter 7 below) concedes the importance of peacekeeping and conflict resolution for the legitimacy of ICJ (Braithwaite, 2002). In much of the debate about the contemporary direction for global governance (Lederer and Muller. 2005; Findlay, 2008b) the importance of state reconstruction is emphasised. It is assumed that post-military intervention in transitional states, conflict resolution community to community will provide an essential peacemaking function. Yet, whether it is through the mechanism of truth and reconciliation commissions or the retributive outcomes of criminal tribunals and special courts, lasting peace will only emerge when victim communities are satisfied that the governance and justice interventions on their behalf have meaning and impact. Peacemaking will be little more than political posturing when communities not at war but victimised through war remain excluded from constructive justice outcomes. Those institutions and paradigms of justice most successful in meeting the widest range of victim interests will obviously, as a consequence, enjoy greater legitimacy among communities that might challenge peace.

Legitimacy of victim interests

Legitimacy for justice and governance emerging out of victim satisfaction is an important underpinning of ICJ. Even with their limited engagement of victim interests and aspirations, the international criminal tribunals and the ICC have been legislated at least to provide victims with information about the substance and impact of their determinations. This will never be enough in itself. Victim communities have identified a desire to see the perpetrators of global crime brought to justice (Albrecht et al., 2006). In many situations, however, this is a symbolic first stage to addressing more restorative and community-centred considerations.

The capacity for victims and the satisfaction of their legitimate interests then to legitimate criminal justice service delivery is more than an ideological attainment. With ICJ institutions identifying conflict resolution and peacemaking as crucial practical purposes, the enjoyment of ongoing peace and good order should first be measured against the victim communities that have suffered from the global crimes in question. Where peace may be won through further alienation and exclusion or consequent victimisation legitimacy will be squandered.

An obvious problem here is to identify legitimate victim interests in situations where several victim communities contest the nature of their victimisation, its origins and what should be done in restoration. Contested victim interests will require the resolution which is discussed in chapters 5 and 6 if the satisfaction of these interests is to afford legitimacy to ICJ. More of this later.

Capacity for victims to make global governance accountability

In our discussion of the two levels of accountability – internal and external – offered for ICJ through the transformed trial (see chapter 6) we identify the important contexts of communities of justice. Communities of justice in each particular incarnation will provide 'boundaries of permission' to determine the nature of justice applied and justified for the conflicts and challenges these communities are facing. The processes of justice employed, the decision-making which they achieve and the outcomes and resolutions that they conclude will be the measures of accountability against genuine communitarian justice aspirations.

The location of justice accountability within communities takes it away from its present and, we would argue, unhealthy reliance on the sponsorship of sectarian political hegemony. This is not to say that ICJ accountability will not have its political dimension. Rather, a more productive place for the political aspect of accountability is grounded in the authority that communitarian justice interests and processes provide.

The nature of the global victim

Once the need for greater attention to a victim constituency in ICJ has been argued, the next issue is to identify and describe in more detail the nature of the global victim. Collectivisation aside, the global victim presents certain unique features in terms of inclusion and exclusion which make victim status not simply designated by proximity to violent harm. Even so, the harm borne by victims arising out of violent exchanges remains a critical determinant of victimisation in domestic criminal justice settings. Globally, the relativity and sectoral designation of violence which is the interest of ICJ means that harms to victims and communities of themselves may not be enough to ascribe legitimate victim status (Findlay, 2007).

Problems caused by victor's justice

The notion of 'victor's justice' suggests the collectiveness and exclusion essential in ICJ inextricably linked to sectarian political hegemony (Findlay, 2008b: chapters 1 and 7).

In terms of victimisation, victor's justice is responsible for the designation of those victims worthy of protection, imbued with the rights of citizenship and therefore standing before formal justice institutions. The consequence of this is the denial of legitimate victim status to those individuals and communities that resist the cultural, economic and political predetermination of this hegemony.

Essential for discriminating those victims worthy of justice outcomes and those not is the attribution of morality or immorality to violence applied by and against particular groups. Morality and immorality in this sense rely in part on awarding the status of innocence to some victims and perpetrators or, at the very least, collaborators to others. Concepts of risk, powerlessness, guilt, injury and blame are empowered where they are awarded on behalf of the innocent victim against those represented as unjustified perpetrators. For example, terrorist communities become victims in very similar contexts to those who suffer terrorist violence, but from the perspective of victor's justice, little regard is paid to their victimisation, evolving as a necessary consequence of justice against terror.

Therefore, the subjective distinction of worthy victimisation depends on the authority of those imposing the label and the 'significant others' on whom the label rests. The process of 'meaning attribution', however, is not all one-way. For any meaning to carry weight it must resonate in the wider audience to which it is directed. The valorised victim may retain the status accorded by our politicised process of meaning, among those significant others (family, friends, civic leaders, etc.) who accept the authority of the labelling agency and its stance on the terror enterprise. Crucial to this process are the victims themselves. Those who might challenge or even modify the nature of this meaning and its authority are quickly marginalised and their valorisation denied.

The morality of the justice response (or the terrorist act for that matter) requires either community respect or superimposed violence (force) to condition its standing and ensure compliance. If the claim for standing relies on force rather than respect, then the resistance of the recipient communities is an important consideration in fashioning the response and expectations for its effectiveness.

If standing is to have an essential influence over the prosecution beyond a particular version of truth or justice, then the arena within which it is claimed must be mutually respected. Particularly at this level, the morality of victor's justice is contested by terrorist violence.

The challenge of jurisdiction and standing caused by selective citizenship

Standing, even in the legal, non-metaphysical sense, has largely eluded analysis in the literature on ICJ and global governance. One reason for this is that if standing is to have a definitive influence over the prosecution of a particular version of truth or justice, then the context within which it is claimed must be mutually respected. The selective application of ICJ currently runs against such mutuality of interest (Findlay, 2007). Particularly at this level of the morality, victor's justice is constantly contested through the violence of resistant communities.

The ambiguity of violence, as both a challenge to and a confirmation of hegemonic domination, is widely apparent in the process of redefining statehood and citizenship on the 'global periphery'. Here, in transitional and separatist states, violence is transacted from the status of terrorist coercion through to legitimate armed struggle, along with the transformation to legitimacy and global recognition.

In the context of the war on terror, crime victimisation and the legitimate claims to global citizenship are conflated. The fissures of exclusion and inclusion are drawn against criminality and victimisation against global communities.

Citizenship is protected through globalisation where it accords with the constructs of the global community, its market economies, liberal democracies, democratic styles of government and allegiance to the modernisation project (Bauman, 1998; Findlay, 1999). The nature and ramifications of global citizenship are clearer in the context of ICJ than they may be in other regulatory frameworks because of the triggering effect of citizenship.

Humanity is represented and protected by the prosecutions before international criminal tribunals. The global community, through the enabling legislation of the ICC and tribunals, carries actionable responsibility for a limited range of harms caused to communities within it. In this regard it is not simply individuals or nation-states that are the subject of tribunal interest, and in fact under the terms of the ICC statute, individual liability is the focus of the justice delivered.[8]

The challenge when conceptualising and actualising global citizenship is to avoid the political partiality demonstrated in global governance as it presently operates. From the regulatory perspective of the dominant political alliance, domestic citizens are cherished if they fall within the political allegiance and jurisdictional boundaries of the alliance and supporter states. Outside these boundaries the protection of the nation-state and citizenship are conditional on risk and security evaluations from the perspective of the dominant alliance and on broader geopolitical significance. These considerations also invest the designation of legitimate victims.

Victims are centred in both supportive and resistant communities

Resistance is sometimes violent with respect to the partial recognition of citizenship within communities where the individualised rights are subservient to communitarian concerns for social harmony (Braithwaite, 2002; Findlay, 2007). Western governance models which promote individual autonomy over community responsibility have not received universal acceptance through globalisation, and in some contexts this has fomented violent resistance. Levi (1997) argues that citizens are more likely to comply and give active consent to imposed democratic governance when the institutions and processes that have evolved are perceived as fair in decision-making and implementation. Along with this realisation, the cultural sensitivity and origination of these processes are also crucial to their acceptance (Findlay, 1999). Inclusivity and community collaboration are conditions which affect the acceptance of imposed governance models.

The same could be said about the response to ICJ as an introduced governance model where community justice is not primarily individualised.

When citizenship is more dependent on the jurisdiction of the secular state than membership of a religious culture or a cohesive community, issues such as territoriality, sovereignty and political authority are determined by the dominant alliance as central risk and security considerations. Communities which value religious culture and communitarian customary practices are over-represented among those victimised by violence internationally, but who, through their resistance to the dominant political alliance, have been denied legitimate victim status.

The necessity to remove international criminal justice as another regulator for social exclusion

It may be correct to assume that concerns about jurisdiction and mandate for ICJ when they are not directed towards victim interests are really centred on the spread of democracy, modernisation and western value systems. In order to promote these priorities for global governance ICJ is focusing on conflict-prone states to assist in state reconstruction. While victim communities in these settings are recognised, particularly by the ICC, as an important interest group for criminal prosecutions, through retributive justice the determination of legitimate and illegitimate victims before the Court is the exclusionary by-product of ICJ.

The valorisation of victims has an essential bearing on which individuals and communities can claim legitimacy in justice resolutions, thereby having a voice and demanding a dominant place for their interests above those of marginalised or illegitimate communities. As mentioned earlier, and to confound conventional considerations of justice, innocence alone may not be the crucial driver for victim valorisation. As with security risks and control responses, it is the nature of the authority claiming the power to distinguish between victims or collateral or resistant communities that confirms this legitimacy. Or at least that is how it operates within the current ICJ dimensions of global governance.

To make such distinctions more striking, the dominant political alliance valorises citizen victims while simultaneously alienating and even criminalising opponents and their resistant communities. Part of this legitimacy project is to neutralise value plurality. There is one model of governance to be fought for, one victim community to be protected, and embodies one prevailing justification for violent justice responses.

Collectivity and distance – who can claim victimisation?

Issues of standing for 'victims' seeking ICJ identify a clear tension between the 'local' and the 'global' contexts of justice service delivery. The criminal justice literature abounds with cautions concerning the uncritical expansion of victim participation and influence in domestic trial deliberations (Fletcher, 1995; Erez and Rogers, 1999). Internationally, however, the ICC and the criminal tribunals have advanced victim interest through a range of pre-trial and trial inclusions. This is a logical consequence of the special position of victim communities in the construction of global criminality. Further, the collective and communitarian contexts of global criminal victimisation defuse much of the domestic debate about distance, harm and legitimacy.

The experience in domestic jurisdictions of trying to identify an appropriate victim voice in homicide trials has raised the specific question of victimisation and the actionable distance from the harm caused by the substantive crime (that is, the original victim encounter). Courts have faced some difficulty in determining in situations where the immediate victim is the deceased to what extent family and friends intimately connected to but removed from the act of victimisation can be considered as victims for the purpose of an impact statement. The conundrum of victim status and distance from harm is likely to be moderated within global crimes such as genocide, where the victim may be perceived as a community, a culture or a race as much as individuals that have suffered directly from crime.

In the context of mass murder trials, Logan (2008) explores the many difficulties that the use of victim statements present. These include:

- demarcating permissible boundaries in terms of victimisation and impact. These are issues for capital (murder) trials in general, but may be exacerbated in the context of mass killings and mass victimisation;
- questions of proximity to the actual victimisation for survivors;
- the forms of harm to be recognised by the Court;
- guarding against popular emotionalism which may affect the personal experiences of victim survivors;
- a range of tactical problems in giving equal recognition or proportional weight to different victim voices depending on proximity, and how these are to be challenged.

For instance, the instrumentality of victim impact statements arising from terrorist mass killings is controversial. Should the victim voice, whether individual or collective, influence sentencing directly, and if so what weight should be accorded relative to other sentencing principles such as general community protection? Further, in the context of widely feared terrorism, how can the interests of the accused fairly be separated from victim impact and community vengeance or mob hysteria?

In terms of extending the reach of legitimate status, what are the dangers for ICJ in preferring victim interests and thereby compromising conventional protections for an accused person? The problems associated with this trend have been rehearsed in detail when considering the domestic jurisdiction of victim impact statements in murder trials (Erez and Rogers, 1999). Therein no victim voice remains, beyond the voices of second parties closely connected to the deceased. This issue of connection to harm is exacerbated when there is more than one voice to comprise a connected victim community. Moving up to a global context, communitarian victim contexts presuppose a more flexible and case-by-case consideration harm 'networking'. After all, this is the essence of genocide.

In the international context, the normative framework around harm and victim location may not be as consolidated as it could be in the domestic setting:

> While the views of natures and cultures can coalesce in matters of broad importance ... they often diverge on questions relating to more specific normative notions of substantive and procedural fairness ... finally is the basic question whether government should be appointed to deploy victims to meet their didactic ends?
>
> (Logan, 2008: 741)

Contextual relativity of victimisation

Another important theme in establishing the nature of a legitimate global victim is the contextual relativity of victimisation. Many violent groups and organisations presently identified as terrorist threats have themselves been victims of harsh repression and counter-insurgency violence. In transitional state conflicts in particular, some sides of the violence hold privileged identity as both victors and victims, and as such claim considerable domestic legitimacy (Bikundo, forthcoming). Sovereign decisions on who is friend or enemy are not grounded in force of violence alone, otherwise the authority for its exercise continues to be denied to those whom it might be directed. More importantly, this distinction depends specifically on the authority of the sovereign and the legitimacy of the distinction between citizen and alien respondent communities. When referring to respondent communities we cover both those that support sovereign authorities and those resistant to it. If the legitimacy or authority of the sovereign is challenged, the valorisation of victims above others beyond questions of innocence may also be challenged and the determination of legitimate victim interests will be contested as a consequence. How is ICJ to resolve this where military and political discrimination has exacerbated the confusion?

Take the contested victim interest themes in our scenario. Following on from the survey of both victim communities by the INGO:

> In common they want offenders brought to justice before an international criminal tribunal, and they want compensation and reconciliation. Most of all they want their stories to be known as truth, and they want to challenge what they see as systematic misinformation from the media and the government, or from their clan opponents.

Besides international commitment, what stands in the way of achieving and perhaps reconciling these aspirations? The clan bias within the nation-state has valued the stories of the Tubus over the Ubu. Victim valorisation is at work. This is compounded by a compromised and politically dependent media. Because the local truth and reconciliation commission is a creature of government, it fails to achieve legitimacy with either victim community and therefore is unable to provide a jurisdictional foundation for any international intervention. Neighbouring states with geopolitical influence advance the cause of the Ubu victims and this makes the partial interpretation of truth dependent on clan context worse.

The formal intervention of the ICC and the manner in which victim witnesses have been managed seem to have done little but reverse the direction of partiality. And this is in the face of the concession by the Chief Justice that the local courts have capacity and interest.

Finally, the local truth and reconciliation commission has made findings and suggested responses to responsibility which go beyond the capacity and interests of the ICC. The question is whether a wider range of victim interests would be satisfied by this approach. Could victim interests from opposing communities be mediated in a context where the rights of both sides were recognised and protected?

Victim valorisation

The valorisation of victims has an essential bearing on which individuals and communities can claim legitimacy in justice resolutions, thereby gaining a voice and demanding a dominant place for their interests above those of marginalised or illegitimate victim communities. As mentioned earlier and to confound conventional considerations of justice, innocence alone may not be the crucial driver for this process of victim valorisation. As with the risks and responses connected to terrorism in particular, it is the nature of authority claimed and exercising the power to distinguish between victims and collateral resistant communities that distinguishes and awards this legitimacy. Legitimacy so conferred, particularly through military might or imposed justice paradigms, will stand as a fragile determinant of victimisation and citizenship where such legitimacy is resisted by violent community reactions.

To make these distinctions more meaningful, the dominant political alliance which currently sponsors global governance valorises citizen victims while simultaneously alienating and even criminalising opponents and their resistant communities. Part of this legitimacy project is to neutralise value plurality. There is one model of governance to be fought for, one victim community to be protected and one prevailing justification for violent justice responses. A narrowly focused and politically dependant regulatory mode resting on military and then justice-based violence always tends to alienate resistant communities.

Democratisation of formal and informal justice paradigms

As we suggested earlier, one reason for the proliferation of informal justice resolutions at both the local and global levels is the aspiration for victim inclusion. A criticism raised concerning the formal justice process internationally through victim communities directly affected by matters at contest is the limitations on access to trial justice. If the transformation of the trial process advocated in this book is achieved, then access, inclusivitiy and integration of legitimate interests will be features of that transformation. In such circumstances the 'democratisation' of formal as well as informal ICJ processes will necessarily result in a heightening of interest in the victim voice.

In addition, as argued in the conclusions to this book, methods and processes of accountability will flourish when situated in a democratic structure of victim responsiveness. That said, we concede, due to the self-interest and partiality of some global communities, that greater access may not result in more universal representation. Even so, if genuine attempts are made to achieve consensus prior to trial deliberations, then more democratic accountability should flow from better reflecting the victim voice.

Victim communities

Crucial to our argument in favour of repositioning the constituency of ICJ towards legitimate victim interests is the recognition of communitarian victimisation. Communitarian incorporation assumes a level of participatory democracy not yet seen in global governance. Communitarian governance will give legitimacy to both the substantive and institutional authority of global governance so far not present beyond normative claims about themes such as rights and justice (Braithwaite, 2002).

We have strategically employed the notion of 'victim communities' not only to emphasise the collective composition of global victimisation, but to identify the structures of relationships which make sense of global crime victimisation and which would be essential in the measure of appropriate restorative and reconciliatory responses (Findlay, 2008b). We next develop the concept of communitarian victimisation in discussing communities of justice. Essential to this discussion is a recognition that victim communities themselves may be in contest over the nature and legitimacy of victimisation. This is one of the principal challenges for legal professionals in the transformed international criminal trial process.

Onto the requirement of identifying victim communities in action, the communitarian context of victimisation engages:

- the communities of these victims which share their harm;
- where wider communities or groups of victims suffer harm;
- where the crime is directed at community cohesion or cultural integrity; and
- when violence is motivated by the destruction of what makes communities or cultures (language, art, religion, family structure, etc.).

The nature of global crime

When discussing our arguments in favour of a victim-centred ICJ constituency we have referred to the unique collective characteristics of global crime identified as the limited jurisdiction of international criminal courts and tribunals. Crimes against humanity, genocide and war crimes all have about them and within them collective composition. Global crime, therefore, assumes the importance of communities that comprise the humanity which ICJ should prosecute and protect in both a normative and a practical sense.

However, as with victim valorisation, the concept of 'humanity' has been limited as a consequence of the segregation of legitimate violence. Oppositional cultures and communities, if resisting in a violent fashion the governance of the dominant political alliance worldwide, will become the subject of criminal prosecution rather than being appreciated in any context of victimisation. Segregated cultures therefore become excluded from any protections of ICJ through association with perpetrators rather than victims. Consequently, the communitarian notion of global victimisation is selective, exclusive and discriminatory. Victimisation is not accorded as a result of violent harm alone. Violence is negotiated in terms of its legitimacy rather than its consequences. With this in mind a theoretical appreciation of the connections between violent crime and violent legal responses discriminating the victim status is helpful (see Findlay, 2007)

Walter Benjamin, in his critique of violence, explicates the relationships between violence, law and justice:

> The task of a critique of violence can be summarised as that of expounding its relation to law and justice. For a cause, however effective, becomes violent, in the precise sense of the word, only when it bears on moral issues. The sphere of these issues is defined by the concepts of law and justice. With regard to the first of these, it is clear that the most elementary relationship within any legal system is that of ends to means, and, further, that violence can first be sought only in the realm of means, not of ends.
> (Benjamin, 1978: 277)

This means/ends distinction distinguishes violence in terms of motivation. However, from the perspective of criminal law, and its influence on ICJ, motive takes on a minor significance in the determination of liability. Whether good or bad, legitimate or otherwise, violence must be lawful or it is for the domain of criminal sanction. As such, both means and ends are criminalised and the rationalisation of violence in any legal/criminal sense is not exculpatory unless it falls within a justification or defence determined by the law.

Jacques Derrida, in his deconstruction of the 'Critique of Violence', explains that 'to ask ourselves if violence can be a means with a view towards ends (just or unjust) is to prohibit ourselves from judging violence itself' (Derrida, 1992: 983). The crucial concern, then, would only be with the application of violence and its contextual relativity, not the nature of violence itself. We would not be able to tell if the latter, as means, is in itself just or not, moral or immoral, without contextual location. Located in our discussion about violent justice responses to global terror (Findlay 2008b: chapter 4) a decontextualised consideration of violence would risk sanitising our analysis in the same way that we criticise the delegitimation of resistance through sectarian retributive justice.

Elsewhere in his work, Derrida observes that in its foundation law can rest on nothing but itself (its own authority) and therefore 'a violence without ground' is neither legal nor illegal, nor even illegitimate or unjust (Derrida and Anidjar, 2001: 242). This provides at the level of political legitimacy alone an argument for locating violent retributive responses to global terror within the pre-existing legality of ICJ, rather than military might alone. This pre-existing authority distracts considerations away from the comparable nature of violence across the legal divide and shifts concern from harm, to sectarian victimisation.

> On the one hand, it appears easier to criticize the violence that founds [the law or legal system] since it cannot be justified by any pre-existing legality and so appears savage. But on the other hand, and this reversal is more the whole point of this reflection, it is more difficult, more illegitimate to criticize this same violence since one cannot summon it to appear before the institution of any pre-existing law: it does not recognize existing law in the moment it founds another.
>
> (Derrida, 1992: 1001)

Benjamin sets justice against legality, describing violent justice as a risk to the legal system itself and not merely its laws. The dangers for the legitimacy and longevity of a legal system posed by sectarian violent justice and para-justice responses are clear:

> It can be formulated as a general maxim of present-day European legislation that all the natural ends of individuals must collide with legal ends if pursued with a greater or lesser degree of violence. From this maxim it follows that law sees violence in the hands of individuals as a danger undermining the legal system.
>
> (Benjamin, 1978: 280)

Such a danger is all the greater when violence is promoted by *illegitimate* (or at least culturally contested) political hegemonies or sectarian military alliances, against certain classes of resistant victim communities. The monopolist claims over legitimate violence through compromised global governance are themselves claimed by victim communities against which the violence is directed. The monopoly on violence is in terms of contested legitimacy and not merely occurrence. Violence may be a force for transition, but rarely can it sustain legitimate governance, whether domestic or global.

However, violence is an essential precursor to more established styles of global governance. In this sense Max Weber's comments on state formation have resonance globally where governance (state- or otherwise-centred) is 'the rule of men over men based on the means of legitimate, that is allegedly legitimate, violence' (Arendt, 1969: 35). Legitimacy, or asserted legitimacy prevailing over contested realities, is the key.

Benjamin saw the legal *ends* of violence as well. Militarist violence claims its legality through the authority of the state, but does not have legality as its principal end. Militarist violence is applied not simply to natural ends but also to legal ends (Benjamin, 1978: 284). Benjamin called the first function of violence the lawmaking function, and the second the law-preserving function (Benjamin, 1978: 284). He concluded that military violence, as well as being primordial and paradigmatic of all violence used for natural ends, had an inherent but not predominant lawmaking character. Therefore, violence, in the context of legality and justice responses for the sake of longstanding legitimacy, would replace militarism (Benjamin, 1978: 280–1).

It would seem that faith in the law, even when coupled with violence as the exclusive means for legitimating governance and order, has its limits:

> A gaze directed only at what is close at hand can at most perceive a dialectical rising and falling in the law making and law-preserving violence formations of violence. The law governing their oscillation rests on the circumstance that all law-preserving violence, in its duration, indirectly weakens the lawmaking violence represented by it, through the suppression of hostile counter-violence.
>
> (Benjamin, 1978: 300)

When governance itself is challenged as a consequence of a sectarian and arguably unjust or illegal application to some victim communities and not others, the limitation of violence as a regulatory capacity is clear.

The nature of global violence

Violence becomes a tool for social exclusion against communities and cultures determined as living beyond and outside the realm of legitimate victimisation. When these communities and cultures become 'collateral damage' through military intervention or violent justice responses, then it is unlikely that the violence directed against them will be determined as suitable for prosecution in international criminal courts.

In the setting of global governance we have discussed in detail the nature and consequences of violent regulatory responses, whether in the form of military intervention or formal and sometimes distorted justice incursions (Findlay, 2008b: chapter 7). There can be little doubt that the perceived danger of international terror has given the United States and its global political alliance the opportunity to expand justifications for military intervention and to augment traditional justice forms to segregate, contain and punish terrorist suspects. A fine distinction between lawful and unlawful combatants aside (Fogarty, 2005), the due process protections of international law could be seen as vulnerable to the evil purposes of global terror, it is argued by the proponents of these justice distortions. However, what challenges any such repudiation of the traditional protections inherent in criminal justice is the reality that the threat exhibited by current terrorism may in fact be no greater than others which have been effectively controlled by the resilient institutions of conventional criminal justice. The Nuremberg and Tokyo tribunals that followed the Second World War are cases in point. However, risk is not a matter here of comparative harm, but rather is redefined in 'the national interest' (Kay, 2004). Violence, therefore, is a common theme in the behaviours which underpin global crimes and the responses which global governance agencies determine as appropriate (Findlay, 2007, 2008b).

War-based governance

Another way in which traditional criminal justice protections, and even international human rights conventions, can be argued away is to identify the principal threats to global security in terms of war and war-making. As we discussed in relation to valorisation, war discourse promotes a clear if questionable division between citizens who deserve the protections of ICJ and the enemies who don't. In this way once ICJ is co-opted into this war analogy, even the conventional justice protections are selectively employed through this conditional citizenship.

The war discourse and its consequences for the purposes of social control as governance are not new. Jonathan Simon (2007) rightly draws our attention to the war on drugs, and even the war on cancer, as policies designed to galvanise and sharpen control on regulatory potential. What makes this new phase of the war on terror interesting, in terms of governance and victimisation, is the manner in which it has justified both military intervention and the distortion of conventional criminal justice when applied to terrorist respondents. War discourse is no novelty as a language of international crime control. Whether it is a war on drugs, a war on vice or a war on child abuse, the conflictual discourse resounds through the political representation of law enforcement as military engagement. Now we are immersed in a war on terror. What distinguishes this discourse from, say, that which relates to the war on drugs is its justification for actual and extensive military interventions. This state of war is more universalised.

The preference in global governance terms for 'law over war' in controlling international crimes such as terrorism may gain greater relevance as international humanitarian law plays a more important role in ICJ (Chadwick, 2003). Modern laws of war evolved in the nineteenth century from reciprocal alliance pacts designed to ensure minimal restraint among civilised people. Any strict contractual approach to mutuality in restraint has been superseded in the current situation of global governance by a more rigid and delineated commitment to global security and order at whatever cost. The cost has emerged as violence to the rights of the offender and victims in the name of risk and other securities.

The violence focus of governance responses to global terror can be seen as harming the rights of offenders and communities as much as their physical integrity. Michaelson (2003) argues that criminal law has been 'bastardised' in the name of control and security. The perversion of human rights in the process is evidence that both law and justice have been subverted. The question is whether the terrorist threat can be viewed legally as posing a sufficient public emergency so that national security legislation is justified in abrogating the common obligations imposed by international human rights conventions.

In the context of the war on terror, crime victimisation and the legitimate claims of global citizenship are conflated. The lines of exclusion and inclusion are drawn against criminality and victimisation across global communities. Governance becomes defined by criminalisation and the restoration of global security through a battery of control institutions (see Simon, 2007). Even so, control within the war paradigm is essentially reliant on violence against violence.

Cultural victimisation

Terrorist communities worldwide currently are clearly delineated in terms of their ideology and political commitments. For instance, fundamentalist Islamic predispositions now are seen as a crucial stimulus to terrorist activities. Almost as it was during the crusades (late eleventh to late thirteenth centuries), Islamic culture has become the enemy of western freedoms and liberal democracy, leading to the wholesale alienation of Muslim communities in the West in particular.

Among other cultures facing simplistic terrorist designation, political separatism may be given legitimate victim status along with credibility in otherwise geopolitically valued states. The 'terrorist' communities are denied the political legitimacy of rational resistance and so violence against these communities is legitimated and resultant harm neutralised. Take for a point of comparison the worldwide condemnation of the Tamil Tigers and their long-standing violent resistance to the Sri Lankan state authorities. On the other hand, in the case of the East Timorese opposition to Indonesian annexation, the world slowly came to the view that this resistance was in itself a struggle for self-determination and cultural identity. Some might say it is an interesting coincidence that Indonesia is the largest of the world's Islamic nation-states and Sri Lanka is seen as a bulwark against the socialist governance of Tamil Nadu.

The social exclusion of whole cultures beyond claims for legitimate global citizenship and resultant actionable victimisation provides fertile opportunities for violent resistance to global governance. Devaluing the critical components of any culture along with violent justice responses to terrorist resistance undermines the capacity of global governance to develop a pluralist and inclusive regulatory framework. Violence breeds violence when cultural integrity as well as community safety is at stake.

Hegemonic violence and sectarian exclusion

Violence against resistant communities, whether in the form of military intervention or violent justice and para-justice (see Findlay, 2008b: chapter 3) responses, has a sectarian and contestable political logic. As examined in our exploration of crime and global governance (Findlay, 2008b), the dominant global political alliance which has assumed a crusading role in the war on terror has consciously sponsored and promoted the emergence of violent control strategies and their delineation. Coalescing this alliance is a hegemony of ideals, preferred governance models, singular economic relations and cultural supremacy. Yet this hegemony is fragile when both confirmed and challenged through terror and violent resistance. The formation and re-formation of hegemonic orders in the context of wars of any type gives disproportionate and dangerous precedents to violence in challenging or confirming order. Hegemony over the war on terror is no different.

It is a characteristic of political hegemonies which struggle to determine and impose a singular cultural and economic order over wide and expanding terrain that violence becomes dominant in control strategies. Violence always produces victimisation. The authority behind violence or its resistance, we argue, critically if often undemocratically discriminates the legitimate and illegitimate victim and the resolutions available to them. Where violence and victimisation become instrumental in determining the limits of a political hegemony and the nature and illegitimacy of resistance to it, then social exclusion in a community and cultural sense is a feature of that order.

Constructive political configurations are less possible or sustainable where oppositional forces are determined through violent risks and countered with more violence than by grant of diplomacy. The security of hegemonic order becomes the overriding aspiration where order is contested and violence is the language of dominion.

At base, global hegemony is presently a political construct. Friedrichs (2005) suggests that global politics are not the same as international politics or relations. Rather, global politics is a meta-concept encompassing political relations among governments in a process of selection and mutual self-interest. As Friedrichs observes, to provide the glue for global capitalism and ordered global community, global governance is sometimes construed as beyond and somehow above politics. That said, violence and victimisation which confirm and confine world order have recently in the global terrorist experience exacerbated violent resistance through sectarian exclusion of communities and cultures from that order.

Legitimate victim interests

Throughout this chapter we have alluded to victim communities in contest. Later we explore a range of pre-trial and trial mechanisms which have the potential to distil and conciliate contested victim interests in order to reduce substantial points of conflict and determine common grounds of legitimacy. It is our belief that legitimacy through compromise is possible as a central precept of trial transformation (Findlay and Henham, 2005). One reason for this are the common features of victimisation (and any essential aspirations that follow) irrespective of its location and those who perpetrate the harm. Whether or not conciliated victim interests are achievable, the process to reach a mutuality of interests will not be without its problems.

Consider the following scenario.

> The rural populations of Cornucopia are organised in a clan structure and live in agrarian villages. Cash economies are a very recent introduction and have little impact on rural life. The clans are divided into two tribal groupings which have a history of violent hostility. Politics has been beset by tribal rivalry and in recent years the UN Security Council sent a peace-keeping force to oversee democratic elections and to prevent tribal killings which might otherwise have resulted.

Is it any wonder that despite similarities in victim community aspirations and a common desire for the truth to be told, either clan group would not want to participate in truth and reconciliation supported by a politically and ethnically partial government. So, is the answer to prosecute the military champion of one side for crimes against the other? Such a response, while having significant declaratory purchase, is only likely to exacerbate ethnic division and compromise the authority of the ICC in the eyes of the community of the accused.

The negotiation and mediation of legitimate victim interests is a central challenge for transformed ICJ. We argue that it is best done in a communitarian justice model of pre-trial conciliation where the issues in dispute community to community will be disentangled from histories of animosity, fear and misperception.

Contested truth

One reason for the distinction of formal or alternative ICJ paradigms is the conceptualisation of 'truth' at the heart of their separate resolution processes. As we examine in chapters 5 and 6, the trial has conventionally focused on admissible evidence arising through the adversarial or inquisitorial treatment of alleged facts. This represents a rather narrow conceptualisation of truth to a point where evidence at trial is better viewed as a prevailing version of contested 'facts' (see chapter 3). In the truth and reconciliation setting on the other hand, story-telling and truth from the mouths of victims is a more fluid, fulfilling, inclusive, sustainable and encompassing representation.

When it comes to considerations of 'truth' in the context of a terrorist struggle, the contested nature of truth is obvious, if also regularly glossed over. Truth is what the suicide bomber is said to die for and what the military and criminal justice responses are set to protect. How can this be the same truth? The relativity of truth in such settings becomes a contested objective of the relationship between terror and justice responses (Findlay, 2007). At the heart of the contest over the meaning of truth is moral legitimacy. In this moral stand either side of a violent conflict or struggle will argue that they have the imprimatur to blame the enemy and so the right to inflict violent retribution with just cause. Again, both sides cannot be right.

Distillation of the truth

It is essential, if competing victim communities in particular are to reach some *rapprochement*, that a context for determining and resolving contested issues into some legitimate agenda for victimisation should be accepted by, and accountable to, the parties involved. If ICJ is to perform this role more effectively, then it needs to move much further from the orbit of global hegemony and the dominant political alliance which, as we have argued, plays a key role in the sectarian divide which leads to violence.

To date it has largely been the alternative justice sector which has taken responsibility for conciliating and mediating contested victim interests. One reason for this might be the more broadly based and locally agreed authority of alternative justice paradigms confirmed by greater access for victims to the resolution process than is available and accepted in the trial proper. Our concept of the transformed international criminal trial addresses access to victims head on (Findlay and Henham, 2005: chapters 7 and 8). It also recognises that to confine conciliation and mediation of victim interests to less structured and sometimes less accountable informal resolution options will expose victim communities to compromises in individual and collective rights (see chapter 1).

We argue that the responsibility for the distillation of victim interests in situations of contested victim communities requires the authority of justice professionals with skills and competencies in this exercise of authority. If this is to occur, then the role of justice professionals and the context in which they operate need to be imbued with a greater level of community legitimacy than those that exist for ICJ at present. Otherwise the involvement of justice professionals is another layer of imposition which exacerbates community segregation and exclusion, and even leads to further violent resistance. The prospect of an effective role for justice professionals in the distillation of victim interests will require some formality. We prefer, as exists in some domestic jurisdictions with pre-trial conferences, a situation where the Prosecutor at least is required to engage with victim stakeholders following the investigation phase. There is obviously a question here about the role of the Prosecutor as an independent officer of the Court, while at the same time attempting to negotiate victim interests. However, within ICJ rules and procedures the Prosecutor has adopted more clearly a role in at least advancing victims' legitimate considerations if not representing them.[9] This role is also consistent with the conventional and traditional criminal justice position that the Prosecutor acts on behalf of the wider community and the state in managing retributive justice.

Consider this scenario:

> The ICC Prosecutor has commenced investigations in Cornucopia. Agents for his Office have been offering potential witnesses 'protection and eventual compensation' in return for evidence against General Lutobu and in particular:
>
> - evidence of recruiting child soldiers;
> - information on the collaboration between the mining company ConCom and the general's troops in the massacre of Ubu villagers;
> - information concerning ethnic cleansing of Ubu villagers by Tubu tribesmen at the behest of the general.

The international community and the UN Security Council want a retributive response. But the neighbouring state where Tubu tribes are in the majority demands that the ICC also prosecute Ubu reprisals if the retributive response is to have wider credibility. The stories of harm and victimisation are not the province of one victim community alone. Yet retributive justice is one-dimensional. It has little capacity in determining liability at least to look at aggression and retaliation. Prosecution in the current trial format is individualised and as such looks to represent the victimisation of one community above another. Yet even the prosecution of the individual accused is not as simple as his actions may suggest. Responsibility carries overtones of wider involvement, as discussed in chapter 4.

> The UN Security Council has given the ICC a mandate to issue warrants for crimes committed by General Lutobu and the Minister for Information. The government has offered to cooperate by complying with a warrant for the general's arrest, in return for proceedings against the minister being suspended. Lutobu, on the other hand, has offered to cooperate with the ICC Prosecutor by giving information concerning the government's and mining company's involvement. He claims that he was doing nothing more than following orders.

Even the carriage of a retributive trial may require bargaining and a trade-off on the part of the Prosecutor if successful convictions are to eventuate. These trade-offs have a further capacity to compromise the impartiality and simplicity of retributive trial justice. They may also compete with legitimate victim interests for the superior aspiration of penality.

There is pressure on the Prosecutor to compromise. There is also a need to offer victim witnesses satisfaction at a level of aspiration beyond the satisfaction of individual conviction. And if deals are to be made with victim communities so that witnesses can be secured, what about competing victim interests in the communities of the accused? Pre-trial mediation and conciliation, therefore, may also take on bargains to secure the wider legitimacy of the selective prosecution and conviction of General Lutobu. Resistant victim communities will also need their interests negotiated and distilled if it is hoped to co-opt their support for the narrower individualised retributive purpose. It could also assist in determining the true contest between the Prosecution and Defence cases.

The distillation process envisaged here would not be dissimilar to determining agreed facts at the start of a trial or in the testing of expert evidence in order to refine points of contest. It is anticipated that in certain situations where contested interests were intransigent, then some independent victim advocacy might be necessary.

Distillation of responsibility

The conventional approach of the criminal law, whether domestic or international, is to focus on determining the individual liability of offenders. In order to facilitate this determination, evidence is presented in adversarial or inquisitorial trial contexts from both sides of the case. The verdict is determined relative to which case and hence which accumulation of evidence is most convincing.

It is well accepted that trial evidence does not necessarily equate with the truth of the matter (see Twining, 1992). In fact, because of the contested nature of trial evidence one might say it is logical that the case which prevails will still rest on the partial and sometimes problematic interpretation of the evidence in question. Criminal liability will therefore be determined on the basis of preferred facts and their probative value relative to the offence charged and any defences or justifications which are advanced against the Prosecution case. As we discuss later, concepts of criminal liability in the major procedural traditions which influence ICJ is almost always considered against the behaviour and culpability of the individual (Norrie, 2001).

In *Transforming International Criminal Justice* (2005) we observe the distinction between criminal liability and wider notions of responsibility in a moral and legal sense. This distinction is not always easy to draw in the context of criminal justice. It remains, however, a useful distinction when looking at the separation of truth and fact. An example may help here. The influence of mental incapacity when determining criminal liability in common law is limited to a very qualified defence of insanity, and considerations of diminished responsibility which focus on notions of abnormality of the mind (Findlay, 2006: chapter 6), particularly when compared with medical notions of mental incapacity, are highly restricted in permitting considerations of the disturbed mind when assessing liabilities. Once a decision on that has been reached, a wider range of implications regarding the mental disposition of the accused will be examined in the determination of sentence. The justification for this is that individualised mental conditions are distinctly relevant when evaluating the morality of someone's actions, the autonomy of their behaviour and its culpability. When looking at sentencing an individual who alleges mental or behavioural disorder, evidence may be presented to form in the mind of the judge the accused's responsibility for his or her actions and the appropriate sentence that should result from such an evaluation. In this case, liability relies on narrow mental constructs, and responsibility is opened up to wider individualised and conditional considerations.

Alternative ICJ paradigms are said to be interested in truth beyond determined issues of evidence which may be contested and restrictively admitted into the trial for liability considerations. Truth and reconciliation commissions, for instance, have as their purpose to provide opportunities for both victims and perpetrators to tell their stories about the conflicts in which they are engaged. Such story-telling sheds light on an historical record richer and more interactive than is permitted through evidence in the criminal trial. This story-telling may be cathartic as much as it enables a diverse range of attitudes, opinions and interpretations to coalesce and hopefully produce a truthful account.

Criminal liability, once determined, usually returns a sanction and a punishment equivalent to the main themes of mitigation and aggravation in the sentencing process. Truth-telling, because it may be accompanied by amnesties and assurances against sanction, has the capacity to indicate responsibility and invite a range of restorative outcomes which may be precluded through the process of retributive justice.

Interestingly, as Aertsen et al. (2008) graphically portray regarding large-scale violent conflicts in Kosovo, the Democratic Republic of the Congo and Israel/Palestine, victims are primarily interested in restorative options through the justice process, while at the same time not being willing to reject retributive justice for the perpetrators where liability attaches. As the contributors to Aertsen et al. (2008) explore, the challenge for restorative justice in the context of mass victimisation is to ensure victim satisfaction and perpetrator inclusion without condoning a wholesale retreat from the consequences of criminal liability.

Until now truth and responsibility frameworks in ICJ have generally been consigned to the alternative justice institutions and agencies, while criminal liability remains within the province of the trial. We suggest in later chapters that through pre-trial conferencing and transformed trial deliberations there exists a greater potential to satisfy the diverse expectations of victim communities through more varied trial outcomes. Responsibility and liability, truth and fact, can coexist in the transformed trial environment to the greater satisfaction of victim community interests.

Mediation

We noted above that a challenge for trial transformation will be to reconcile competing and contested interests emerging from oppositional victim communities. War and mass conflict rest on communities in contest. Military victory or political subjugation rarely produces lasting concessions or reconciliation between opposing communities and cultures. In fact, the victory of one side over the other is likely to exacerbate the pre-existing differences which fomented violence and military conflict. Little wonder, then, if victim communities were to come to the transformed trial embracing oppositional viewpoints that these differences might have a tendency to undermine the possibility of achieving legitimate victim expectations.

Our scenario poses just this challenge. And it has been exacerbated by the manner in which a formal justice intervention has been constructed with all the appearances of partiality when viewed from the communities of the accused.

> The global community has exerted significant pressure on the government to prosecute General Lutobu for genocide. No international reference has been directed against the leaders of the Ubu reprisal raids. The Prime Minister has indicated that in the face of the public unrest that genocide charges against Lutobu would generate, the local criminal courts do not have the capacity to process any such prosecutions. The Chief Justice, on the other hand, has told the international media that the courts are willing and able to handle the matter.

Any discussion of mediated victim interest is against this background and some might say thwarted by the retributive purpose.

When discussing the trial project in later chapters we posit situations in trial decision-making sites which are the progress of trial deliberations where mediation might become the best alternative. Very briefly here, the thinking is that juridical professionals (the Prosecutor or judge) may see through the nature of the issues in question and the manner in which attempts to determine liability are playing out that important legitimate victim interests would be sacrificed by restricting access to truth for the sake of the integrity of probative evidence. In such situations, and against the recognition of legitimate victim interests, we suggest the possibility of diverting the course of the trial into mediation mode where truth and responsibility might be serviced and resolved for the sake of a restorative outcome.

In common law the use of mediation in a criminal trial is extremely rare. In fact, trial lawyers would argue that it is considerations such as mediation that distinguish criminal jurisdiction from civil. In civil claims, particularly with the recent popularity of civil justice in the UK, judges are either encouraging or requiring claimants to engage in mediation first so that only key and irreconcilable areas of dispute take up the time of the civil courts. There is more to this than cost-saving. Judges are well aware that much time can be wasted and resolutions confused by opposing parties prolonging disputation to wear down the other side or in the hope of extracting concession as the trial proceeds.

While mediation may not be practised within the confines of some criminal trial traditions, through recent interest in discovery, pre-trial agreed facts and the reconciliation of expert evidence, conferences before the trial which possess a mediatory slant are growing in popularity. A good example of this is pre-trial discussions between the Prosecution and Defence to narrow down and determine essential facts in dispute. Pre-trial conferences are common now so that by the time the trial commences the judge can be assisted by agreement as to a range of facts which both cases consider to be outside the adversarial contest.

In the transformed criminal trial we would argue that, especially in situations where victim communities as stakeholders in the trial process and outcome are at loggerheads, there is much to commend the pre-trial conference as a venue for the Prosecutor in particular to invite mediation so that only critical themes in dispute may complicate trial decision-making. Having looked at much of the empirical research on victim interests in mass conflict we have been struck by the commonality in expectations among communities. Disputes arise not so much about the mechanisms for resolution but rather over which side of the victim divide merits retributive and which restorative justice. Therefore, it may be a simpler process to gain agreement about the trial outcome at hand and leave to the adversarial contest disputes over facts as to merit.

The major challenge to incorporating mediation in criminal justice is the consideration of parity. Much of the critical literature examining juvenile conferencing in restorative justice (e.g. Barton, 2003) discusses the pressures exerted on an accused for contrition and participation. In many respects it could be said that even the 'community of significant others' in the restorative conference creates a coercive environment wherein the offender, and to a lesser extent the victim, are not truly voluntary participants. Similar difficulties may arise in mediating victim conflict pre-trial or through trial diversion if access and inclusivity are not ensured by respecting in a procedural sense the victim voice and victim advocacy.

In those jurisdictions where mediation is available for lesser offences in the criminal trial process such as, in principle at least, in China (see Findlay, 2008b: chapter 8), situations where professional trial participants dominate the mediation environment bring into question the reality of conciliation against status-borne coercion.

Recognition

When examining the distillation of truth as opposed to the admissibility of fact, we have suggested the importance of story-telling as a technique for activating the historical record. Freeman (2006), in his work on truth commissions and procedural fairness, reflects on Shakespeare's 'For truth is truth to the end of reckoning'. Even so truth-telling for the purpose of historical record is in the experience of the truth and reconciliation commissions a process of negotiation. Richard Goldstone identifies:

> One of the challenges facing truth commissions is the fairness of its proceeding. It is all too easy to allow it to be used as a political platform to castigate the former regime. It is a complex and sensitive process to ensure victims that they will receive protection and respect for their dignity when they testify. It is no exaggeration to state that the success or failure of truth commissions will crucially depend on the fairness of its proceedings.
>
> (Foreword in Freeman, 2006: xi–xii)

The truthfulness of stories is one measure in determining fairness. However, truth is contested particularly between victim communities with long-standing disputes and entrenched traditions of animosity. The art of truth and reconciliation is to recognise these differences and, through concession and compromise, to interweave different stories into an historical record which may be complex but convincing. The experience of the Truth and Reconciliation Commission in South Africa was that the record of its proceedings often portrayed differing cultural and community interpretations of events, which were no less compelling as a record and no less distinct from narrow legal transcripts which plot the course of evidence - contested or otherwise – in a criminal trial.

The experience of witnesses before the truth commissions has often been in large part a sense of relief at having the opportunity to recount their version of events and to have their story taken seriously. An ancillary but no less significant by-product of story-telling has been to produce concessions between disputants concerning truth and responsibility, which may not have been possible in an environment where such concessions would have led to retributive outcomes.

Reconciliation

Reconciliation is one of the central considerations of restorative justice. As we have mentioned in the sense of difficulty for mediation and the challenges for truth-telling, reconciliation should originate for victim communities as stakeholders in the international criminal trial within the mediation and truth-telling environment. This aspiration is not meant to exclude the alternative justice opportunities for truth and reconciliation. Rather, it is to provide an additional situation or the realisation of legitimate victim interests, particularly where rights are ensured.

Our model for trial decision-making is something we refer to as 'pathways of influence' (Findlay and Henham, 2005: chapter 3). These pathways are what make function different and important decision sites in the trial. Whether it be through conventional adversarial process or in transformed trial justice by way of the other modes of determination, principal stakeholders involved in particular decision sites should be required, where appropriate, to reconcile disputes or at the very least accept the reconciliation offered through the judge's decision.

Reconciliation, therefore, exists as a feature of conventional trial practice, even if it is largely an undeclared one. The transformed trial process will incorporate and expand opportunities for reconciliation pre-trial at central trial decision sites and through the expanded options for trial determination.

Restitution

Again, in conventional criminal trial practice, monetary compensation or restitution is not common. Criminal compensation schemes sometimes follow contemporary trial practice but usually as an ancillary concern and rarely do they reflect the true value of the harms perpetrated. Critics suggest that such criminal compensation is more symbolic in its intentions and purposes than it is true restitution.

In the international criminal context, large-scale violent conflicts produce expansive harm and deep levels of community victimisation. Restitution, therefore, is both a material and a communitarian concept. Ethnic cleansing and community displacement are rarely responded to through the satisfactory restoration of refugee communities to the lands from which they were forcibly ejected. Permanent refugee camps in Palestine and across northern Africa attest to the absence of spatial and temporal restoration for the victims of endemic and ongoing large-scale violent conflicts.

Restitution is an essential expectation of most victim communities (Albrecht et al., 2006). It involves material compensation and a range of other community restructuring and servicing to restore the dignity of expelled communities. Tschudi (in Aertsen et al., 2008: chapter 2) argues for a restorative justice model focused on dignity but ensured through individual and communitarian empowerment. His argument recognises dignity as a core value of restorative justice and the failure of deterrence measures in response to terrorism, but does not shy away from the importance of material compensation to restore communities and their faith in peace and security. As an essential precursor of this process Tschudi describes a dialogue to be put in place which values humility and respect over egocentrism. The challenges facing such a dialogue in contexts where conflicts are deep-seated recognise a sometimes risky commitment to building personal relations on faith and goodwill. The example of restorative justice peacemaking in Bougainville resonates here. John Braithwaite has worked extensively to achieve restorative justice outcomes in Bougainville and he describes how through a 'slow war' during which whole generations have failed to see the inside of a school or other community consolidators which we take for granted, confidence-building and restoration is more than just money and aid. Tschudi makes the point that 'Building viable relations requires mutual resonance, the rediscovery of joint humanity and global harmony' (Aertsen et al., 2008: 57).

Where such dialogue fails, deterrence and retribution have their place in the regulatory response pyramid (Braithwaite, 2002). However, well before a reluctant recourse to deterrence, retribution, war and even vengeance, restoration holds out great possibilities reliant on constructive discourse and mechanisms designed strategically to generate trust.

Communities of justice – making victim focus work

Throughout our discussion of the transformed trial process (Findlay and Henham, 2005) and our analysis of crime and global governance (Findlay, 2008b) we have underlined the importance of a communitarian justice model as a focus for ICJ and as its vibrant accountability framework. Essential to this communitarian model - what we call communities of justice – is a discussion of victimisation suggesting the nature, composition, location and integration of such communities. But what are communities of justice? In essence, they are a meeting of principal stakeholders in ICJ, a context wherein legitimate interests can be identified and features in dispute narrowed down with the assistance and oversight of legal professionals and the protection of a trial justice tradition.[10]

But what are communities of justice?[11] Communities of justice are more than just a venue for negotiating particular or mutual interests. They are also essentially communitarian in nature, intent, discourse and diversity. As true communities, these coalesce with an eventual common purpose: the achievement of *humanitarian justice*. We anticipate that if the conditions for communitarian justice are ensured[12] (trust and mutual respect being essential to these), then a shared notion of humanity may override the tensions of self-interest. This outcome will eventuate within communities of justice provided that the rewards available through trial access, inclusivity and integration are both observed and real (chapter 6).

It would be naïve not to identify the very different starting points for stakeholders on the road to a justice communion. Therefore, the mechanisms which we have proposed for the achievement of that identification and its mediation will be crucial to establish a common framework from which communities of justice will evolve.

In our scenario, the pressures for reconciliation also realise the importance of context, perspective, perception and outcome:

- *Context* – mediation of interests in a pre-trial environment suggests safety in the presentation of a particular position and rights protections for parties against known principles of due process.

- *Perspective* – to ascertain the bargaining position of any stakeholder it is essential not simply to know where they stood in the history of the conflict, but to recognise how they have interpreted other positions and authoritarian interventions.
- *Perception* – parties see things differently but also appreciate the way they are viewed and represented in very different, and often conflicting, ways.
- *Outcome* – in all mediation settings the question 'what's in it for me?' is central. In that respect, pre-trial inducements must be openly and accountably connected to liability or responsibility determinations. Flowing from this is the recognition that legitimate victim interests need to maximised once they are mediated to give credibility and teeth to the mediation exercise and encourage positive participation.

In addition, a sophisticated understanding of actual communities of justice wrestling with the sort of contentions apparent in our problem scenario demands close attention to important decision sites on the way to shared justice resolutions. These decision sites are apparent in our model of the trial process (Findlay and Henham, 2005: chapter 3). Fortunately, in recent years brave and insightful empirical studies have emerged to give life to communities of large-scale violent conflicts and their transition on the road to justice or its frustration. Communities of justice, therefore, may be charted and predicted against the trial transformation model that we advocate.

As with our trial model, as a series of crucial decision sites where 'pathways of influence' are constructed by crucial stakeholders, victims included (Findlay and Henham, 2005: chapter 3), communities of justice will centre on decision sites essential for the identification and achievement of justice outcomes. Pre-trial and trial contexts will enable the mediation of disputes which would otherwise complicate and confound the decisions that emerge progressively in this model.

These decision sites will also be influential in the type of communitarian justice resulting from the various regulatory mechanisms resorted to by any community of justice to solve its justice requirements. Outside the trial, for instance, the crucial process of victim compensation in the ICC framework would be significantly impacted and facilitated by the mediation of victim interests through communities of justice resolutions pre-trial and at trial. This process assumes that in a community of justice a single regulatory model will not be appropriate and that a variety of regulatory alternatives should be offered for negotiation and resort, even in the trial itself (chapters 1 and 7).

A detailed contextual interrogation of how any particular community of justice reaches consensus will also require getting to know the parties and relationships from which pathways of influence to crucial decisions in the trial may evolve. In order that such an interrogation will be valuable and predictive, the obligations of trial professionals to facilitate communities of justice need to be clearly designated and uniformly required (chapter 7).

Communities of justice and accountability

We argue in more detail later in this text that communities of justice, as well as providing the framework for a more conciliatory justice resolution respectful of legitimate victim interests, will also act essentially as a background to test the accountability of ICJ. How, then, does the community of justice promote international justice as an accountability pillar in global governance?

- As with all communities, it provides 'boundaries of permission' within which discretion can be exercised and decisions have their acceptable reach.
- These boundaries are qualified by the same normative framework as that confirming the justice for which the community strives.
- For this justice to be confirmed and to continue it must have legitimacy within the community.
- This legitimacy is crucially dependent on an atmosphere of peace and order which global governance is charged to ensure.
- The capacity of global governance to achieve peace and good order, and to maintain their benefits, relies on the widest support of the cultures and interests which contest in any community of justice.
- Therefore, good governance is only achieved when the instrumentalities and processes of governance are responsible to the legitimate interests within those communities.

Communities of justice and legitimation

Concluding the analysis in *Crime and Global Governance* (2008b) is a recognition that communitarian justice holds out powerful potential to legitimate ICJ and the governance within which it is included. But for such legitimacy to be more than superficial, communities in dispute need at a minimum to have a common regard for the reconciliatory capacity of ICJ, its institutions and agencies.

The achievement of a resounding and resilient legitimacy which is community-focused takes us back to a consideration of the normative framework for a transformed ICJ and the manner in which it is to be actualised. Access to justice is central to this achievement. That access needs to be much more inclusive than is possible for victim interests in contemporary domestic criminal justice models. Inclusivity means more than appearance and much more like actual involvement. To confirm the reality of access we argue that with inclusivity comes the need for integration at all stages of the pre-trial and trial decision-making process. If this is achieved, then victim interests should be recognisable in each important pathway of influence as any pre-trial and trial decision site within the transformed trial process.

We have recognised the challenges inherent in a victim constituency for ICJ. Communities of justice will not be achieved simply by a loose recognition of a new normative framework around access, inclusivity and integration. The reality of communitarian justice for ICJ will rely on if and how justice professionals, Prosecutors and judges in particular engage with and promote the victim voice, and confront and confound the challenges that enabling a victim voice will always present.

Notes

1. This is not to suggest that the ICC has no concern for restorative, victim-centred considerations. Such considerations feature in the recent decisions to join victims' interests with the prosecution appeals against disclosure, and release of the accused in the Lubanga trial proceedings. See ICC Appeals Chamber No. ICC-01/04-01/06 0A 13, 6 August 2008.
2. For a very comprehensive summary of the ICC's victim obligations, see Human Rights First, 'The Role of the Victim in ICC Proceedings', http://www.humanrightsfirst.org/international_justice/icc/VICTIMS_CHART_Final.pdf
3. See, for example, Rule 50 on victim witnesses and Rules 89–91 governing the participation of victims in the trial process.
4. This is a challenge recognised by the ICC in the pre-trial deliberations in the Lubanga prosecution.
5. Crimes of aggression are to be incorporated along with war crimes, crimes against humanity and genocide in 2009 as appropriate for prosecution before the ICC. Consistent with our argument as it relates to the collectivisation of victims for the already existing crime types, crimes of aggression more often than not are directed against victim communities.
6. For a detailed modelling of the international criminal trial in terms of sites for decision-making and consequent pathways of influence, see Findlay and Henham (2005: chapter 3).
7. We are wrestling with the details of trial transformation, particularly in terms of a 'developed trial programme'. In particular, the analysis focuses on the repositioning of fact and evidence in the determination of responsibility, and a realignment of trial outcomes away from the limits of penality as the consequence of adversarial argument. See chapter 6.
8. For a critique of this position against the need to collectivise liability, see Danner and Martinez (2005).
9. It would be fair to say that the pre-trial debate regarding disclosure in the first trial before the ICC (see chapter 8) exposed the conflict of interest at the heart of the prosecutor-victim pre-trial conversation.
10. We do not here intend to overstate trial rights protections. If these are retained in their conventional form, then the focus on accused persons' rights (EU Convention, Article 6) offers little comfort to victim participants. A feature of trial transformation as we see it is the actualisation of victim participant protections which do not discriminate against the accused.

11. The concept is explored in the context of democratic global governance in Findlay (2008: chapters 7 and 9).
12. Put simply, communities of justice in a trial attachment will be determined through pre-trial conferencing in a mediation format. It will be similar in process to the way in which agreed facts are settled before any trial. The Prosecutor, and where necessary victim advocates, will mediate conflicting interests in order that commonality can be passed on to the trial proper and the key issues in dispute can progress to adversary resolution within the trial.

4
Truth and Responsibility vs. Fact and Liability

Introduction

There is no pure adversarial or inquisitorial trial. Contemporary trial traditions either exhibit derivations of either paradigm or are hybrids incorporating essential influences from one and both traditions. Nevertheless, the adversarial and inquisitorial models exercise a strong influence over the nature of evidence and the standing of 'fact'.

An adversarial trial values the supremacy of contested evidence.[1] 'Fact' in the trial is established when one 'case' and its version of the evidence are preferred over another. The essence of the adversarial trial is two sides of the story. The prevailing story arguably might resemble or equate with some objective truth, but that is not what makes it fact. Nor is the search for truth, contrary to popular understanding, a search for truth. Probative evidentiary rules, depending on the trial tradition in play, determine what evidence can be admitted into contest and from there, what is evaluated by the fact-finder as predominant.

Inquisitorial trial is no less interested in facts. The pre-trial investigation and distillation process is designed to produce, where possible, documentary evidence which, if it proceeds to trial, will gain status of fact through procedures of contested validation.

The need for prevailing contested fact to be proved through critical interrogation explains the adversarial dedication to oral evidence presented in the trial and the inquisitorial preference for documentation. Oral traditions want the witness voice to be challenged and tested to the rank of fact. Documentary traditions celebrate the evidentiary power of the narrative.

Neither the adversarial nor inquisitorial trial tradition is exclusively oral or documentary in its approach to evidence and fact. It is wrong to assume that adversarial fact is the exclusive outcome of oral testimony. Whatever its form, 'fact' is the result of the didactic elimination of oppositional, 'reasonable' doubt. It is never doubt-free.

The place of 'reasonable doubt' in trial fact-finding should not be underestimated. Evidence can stand as fact provided the doubt it raises is below the probative upper limit of reasonable tolerance. Truth, on the other hand, cannot accommodate doubt and as such is not the natural by-product of didactic trial, oral or written in evidentiary context:

> the trial procedure does not constitute legal truth ... rather it forms a 'truth certifying procedure' ... or knowledge of truth and the 'facts of the matter' is inexorably linked with the procedure we adopt for certifying it, which itself determines the outcome.
>
> (Bankowski, 1988: 17)

The essential connection between trial procedure and truth certification, rather than truth-finding, is revealed in different verdict delivery scenarios. In Scotland, for instance, there is a third verdict possibility: 'not proven' (Maher, 1988). This covers the uncertain circumstance where evidence exists pointing to the accused's guilt, but is not sufficient to breach beyond reasonable doubt. It gives comfort to the Prosecution case, while accepting that the presumption of innocence has not, through the facts revealed, been rebutted.

In justice paradigms where historical truth is preferred, the adversarial contest gives way to mediation and concession.[2] Truth and reconciliation commissions, for instance, were established as an alternative not simply because access for the many to the trial process was limited (Freeman, 2006), but, along with enhanced access, these commissions offered opportunities to tell the truth without facing the adversarial rendition and its consequences if the individual's version of the facts is not accepted.

The other attraction of 'truth-telling' paradigms is the chance to put history right. In that respect competing or contested histories can be laid out without the need to rule one over the other. The possibility to tell the story from the perspective of the victim or the perpetrator has been shown to be cathartic and conciliatory.[3] It has also offered a safe space for degrees of responsibility to be arrayed and restorative outcomes to follow.

We suggested in chapter 3 that, despite the challenges, victim interests need to be better recognised and restored through international criminal justice (ICJ). In earlier work (Findlay and Henham, 2005) we detailed the argument why, along with the expansion of transitional and alternative justice options, both restorative and retributive victim aspirations must be encountered and managed within the transformed international trial.[4] Arguments against this, when it comes to the tools for trial decision-making, include:

- the suggestion that historical recording is not for trial narrative and that judges, confronted with contested fact, cannot be historians;[5]
- that adversarial argument depends on evidence substantiating fact, and in some situations the rules governing this will work against the presentation of alternative histories from diverse stakeholders;

- that truth and fact are not essentially compatible and coexistent within the trial because they can be established quite differently and their presence may lead to divergent outcomes; and
- the fundamental procedural differences between fact and truth as they are managed with the contemporary institutions of ICJ mean that they should remain separated.

Even so, the trial offers a 'due process' procedural environment in which truth can be contested with equanimity and safety for all parties. We leave the consideration of the last assertion (but see, for instance, chapter 8) as it is our purpose in this chapter to examine what the consequences of this segregation are for the possibility of trial transformation, assuming fact and truth can be (if not is always) distinct within the criminal trial. What can be done in a practical sense to recognise and reconstitute this difference, without destroying the adversarial environment where necessary, to enable truth and fact to coexist within the trial? From such harmony, or at least procedural tolerance, can retributive routes from liability and restorative outcomes from the attribution of responsibility exist within the transformed trial where truth and fact have space?

Our scenario identifies the options and potentials for truth-telling as well as fact-finding. Truth and reconciliation, insofar as our scenario is concerned, remain uncomfortably and incontrovertibly outside the transformed trial.

> As a compromise the government has established a truth and reconciliation commission to investigate the events. However, the victim communities on both sides have expressed no confidence in it and have refused to cooperate.

Even recognising this climate of reluctance and suspicion:

> Regarding contested victim interests, in common they want offenders brought to justice before an international criminal tribunal, and are seeking compensation and reconciliation. Most of all, they want their stories to be known as truth, and to challenge what they see as misinformation from the media and the government, or from their clan opponents.

The issue here is this: should truth-telling remain outside the trial framework, currently sequestered for fact and evidence?[6] If they can be brought within the boundaries of the trial, what will this do for the popular appreciation that trials determine truth, and fact is the mechanism?

Facts' adversarial home – a place of mythical distinction

Research on juror comprehension[7] has established that lay fact-finders are perplexed by the inclusion and exclusion of evidence, courtesy of procedural convention. For instance, in common law jurisdictions, detailed legal debate over issues such as the admissibility of confessions will be heard in the absence of the jury. Jurors so excluded tend to second-guess what the lawyers have been arguing. This further compounds the frustration of lay decision-makers that issues which they suspect would be helpful to them are not adduced by witnesses from either side or commented on by the judge. 'Why is this so?' they ask. 'What are they hiding?'

It is not only the need to confine trial evidence within strict and constructed procedural traditions which tends to exclude the emergence of contested 'truths'. The adversarial trial process itself, managing the temporal delivery of evidence as it does, what is and is not told, has the potential to create a frame of reference against which fact-finders will reflect on other 'versions' of the facts. Evidence initially presented by one side offers fact-finders an organising framework for the subsequent reception and processing of information.[8] In addition, where the evidence comes from an expert, and particularly regarding forensic science, the legitimacy of the framework becomes as challenging as the evidence to contest.[9]

In this 'fact-finding' environment, aspirations for neutral, objective or negotiated 'truths' may be inappropriate or far-fetched. The 'two cases' approach will always deliver a resulting judicial narrative which appears Janus-faced: attentive to incriminatory and exculpatory evidence from two opposite directions (Twining, 1992). Part of the problem here lies with what we shall address later: the conflation of languages of capacity, liability, justification and excuse, and culpability (mitigation or aggravation).

The theory of the neutral fact-finder, professional or lay, is flawed in practice. The verdict delivery is considered to be separate from the law and yet it is judicial interpretation of law which designates factual relevance and significance for the fact-finder. In our scenario, when the ICC indictment is tried, the nature of the case before the Court will not be a free-flowing and elaborated contest between two tribal legitimacies. Rather, it will be what the Court admits as evidence that will face the distillation of verdict delivery – nothing more and nothing less. No doubt this will fall short of the 'truths' which victim witnesses believe should be debated.

The adversarial process is centrally complicit in this search for mythical objective and objectifiable fact distilled from partial and sectarian argument. Selective and sequential delivery of evidence creates a procedural dynamic where partiality prevails, for interests which adversarial contest rewards:

> No wonder when truth is expected to emerge from two competing vectors their sum is skewed whenever one side exaggerates when the other-side refrains from doing so.
>
> (Damaska, 2008: 338)

The adversarial sieve is refined through probative concerns, concerns themselves not separable from impressionism and populist perception. Factual refinement (and its influence over decisions of liability or otherwise) is exacerbated when forensic or circumstantial considerations are mediated through popular culture. Juries are particularly susceptible to overestimating the probative significance of DNA evidence due to attitudes largely constructed by their consumption of American crime investigation television shows (Findlay, 2008a).

It is because the form and process of the adversarial trial has the capacity to distort truth for fact that we argue in favour of trial transformation. The harmonisation of truth and fact is not a reason in itself for transformation, but rather our commitment to a victim constituency for ICJ requires procedural and contextual compatibility from which the trial should not be excluded. To the contrary, if trial-based justice is to continue as a centre-piece of ICJ, the reality of victim constituency will be measured in no small part by the way in which the trial satisfies legitimate victim interests. As we have put in terms of victim-centred international justice aspirations (see chapter 3), retributive and didactic determinations alone in the adversarial trial are in no small measure a product of tight evidence regimes. Deconstructing the impediments to fact meeting truth should advance the possibility of achieving, through mediation, restorative outcomes pre-trial and at trial. These are the framework aspirations of trial transformation.

Sourcing trial transformation

Our vision of transformative justice is based on the moral foundations of humanitarianism (see chapter 1). Deriving the moral justifications for intervening in the lives of others from the notion that that conflict is essentially destructive of humanity, ICJ comprises processes seeking to resolve conflict by peaceful means which are intrinsically good. The ICC declares these essential purposes. Peacemaking through trial justice suggests an engagement with competing 'truths' in ways similar to conventional trial fact-finding through adversarial argument. The search for truth within the trial need not be an unattainable aspiration or distracted normative commitment. Nor should it be consigned to non-trial restorative resolutions.[10] It can take on, through trial transformation, as much of the operational reality and procedural appropriateness as verdict delivery within the trial process. Truth will thereby give a more legitimate and viable foundation for state reconstruction than retribution and deterrence as didactic and unproven consequences of penality. Truth-telling becomes a purpose as well as an outcome of the transformed trial process.

Some say that to attach conflict resolution to the central aims of the international criminal trial is asking too much and so is doomed to frustration.[11] These criticisms have merit if the trial model under review is a narrow and constrained reflection of adversarial decision-making.[12] Even without the trial transformation we envisage, the ICC pre-trial and trial models have moved away from an unreconstructed adversarial frame. For better or worse, the juridical professionals in the ICC reiterate the Court's exemplary function motivated by wide peacemaking aspirations. These are beyond individual deterrence and concerns about impunity. They represent a fundamental belief that, through strategic prosecution, the ICC may have a much more extensive conflict resolution function than the consequences of prosecuting individual liability in domestic courts might anticipate.

However, exemplary prosecutions and penalties cannot of themselves claim restorative potential. To maximise the restorative dimension of formal ICJ, the normative foundations of the trial transformation process must reflect a number of humanitarian principles. The most fundamental of these involve equal treatment and tolerance of human difference and frailty. The justice system and the trial in particular must not be used as a tool of oppression where the law and its execution evoke a theory of social control by force and violence. Further, the humanitarian normative foundation advances the legitimate interests of victim communities over the sectarian priorities of a limited cultural and political hegemony.[13]

It could be argued that the diversionary pathway to trial litigation and the deductive process of evidence accumulation and presentation favour justice through institutional and social exclusion. Added to a trial context where access is much constrained and inclusivity formalised, the conventional criminal trial is a discriminatory regime. This explains why the normative repositioning of ICJ which respects restorative as well as retributive paradigms requires humanitarian foundations confirmed through improved procedural access, inclusivity and integration.[14]

Retributive ICJ now administered through a largely adversarial process is rationalised by substantive norms of law and procedure that conventionally ignore the essential qualities of humanity at large, even though presumptions of equality before the law overlie trial fairness. This rationalisation is itself justified by a notion of trial fairness where the accused person is protected from the vengeance of victim communities and the domination of the state.[15] In this paradigm we have argued[16] that a strong justification for locating even limited restorative determinations within the international criminal trial is to benefit from measures of procedural fairness. The selective 'rights focus' of the trial should also be an important expectation for victim interests seeking restoration, whether or not these rights take second place to the accused's protections. It is the recognition of procedural fairness (in a more balanced setting than conventional adversarial trial fairness) and juridical accountability over humanity's interests which can be didactically asserted and valued through the transformed international criminal trial. Once so enunciated in trial transformation, procedural fairness and the rights it recognises may act as a comparative normative framework for the processes of alternative institutions which will continue to have a much wider restorative remit in ICJ.

The 'rights protection' paradigm characterising the transformed trial:

- Is committed to communitarian rather than individual rights recognition.
- Respects the preferred rights of accused persons in the adversarial trial mode, while victim voice will be given significance in pre-trial and trial fact determinations as well as in sentence.
- Is where the restorative/mediatory role of the victim voice will be given equal standing as any other key truth-teller (and contesting victim voices will be free to dispute the stories told).
- Is where the sanctity of the trial and the pre-trial context, as it protects witnesses and values evidence, will prevail in both the retributive and restorative modes, and will value and protect the process of truth-telling in the same way as it validates and protects witness evidence.
- This in turn is injected into restorative 'truth-telling' within and beyond the transformed trial expectation for the recognition and delivery of communitarian rights in which the juridical professional ensures agency.

Transformed trial process will also produce a new justice ordering where real institutional involvement will be accorded to the victim voice. Integrating victim interests in a more sophisticated, even if only practically didactic, fashion within the transformed international criminal trial will open up the prospects for 'fairness' as a measure of the humanity of justice processes. Communitarian integrity and, more importantly, an awareness of the contexts that give rise to cultural differences based as these may be in alternative world views of fairness, competing conceptualisations of primary knowledge, valuable normative traditions and community virtues are picked up by the 'truth-telling' opportunities in a transformed trial framework. In this regard, trial fairness will not simply be secured through the concern for the accused on the adversarial context, but more widely balanced in restorative opportunities for the victim and the offender.

Our conception of transformative justice offers the possibility to reconcile differences of approach exemplified in the dialect of retributive and restorative justice. This dialectic is resolved through trial transformation. The transformed trial, as a centre-piece within this transition, transcends this debate by recognising difference, much more than adversarial differences do, when seeking to resolve conflict by using rules of law and procedure to facilitate such outcomes.

Having said that, as with the international criminal trial at present limited to retributive considerations, prosecutions are very selective and the interests covered are as symbolic as they are significant. Opening up the trial to restorative possibilities will not invite a flood of victims to enjoy this new atmosphere of procedural fairness and retributive/restorative resolve. The vast majority of victim interests will still await recognition and resolution in the alternative justice domain. The limited resources of the juridical professional and the progressive politicisation of the prosecution process will confirm this.

If this limited didactic role for the international trial will prevail, why do we justify, or even require, trial transformation embracing new restorative possibilities and the 'truths' on which these are founded? Is this not expecting a radical repositioning of the trial without adequate victim coverage? Perhaps this is a sound criticism in the context of contemporary trial practice. But, as Damaska (2008) concedes, even for the retributive adversarial trial, it is a dominant and valuable didactic rather than a reconstructive enterprise. In this sense trial transformation may not always or necessarily change this exemplary purpose into more actual reward. Were such and expansionist impact of trial transformation required to maximise didactic impact, then the control function of the superior courts as social engineering exercises could all be impugned.

Truth-telling and historicising may necessarily replace guilt and penalty without essentially enhancing the possibility of individual responsibility. That is why collective perpetration and victimisation suggest a more vital arena for trial histories as a means to identify and apportion moral responsibility.

In light of the practical limitations of the international criminal trial ongoing (transformed or not) as a general context for examining the interests of humanity, how can we argue for access, inclusivity and integration in a more didactic sense? (See chapter 1.) The answer lies in the realisation, we argue, of the representative the inclusion of 'interests' rather than armies of victims. In that, a transformed trial recognises the needs of humanity as central 'pathways of influence' (Findlay and Henham, 2005: chapter 3) in a decision site model, even if the trial outcomes could only ever satisfy these interests at the most symbolic level (as is the case with retribution). In this expressive and truth-telling form, victim communities are championed in a small number of transformed trials for the wider restorative impact in associated alternative (fairer?) justice paradigms. In addition, if collective responsibility is better enforced within the transformed trial setting, then victim community interests are more likely to be achieved.

The transformed trial, selective as its resolutions will be, opens up exciting new possibilities to the victim interests identified for access, inclusivity and integration. To achieve this, liability and responsibility will be offered, enunciated through fact and or truth sources. In light of negotiation through judicial discretion (see chapter 5), the dichotomy of truth and liability vs. fact and responsibility (discussed later) can be viewed as false at the level of both ideology and process if the transformed trial breaks free of its adversarial straitjacket and recognises and values cultural plurality. A more central place for victim communities within the transformed trial will automatically deliver this harmonisation.

As Tamanaha (1979) suggests, fact and value are essentially cultural entities, through which they receive real social location. In this respect a fresh approach to fact and value as coexisting non-problematically (or at least outside adversarial discrimination) opens up the opportunity for transformative justice holistically, focusing on humanity and its protection. If there is a paradox between fact and value within ICJ, it may lie in the recognition that transformed trial processes must integrate retributive and restorative justice to provide a wide normative context capable of satisfying different and sometimes contesting demands for justice (see chapter 3).

Given the unrealistic prospect of completely redesigning international trial justice as transformative *de novo*, in what follows we suggest ways in which retributive and restorative forms of justice can be reconciled and integrated into the normative framework of existing international criminal court procedures in particular, so that transformative aspirations will be realised. In suggesting the transformative path we accept the following reservations:

- limitations in victim access, inclusivity and integration depending on the political and prosecutorial dynamics of case selection and management;
- the significance of 'humanity' over partiality and sectarianism in focusing trial constituency and the interests it should reflect;
- the continuing need to develop alternative, transformative and restorative justice processes and resolutions to satisfy victim interests outside the didactic and conciliatory capacities of trial decision-making.

As we explain later, trial transformation envisages an adversarial and mediatory phase of the trial where fact and/or truth will be established for transformative purposes. However, it would be wrong to suppose that retributive or restorative objectives will predominate in either mode because the transformative rationale depends on negotiating, recognising and managing legitimate victim interests at any stage pre-trial and at trial (see chapter 3). These may or may not approximate retributive or restorative concerns. What it does mean is that conventional adversarial concepts of liability, the nature of the evidence required for liability attribution, and how much truth and fact are admitted for any purpose, need to be detached from their primary association with retributive outcomes.

The truth/fact divide. Much ado about nothing?

Before embarking on a brief interrogation of the separation of truth and fact, an observation of the place of truth within the trial is merited. In his illuminating essay 'The Jury and Reality', Zen Bankowski (1988) explores the search for truth within the trial. He suggests that any such search is based on epistemological premises requiring further testing. Bankowski challenges any assumption that the trial is about 'finding' truth in the same way that an explorer discovers a new land. In his view the context of the adversarial trial not only restricts this, but was never designed for any such eventuality. As a purposive exercise, fact-finding is about not finding facts (or for that matter truth) in the trial at all. Rather than an epistemological exercise of uncovering what 'is', the trial suggests to the jury what 'ought to be' in a normative sense. Allan Norrie (2001) confirms this view in his critique of the subjective interpretation of the 'guilty mind'. It is an inductive rather than empirical process of psychopathology.

Bankowski next suggests that there is a 'sociology' (or social interaction) that is the adversarial trial which gives a particular impetus to truth in the trial. In discussing the 'coherence of the case', Bankowski identifies fact as the outcome of decisions about persuasion and the minimising of doubt. Can the outcome be truth? From here the trial of fact becomes at the very least a 'truth-certifying' process, a game adjudicated by the rules of evidence where one side wins the contest over guilt or innocence by clearing predetermined hurdles of proof or countering these with justification or excuse. Is the product necessarily truth? Bankowski concludes that fact-finding mechanisms within the conventional adversarial system say more about our aspirations for society and its governance than it does the achievement of epistemological truths.

The consequences of the truth/fact alternative trial sources within a more inclusive trial process are discussed in what follows and these will lead on to the enhanced role of the judicial professional, which is expanded in later chapters. The analysis suggests that truth as much as fact has a vital place in the discourse and narrative of international trial justice. This means that the adversarial model of trial fact-finding will come under the influence of mediation processes that are more commonly found in a truth and reconciliation environment (Trankle, 2007). The conditions in which mediation may be the preferred approach in trial deliberations will obviously depend on where truth in place of contested fact is deemed through judicial discretion to best determine prevailing victim interests at any point in the process. The shift from fact to truth, and adversarial to mediation styles, will evidence the dynamic process of transformed trial justice. This chapter provides examples of where similar trial practice operates at jurisdictional levels, particularly in hybrid criminal justice traditions (Findlay, 2008b: chapter 8).

Truth, as much as fact, has a vital place in the discourse and narrative of international trial justice. This means that the adversarial model of trial fact-finding will come under the influence of mediation processes more common in the truth and reconciliation environment. The preferred approach will obviously depend on where truth in place of contested fact is deemed through judicial discretion to best determine prevailing victim interests at that point in the process. The shift from fact to truth and adversarial to mediation styles will evidence the dynamic process of transformative trial justice. Examples of where similar trial practice operates at jurisdictional levels will be explored in what follows.

If judicial discretion is to be mobilised in this way, it will need to become familiar with techniques that encourage compromise and truth-telling to promote healing, as well as apportioning individual blame on the basis of legally defined harm. This choice will be determined by whether the revelation of truth or the determination of fact predominates at any decision-making stage (see Findlay and Henham, 2005: chapter 3), leading on to alternative concerns for responsibility and reconciliation or liability and retribution.

The essence of the trial as such is fact. Value needs inclusion if contested fact is to assume the status of truth. The role of the judge in any such transition is crucial if the trial is to provide its context. These imperatives envisage a decision paradigm where the attribution of value to fact through the exercise of discretion provides the power for change. So the judge will have a pivotal role in deciding whether truth supports a determination of responsibility or liability, and their appropriate outcomes, and how fact and value should merge for these purposes. Judicial discretion will also negotiate how the choice and selection of outcomes may be derived from what is accepted as definitive truth and the ways in which legitimate victim and community interests will be recognised to drive the choice of alternative resolutions and their outcomes.

Different contexts and aspirations for truth and fact

Our scenario raises several fundamental questions where fact and truth are contestable:

1. Was the general acting on his own initiative or with the agreement of the government? He suggests that he was doing nothing more than following superior orders.
2. Event 1: Did the Minister for Information minimise the extent of the horror enabling the government's categorical denial of genocide?

Some of the women from the village who had been repatriated after the violence denied the minister's account that responsibility for violence lay with a group of disgruntled villagers who had been in dispute with the village elders over landownership. Is this version of events correct?

3. Event 2
   - Did the mercenaries and the general's troops commit acts of unprovoked violence against villagers and their property?
   - Did villagers mount unprovoked (or provoked) reprisals against the other clan's settlements in the region as a consequence?
   - Did the media and the government systematically provide misleading misinformation about the activities of their clan opponents?

To illustrate the issues at stake it would be helpful to look at these questions in terms of how they might be dealt with in an adversarial/retributive context and contrast this with opportunities for fact/truth determinations, which might be presented in a transformative trial context. Here we are suggesting a choice to seek truth through mediation and conciliation which could confirm stories told and the consequential responsibility. On the other hand, there is the conventional testing of conflicting 'cases' to determine which evidence prevails and if so, whether the burdens for liability are met. Such a comparison enables informed speculation as to the possible impact of different resolution and deliberation contexts on responsibility/liability determinations at particular stages in the criminal justice process.

Take as an example the issues in 1 above and the consideration of superior orders or command responsibility. Even in terms of complicity, adversarial criminal law is not comfortable allocating liability (or even responsibility) on the basis of contribution. Unlike civil law considerations of contributory negligence, the criminal law ties the liability of secondary parties to the acts of the perpetrator and to collective criminal minds founded on agreement or inferred contemplation. In this sense, superior orders are treated as a very limited justification or excuse for criminal participation (see Ambos, 2007).

Shared responsibility and the culpability of higher-order directors are much more easily managed through truth and reconciliation, and mediation. Fault can be more accurately calibrated and apportioned when cut free of artificial links to shared perpetration and common minds.

In the scenario, various stakeholders advance different stories which they allege to be truth. In an adversarial trial context, these versions will be tested through oral or documentary evidence and a decision by the fact-finder will determine which story, if any, is accepted as probative evidence. For those whose stories fall outside this determination, no matter what elements of 'truth' they contain, it is unlikely that the trial will satisfy their claims for voice or their need to see responsibility shared.

Pre-trial mediation or conciliation does not necessarily produce such exclusion and frustration. As the truth and reconciliation processes have shown, mediation in a formalised adjudication, beyond the strictures of adversarial trial, has the capacity to tolerate disparate stories and negotiate responsibility even where perceptions of truth may differ, but identification of harm and those involved is agreed.

Harmonisation possibilities: liability vs. responsibility

Trial transformation is as much about diversifying trial decision-making processes as it is about opening up alternative outcomes. A crucial indicator of trial transformation as we have proposed it so far will be the radical and applied 'harmonisation' of two crucial decision-making paradigms. The first is the nexus between fact and liability around which the adversarial trial conventionally revolves. The next is the broader concern for truth and responsibility which have featured in alternative international criminal justice resolution frameworks such as truth and reconciliation commissions.

The merging of these two paradigms is the natural, if not challenging, consequence of introducing restorative justice possibilities into a retributive trial process (Findlay and Henham, 2005). At the very least this means a reconceptualisation of the foundations of trial decision-making such as 'fact' and 'evidence' against wider interpretations of 'truth'. We indicate in *Transforming International Criminal Justice* that evidence as both a facilitator and an outcome of trial decision-making will be re-envisaged through transformation so that it may be employed for retributive and, where appropriate, restorative deliberations.[17]

In what follows we explore some of the well-known themes germane to fact/value debates which have long fuelled socio-legal critique (Tamanaha, 1997: chapter 2). With this as a background, the discussion of the purposes of 'evidence' within the transformed trial structure where the normative constituency is 'humanity' and the deliberative outcomes can be either retributive or restorative will critically proceed.

The current divide in ICJ is between liability-focused trials and restorative, truth-centred commissions. This is an unhelpful institutional and process divide, which, as we established in chapter 3, fails at least to encapsulate and broadly satisfy the diverse and legitimate interests of victim communities. Building on the case for integrating restorative and retributive justice within the international criminal trial (Findlay and Henham, 2005: chapter 7), it is logical here to open up the manner in which facts and truth can be established and applied for different but not inconsistent trial purposes. The widening application of what until now, in the adversarial context, might be viewed as incompatible sources necessitates unlocking the trial from narrow notions of liability and its retributive outcomes, without diminishing or dismissing these as they represent legitimate victim interests. In chapter 5 the domain of juridical discretion is proposed as a constructive and creative context where evidence and truth can coexist for enhanced trial objectives. The transformed trial may be as interested to explore the stories which need to be told by victims and the truth which needs to be negotiated for community reconciliation as, conventionally, the trial objective has been to focus on liability and not the broader forms of responsibility. Again, the challenge here is to introduce a more active victim voice, along with the establishment of truth and the responsibility which follows, but not at the expense of retributive punishment where liability also stands. Until now, these objectives have remained corralled in ICJ in distinctly separate contexts of legal determination and regulation (Roche, 2005). Already there has been some detailed discussion of the way in which negotiated justice could apply to pre-trial situations in ICJ, particularly with plea bargaining (see chapter 3 above; Damaska,

2005). In this chapter we extend these considerations to the foundations of the trial itself and the process of its essential decision-making sites.

By utilising juridical discretionary power (see chapter 5), the trial also can become a vehicle to explore the stories which need to be told by and on behalf of victim communities. Consequentially, truth and responsibility may be the appropriate negotiation at the expense of liability through adversarial contest within a new decision-making trial format. Hence, notions of individual criminal responsibility will need to be broadened beyond individual culpability, so recognising that conventional concepts of individual and collective fault must be argued for, against the contextual understandings of what this means for victims and communities of justice.

The first hurdle – jurisdictional challenges

Particularly in Western Europe, victim/offender mediation (VOM) is a common precursor to the adversarial trial. In a detailed qualitative study of VOM in Germany and in France, Stefani Trankle (2007) presents problems which contradict the aims and working principles of VOM as well as the legal rights of participants, even if an agreement between the parties has been reached. Trankle ascribes the essence of the problem to VOM being unable in practice to secure its specific *modus operandi* in the framework of penal procedure. She argues that the informal and pedagogic logic of mediation is constrained by the penal framework, namely its power to impose its formal and bureaucratic logic on the mediation process. In her study it was the penal law that dominated the procedure of VOM and impeded the interaction process.

Trankle's research highlights the conceptual and procedural impossibility of successfully incorporating even early stage VOM in a trial process not subject to transformation. The integration essential for mediation to work in any true sense of parity will be thwarted by the functional and structural imperative of adversarial trial justice where prosecutorial dominance and victim marginalisation undermine the conciliatory nature of mediation. Trankle concludes that VOM in the two jurisdictions targeted in her research does not work well within a system of penal law. VOM is based on ideals that are not easily compatible with the structural conditions laid down by the judicial framework in an adversarial and retributive model.

> From my point of view the main problem is the structural link between mediation and the penal system. The empirical problems described (in the study) add up to the question of whether victim/offender mediation ought to be institutionalised within, or outside, the penal system. The question is how much 'shadow of leviathan', that is how much formality and power control is necessary to guarantee procedural rights and how much mediation can endure without losing its specific character.
>
> (2007: 411)

The issue of destructive tension between mediation paradigms and penal decision-making frameworks has been widely discussed in the literature of legal sociology (see *inter alia* Spittler, 1980; Von Trotha, 1982; Jung, 1998, 1999; Trenzek, 2002, 2003, all in Trenkle, 2007). It is recognised that the more informal mediation is the more elements that do not belong to the penal procedure are introduced as such and the less it can be controlled.

If the judiciary is to keep control over VOM and in so doing retain the conciliatory integrity of a restorative mode, then both the nature and framework for exercising judicial discretion need to be transformed (see chapter 5). The judiciary, in a conventional trial model, has at its disposal sufficient power to exert control over mediation officers and the progress of the mediation they deliver. On the other hand, too much control by the judiciary or trial professionals will so adulterate the restorative context of mediation as to make the essentials of parity between the non-professional parties impossible.

Trankle discusses the possibilities of improving VOM within a penal system of trial justice. However, she does so within a very limited reform framework, not one that envisages the possibility or achievement of wholesale trial transformation. She warns against confusing a penal and psychological procedure which will tend to confuse participants regarding what it includes and excludes. In this sense the extension of the study is to:

- identify the impracticality of restorative justice within a conventional penal model;
- highlight the significance of judicial discretion in the management of restorative trial opportunities (conventional or transformed); and
- identify the particular relationships in a restorative enterprise which would need to transform its decision-making pathways to avoid the constrictions of retributive penality, and at the same time embrace restorative possibilities within a rights protection trial framework. The essential consideration here is the management of alternative trial sources at reconstituted judicial discretion.

Once jurisdiction for whatever intervention is preferred has been settled, the issue of attributing liability or responsibility presents itself. For collective liability in particular, the legal individual remains the unrealistic focus of conventional international criminal trials. Crimes by groups against groups necessitate a broader engagement either for liability and punishment to follow or at least for truth and responsibility to be attributed.

The second hurdle – collectivising liability

In the Introduction we identified the challenge faced by international criminal law in more effectively bringing together collective victimisation and collective liability. International victim/offender interaction in the context of crimes against humanity or genocide realistically demands collective rather than individual engagement. Despite the reluctance of international criminal legislation and its instrumental processes to venture outside the crimes of the individual (and tortuous interpretations of liability through association), collectivised responsibility has been a major consideration in truth and reconciliation settings.

The ICTY in a number of decisions wrestled with the scope of 'joint criminal enterprise'.[18] The intention behind this doctrine is to construct, through the commission of similar or collaborative acts agreed to or contemplated, a culpable association with the perpetrator. In this way it is a doctrine to impute individual liability through association across a group. From an evidentiary standpoint, the doctrine saves the Prosecutor the necessity to prove communicated agreement or a causal link to the perpetration of the criminal act.

As Damaska concedes:

> its animating idea – that of reaching the criminal masterminds – is sound. It responds to the fact that most international crimes are committed in an organisational context, so that looking for principal culprits beyond hands-on perpetrators makes eminent sense. It is the elaboration of that idea that causes concern. Under the presently prevailing understanding, the scope of membership in the enterprise, as well as its spatial and temporal range, are uncertain and liable to arbitrary extension.
>
> (2008: 352)

The sharpest criticism of 'common purpose' or joint criminal enterprise approaches to collective liability has been in circumstances where agreement is inferred from foresight of the consequences of being within the accused's contemplation (Cassese, 2007). The slippage between judicial hindsight and actual foresight (or not) within the pressures and confusions of conflict and armed struggle tends to dislocate evidentiary construction from truth (Rachlinski, 2007).

The difficulties facing courts in being satisfied that degrees of involvement equate with perpetration and individual liability highlight the tensions when forcing inclination, impression and predisposition into a form of evidence equating with the guilty mind of the individual. The legal wrangling over the interpretation of superior orders (Ambos, 2007), command responsibility (Danner and Martinez, 2005) and equal culpability (Ohlin, 2007) emphasises the impossibility of collective liability being viewed outside the constraints of the individual and his or her 'mind'.

Amann (2002) looks at the problem of collective liability with particular reference to genocide. The state of mind required for the crime is the intent to destroy, in whole or in part, a national, ethical, racial or religious group as such,[19] much more than mass killings. Conviction requires that the victim belongs to one of four designated protected groups. Evidence of the intent to destroy can take other crime forms, but it must be directed against the designated protected group. Therefore, liability is essentially dependent on harming a specific victim community. Here, the group mentality in question is not merely that of certain perpetrators. It is also the collective mentality which binds the protected group that gives purchase to the prosecution and punishment endeavour.

The question is asked with respect to genocide as against other forms of collective harm: so what? Does calling an act genocide bring it any added significance. Amann holds that it does because international and domestic laws against collectivised harm and victimisation, it is argued, 'operate as a means for articulation and nourishment of social values'.[20] To this extent the declaratory purpose of criminalizing, or even holding responsibility for, genocide is as important as the punishment of the individual or the group:

> This expressive function has special force in international criminal law, only now entering an era in which ongoing international criminal tribunals reinforce pronouncements of norms, such as the proscription against genocide in the 1948 Convention.[21]

Even so, for genocide to be recognised as a unique form of criminal liability, the limited number of protected groups affected by the collective harm to qualify as genocide resists upsetting the singular status of the designation. For groups falling outside the protected range, with individual liability not sufficiently answering other heinous forms of collective victimisation, responsibility may await truth-telling and restorative interventions beyond failed punishment.

If collective liability remains a narrow, legal construct in international criminal law, then the argument to include considerations of truth and responsibility within the transformed international trial become a clearer aspiration. The attribution of responsibility depends on truth-telling beyond adversarial argument. The tensions inherent in adversarial contest are exacerbated when victimisation and perpetration are collectivised and cases are multiple. Contrary accounts are difficult enough to resolve as truth when there are two self-interested individuals in the frame. Multiply that through collective liability, and even legal fictions such as reasonable contemplation will not produce a credible, truth-telling environment. As Haack (2004: 49) suggests, truth is not a consequence of the 'clash of bias and counter-bias' because, as with collective liability determinations, the more complex the investigated question, the more partisan polarisation becomes the straitjacket of historians.

The third hurdle – criminalising organisations

In Australian domestic jurisdictions there are several models for the criminalising of organisations within which collective liability can be constructed.

Kyriakakis (2007) suggests that the integration of ICC crimes within the Commonwealth Criminal Code, aligned with the Codes approach to corporate liability, has created an opportunity to prosecute corporations for global crime, even under the universal jurisdiction principle.[22] The possible reach of the Code when testing Australian international crimes provisions against its framework of corporate liability might, it is argued, fill the void left by the ICC's restriction to the individual legal personality. The Code (Part 2.5, section 12.1) makes it clear that all offences contained therein apply equally to bodies corporate as to natural persons.

The possibilities under the Commonwealth Code for making corporations responsible for the harm they cause may be wider than what is offered through the civil reparations route of the US Alien Tort Claims Act 1789,[23] provided the Code is given an offshore reach. The Code would not need to rely on the law of nations or customary international law (Joseph, 2004) in order to move corporate responsibility to a determination of criminal liability.

In the Code, drafting conventional notions of the mind of the company are relied on to establish liability through identification and transference. Constructing the mind of the company for the purposes of criminal liability is not possible, however, through aggregating individual 'culpabilities' exhibited by groups of individuals in the company. The unique feature of determining liability which would particularly lend itself to global crime is the notion of 'criminal corporate cultures'.[24] Part 2.5, s. 12.3 of the Code provides two routes to proving fault where culture is concerned. A company can be liable where:

1. a corporate culture existed within the body corporate that directed, encouraged, tolerated or led to non-compliance with the relevant provision; or
2. it is proved that the body corporate failed to create and maintain a corporate culture that required compliance with the relevant provision.

It cannot be said that the Code criminalises organisations *per se*. Rather, it either identifies either the mind of the company or a criminal culture that influences that mind. Interestingly, the criminalisation of the organisation was not the stated purpose of the recently enacted Crimes (Criminal Organisations Control) Act (NSW) 2009. This legislation was a criminal justice response to an outbreak of biker gang violence in New South Wales. The Act claims extraterritorial operation in part to have organisations 'declared' which will have criminal consequences for membership and association. A judge making a declaration needs to be satisfied that members associate 'for the purpose of organising, planning, facilitating, supporting or engaging in serious criminal activity or the organisation represents a risk to public safety and order' (s. 9). Proof is only required on the balance of probabilities.

Associated with a declaration is the facility for the court to make control orders against individuals who associate with the organisation.

This is not the place to analyse the many problems associated with proving and prosecuting membership or association as determined in the Act. For the purpose of a concern with collective liability and the transferability to international criminal law, the issue of *association* is crucial. The Act views association as being in company with, or communicating with, a member. Association becomes a criminal offence. It would appear under s. 23 of the Act that association is a status offence; that is where criminal conduct is confirmed through the act of association. It is not clear whether an accused is also required:

- to share the objectives of the organisation regarding serious criminal activity;
- to agree with others to share these objectives, or to have this agreement implied;
- to have agreement or shared objectives inferred as a natural consequence of association; or
- to intend to associate for any serious criminal purpose, or otherwise.[25]

It would seem, however, that some mental state is required for liability. This assumption can be drawn from the construction of defences to a charge of association. On the one hand, s. 26(5) lists certain types of association (such as close family membership or in the course of lawful occupation) which might be disregarded for the purposes of the offence. While it can be assumed that the onus shifts to the accused to raise these issues in justification of association, the motive or intention for association outside the charge on the part of the accused is an essential proof. Beyond denying association or that an associate was a member of a declared organisation, the other defence against association would be that the accused knew that the organisation had been otherwise authorised to conduct activities which would in ordinary circumstance be considered seriously criminal or a challenge to order.[26]

If little else, these two legislative approaches to collective liability identify the challenges in directing international criminal law away from approaches dealing with joint criminal enterprise, command responsibility or common purpose. Is it then best for the ICC to move more in the direction of considerations of the collective challenge to human rights? In answering this question we continue to address corporations as criminal organisations rather than, say, political resistance groups in transitional state conflict. Despite the obvious and documented impact of multinational corporations in fomenting civil unrest, corporations represent a legal fiction as individual legal entities, but resist criminal liability because of their collective and incorporated form. This increases the challenge for conventional criminalisation through prosecution and trial processes.

The fourth hurdle – agency against collective human rights abuses

Schabas (2001) considers general principles of international individual criminal responsibility – accomplice liability in particular – and how they could be employed to prosecute 'economic actors' who participate in international crimes. In the context of corporate crime, these principles might be applied to the prosecution of individuals within the body corporate. As Schabas argues, Article 25 of the Rome Statute has at least two potentials for linking accessorial liability to the nexus between business and international crime:

1. article 25 does not stipulate that the assistance provided (economically or through business) should be substantial in order to constitute aiding and abetting;
2. the wording of the article entitles the prosecution of an individual on the basis of having acted through a corporate entity to commit an international crime.[27]

The problems associated with working from the liability of the individual to that of the corporation in the economic sphere challenges a broader consideration of morality and good global citizenship. As Braithwaite and Fisse (1993) suggest, for punishing corporations the complexity of collective responsibility requires rethinking conventional responses which might be appropriate for individuals, but not corporations. How can it be right that corporations profit from what would be considered criminal for individuals simply because the law of global liability cannot find the technology to encompass the company perpetrator? Legal incapacity could never be equated with innocence or, to a lesser extent, moral probity and hence impunity.

McCorquodale and Simons (2007) argue that states routinely support and assist their corporate nationals in prosecuting and advancing global trading interests. Even though states may not advocate human rights violations as a consequence of these extraterritorial adventures through acts or omissions, states may unwittingly contribute to corporations violating rights off-shore. Therefore, is there a case for home state responsibility in situations of rights violations?

Corporations do carry human rights obligations. The nature of transnational corporations and their impact on the international legal system in a commercial sense at least is premised on good corporate citizenship. Where states carry human rights obligations for actions of all corporations within the state's territory, global governance requires that international human rights law (IHRL) has purchase over human rights violations by corporations taking advantage of extraterritoriality.[28]

It could be argued that states become internationally responsible[29] for rights violations by their corporate citizens where:

- a corporation is exercising government authority, including where it has exceeded that authority;
- a corporation is acting under the instruction, direction or control of the state, including where it has ignored or contravened instruction;
- a state aids and assists the corporation with its activities in the knowledge of circumstances of unlawful activity.

A state may have international responsibility for a foreign subsidiary of a corporate national where:

- state practice shows that the state's relationship with transnational corporations is not territorially limited; and
- a duty of due diligence to protect from harm applies to the state, whether knowledge is actual or constructive, and the state facilitates that duty.

International organisations such as the Organisation for Economic Cooperation and Development recognise the need for states to shoulder responsibility through their domestic jurisdictions (state responsibility), for rights violations by corporations where international law alone may not have clear purchase.

> (States should encourage corporate nationals) to respect human rights of those affected by their activities consistent with the host government's international obligations and commitments.[30]

In this guideline the seeds of its own impotence may lie. If international law fails to regulate corporate rights violators, why should we believe domestic regulations will be any more effective if the domestic jurisdiction has a checkered rights record through a reluctance to act on international rights obligations? Isn't this a more fundamental challenge to the state as the holder of both rights and obligations? Perhaps the notion of state responsibility in international law needs to give way, as far as global crime is concerned, to considerations of collective liability or responsibility effectively determined through a transformed ICJ. Once again, the call for corporate responsibility may rely on histories of truth and costly revelations against corporate reputation.

Imperatives for truth and the historiography of justice

Recording history as an aim of ICJ is closely connected to wider concerns for conflict resolution. Cassese (1998: 6-7) identifies the enunciation of an accurate historical record so that 'future generations can remember and be made fully cognisant of what happened' as a worthy purpose of ICJ.

This is no simple task. Contested histories proliferate as much in the experience of truth and reconciliation commissions as alternative facts fuel adversarial examination. Even so, the didactic purpose of justice is undeniable in the widest presentation of the story at issue. The question remains whether the trial is the place for this 'truth-telling' and if so, how it is to be managed.

Damaska denies the validity and possibility of judicial historiography because 'judges cannot sufficiently disentangle themselves from the web of legal relevancy' (2008: 336). Even if this is so, it acts not as a denial of historical record for the achievement of ICJ, but rather as the need for trial narrative to break free from the procedural strictures of fact-finding.

We assert that trial transformation makes truth-telling possible and appropriate. Why?

- It acts as a precursor to restorative outcomes which address significant victim interests.
- It may produce justice understandings that adversarial evidence rules can conspire to restrict or conceal.
- It gives an expanded victim-voice which if not leading on to liability determinations will not necessarily compromise the rights of the accused.
- It opens up possibilities for judge-led mediation and conciliation where retributive outcomes are unlikely or inappropriate.

The effect of the 'truthful' recording of history which promotes reconciliation was referred to in the ICTY case of *Plavsic*. On this issue the tribunal stated:

> The Trial Chamber accepts that acknowledgement and full disclosure of serious crimes are very important when establishing the truth in relation to such crimes. This, together with acceptance of responsibility for the committed wrongs, will promote reconciliation. In this respect, the Trial Chamber concludes that the guilty pleas of Mrs Plavsic and her acknowledgement of responsibility, particularly in the light of her former position as President of the Republika Srpska, should promote reconciliation in Bosnia and Herzegovina and the region as a whole.[31]

The *Plavsik* declaration of responsibility is all the more remarkable in an adversarial context, even if rewarded with sentencing concessions for contrition. It was a concession which admitted to the record a wealth of 'stories' that would otherwise have been excluded in a contested trial.[32]

In the appeal from the trial of *Drazen Erdemovich* the tragic case turned on a soldier's responsibility when forced by threats of his own death to kill innocent victims under superior orders.[33] The accused's conviction was as much due to the legal/moral convention that it is better to sacrifice your own life than the lives of others rather than any undisputed determination of a criminal mind.

Generally, on the purposes of the criminalisation in this instance the majority judgment observed:

> one of the purposes of international criminal law is to protect the weak and vulnerable in armed conflict situations. Judges McDonald and Vohrah, therefore, seek to facilitate the development and effectiveness of international humanitarian law and not to impede it. Thus, they 'give[s] notice in no uncertain terms that those who kill innocent persons will not be able to take advantage of duress as a defence and thus get away with impunity for their criminal acts in the taking of innocent lives'.[34]

On the issue of responsibility, in dissenting with the majority view, Judge Sir Ninian Stephen emphasised the contextual relevance of responsibility in the face of immutable, if harsh legal principle:

> Whatever [the appellant] chose, the lives of the innocent would be lost and he had no power to avert that consequence. Hence, since the common law authorities - but for which one could say that the general principles of law favoured duress as a defence to all crimes - did not address the issue at stake, and since their underlying rationale did not justify excluding duress as a defence to unlawful killing in circumstances such as those facing the appellant, the general principles of law would allow duress to be raised as a defence even to a charge of unlawful killing.

Moral responsibility and pragmatic rationality, in this judge's view, argued against the unqualified application which imposed liability no matter at what cost. Interestingly, the accused initially pleaded guilty, even though he believed he was neither liable nor culpable, on the advice that duress did not apply. This was the only appeal point that succeeded.

The experience of corporate criminal liability has been that stories of responsibility against histories of reputation may have a far greater punitive impact than conventional sentencing options. Imprisoning corporate executives when they can be replaced, fining companies when the cost is passed on to the consumer, restricting the capacity to trade when it hurts shareholders all problematise the liability/punishment nexus transferred without creative adjustment from individual to collective liability. Braithwaite and Fisse (1993: chapter 6) suggest that corporate compliance is best ensured by challenging and negotiating otherwise marketable reputations and respected organisational and trading histories in order to ensure responsibility.

Responsibility flowing from the revelation of truth, contested or otherwise, surely represents an aspiration for more inclusive trial justice and not simply its denial within the context of evidence and fact trial 'languages'. If so, how does one represent a more balanced consideration of responsibility when the discourse of individual liability dominates ICJ? Part of the pathway to a more inclusive discourse on truth and responsibility is to touch on the failed 'language' of individual liability as the restrictive 'narrative' of international criminal law.

Languages of capacity, liability, justification and excuse, and culpability

There is no space here to interrogate adequately the language of the law as it relates to fact-finding, evidence-testing and liability attribution. We shall restrict our consideration of language in the way it binds and ties fact, while at the same time denying the primacy of truth, to the importance of judicial narrative. The reason for this is the reiteration of juridical discretion in the achievement of trial transformation and the essential place of judicial narrative in holding the exercise of such discretion accountable to victim interests. Through the process of accountability, we argue, the legitimacy of ICJ will be more significantly ensured (Findlay, 2008b: chapter 9).

Trial transformation enables an engagement with truth at stages where the juridical professional determines that adversarial justice (and its fact fascination) are inappropriate for the achievement of significant victim interests. In talking from evidence to truth, the judicial narrative will chart an exercise of discretion no longer essentially concerned with factors determining or denying liability. In fact, by admitting the wider histories of truth, judicial narrative will breach essential rules of evidence and compromise the search for liability in a sufficiently probative sense.

Capacity will take on new meaning. No longer will it be communicated in terms of volition to commit the criminal act. Instead, it will carry a more moral meaning, referring to responsibility rather than liability. The consequence of this will be that justifications or excuses will be crafted not to deny the evidence of the Prosecution, but to qualify or mitigate responsibility, particularly where contested histories are offered.

Culpability will give way to responsibility. Guilt will not be the essential outcome of liability proven. Culpability can take on contributory and conditional forms. This will certainly enable a language of collective responsibility that is more compatible with restorative outcomes which until trial transformation remained the province of alternative justice discourse.

In the context of a discourse on the 'right to truth' for victims of international armed conflict, Naqvi discusses the significance of 'legal truth'. She holds that legal truth is merely a by-product of a dispute settlement mechanism. We agree and argue that trial transformation must precede the more convincing approximation of legal truth.

> In trials dealing with international crimes, however, the significance of this bi-product of legal truth has taken on a new dimension owing no

> doubt to the unique objectives that international criminal law is supposed to fulfill and that go way above and beyond merely finding guilt or innocence of particular individuals ... this legal concept intersects with international criminal processes in various ways, at times strengthening the intended purpose to prosecute persons accused of international crimes and at times overriding the focus on the individual defendant and instead turning the attention of the case to the broader implications of international criminal trials. The desire for truth may even be used to justify non-prosecution of certain alleged offenders in an 'amnesty-for-truth or 'use immunity' situations.
>
> (2006: 246)

Conclusion? Victim-driven truth and fact

Damaska represents the adversarial trial as sometimes progressing dysfunctionally 'when fact finding is organised as a sequence of two partisan cases' (2008: 337). If one remains contained within an adversarial model, the suggestion that fact and truth should coexist in the evidentiary and proof project is dangerous indeed. One likely casualty is independent and impartial juridical decision-making, and then the potential to transform the trial into a more efficient deliberative environment:

> Judicial interference with partisan management of cases (for the purpose of historiography) deflates partisan incentives to develop more effective trial strategies, and may also appear to help one side, compromising the court's neutrality *inter partes*.
>
> (2008: 333)

In an ideal world, as Damaska denies its possibility:

> there would be no reason to balance (accused's rights and victim interests) – they would coexist in harmony. But in the real world, painful tradeoffs between them must be made.
>
> (2008: 333)

It is here that our analysis parts company. Those who suggest, despite its ennobling humanitarian foundations, that telling victim-centred truths beyond the confines of evidence in the trial format is misconceived, do not go the next step to ask: Why not? To exclude an essential humanitarian focus under the guise of coherence with procedural conventions is to ignore the potential through trial transformation of attaining the unattainable. It is more than an inevitable tension between wide communitarian and victim-centred rights aspirations and the definitive trial focus on the rights of the accused (which are today constantly compromised for far less noble intentions), that makes trial transformation heretic (Zedner and Hoyle, 2007).

In this chapter we have used the collective perpetration and legitimate interests of victim communities which define global crime as the imperatives for trial transformation. In so doing we have shown how conventional exceptions to individual liability are not creating a novel and effective international criminal jurisprudence. Further, the commendable attempts of the nation-state through extraterritoriality are not effectively requiring responsibility from corporate and collective violators even through the exercise of state responsibility required by international law.

We return to the simple potential of trial transformation and its engagement with truth and responsibility as a route to satisfying victim communities collectively violated. This may not produce retributive declarations or the imprisonment of otherwise criminal corporate executives, but the wide vista of restorative outcomes will be available within the due process protections of the transformed international trial to satisfy more victims collectively harmed.

Notes

1. This comment should not be taken as an indication that we see the international criminal trial as an exclusively adversarial enterprise. In addition, we have previously questioned the existence and prevalence of a model and uniform adversarial tradition. International criminal trial in the ICC is in substance adversarial with strong inquisitorial pre-trial and victim voice influences.
2. This is a reason why, as Roche (2005) suggests, restorative justice has aligned itself with truth-telling mechanisms. The transitional justice movement equally values justice based on truth-telling.
3. Claims for this success measure were at least made for truth and reconciliation in the restoration of democratic governance to South Africa, where retributive prosecution and selective immunity may have fractured that aspiration.
4. Unfortunately, it is not uncommon in adversarial trial models for victim interests to be marginalised in the sentencing equation or will be bungled in efforts to provide a limited voice in the pre-trial and trial evidence delivery. In international criminal trials, this often arises out of an incapacity to realise for victims ambiguous procedural rights in the context of a wider desire to satisfy legitimate victim interests.
5. For a detailed discussion of this critique, see Damaska (2008: 235–8).
6. We discuss this in more detail in chapter 8, and argue against it in response to Damaska's contention that truth-telling is and should remain incompatible with the purposes and procedures of adversarial trial.
7. See, for instance, Findlay (1994), where the impact of *voir dires* on juror 'second-guessing' was identified.
8. Forensic psychology confirms that, in the mind of judges and other fact-finders, initial beliefs tend to persist. See Goldstein (2006).
9. In the case of DNA profiling evidence and juror comprehension, see Findlay (2008a).

10. As discussed later, Damaska (2008) opposes this view.
11. See, for instance, Damaska (2008).
12. This could not be said of the procedural hybrid form of the ICC.
13. For a discussion of the connection between humanity and hegemony, see Findlay (2008: chapter 3).
14. This is discussed in greater detail in Findlay (2008b: chapter 1).
15. See, for example, of European Convention on Human Rights, Article 6.
16. Findlay and Henham (2005: chapters 7 and 8).
17. There will be particular difficulties, however, in the status of evidence once applied to restorative contexts such as mediation if it is to return to its procedurally recognised standing in adversarial argument.
18. For a discussion of this, see Haan (2005: 169–94). Recent judicial discussion can be found in the *Prosecutor v Brdjanin*, Case No. IT-99-36-A, Judgment, 357–450 (ICTY Ap. Ch. 3 April 2007).
19. Convention on the Prevention and Punishment of the Crime of Genocide, Article II.
20. p. 95.
21. Ibid.
22. Kyriakakis refers to the investigation by the Australian Federal Police into the possible role of Anvil Mining Limited in facilitating a military offensive in the Democratic Republic of the Congo. This investigation, she alleges, indicates that Australia, like many other nations, is grappling locally with the possibility of corporate involvement in International crime.
23. 28 USC 1350.
24. 'Corporate culture' means an attitude, policy, rule, course of conduct or practice existing within the body corporate generally or in the part of the body corporate in which the relevant activities takes place.
25. Section 26(6) relieves the prosecutor of the necessity to prove that the defendant associated with any particular purpose or that the association would have lead to the commission of any offence.
26. See s. 27(6) for the circumstances of authorisation.
27. For an expansion of this position, see Chapman (2004).
28. It should be remembered that IHRL is seen often more as legitimating rights violations through armed conflict rather than presenting a framework of rights protections.
29. In methods similar to states responsibility in international law, rather than through the domestic enactment of international criminal law.
30. OECD (2000) *Guidelines for Multinational Enterprises*, para. 11.
31. *Plavsic*, ICTY Ch III, 27 February 2008, para. 80.
32. This should be put against an expectation of full disclosure, which in turn might have increased the sentence.
33. *The Prosecutor v. Drazen Erdemovic*, Case No. IT-96-22-A, A. C., 5 May 1997.
34. http://www.icty.org/sid/7463.

5
Transformed Process through Enhanced Discretionary Power

Introduction

This chapter advances our thesis that discretionary decision-making in international trials should be seen as the appropriate locus for developing more integrated and inclusive forms of ICJ by making concrete procedural reforms (Findlay and Henham, 2005). We have suggested that the perceived legitimacy of international punishment will be enhanced by making trial justice more inclusive to victims and the relative demands for justice of post-conflict societies. Within this context the gathering of evidence and fact-finding are identified as key areas for procedural transformation. The chapter explores as a specific example how the factual basis for sentencing in international criminal trials might be reconceptualised as part of an agenda for trial transformation.

The mobilisation of judicial discretion will depend on a cooperative project to reposition the international criminal trial and reflect a more restorative and inclusive influence. Such a project will be possible only if the normative structures that are put in place are developed from a strong ideological foundation to which the relevant state parties and international judiciary are formally committed. Each scenario will bring its own difficulties in this respect. We argue that it is not feasible to move from a situation of judicial diversity to one of coherence without this ideological commitment. The dependent normative structures should then provide a platform *de novo* where the diverse traditions, practices, attitudes and penal philosophies international judges bring with them have a chance to gel, since ideology and practice will merge (fact and value) in the transformative environment of the trial. Once freed from the restrictions imposed by the retributive dynamic of ICJ, judicial discretion will become a driving force for developing crucial issues within the new normative framework, such as lay/professional interaction and victim inclusion, as well as the distinction in the use and style of 'facts' in the trial proper.

Within this context the broad aim of the chapter is to draw on existing knowledge of the relationship between decision-making and structure in criminal trials in terms of its impact on determining the factual basis for sentence. In order to do so it takes the view that judicial discretionary power and the normative structure within which it is exercised are crucially interrelated dependent variables. The ideological rationales which shape decision-making structures and trial relationships must also be taken into account. In short, the chapter aims to achieve an understanding of the relevant trial procedures within their broader contextual influences and make suggestions for transforming aspects of international criminal procedure as part of the wider agenda for trial transformation referred to earlier.

More specifically, the chapter's thesis is developed in three sections. The first emphasises the need to appreciate the significance of sentencing norms and practice within different jurisdictional contexts and trial traditions, exploring the broader context in which information is attributed as fact for the purposes of sentence. It critiques conventional approaches for describing the process of sentencing and deconstructing punishment rationales in a comparative context and assesses the implications for ICJ.

The second section examines particular procedural questions in greater depth, highlighting areas of difficulty and points of tension and ambiguity which currently frustrate the task of trial transformation. It focuses specifically on problems associated with conventional approaches to establishing the factual basis for sentence and considers differences between adversarial, inquisitorial and hybridised forms; issues of procedural expediency and procedural fairness; substantive law issues and their impact on sentence determination; the significance of the verdict in excluding evidence relevant to sentence; the problem of previous convictions; mechanisms for resolving disputes; and the role of victims and trial professionals.

The chapter's final section seeks to elaborate the case for change from three interconnected perspectives:

- *Reconceptualising* – changing trial ideology and norms; retaining the balance between retributive and restorative goals for transformation; clarifying the role of facts in establishing 'truth' – 'liability' and community responsibility rather than individual guilt; elaborating notions of integration and inclusive sentencing.
- *Repositioning* – changing the rules for admissibility; providing different levels of probative value to reflect the sources, nature and possible utility of trial evidence; collapsing the two-stage (verdict/sentence) distinction; developing new strategies for intervention; conceptualising and formulating a transformative agenda for judicial discretionary power.
- *Operationalising* – developing new techniques for rationalising law and legal knowledge; using discretion as a force for developing transformative outcomes and dealing with inconsistency, appeal and enforcement.

Understanding sentencing comparatively

Conventional paradigms for evaluating punishment in both common and civil law jurisdictions attach great symbolic significance to the formal pronouncement of sentence and the elaboration of its rationale by the judiciary in individual cases (Henham and Mannozzi, 2003). The rhetoric and symbolism of the moment not only marks the conclusion of the trial process by acknowledging the extent of criminal liability through appropriate punishment, it also signals an apparently natural break between the determination of guilt through verdict delivery and the consequences of its pronouncement.

Furthermore, the conventional trial recursively reinforces relationships of power and subjugation existing within the jurisdictional boundaries of states and appropriates presumed mandates for punishment. Such mandates are normally based on an ideology and rationality for punishment forged *ex post facto* following analysis of the causes and consequences of war or social conflict, but are nevertheless generally taken to represent coherent and legitimate rationales for depriving individual citizens of their liberty through formalised punishment. Consequently, as Garland (2001) suggests, the ideology of freedom and liberty is often replaced by that of control, so the processual reality of the trial may bear little resemblance to its proclaimed rationale or the social context in which it operates.

Such an interpretation forces us to confront the dichotomy between objective representations of the trial and its relative reality for lay and professional participants and the wider social audience. In the present context, for example, do the different phases of the trial actually represent key moments which have some moral or normative significance extending beyond its boundaries, so that they can be said to connect in some profound moral sense with what citizens deem to be necessary requirements for justice delivery?[1] Alternatively, are such processual divisions devoid of any substantive ideological relevance, and, if so, does this matter?[2]

Recognising that our experience of law and the power of normative judgments is relative and reflective of value pluralism means that the answers to these questions can no longer be reached by testing social reality against conventional paradigms of trial justice.[3] Conversely, they are unlikely to be answered by an approach that fails to question the moral integrity of law and its ideological foundations.[4] We are therefore left with the apparent paradox that any comparative understanding of criminal procedure must be approached from a perspective tolerant of context (Vogler, 2005) and its effect on the social reality of discretionary decision-making for trial participants and their relevant social audience.

Henham and Mannozzi's (2003) comparative contextual analysis of victim participation in sentencing in England and Italy provides a useful illustration of this paradox and its implications for understanding the relationship between ideology and discretionary decision-making. It also serves to illustrate that our perception of trial norms and the procedural goals they serve are the conditioned effects of context. In essence, their research concludes that it is the instrumentality of judicial discretion which distinguishes the English and Italian sentencing paradigms. In Italy, the neoclassical form of retributive justice embodied in the framework for decision-making[5] has been judicially interpreted within a civil law, non-adversarial paradigm and jurisprudential tradition that regard the creativity and interpretative function of the judiciary with circumspection. In England, by contrast, the reverse holds true, since from the outset of the liberal enlightenment project in criminal law and justice, the instrumentality of judicial discretionary power has been integral to maintaining the pre-eminence of the judiciary as lawmakers and *de facto* determiners of sentencing policy (or executive attempts to direct it).

In Italy, discretion has not been instrumental in shaping the criminal process since, historically, this has not been a crucial factor in the development of the judicial role. The emphasis on procedural form and the failure of legislative or juridical attempts to rationalise contemporary punishment justifications has been countered defensively by the Italian judiciary and seemingly exacerbated by the more recent hybridisation of the Italian trial process through the incremental introduction of adversarially inspired 'reforms'.

No conceptual distinction is made in Italy between the procedural contexts for receiving information relevant to sentence which might serve to differentiate the qualitative nature of the evidence for the purposes of either verdict or sentence. The sentencing phase of the Italian trial is characterised by form,[6] with any allusions to sentence justification being merely declaratory of the court's considered view without further elaboration. These apparent differences in structure and form between Italian and English sentencing are also paradoxical for victims in the sense that Italian law imposes no substantive limits to the possible extent of victim participation in sentencing, whilst English sentencing law has conventionally envisaged no substantive rights at all and has only recently succumbed to the notion of victims' 'personal' statements which aim to satisfy purely 'service' rights.[7]

Significantly, it is the legal culture and the broader socio-political context of criminal justice that has conditioned the response of the Italian courts to victims. Such factors account for the circumspection with which victim evidence is received and treated by the Italian judiciary. The Italian sentencing process is typified by legal formalism and the restrictive judicial interpretation of particular procedural constraints regarding the appropriation of information that might be deemed relevant to victim participation in sentencing decisions. This narrow ideology consequently delimits the appropriate terrain for victim participation in sentencing in terms of due process and the potential for restorative justice themes to be developed. By contrast, in English sentencing, the principle of judicial independence has, by convention, placed the judiciary in the vanguard of determining the ambit of substantive and procedural sentencing law and the parameters of policy. Furthermore, the context in which this judicial discretion has been exercised has been one that strongly supports and sustains the concept of individualisation in sentencing.

The above example, therefore, serves as an important reminder of the need to appreciate the influence of legal and social variables in formulating understandings of the objectification of trial structure and human action within specific jurisdictional contexts. As Henham and Mannozzi (2003) suggest, the objective reality of trial process is fluid, dynamic and recursive; it is an actuality constituted largely through instrumentally exercised judicial discretionary power. Common experience of what constitutes the normative and processual reality of the trial is therefore firmly grounded in context. This insight has particular relevance where, as is the case with international courts and tribunals, those exercising discretionary power are themselves drawn from diverse legal cultures and personal and social backgrounds. Thus, the challenge of understanding how rationales and motivations for judicial behaviour influence discretionary decision-making within the context of international criminal trials is crucial to initiating the project of trial transformation and establishing trial cultures which are responsive to restorative justice ideology and practice.

Establishing the factual basis – conventional approaches

This section draws attention to some of the salient features of approaches to establishing the factual basis for sentence in both national and international contexts. It forms the basis for understanding the section that follows where suggestions are made for modifying structures and relationships which influence the exercise of judicial discretionary power over the determination of factual evidence for sentencing in the transformed trial.

Adversarial systems are driven by the overwhelming need to make a formal determination of guilt, whether or not this results from the plea or verdict. Unfortunately, neither outcome necessarily establishes a sufficiently precise factual basis for the sentencer to assess the culpability of the offender. In addition, according to Ashworth (2005: 342), the problem is likely to be exacerbated (particularly following a guilty plea) where the system of criminal law is based on broadly defined offences.[8] As Thomas (1979) suggests, the facts on which the sentence is based must be consistent with the formal determination of guilt. Consequently, if the offender is acquitted of a graver charge or pleads guilty to a lesser offence, the sentencer must accept this as forming the factual basis for the determination of the sentence. However, sentencers normally have discretion regarding whose version of events to believe where there are conflicting accounts as to whether the offender was engaged in a continuous course of conduct, as long as they do not assume the existence of facts clearly negated by the formal finding of guilt.

A crucial question that arises in this context is the extent to which general principles relating to the burden and degree of proof apply in reaching a decision as to whether a fact is relevant to sentence. This issue gains in significance where the sentencing phase of the trial is separated from that which determines guilt or innocence, and its form is determined by conventions, principles, relationships and interactions which differ from the main body of the trial. In England, for example, not only has the sentencing phase of the trial traditionally been one where the principle of judicial independence has found its fullest expression, it has also developed its own philosophical rationales, procedural rules, sentencing principles and policy.

The separation of verdict from sentence, whether within a unified or two-stage process, also poses a significant structural question: What is the most appropriate processual context for realising the constructive potential of discretion as an instrumental force for influencing praxis and thereby advancing the integration of restorative themes in trial decision-making as a recursive reality?

One of the most significant practical consequences resulting from the separation of verdict and sentence concerns the need for evidence to be reconstructed to serve the purposes of the sentencing phase. For example, evidence relevant to sentence (such as provocation) may not be sufficiently explored, even during a full trial. Where the offender pleads guilty, these difficulties are exacerbated, since the Prosecution and Defence accounts of the facts may differ considerably. Yet this phenomenon may also occur within an integrated criminal process model. In Italy, for example, specific criteria establish the boundaries for the exercise of discretionary power relevant to sentence, but it is witness testimony elicited during the trial phase that is evaluated against these legal constraints. Judicial deliberations follow immediately after the close of the trial and, after considering any unresolved preliminary matters and/or procedural issues, judges must consider each issue of fact or law, as well as the appropriate sentence. Needless to say, such abbreviated proceedings and procedures may facilitate sentence bargaining and distort the extent to which the facts on which sentence is based actually correspond to those that occurred. Similarly, rights accorded to victims[9] are directed towards the trial (verdict and sentence) rather than to sentence alone.

Whether a distinction should be made between verdict and sentence, or provision made for a separate sentencing phase, is one of the most important issues to impact on sentence decision-making in international criminal trials – a decision that has fundamental evidential repercussions for the sentencing outcome. The current position is that both the ad hoc tribunals for the Former Yugoslavia and Rwanda and the ICC have a predominantly unified structure. However, this was not initially the case with the ad hoc tribunals where the respective Rules of Procedure and Evidence (RPE) for the ICTY and ICTR (Part 6, section 4) implicitly provided for a system where evidence relating to sentence could be heard only once the decision as to guilt or innocence had been made.[10]

Early ad hoc tribunal cases such as *Tadic* (ICTY)[11] and *Akayesu* (ICTR)[12] even went as far as to hold separate sentence hearings, but their respective rules were later amended to remove this possibility. The rationale for this was essentially the bureaucratic and administrative one of greater speed and efficiency. The new procedure ensured that the presentation of evidence and pleadings on sentencing matters occurred *before* the verdict was determined, with the result that both phases of the trial are now reflected in a single judgment. Rule 86(C) of the ICTY and ICTR RPE effectively provides that after the presentation of all the evidence pertinent to the trial of the issues the closing arguments of the Prosecutor and the Defence must 'address matters of sentencing'.

The ICC Statute adopts a similar model. Article 76(1) provides that, following a conviction, the Trial Chamber should move on to sentencing, taking into account evidence presented and submissions made *during the trial* that are relevant to sentence. Significantly, in Article 76(2)[13] it goes on to provide that, in contested cases only and before completion of the trial, the Trial Chamber may direct (or must, if requested by the Prosecutor or the accused) a *further hearing* to hear any additional evidence or submissions relevant to sentence.[14] Schabas (2007: 305) suggests that this procedure creates a strong presumption in favour of a distinct sentencing hearing following conviction, but this has not been the experience of the ad hoc tribunals. Notwithstanding, Zappala (2003: 198) argues that the position regarding the ICC remains unclear as to whether there should be one decision containing both verdict and sentence, or two separate decisions.

Clearly, evidence relating to mitigating and aggravating factors will be heard in so far as it relates to the commission of the crime. In the case of the ad hoc tribunals, Rule 85(A)(vi) of the respective RPE provides for the presentation of 'any relevant information that may assist the Trial Chamber in determining an appropriate sentence' after all other evidence led by the Prosecution and the Defence (or otherwise ordered by the Trial Chamber) has been presented, unless otherwise directed by the Trial Chamber in the interests of justice. Significantly, since the removal of Rule 101(B), there is no implication that the Defence should present evidence pertinent to mitigation of sentence on the basis of the accused's guilt, but rather that its emergence should be part of the normal course of the trial and, therefore, directed towards assisting the tribunal determining the relative merits of the case against the accused.[15] Since the Rules refer to the submission of 'all relevant information' there is some doubt regarding the exact nature of the evidential material permitted and whether it may be treated as equivalent to evidence submitted in accordance with the Rules.[16] Similarly, whether trial rules on the submission and admissibility of evidence also apply to the Trial Chamber's deliberations during the sentencing phase is a matter for conjecture.

Arguments in favour of holding a separate sentencing hearing after conviction are considerable. For instance, in a mono-phase hearing, the necessary omission of mitigating evidence during the trial stage may prove prejudicial to the Defence when it comes to sentencing because it restricts information concerning the accused's personal role in the commission of the crime and its immediate aftermath. The introduction of such evidence may also impact adversely on the accused's rights of silence and protection against self-incrimination. In particular, the Defence may be induced to introduce more witnesses during the trial process in order to establish the accused's good character and personal circumstances.[17] Alternatively, from the Prosecutor's point of view, a second hearing is likely to permit the introduction of aggravating factors (such as the accused's criminal record) that might be considered inadmissible for reasons of irrelevance during the trial proper (Schabas, 2007: 306).[18] In any event, the range of admissible material for sentencing purposes is potentially considerable.[19]

At first sight, the foundation instruments of the international institutions, particularly the ICC, go much further than many domestic legal systems in providing procedural safeguards to ensure the fair trial of the accused has a fair trial and for the participation and protection of victims and witnesses at all stages of the criminal process. For example, Article 67(1)(a) of the ICC Statute is unequivocal in stating that the accused must be informed promptly and in detail of the nature, cause and content of the charge in a language he or she fully understands and speaks. Yet, these kinds of safeguards are largely absent when it comes to the deliberation and pronouncement of sentence. The conventional practice, now adopted by both the ad hoc tribunals and prescribed for the ICC, is that all evidence relating to trial of the issues and sentence is heard before the verdict and sentence are delivered.[20] Furthermore, although sentence is pronounced publicly and, wherever possible, in the presence of the accused (ICC Statute, Article 76(4); RPE, Rule 144(1)), deliberations are held *in camera* and there is no obligation for the reasons and an account of the process whereby the decision was revealed to be made public. This contrasts with the position on verdict delivery where Article 74 of the ICC Statute provides specifically that the decision must be in writing and give a full and reasoned statement of the Trial Chamber's findings on the evidence and conclusions. However, only a summary of the decision need be delivered in open court. Consequently, as far as sentencing is concerned, whilst the matters the Court is required to consider are set out in some detail in Rule 145 of the ICC Statute, the legislative instruments do not go further than requiring that they should be taken into account during the private deliberations of the Trial Chamber.

Although, of course, the international courts have, in many instances, delivered consistent and lengthy accounts of their reasoning in sentencing offenders, the absence of any obligation in this respect is a significant procedural limitation given the normal absence of a separate sentencing hearing.

The existence of such hearings promotes the creation and development of a sentencing jurisprudence, one that encourages a culture of judicial transparency through the public reception and rational evaluation of evidence. As the International Law Commission made clear in its comments on the work of its 46th session,[21] the procedural guarantees inherent in the concept of a fair trial should be extended to a separate sentencing hearing (as was then proposed) since its purpose is to determine an appropriate punishment for the *individual* as well as the crime. In the absence of any obligation to hold such a hearing, an even stronger argument for transparency in sentence decision-making surely exists. Again, the absence of any mandatory procedure for transparency in sentence decision-making can be said to stem from the major systemic weakness of the entire international criminal trial process, namely, that the procedural safeguards are more apparent than real because there is no need for them to be otherwise. Justifications for punishment do not have to extend beyond the limitations imposed by the philosophies of limited retributivism and deterrence.

There are, however, broader issues raised. First, there is an argument for supporting separate sentence hearings for symbolic reasons; that marking out as distinct from the verdict the public deliberation and pronouncement of sentence has an enormously powerful symbolic effect in drawing attention to and dramatising the punishment, as well as promoting psychological and emotional feelings relating to atonement and closure.[22] Arguably, a mono-phase process encourages obfuscation in the justification of sentences.[23] Since it does not promote an alternative context for sentencing, a mono-phase process is likely to negate and stultify those arguments that might explore issues relating to the constructive engagement of sentencing outcomes in favour of those that sustain the status quo.

Secondly, an argument can be made for suggesting that a two-stage process serves to emphasise the qualitative distinction between the pre- and post-conviction phases of the trial by signifying that different substantive and procedural norms apply. It is significant that in the English context where similar wide judicial discretionary powers in sentencing exist within a mono-phase process, the sentencing phase of the trial is often used by judges to make what Ashworth (2000c: 306) refers to as 'moralistic homilies', and that the systematic analysis of relevant aggravating and mitigating factors is associated with or developed within this process culture. Arguably, such a tendency is fostered through a mono-phase trial process, particularly where, as in the international criminal trial institutions, the process is dominated by a predominantly retributive ideology which does not encourage transparency or the reasoned analysis of evidence for sentencing purposes.

Failure to clarify the relationship between substantive offence elements and sentencing principles exacerbates these difficulties. The conventional common law approach for dealing with the conceptual problems of culpability and harm has followed the notion that the substantive law exists to fix the minimum conditions for criminal liability whilst sentencing principles should determine the degree to which any offender can be held responsible for the consequences that follow from his actions (Ashworth, 2006: chapter 1). The moral distinctions between offences are drawn through the framing of substantive offences with specific factors which have a bearing on an individual's responsibility for harm and culpability being reserved for sentencing purposes.

In *Aleksovski*[24] the ICTY endorsed the approach adopted in the *Celebici* and *Kupreskic* judgments to the effect that the inherent gravity of the accused's criminal conduct must be reflected in the sentence, and that the determination of gravity requires a consideration of the particular circumstances of the case, as well as the form and degree of the accused's participation in the crime. However, this approach collapses what Carcano (2002) identifies as an important distinction; the determination of gravity *in abstracto* and *in concreto*:

> The gravity *in abstracto* is based on an analysis, in terms of the criminal law of the objective and subjective elements of the crime. The gravity *in concreto* depends on the harm done and the degree of culpability of the offender. ICTY and ICTR case law reveals divergences in the application of these concepts. The former focuses mainly on the concrete gravity of the crime inferred from the circumstances of the case. The latter assessment has been broader in that both the gravity *in abstracto* of the crime and its gravity *in concreto* were taken into account
>
> (Carcano, 2002: 609)

The ICTY and ICTR have failed to differentiate clearly or consistently between notions of gravity and seriousness for the purposes of the trial and sentence. The 'gravity'[25] of an offence in substantive terms depends on satisfying different criteria from those applicable to sentencing. For sentencing, 'gravity' is a primary criterion for assessing the nature of the penalty and crucial in determining the appropriate sentence. In trial terms, the notion of 'gravity' is integral to satisfying the requirements of substantive offence definitions. Although the sources of evidence may be the same, its disclosure, presentation, testing, admissibility and prioritisation satisfy distinct purposes. In the same way that moral and political ideology influences the framing of the criminal law, so it correspondingly determines how offences are to be perceived for the purposes of punishment, involving crucial decisions about the relative severity of penalty scales (cardinal proportionality) and how offences are ranked according to seriousness (ordinal proportionality). Obfuscation results from a failure to differentiate the consequences of assessing offence gravity for the purposes of determining the substantive issue of criminal liability from that of determining sentence.

Despite the fact that the notion of the individualisation of sentences is apparently enshrined in Article 24(1) of the ICTY Statute (and ICTR Statute, Article 23(1)) through the reference to 'individual circumstances', the parameters of this concept are not elaborated. As a result, confusion also persists in the sentencing decisions of the ad hoc tribunals regarding the interpretation of 'individualisation' as a sentencing concept. Zappala (2003: 204), in particular, seems to elevate 'individualisation' for crimes under international law to the level of a due process right on the basis that it is instrumental in defining the limits of individual criminal responsibility[26] for acts committed during the course of armed conflicts, although falling short of recognising a concomitant right to rehabilitation on the part of the convicted person. In any event, the precise ambit of the 'individualisation' concept and its relationship to rehabilitation as a possible sentencing objective for the *ad hoc* tribunals remains conjectural.

It is difficult to see how individualisation as a philosophical approach to the resolution of the conflicting demands of sentencing can be conceived in terms of a legally enforceable right in international sentence decision-making. This would only be possible should the rationale(s) for sentencing international crimes accommodate such an approach. As things stand, the predominantly retributive and deterrent ideological framework for international sentencing suggests a particularly narrow interpretation of individualisation; certainly not one that engages constructively with the wider social context of sentencing outcomes.[27]

Where offences are broadly defined (as in international criminal law) the tendency for evidential matters relating to sentence to be ignored or treated superficially is accentuated. The problem is exacerbated where a plea of guilty has been entered to some or all of the offences charged. The implications are considerable since the absence of substantive uncontested material relating to sentence may encourage inconsistency in sentencing and injustice in particular cases.[28] Where a guilty plea exists, a dispute regarding the nature of the factual evidence contended as relevant by the Defence for mitigation of sentence may need to be challenged by the Trial Chamber, either in terms that require the Defence to adduce further evidence to substantiate their version of events, or through the instigation of some kind of procedural device[29] whereby various approaches are adopted in order to elicit an agreed version of the facts before proceeding to sentence.[30]

Additional difficulties result from the compromising effect of plea agreements in this context. A specific criticism illustrating the distorting effect of plea agreements and their capacity for downgrading the 'truth' in terms of how the trial marks the seriousness of what has taken place through punishment concerns the factual basis underlying the conduct charged. This difficulty was particularly evident in *Momir Nikolic*[31] where the defendant was originally charged with numerous crimes, including genocide. Following an amended plea agreement the defendant eventually pleaded guilty to the lesser charge of persecutions (a crime against humanity), and all remaining counts on the indictment against him were dropped. In considering Rule 62 *bis*[32] of the ICTY's RPE, the Trial Chamber observed that it was satisfied that the factual basis on which the charge of persecutions was based reflected the totality of the defendant's criminal conduct (para. 51).

Whilst the sufficiency of the factual basis for the crime eventually charged and the accused's participation in it is not in doubt, the application of this rule ignores the fundamental capacity of plea and other forms of negotiation for manipulating evidential 'truth' to suit processual goals. Not only does the plea deny the possibility of testing the evidence in open court,[33] the acceptance of a charge as reflecting the totality of the accused's criminal conduct effectively denies the Court the opportunity to give full expression to the totality of that criminality through the imposition of a penal sanction which adequately reflects the seriousness of the crime(s) and the culpability of the offender. The effectiveness of international penality in terms of its undoubted capacity for symbolic public expression and denunciation of past breaches of international criminal law is seriously compromised if the totality of the punishment is not seen to be proportionate to the totality of the defendant's criminal conduct.

Such an outcome was evident in the ICTY case of *Deronjic*[34] in the powerful dissenting judgment of Presiding Judge Wolfgang Schomburg[35] regarding proportionality and the compromising effect of plea agreements. Schomburg's objection to the sentence of ten years' imprisonment imposed on Deronjic for a single conviction for persecutions (a crime against humanity) was that the factual basis for the conviction was enshrined in a plea agreement which provided an arbitrary selective account of what took place and in no way reflected the accused's undoubted participation in a much larger, premeditated criminal plan of ethnic cleansing by a relatively high-ranking perpetrator. Whilst accepting in principle the arguments advocating the utility of plea agreements for reasons of judicial economy and limited resources, Schomburg's chief objection lay with their possibly detrimental effect on the quality of justice subsequently administered by the Court:

> The test should be, whether individual separable parts of an offence or several violations of law committed as a result of the same offence are not particularly significant for the penalty to be imposed. In those cases the prosecution may be limited to the other parts of the offense or violations of law.
>
> (para. 8)

Schomburg was also uncompromising in his attribution to the Prosecutor of a clear duty to safeguard justice by ensuring that 'there is no arbitrary selection of persons to be indicted and no arbitrary selection of charges or facts in case of an indictment' (para. 10). Regarding the significance of the guilty plea *per se*, after taking into account the comparative evidence (Sieber, 2003), Schomburg was unequivocal in his rejection of the notion that a guilty party should be capable of derogating from the gravity of a crime (para. 14(a)(b)), and showed particular concern for the fact that 'no victim or person has been given the opportunity to address the Trial Chamber in person' (para. 20). Hence, the clear message conveyed by Schomburg was his insistence that the ICTY would be failing to fulfil its mandate if it did not adhere to the fundamental principle that a perpetrator deserved a sentence proportionate to the gravity of the crime and that the mitigating effect of post-crime conduct should be strictly limited.[36]

Plea agreements and their increasing use in international criminal trials reflect the way in which procedural norms and processes in conventional adversarial and, to an increasing extent, inquisitorial trial paradigms distort the 'real' facts to produce a version of the 'truth' which conforms to the exigencies of the trial context rather than the real experiences of the offenders, victims and the communities in which they live.

Changing the factual basis – an agenda for trial transformation

Reconceptualising

Conceptions of restorative justice, whilst being more suggestive of non-adversarial procedures, are not necessarily at variance with deserts-based retributive sentencing (Dignan and Cavadino, 1996). Furthermore, as Zedner (1994: 248) suggests, both reparation and retribution are predicated on notions of individual autonomy, although ignoring the impact of structural inequality, power and social control variables (see further Braithwaite, 2002). A potential difficulty lies in the fact that, whilst retribution equates proportionality with an objective assessment of offender culpability (and harm), reparative justice is proportionate to victim harm, thereby suggesting a process of social intervention that goes beyond the normal boundaries of conventional crime prevention. However, it is precisely the need to address such significant structural and ideological concerns that characterises those crimes of the magnitude with which we are concerned. Thus, notions of criminality as reflective of destruction, disintegration, conflict and breakdown go beyond traditional models which equate crime with social injustice. Instead, they lead directly to imperatives for reconstruction and reparation compatible with restorative justice principles aimed at increasing understanding, empowering victims and citizens and increasing their potential for participation and the resolution of conflict.[37]

Certainly, in the arena of conventional crime, restorative justice principles are seen as potentially capable of re-empowering citizens and a force for social cohesion. Whatever the potential for restorative justice, its value and relevance in the present context lie in its capacity to challenge conventional notions of the relationship between retributive justice and other conceptualisations of penality in international sentencing. This includes a recognition that restorative objectives are necessary for the resolution of social conflict and that notions of reparation and reconciliation should inform sentencing rather than be accommodated by inconsistent retributive practices so lacking in any coherent philosophical basis as to threaten their legitimacy.

The mere clarification of the philosophical justifications for sentencing in international criminal trials is insufficient. It is necessary to develop such rationalisations with a firm commitment to ground rationality in context; to relate the justifications for punishment within a unitary paradigm which connects the global and local. An important illustration of the need for such an inclusive paradigm is provided by the sense in which utilitarian rationales in the ad hoc tribunals have remained disconnected. For instance, part of the obfuscation that exists is precisely because of a failure to engage with the notion that individual and collective rehabilitation are fundamentally interrelated concepts. Traditional postmodern conceptions regard rehabilitation as essentially reductivist in promoting crime reduction, the ethos of the justification being that it suggests the provision of 'curative' or 'healing' disposals and outcomes. The ad hoc tribunals have clearly failed to connect with the notion of rehabilitation in the wider context of the potential for its conceptualisation as an individual and collective endeavour.[38]

Mathiesen (1990: 29) makes an important point relating to the relative moral influence of rehabilitative ideology within the prison system, and, more particularly, that the rationality of this ideology has been maintained to fulfil the demands of system interests. We would argue that these observations are just as pertinent to the characterisation of rehabilitation in international penality through its failure to exploit the nexus between individual and social rehabilitation within a more far-reaching and inclusive paradigm for punishment, one that is tolerant of process and outcome. In so doing, the relationship between rationalisations supporting rehabilitation and those supporting the institutions of hegemonic power cannot be ignored. This is exemplified by Article 33 of the Socialist Federal Republic of Yugoslavia Criminal Code, which includes the following as two of its three reasons for the imposition of sentence: '(1) preventing the offender from committing criminal acts *and his rehabilitation*; (3) strengthening the moral fibre of a socialist self-managing society and influence *on the development of the citizens' social responsibility and discipline*' (emphasis added).

Whilst the notion of social rehabilitation advocated in this extract carries a covert political message, we would argue that it has much wider significance in suggesting what might be involved in reconceptualising the ideology of international criminal trials in a more relational sense. By this we mean that, whereas conventional notions of rehabilitation focus on relating the offender's criminality to its social context, trial transformation demands the notional transposition of social context into the ideology of the trial.

Consequently, the self-serving system interests of symbolism and retributive ideology are redefined by a vision which envisages sharing responsibility for social equality and control and the equal distribution and enforcement of rights in terms that balance restorative and retributive demands for justice.

If we accept that the rationality of international penality should be informed by adopting a relational approach to the conceptualisation of justice rather than through the imposition of external rationales foreign to local priorities for truth and restoration, it implies that localised notions of moral legitimacy ought to be mirrored in national and international structures. Seen from this perspective, conceptualising rationales which facilitate the individualisation of sentences in international criminal trials provides an opportunity to develop a relational framework for sentencing driven by the need to reconcile the moral justification for process with its perceived moral legitimacy. Consequently, the context for restorative outcomes is conceived through moving beyond conventional conceptualisations that envisage 'communities' purely in terms of victimisation towards one that sees process as a context for their holistic restoration.

Sentencing can provide an operational context for conflict resolution or relational justice according to whatever interpretative category sentencers are asked to work with. Rationality alone, in terms of prioritising moral values and their expression as general justifications, does not qualify for this task. It provides 'ought' statements – desirable states of affairs (value principles). It is only when values are operationalised (become instrumental as normative principles) that they have the capacity to influence individual thought and social action. In the context of international penality, the relationship between ideology and norms is likely to take the form of a definite sentencing policy, such as just deserts/proportionality, which has been predicated on rational principles derived from a modified version of retributivism. However, it might equally arise through the incorporation of a set of autonomous rights principles, whose underlying values are enshrined in a foundational statement of intent. The crucial empirical question is this: How far does practice (process) give effect to those values which originally inspired the norms embodied in the relevant instrument or rights paradigm?[39] This implies that for restorative themes to impact on international penality requires the link between the moral justification for penality and its perceived legitimacy to be forged through processual norms by instrumental discretionary decision-making.

Any ideological reconceptualisation for international criminal trials which seeks to balance retributive and restorative aspirations must be reflected in a paradigm for justice delivery which recognises that:

- The involvement of victims and communitarian interests requires a process intended to have both empowering and healing potential.

- It will involve a principled delegation of power from the state parties to the relevant community.
- The mechanism of the trial process must be transformed to enable solutions aimed at peace and reconciliation.
- There should be empowerment of victims and communitarian interests to formulate acceptable strategies for achieving aims.
- Policies and structures should exist for monitoring implementation and enforcement.

The predominant retributive paradigm generally reflected in adversarial systems of criminal justice currently produces a process where facts are distilled through adversarial argument and interrogation. Similarly, guilt or innocence is based on an allocation of individual responsibility derived through prevailing argument, with the victim being vindicated by state intervention and community interests supported by retributive punishment. By contrast, in a restorative process, the establishment of those facts constituting truth is derived through mediation and reconciliation, the objective being to empower victims and communities of interest by establishing harm and the needs of victims through confrontation and compromise. Rather than the process allocating responsibility in a seemingly autonomous manner, a restorative process concedes responsibility and tolerance and promotes reparation and restoration. By establishing the truthful story, restorative outcomes effectively vindicate the victim through community intervention and confirm community interests through restoration.[40] In general terms, therefore, restorative process enables victims to re-establish dominion by asserting their full rights as citizens. By extending the notion of victim to community it allows victims and communities to claim ownership of conflict and achieve closure. Restorative justice models tend to diminish the tendencies for adversarial systems to encourage system efficiencies and standardisation and threaten notions of consistency and proportionality typical of deserts-based sentencing regimes.

Any synthesis of the ideologies underpinning retributive and restorative trial justice will require a reconceptualisation of the nature and meaning of truth-finding within the trial. For example, the concept of individual responsibility and its association with the allocation of blame and guilt should be replaced by a more instrumental notion of fact-finding which promotes the emergence of truth from a process of compromise driven by the desire to regulate relationships of community, rather than a celebration of the subjugation of the offender and the vindication of the victim as part of an apparatus of social control. Professional actors in the trial will therefore be instrumental in protecting the interests of victims and community interests, so reducing formalism and promoting inclusivity. In this, the discretionary power of the judge and his or her ability to recognise the interests of the victim and the community and to ensure that their voices are heard will be pivotal. This will also involve increasing thenumber of those who might be made accountable under the overriding direction and supervision of the judge.

It is necessary to provide an overview of the sentencing decision-making process before elaborating the nature of the specific changes required to the factual basis for sentencing in the transformed trial in order to identify the essential dynamics of those decision sites where significant relationships operate. Such an overview reveals three distinct possibilities.

Procedure before sentence

This concerns the way in which information is tested, filtered and accepted throughout the trial phase in order to establish its validity in the context of whether the defendant is guilty of the substantive offence(s) alleged in the indictment. Thus, the construction of this evidence is in terms of its relevance for criminal liability rather than punishment. In order to further the interests of legitimacy the issue here is how such information can be interrogated in terms that facilitate the production of outcomes based on a broader and more flexible conception of the purposes of the trial.

Determination of sentence

In this phase information is reconstructed to reflect sentence-specific criteria, such as seriousness, gravity, mitigating and personal circumstances, and broader social purposes. Again, it is legitimate to consider what purpose this serves. Essentially, it is done in order to meet the requirements of the sanctioning process. However, if the process is not envisaged as being concerned with sanctioning, but rather as contributing to the production of positive legitimate outcomes for victims and communities, the focus might then move on to trial professionals being encouraged to perceive and utilise factual information in a more selective and constructive way,[41] rather than by unquestioningly continuing to devote their efforts to facilitating the kinds of outcomes prescribed by the rules of adversarial trial.[42] Instead, directed by the judge(s), opposing trial professionals will need to refocus their discretion by using and developing the relationships they have with both lay and professional participants in order to test the possibilities and parameters for producing positive outcomes, instead of promoting trial norms, underpinned by professional codes of conduct, designed to negate or underlie those aspects of trial information which do not support the particularised adversarial versions of reality – and therefore 'truth' – which they are endeavouring to create.

Pronouncement of sentence

If the first two stages are collapsed into what one might call an *outcome phase*, there would be less need for judges and trial professionals to externalise the adversarial ethos of international criminal trials by focusing disproportionately on issues of transparency, homily and accountability. This helps to reinforce the ideology of retributivism. Instead, the processes of discretionary decision-making which determine the penal outcome of international trials should themselves be designed to move incrementally towards this end as the natural outcome of the criminal process. In other words, the theatricality, symbolism and denunciation characteristic of publicly pronounced punishment would no longer be needed. In so far as retribution and deterrence were given prominence, this would be in recognition of a collective desire for punishment reflecting victim and community interests rather than some symbolic vindication of the victim.

Describing those decision-making sites relevant to sentencing in this way allows us to identify the contexts for change. It illustrates the broader contexts underlying the normative framework of sentencing and allows the discretionary decision-making process to be appreciated as an aspect of social reality where predetermined social roles and expectations are played out. For instance, the capacity for victim impact in the evidential or sentencing phases of the trial is not simply structured through norms of access; it is operationalised by trial actors who exercise their normative responsibilities within the pragmatic contexts afforded by individual cases and the constraints of trial relationships This is evidenced, for example, by the limited opportunities presented to the Prosecution or the Defence to address matters relevant to sentencing within the context of a mono-phase sentencing system such as the ICTY. Similarly, where facts for sentence are in dispute, it is important to know who can raise the issue and what mechanisms are in place for its resolution. If evidence relating to previous convictions is permissible, what are the normative requirements for timing and content? When can such evidence be admitted during the course of the trial? Who can challenge admissibility and/or content, and on what basis?

The resolution of all such questions depends on ensuring that actions are linked by coherent strategies for the achievement of desired outcomes for the trial. Crucial to the success of such strategic action is the recognition that trial relationships determine how discretion can influence outcomes. More specifically, it stresses the cultural contexts in which significant trial relationships are created and merge to determine the exercise of discretionary power at significant decision sites for sentencing in the trial process. The analysis, therefore, moves beyond the notion of decision sites and their relative significance as process variables and focuses on the context of the trial itself.

Repositioning

We now turn to consider the nature of specific changes that could be made to the legal and process norms that govern international criminal trials in order to promote a different approach to the treatment of trial evidence, one that is more consistent with advancing a restorative and victim-centred resolution to the trial process. The ICC is taken as the focus for exploring how these suggestions could impact on the way in which the factual basis for sentence might be reconceptualised within such a transformed trial.[43]

Changing the rules for admissibility

The rules governing the admissibility of evidence in the ICC reflect a hybridisation of adversarial and inquisitorial approaches.[44] The approach is adversarial in that the procedural norms are chiefly concerned with establishing a version of the facts that will either vindicate or negate the Prosecution's allegations of guilt made in the indictment. In other words, the trial as a context for determining guilt or innocence ensures that the norms that control how factual information is admitted to the record are selectively perceived to conform to this overriding need to establish individual criminal responsibility for what is alleged.

However, the perception of this information is not simply a matter dictated by the nature of the legal process as a juridical form. Social context and social norms influence how trial information is selectively perceived within the trial and also within the wider community, however this is defined. Within the trial context, social norms may well be particularised as norms of legal culture.[45] Where the rules for admissibility are a hybrid of adversarial and inquisitorial rules, as with the ICC, and the judiciary and trial professionals themselves reflect a broad spectrum of legal and social backgrounds, notions of guilt and innocence will consist of a complex mix of perceptions. They will be determined in part by the legal cultures of the trial professionals, in part by their perceptions of the mission with which they have all been entrusted, and in part by the emerging legal culture of the institution itself as its jurisprudence develops.

The influence of legal culture is a matter for conjecture.[46] However, there are significant differences between adversarial and inquisitorial approaches to the role of trial evidence which merit further consideration in the context of trial transformation. One of these concerns the way in which civil law systems generally view the notion of 'legal proof' with circumspection, preferring instead a more intuitive approach to the determination of guilt, as exemplified by the French concept of *intime conviction*.[47] This has its roots in the social contractarianism of the Enlightenment, as developed by writers such as Cesare Beccaria in relation to the administration of justice (Radzinowicz, 1966). Although its practical effect may, as Spencer (2002) suggests, be similar in requiring a level of certainty which amounts to something equivalent to the common law standard of proof 'beyond all reasonable doubt', it is essentially based on the principle that the guilt of the accused and any consequential deprivation of liberty should result from the intuitive exercise of judicial discretion and not be obscured by the strictures of legal form and lack of transparency.[48]

Reliance on the principled exercise of judicial discretion is similarly fundamental to the development of notions of justice in international criminal trials (Henham, 2003a). This is facilitated by the largely unfettered judicial discretion bestowed on sentencers by the foundation instruments of the ad hoc tribunals and the ICC, which encourages individualisation in sentencing and reliance on oral testimony. In normative terms, it also impacts on the admissibility and relevance of evidence concerning guilt or innocence,[49] its probative value and likely prejudicial effect.[50] The general rules for the disclosure of evidence, including reciprocal disclosure, and the nature of permissible evidence are similarly much more innovative and flexible than those normally found in common law jurisdictions (Findlay, 2001). Hence, it is arguable that the ICC already has the institutional capacity to develop judicial discretion as a positive force directing the nature and course of the trial process. At present, its penality simply lacks the rationale and strategic direction that would come from trial transformation. This is exacerbated by the artificial dichotomy between the verdict and sentencing phases of the trial drawn by Article 76 of the Rome Statute.

The discretionary rules reflect their contextual origins but are essentially neutral as regards how they might be used instrumentally within the trial as a force for change. Human agency through trial relationships, especially those involving the judge and victim, will determine this. Nevertheless, viewed as instrumental norms, the basic principles of admissibility must allow the transformed trial to function in such a way as to permit the balancing of retributive and restorative justice demands. Hence, the objective purpose for admissibility and the testing of evidence should exist not just to determine individual criminal responsibility but to engage in a broader purpose wherein the concept of individual responsibility is effectively replaced by – or at least utilised in conjunction with – an idea of community or social responsibility which embraces the collective need for social accountability for what has happened and seeks to repair the damage done, albeit that this may involve the use of retributive justice. In this sense, the notion of liability[51] rather than responsibility may be a more appropriate concept through which to diffuse the attribution of blame and punishment, and therefore justice.

For the ICC, a reconceptualisation of the notion of responsibility would mean that Article 25.2 of the Rome Statute[52] would have to re-evaluated and recast in terms that reflect a broader purpose for the transformed trial. However, the issue is not straightforward because the intention is not simply to replace the concept of individual criminal responsibility, but to site it within a broader notion of what responsibility means for victims and communities of justice in post-conflict states. Thus, the designation of when criminal responsibility will be taken to exist for the purposes of retributive justice[53] remains relevant because retribution will always be a significant component of what people regard as justice.[54] Retribution not only focuses on the individual offender's need to atone for the harm done, it is the legal authority's symbolic affirmation of a sense of opprobrium which resides in the wider community. Whether that moral disapproval is representative, temporally or actually, is a matter for conjecture.

A broader reconceptualisation of responsibility in terms of liability which emphasises the context of the (perceived) criminality will allow the objective norms of the substantive offences to be related more effectively to the social, political and historical contexts in which the behaviour occurred. Therefore, the ICC's normative framework would need to be expanded to suggest how individual criminal responsibility should be related to a more inclusive appraisal of community liability which focuses on rebuilding trust and relationships.[55] Rather than being seen as mutually exclusive, these trial objectives should be seen as mutually dependent. Thus, for example, where Article 25.3(e) of the Rome Statute includes criminal responsibility for direct and public incitement to genocide as a crime within the jurisdiction of the Court, there might be added a normative *obligation* within the Rules which tasks the ICC to ensure that the process provides adequate opportunity to explore explicitly why and how this came about.[56]

This does not mean that the ICC would be obliged to engage in some form of socio-historical process of truth-finding in the nature of a truth commission. What is envisaged is a normative structure that enables the judiciary to explore the broader sense of what the attribution of criminal responsibility signifies in terms of establishing accountability, healing and closure for victims and their communities. In this way, factual reconstruction will be circumscribed by procedural norms that require the Court to balance *inter alia* retributive and restorative conceptions of responsibility through appropriate access and rights protection, so that the final resolution of the case represents a meaningful engagement with a more representative and relevant form of justice.

Reconsidering the burden and standard of proof

Any reconsideration of the appropriateness of the concept of individual criminal responsibility as a basis for international trial justice and its possible modification to correspond with a concept that examines individual responsibility within a communitarian context raises the possibility of adopting a civil (or other) standard of proof at particular stages within the trial process, depending on the source, nature or utility of the evidence.[57] Clearly, the unprincipled, indiscriminate and unfettered use of discretion on the part of the judge to change the burden or standard of proof which depends on how useful the evidence is perceived to be for the achievement of particular objectives, however desirable, is fundamentally ill-conceived and contrary to the principles of natural justice and human rights.

As currently drafted, Article 66 of the Rome Statute is unequivocal in asserting the primacy of the presumption of innocence and establishing that the burden of proof is on the Prosecutor to prove the accused's guilt beyond all reasonable doubt. Article 30 deals with the mental element necessary to establish criminal responsibility, emphasising that the trial is concerned with the intent and knowledge of the accused in relation to the conduct and its consequences. There are no norms which countenance the possibility that a true understanding of the accused's state of mind and its broader social significance might only be achieved by introducing other kinds of more locally or community-based evidence, or that this might have to be admitted and evaluated in a different way.

A good example of the difficulty this might cause arises in the case of the Rwandan genocide, where tribal culture was responsible for inciting the hatred and killing of Tutsis by Hutus, so apparently negating the relevance of individual criminal responsibility, or indeed the criminality of the genocide itself. This might lead some to question the impact or relevance for the Rwandese themselves of individual findings of guilt and the imposition of retributive justice by an externally imposed international criminal tribunal (Drumbl, 2000). There is no doubt that within the constraints of the ICTR's adversarialised trial structure evidence of the broader socio-historical causes of the Rwandan genocide has been admitted. However, it was, and has only ever been, admitted within the normative constraints imposed by the existing form of trial and its underlying rationale. What is being argued for in the case of trial transformation requires something more than this. It requires a normative structure that allows for the connections between individual and criminal responsibility to be explored within a broader framework of penal objectives which includes restorative justice. In order to facilitate this, the criminal process will need to be broken down into key decision sites or points where evidence crucial to enable the trial to contribute to the achievement of these objectives can be admitted and tested appropriately.

Article 69.3 of the Rome Statute suggests that the ICC already has the ability to admit evidence submitted by the parties and that: 'The Court shall have the authority to request the submission of all evidence that it considers necessary for the determination of the truth.' In addition, Article 69.4 states that:

> The Court may rule on the relevance or admissibility of any evidence, taking into account, *inter alia*, the probative value of the evidence and any prejudice that such evidence may cause to a fair trial or to a fair trial evaluation of the testimony of a witness, in accordance with the Rules of Procedure and Evidence.

Of course, both these provisions are consistent with the ICC's stated rationale, affirmed in the Preamble to the Rome Statute, which declares that international crimes must not go unpunished, and a determination 'to put an end to impunity ... and thus to contribute to the prevention of such crimes'. However, the crucial difference between the ICC's existing Article 69 powers and what will be demanded from the transformed trial is that the nature of the evidence and its probative value in determining the 'truth' will be evaluated within a changed rationale and normative structure agreed by the state parties.

We would suggest that the relevance and probative value of the evidence and hence its credibility should be determined initially by reference to the current evidential rules for the determination of individual criminal responsibility, but that ICC judges should be empowered[58] to use their discretion during the course of either the Prosecution or the Defence case (and subsequently during closing statements) to ask for and admit evidence to the record which has been tested against a lesser civil standard of proof where that evidence can, in the opinion of the Trial Chamber, be used to promote a greater understanding of the broader social context of the crimes alleged in the indictment.

The reliability of this evidence will be capable of being established through direct questioning of witnesses by the judges alone, or by questioning on behalf of all trial participants (either directly or through the presiding judge), subject to procedural directions from the Court. This broadened discretion will operate against the background of a transformed trial rationale and participatory rights for victims and community representatives, which will allow them to exercise a direct influence on the direction of the trial and the purpose of the proceedings. Thus, the standard of proof and the probity of the admitted material will need to be judged against understandings of the truth that are essentially grounded in community values rather than constructed and interpreted through the rigorous application of formal legal rules and processes.[59]

International trial judges have shown themselves capable of effecting innovative evidential solutions and developing existing procedures to suit the circumstances of particular cases. For example, the ICC could encourage more oral argument before the bench. However, there would need to be safeguards in place to guard against the more recent tendency of the ICTY to curtail oral evidence in favour of affidavit evidence on the grounds of cost and practicality where the latter may be inadequate. An example of the potential for developing oral process was the ICTY's first application of the amended Rule 98 *bis*[60] in *Oric*.[61] In this case, Trial Chamber II dealt with the question of whether there was sufficient *prima facie* evidence to support a conviction, using an entirely oral, non-party-driven procedure to review the evidence and making an oral determination as to the accused's guilt. Similarly, in *Tadic*,[62] an earlier Trial Chamber had used a device akin to a status conference for resolving various aspects of rule interpretation in the pre-trial phase. As Findlay (2001: 44) points out, the ICTY could have chosen to extend their interventionist role to resolve issues regarding the interpretation of the charges on the indictment. In fact, Findlay (2001: 46) suggested a number of problematic evidentiary areas, including access to justice, lack of specificity in charges, corroboration,[63] the status of victims as witnesses, identification evidence, testimony of hostile witnesses and hearsay evidence[64] where issues of dissonance and synthesis between common law and civil law approaches raised the potential for constructive interventions by Trial Chamber judges. Nevertheless, as we have argued, rationality and principled normative guidance are necessary precursors to any effective development of judicial discretionary interventions in international criminal trials.

Collapsing and merging process

For the reasons discussed earlier, there is a strong case to be made for merging the verdict and sentence phases of the transformed trial, primarily to ensure that no artificial distinctions are drawn between the purposes for which factual information is admitted which result in its selective appropriation. Since the purposes for the trial are broader than those concerned with establishing individual criminal responsibility and extend to a consideration of the contextual significance of the commission of any substantive offences for the determination of the trial's outcome, it will be crucial to remove the artificial restrictions imposed on the relevance and admissibility of evidence created by the distinction made between substantive and sentence-related facts.

Consequently, we would argue that the kind of mono-phase hearing which maintains a substantive division between verdict and sentence is counterproductive to synthesising the evidential basis for sentencing in the transformed trial. By this we imply that, whilst verdict and sentence should remain key decision points in the criminal process, this should not involve considerations which influence the introduction of evidence at particular points in the process based solely on whether or not it might involve some tactical advantage or disadvantage for the Defence or the Prosecution. If the scope for introducing material which might otherwise be regarded as prejudicial to the Defence or Prosecution case is widened, it will be on the basis that the potentially prejudicial evidence is no longer threatening because the underlying reason for the threat has been removed.

Hence, Article 76 of the Rome Statute which permits the ICC, following conviction, to 'take into account the evidence presented and submissions made during the trial that are relevant to the sentence' will take on a somewhat different function. For example, the Prosecution might wish to introduce evidence of other alleged crimes or previous behaviour or convictions on the part of the accused which goes beyond the scope of what is necessary or permissible to prove the crime(s) alleged. Similarly, the Defence may wish to introduce material that contradicts this aggravating evidence, something which would normally be allowed if the issues involved were contested during the sentencing phase. Alternatively, the Defence might wish to adduce evidence of good character in mitigation which would normally be reserved for the sentencing stage. If this were to be introduced at an earlier stage because it bears on the issue of individual responsibility, it would, under normal circumstances, lay the Defence open to cross-examination by the Prosecution and the possible introduction of counter-evidence which may prove prejudicial.

Were the context of admissibility to be broadened as suggested, aggravating factors and mitigation would take on a more instrumental role in determining the outcome of international trials because the Court will be under a duty to relate these variables more directly to the social context of the alleged criminality. They would not be introduced on the basis of gaining a narrow tactical advantage over the determination of punishment, but would be admissible during the course of the trial (subject to judicial direction) whenever the Court felt that some engagement with more nuanced accounts of the social context of the criminalised behaviour was imperative in order to arrive at a constructive case outcome.

There is the additional difficulty of whether or not to draw a distinction between evidence which is admitted as reliable because it has been proved beyond all reasonable doubt during the trial stage and that which relates to mitigating factors established on the balance of probabilities during the sentencing phase. As discussed earlier, if the rationale for these conflicting standards were removed because the rationale for the trial as a whole had shifted from a largely adversarial and punitive to a more problem-solving approach, the introduction and admission of potentially prejudicial evidence would be regarded as potentially risk-free[65] and, more importantly, as contributing to the overriding mission of the Court to pursue its goal of promoting trial outcomes which produce constructive and inclusive outcomes for post-conflict societies, including retributive justice.

If the trial objective is concerned with the individualisation of justice within a broader community of interest, this should be reflected in the capacity of the ICC to pursue an integrated approach to sentence determination. Hence, Article 78[66] of the Rome Statute and Rule 145 of the ICC's RPE which currently deal with the determination of sentence should be reconsidered in this light. It is particularly instructive to reflect on Rule 145 in this respect. Rule 145.1, for example, refers, *inter alia,* to the issues of proportionality between the totality of the sentence and individual culpability and also stresses the need to balance all the relevant factors while considering the offender's circumstances and those of the crime. It also contains an exhortation for the judges to give consideration to specific aspects of the harm caused as they relate to the victims and their families, the nature of the unlawful behaviour and the means of execution, the degree of the offender's participation, intent, circumstances of manner, time and location, as well as his or her age, education and social and economic condition.

These provisions as they currently stand take the individual as their focus and consider the relevance of broader social variables purely in the context of that paradigm. The issue of proportionality as between sentence and culpability, for example, might be central to a retributive deserts-based sentencing rationale, but has less relevance to a more communitarian approach to sentencing. Indeed, one of the most intransigent problems for advocates of restorative justice in formulating penal policy is convincing hard-line retributivists that the introduction of restorative rationales and principles will not seriously damage the operational framework of ordinal and cardinal proportionality so central to just deserts philosophy. Circumvention of this dilemma at the philosophical level is problematic and undoubtedly requires a reconceptualisation of what should form the basis of liability for penal sanctions.

We suggest that Zedner's (1994) seminal article on the significance of the relationship between retribution and reparation in the criminal process may be instructive in this respect.[67] Zedner identifies the need for a theoretical reorientation to achieve a greater integration of retributive and reparative forms of justice[68] based on the abandonment of culpability as the central focus for sentencing and paying much closer attention to the issue of harm and its social distribution. Her argument for a move away from culpability to a broader-based conception of social harm is founded in part on an appreciation that crime infringes rights held in common socially and that the conception of harm should be widened since citizens have rights to a presumption of security.[69] These arguments have a resonance for the notion of trial transformation through the merging of retributive and restorative forms of justice, with the following caveats and observations:

1. The reconceptualisation of the trial form we propose is not rights-based but rights-protected. By this we mean that the rationale for trial transformation is founded on a perceived need to give formal recognition to the different perceptions of what constitutes justice by all the relevant players in international criminal trials. It is essentially to do with how the trial outcome can engage with competing moral values and seek legitimacy for its outcomes. Rights are therefore seen as a corollary for maintaining this legitimacy.
2. The rights of individual citizens to a presumption of security can clearly be extended to actual and potential breaches of international humanitarian law. However, as has been argued here, the reconceptualisation of individual criminal responsibility we propose advocates a broadening of the concept of individual culpability because it recognises that formalised notions of individual and collective fault embodied in the norms of substantive law need to be argued against contextualised understandings of what this means for victims and communities seeking justice following social conflict and war.
3. Ultimately, Zedner sees some rapprochement between reparation and retributive forms of justice. She distinguishes both from consequentialist forms based on rehabilitation and deterrence, suggesting their commonality on the grounds that each is predicated on notions of

> individual autonomy and the fact that they both derive their 'authority' from the offence itself and impose penalties on the basis of the seriousness of the crime. However, the use of the term 'authority' is problematic. If it refers to a narrow form of 'legal authority' in the Weberian[70] sense of representing a substantively rational, closed and formalised normative structure, this ignores the importance of social context as a key source of legitimacy for that legal authority. If, on the other hand, Zedner envisages a form of authority which goes beyond the integrity of formal law and seeks to engage with notions of 'moral authority',[71] then we would suggest her analysis fails to address the nature and relevance of competing moral values and their relative demands for justice.

Zedner examines questions of fairness, consistency and proportionality in sentencing within the conceptual parameters imposed by her proposed rapprochement between retributive and reparative forms of justice. Whilst Zedner suggests that social inclusion should provide the rationale for fairness in reparative justice, we argue that ICJ should be proactive through differentiation, identifying interests, providing opportunities for participation and encouraging individual and social responsibility which effects genuine social change. In practical terms, recognising difference (see Hudson, 1998) and reflecting these aspirations in the norms of procedural law are problematic for desert theorists.[72] Achieving consistency and proportionality are both difficult objectives for retributive and consequentialist forms of justice, but for different reasons. For the former, the rationale for attributing fault depends on individual culpability attached to prohibited conduct; for the latter, responsibility attaches to harm and the consequences of prohibited conduct, rather than the conduct itself (see further von Hirsch, Ashworth and Shearing, 2003).

Rejecting exculpatory and mitigating evidence on the basis of its relevance to the distinct phases of trial and sentence serves to reinforce an anomalous procedural dichotomy whose rationality is founded on the theory that establishing individual fault and responsibility is the primary concern of the criminal trial. The conventional distinction therefore ignores the possibility that such evidence might be admitted on the basis of its relevance for a wider purpose, where notions of individual fault are replaced by an approach that looks at individual and collective culpability, explores contextualised understandings of crime causation and seeks to establish a constructive outcome where responsibility for harm is established.

We have argued for the need to establish an evidential basis for sentence according to a procedurally fair examination of the evidence and that notions of procedural fairness should be based on an ideology of substantive fairness. Desert arguments for proportionality and consistency posit an essentially closed and unresponsive criminal process based on a narrow conceptualisation of individual culpability.[73] Ultimately, whether one considers this approach to be fair in any substantive sense is a question of moral conviction (see chapter 1). The point about the ideology of trial transformation we advocate is that it recognises a fundamental need to accommodate different moral views about what outcomes constitute justice within the fabric of the trial's normative structure, if necessary at the expense of objectified notions of consistency and fairness perpetuated by formal law and narrow approaches to penal solutions.

Intervention and diversion

Procedural opportunities for intervention and diversion within the context of the transformed trial will be facilitated by the adoption of an inclusive and constructive trial rationale. The rationale will be inclusive in the sense that the pre-trial and trial context will be seen as a forum for integrating and giving effect to the legitimate expectations for justice of victims and communities of justice. It will be constructive because the purpose of the transformed trial will be the positive and forward-looking one of merging alternatives and dismantling barriers between investigation and trial. Hence, interventions will be conditioned by changed perceptions and expectations for the outcome of the trial which go far beyond the narrow strategic goals of adversarialised process. Similarly, the rationale for diversion will be transformed. Instead of being seen as a route out of one justice paradigm into another because of inappropriateness or inadequacy, it will be perceived as a crucial pathway to the integration of restorative outcomes at particular sites for trial decision-making.[74]

Prosecutorial decision-making, rather than focusing largely on issues of charge and plea, might involve strategic negotiations with Defence advocates and victims' representatives to determine how the trial process might best determine their relative demands for justice.[75] For the ICC, this would require early involvement and impact on the investigative and prosecutorial rationale and functions of the Prosecutor. For example, the initiation of investigations and duties and powers of the Prosecutor with respect to investigations under Articles 53 and 54 of the Rome Statute will require modification. Whilst Article 53 makes several references to the interests of victims in relation to deciding whether or not the initiation of a prosecution would be in the interests of justice,[76] the point about trial transformation is that its rationale will determine the notional parameters for deciding what those interests might consist of. In other words, the rationale for trial transformation is one that embraces the need to establish individual and collective responsibility as the foundations for social change. This will demand the involvement of victims' representatives in the decision-making process which determines the initiation of an investigation.[77]

Similarly, as currently drafted, Article 54.1(a) emphasises that the focus for an investigation should be with a view to assessing whether there is criminal responsibility under the statute and, although Article 54.1(b) cautions respect for 'the interests and personal circumstances of victims and witnesses', these parties are not automatically represented in the decision-making process.[78] Again, it is important to emphasise that the active inclusion of this constituency in decision-making is not to undermine or weaken the Prosecutor's authority, but to ensure that the justice demands of those personally affected by the alleged criminality and having legitimate 'interests' in the transformed process contribute to the vital pre-trial stages of decision-making. Decisions reached by the Prosecutor at this stage would therefore extend to formulating recommendations for the pre-Trial Chamber about the form and objectives of the trial process to follow.[79]

Those findings concerned with the formulation of trial objectives could be incorporated in the pre-Trial Chamber's deliberations under Article 61 when the charges on which the Prosecutor intends to seek trial are confirmed. Article 61 already contains several provisions which deal with questions relating to the disclosure and admissibility of evidence necessary to substantiate the allegations made against the accused in the indictment. These evidential requirements could be broadened to include a requirement[80] that the pre-Trial Chamber should, where charges are confirmed, briefly indicate the proposed objectives for the trial process and the form it should take. This is not intended to subvert the criminal indictment by moving the issue away from establishing guilt and responsibility, but rather to indicate how the particular trial process in question will accommodate the rationale for trial transformation in practical terms.

Through their previous involvement in the investigative process, the Prosecutor will already be aware of the outcome expectations for the trial of victims and victim communities. Consequently, one objective for the pre-Trial Chamber will be to ensure that the trial process to follow provides opportunities at designated sites of decision-making to consider the broader social context of their demands. These sites may follow the conventional trial paradigm, or the opportunity may be provided for more detailed interventions on behalf of the relevant parties at specific points. For example, form and process may be suspended, as directed by the presiding judge, to allow for more informal, directed deliberations to take place, utilising alternative media or other methods of communication, as appropriate.

A broad agenda for any diversionary process could also be provided and suggestions made as to how the objectives of the session would assist in achieving a more constructive and restorative outcome for the trial process as a whole.[81] At this stage the pre-Trial Chamber could also formulate specific practice directions for the conduct of the trial. These might cover:

- the nature and function of interventions;
- rules governing the exercise of the discretionary power to intervene;
- rules for the conduct of diversionary processes, including justifying who will be represented and by whom;

- how such input might help to achieve specific goals for healing the wounds caused to individual victims and relevant victim communities by the alleged criminality.

The actual timing and stages for intervention or diversion will depend on the dynamics of each case. More specifically, there will be certain indicators or triggers for case planning and judicial intervention based on such factors as whether the offender acknowledges guilt, expresses remorse and is willing to repair harm, on the one hand, and the victim community's willingness to accept apologies, extend forgiveness, accept reparation and work towards a collective resolution which favours peace and reconciliation, on the other. However, as Braithwaite (1989) suggests, a critical feature of communitarian societies is that they should be more capable of shaming which amounts to stigmatisation and less willing to condemn deviance. Clearly, this will vary so that the degree to which any justice process – whether trial-based or an alternative – can respond to communitarian demands for justice and the possibilities for achieving them will depend on how it comes to perceive what they are. In this there is a crucial role for victimisation studies in war zones and post-conflict states, such as that recently carried out in the regions of the Balkans and Palestine by Kiza and Rohne (2005). The Balkans study provides a detailed examination of factors such as the basic forms of victimisation during wartime, the perception of victimisation by the victim, the needs of victims during victimisation and the attitudes of victims to punishment and reparation. Whilst generally holding punitive attitudes in demanding prosecution for international crimes, citizens of post-war societies can be distinguished by their different demands for punitiveness, and show a preference for monetary compensation. However, in terms of purpose, respondents from the Balkans sample were mainly in favour of revealing 'the truth' as they saw it; only a small percentage explicitly sought revenge.

Such research confirms the need for comparative contextual analyses to reveal the socio-political and historical realities of victimisation in war-torn states. More significantly in the present context, such reports can form the basis for making informed policy decisions about victim expectations and demands for justice which can be worked through in the development of a responsive normative regime for the trial, underpinned by broad support for the ideology of trial transformation. For example, the important differences between Kosovo and Bosnia-Herzegovina with respect to the emphasis placed on revenge as a measure of punitiveness is highly significant because it clearly supports the case for merging retributive and restorative justice in international trials we have advocated (Findlay and Henham, 2005).

Developing judicial discretionary power

The single most important stimulus for trial transformation will be the principled development of judicial discretionary power. However, since the broader context of international penality informs the instrumentality of judicial discretion rather than trial structure and form, the potential for individualised sentencing to engage with restorative concerns and collective demands for justice is presently inhibited by the retributive dynamic prevalent in international trial ideology. Consequently, instead of international judges being free to utilise their wide discretionary powers to develop a sentencing jurisprudence which promotes consequentialist objectives, individualised sentencing is excessively constrained by the focus on individual criminal responsibility and the need for proportionality. Notwithstanding this, the potential exists for ICC judges to individualise sentences which reach beyond the justificatory rhetoric, symbolism and procedural imperatives of retribution and deterrence to engage with alternative paradigms.

There is no doubt that research suggests sentencing decisions are individualised through the selective appropriation and interpretation of legal and social constraints in the context of perceived audience expectation, and that sentencers *appear* to share similar, uniform and comparable images of relevant case material and legal rules (Henham, 2001). For international sentencing this decision-making paradigm is complicated by the fact that the judiciary are drawn from diverse legal cultures and jurisdictional backgrounds. This inevitably affects their perception and interpretation of information and therefore weakens the extent to which they can be regarded as sharing comparable understandings and expectations.

Ultimately, the mobilisation of judicial discretion will depend on a cooperative project to reposition the ideology of the international criminal trial in order to reflect a more restorative and inclusive influence. This will only be possible if the normative structures put in place are developed on a strong ideological foundation to which ICC judges are formally committed. We do not believe that it is possible to move from a situation of judicial diversity to one of coherence in the long term without this ideological commitment. The dependent normative structures put in place will thus provide the launch-pad, a sort of *de novo* platform, where the diverse traditions and practices, attitudes and penal philosophies judges bring with them will become reconciled within the transformative context of the trial process.

Nevertheless, although the ideological rationale which informs the normative framework for transformation is fundamental to its delivery, it is axiomatic that discretion will continue to operate no matter what the normative framework and so will give life to the norms. It follows that both may be developed simultaneously so that the judges will be instrumental in embedding and activating the emerging normative framework. Once at liberty to look beyond retributive justice alone, judges will become a driving force for developing other crucial issues within the new normative framework, such as lay/professional interaction, victim inclusion and distinction in the use and style of 'facts' within the trial. In this sense, discretion will help to materialise a developing normative framework. In short, such a scenario implies two phases: Phase 1 will involve a commitment by ICC judges to aim for a more inclusive form of decision-making: Phase 2 will involve a commitment by relevant state parties to review progress on normative development and proceed towards whatever normative change is appropriate to facilitate trial transformation.

However, the reconciliation and assimilation of different judicial cultures as a phenomenon through discretionary decision-making in international trials may be problematic. Mills and Stephens (2005) have critiqued theories for the creation of international judicial communities and their dialogue and propose difficulty in assuming a productive and communicative international judicial community and culture. Such reservations raise important questions about how judges at the international level might assimilate their developed and expansive new discretion and what might be the impediments to entrenching this in judicial practice. It also leads us to speculate on the ways in which an international judicial 'collaboration' (community or profession) might draw on its diverse procedural origins so as to develop and empower the frameworks for this new discretion.

Mills and Stephens (2005: 21) make some perceptive points. For example, they suggest, rightly, that there are problems with Slaughter's view that the substantive values necessary for the moral consensus which should support a global community of law will somehow emerge automatically from transnational dialogue. More importantly, Mills and Stephens contest the idea that out of the conventionally conflictual relations of the international legal community:

> will emerge greater dialogue and ultimately a doctrine of 'judicial comity', under which judges will defer to their foreign judicial colleagues, provided that they 'measure up to minimum standards of international justice. The existence of such standards, however, is precisely what is supposed to emerge out of this legal community – which suggests that Slaughter underestimates the problems in achieving communication and agreement between judges with different traditions and values ... Increased transnational communication may be an attractive ideal, but unless the processes through which this will occur are carefully structured and designed, it may simply become a form of transnational contestation. The shared procedural norms which Slaughter postulates will not prevent (indeed they will legitimate) the reality of transnational communication as an exercise of private power.

Similar cautionary comments are made by Romano (2002) when considering the nature and significance of the relationship between international and national trial structures in an internationalised context. The most important aspect of this relationship for sentencing concerns the interaction between international and national norms and their manifestation in hybrid trial processes.[82] Romano suggests that the key factor is how individual judicial discretion modulates this effect to conduct the process of criminalisation. He argues that 'local' judges will exercise a kind of 'local' discretion, embedded in local norms, and 'international' judges a generalised or abstracted 'international' discretion, freed from any particular perspective that would threaten its impartiality.

Notwithstanding the fact that such an analysis appears to ignore the possibility that so-called 'international' discretion is partial rather than generalised and unfocused, Mills and Stephens would no doubt argue that the alternative scenario envisaging the fusion of two normative orders to constitute a uniform unilateral criminalisation of the conduct in question seems an equally remote possibility. More likely, where mixed benches are involved, is that there may be multiple trial processes (rather than one) occurring in each trial in these hybrid tribunals.

However, as argued here and elsewhere, the crucial issue surely remains one of understanding what this process of criminalisation actually signifies (Henham, 2003b). In other words, whilst the international – and internationalised – judiciary may be the mediators of some form of penality, the implications of this cannot be worked through without a consideration, on the one hand, of what the constituent elements of that penality mean and signify in ideological and political terms, and, on the other, the extent to which the exercise of judicial discretion in sentence decision-making is transformative of the morality and normative framework such penality represents. As discussed, this conceptualisation requires us to make certain assumptions regarding the nature of law and the process of legal reasoning in sociological terms. However, it also forces us to address the *legitimacy* of the penality which relates to international (internationalised) institutions because it seeks to make connections between the ideology of punishment and its moral legitimacy.[83] The latter is considered at the level of the moral values that underpin the normative principles embodied in the institutional frameworks of international (internationalised) criminal processes and the connections that can (and should) be made between these and the penality of post-conflict societies. Consequently, a major theme implicit in trial transformation is directed towards understanding the linkage between the conditions of moral and legal pluralism and their implications for international punishment.

Operationalising

If restorative and retributive forms of justice were to be embraced as desirable aspirations for punishment in international criminal trials, the present conceptualisation of individualisation and its potential for engaging with restorative concerns and collective demands for justice is inhibited by the retributive dynamic which pervades international trial ideology. In terms of individual decisions, this means that the individualisation of sentences is constrained by legalistic criteria. Although international judges have wide discretionary powers that could be used to develop sentencing principles which promote consequentialist objectives, the individualisation of sentences as currently practised focuses on the issue of individual criminal responsibility and its clarification in the context of the need for proportionality.[84]

The paucity of sentencing guidelines is a reflection of the failure on the part of successive Preparatory Commissions to settle questions relating to the relative gravity of international crimes and, consequently, the issue of cardinal proportionality for the punishment of such crimes. The philosophy of just deserts is strongly reflected in the sentencing model prevalent in international criminal trials. Unfortunately, an unresolved weakness in deserts theory is that the approach is unable to distinguish convincingly between different degrees of responsibility or quantify harm (Ashworth, 1983: 173–81; 1989: 346); Therefore, whilst deserts theory recognises that sentencing policy must consider the extent to which deserved punishment is applied in individual cases, it fails to provide a rational framework for scaling punishments or ranking them in terms of offence seriousness. The result is that judicial discretion in the ICTY and ICTR has been employed to rationalise the question of offence gravity on a case-by-case basis, rather than through the principled application of universally agreed norms embodied in their respective foundation instruments.

In consequence, the concept of individualisation, so enthusiastically endorsed by judges, is circumscribed by the pervading ideology which underpins the substantive and procedural framework for trial and sentence in international criminal trials. This retributive and deterrent ideology not only militates against the development of sentencing guidance which embraces a more broadly conceived and constructive conceptualisation of individualisation, it crucially hinders that objective by facilitating the use of procedural devices such as plea bargains which limit the possibilities for principled intervention on the part of the judiciary.

If judicial discretion is to be mobilised for trial transformation, it will require not only a reconceptualisation of trial ideology and substantive normative change, but also the development of new techniques for advancing the jurisprudence of sentencing within this changed environment. These techniques should prioritise principles on the basis of the following criteria, recognising the need for international sentencing to:

1. Encourage compromise to produce truth-telling that promotes healing, as well as reflecting the apportionment of individual blame on the basis of legally defined harm.
2. Regulate, balance and prioritise the interests of victims and communities of interest and develop principles which give effect to their participation in decision-making relevant to sentencing, in addition to the determination of sentence itself.

3. Expand the scope of judicial power and accountability beyond adjudication to include the supervision and enforcement of sentencing outcomes.
4. So far as compatible with balancing retributive and consequentialist rationales for trial justice, promote a consistent and proportionate approach to sentence decision-making.
5. Through the extended use of practice directions, promote arrangements for reducing formalism and giving equal effect to lay and professional voices.
6. Distinguish principles on the basis of offender characteristics which differentiate capacity and responsibility.
7. Rationalise the development of procedural norms on the basis of their capacity to contribute to trial transformation rather than expediency and purely systemic concerns.

Notes

1. The relationship between sentencing and legitimacy has received limited attention in recent analyses of the role of the criminal trial. See, for example, Duff et al. (2004, 2006, 2007). This lacuna is especially marked in the developing discourse on the future for ICJ and, more particularly, the ICC. Although legitimacy has received significant attention in theoretical writings and empirical research across a variety of disciplines in the present context (see Tyler, 2008), these generally fail to explain how the trial process might be implicated in delivering more inclusive forms of sentencing; for important contributions (see Hutton, 2008; Indemaur, 2008).
2. Some would argue that the notion of legal closure precludes any consideration of the relevance of moral views in evaluating the validity and authority of law and legal norms.
3. For example, Packer's (1968) dichotomous due process and crime control model. See also Mansoor (2005).
4. For example, purely doctrinal positivist analyses of sentencing law and practice. See Thomas (1979) in the English context.
5. This is provided in Articles 132 and 133 of the Italian Criminal Code (1930).
6. Articles 533 and 535 of the Italian Code of Criminal Procedure (1988).
7. A Victims Advocates Scheme (now replaced by the Victim Focus Scheme) was recently piloted in five Crown Court centres. For evaluation, see Garcia-Sanche et al. (2008). However, this is not intended to have any impact on sentence.
8. The issue is significant because it may impact directly on the choice between a custodial or non-custodial sentence, or the length of any prison sentence.
9. Under Article 90 of the Italian Code of Criminal Procedure (1988).
10. 'Rule 100: Sentencing Procedure on a Guilty Plea. If the Trial Chamber convicts the accused on a guilty plea, the Prosecutor and the Defence may admit any relevant information that may assist the Trial Chamber in determining an appropriate sentence. The sentence shall be pronounced in a judgement in public and in the presence of the convicted person ...'
11. *Prosecutor v Tadic* (Case No. IT-94-1-S), Sentencing Judgment, 14 July 1997.

12. *Prosecutor v Akayesu* (Case No. ICTR-96-4-T), 2 September 1998.
13. See Rule 143, ICTY RPE.
14. Article 76(4) confirms that, wherever possible, the sentence must be pronounced in public in the accused's presence.
15. As would be consistent with an inquisitorial truth-finding purpose for the trial.
16. ICTR decisions have attempted to clarify what information relating to aggravation and mitigation is relevant to sentencing and the appropriate burden of proof. For example, in *Prosecutor v Niyitegeka* (Case No. ICTR-96-14-T), Judgment and Sentence, 16 May 2003: 'It has to be borne in mind that the principle according to which only matters proved beyond a reasonable doubt are to be considered at the sentencing stage extends to the assessment of any aggravating factors, while mitigating factors are to be taken into consideration if established on a balance of probabilities. This Chamber reiterates that a particular circumstance shall not be retained as aggravating if it is included as an element of the crime in consideration' (para. 488). This approach is consistent with domestic adversarial trial practice.
17. As Zappala (2003) suggests, this is hardly likely to prove expeditious.
18. This does not permit the Prosecution to call evidence for the purposes of establishing the commission of offences other than those which have been proved, regardless of their nature and gravity.
19. This includes the detailed consideration of expert medical, psychiatric and personal circumstances reports and witness testimony that are admitted and evaluated purely for sentencing purposes.
20. Notwithstanding the ICC Trial Chamber's power to hold a further hearing on matters related to sentence under Rule 143, ICC RPE.
21. Comment to Article 46 'Sentencing' Yearbook of the International Law Commission (1994).
22. This is consistent with the sociological insights of symbolic interactionism; see further Sudnow (1965) and King (1978).
23. As the Italian experience tends to suggest.
24. *Prosecutor v Aleksovski* (Case No. IT-95-14/1), Judgment, 24 March 2000, para. 182.
25. The concepts of 'offence gravity' and 'offence seriousness' and 'crime' and 'offence' appear to be used interchangeably in the jurisprudence of the ICTY and ICTR.
26. Damaska (2008: 332) suggests that it does so by emphasising the avoidance of collective responsibility. See chapter 8 for fuller commentary on this paper.
27. An earlier study by Schabas (1997) also considers the general applicability of the provisions of the Universal Declaration of Human Rights (1948) and the International Covenant on Civil and Political Rights (1976), especially Articles 7, 10 and 15. Schabas suggests that Article 7 'encompasses the notion of proportionality in criminal punishment', whilst Articles 7 and 10 effectively insist on the importance of rehabilitation. Again, the normative significance of these aspirations is ignored, as is the possibility of their realisation within the existing philosophical context of international penality.
28. This may constitute a breach of Article 14.1 of the International Covenant on Civil and Political Rights (1976). See Kittichaisaree (2001: 291) for further discussion in the context of the ICTY and ICTR.
29. Such as England's so-called 'Newton hearings'. See further Ashworth (2005: 345).
30. Rule 69, ICC RPE provides that any prior agreement between the Prosecutor and the Defence not to contest an alleged fact is subject to the overriding discretion of the Trial Chamber to order a more complete presentation thereof in the interests of justice (particularly those of victims).

31. *Prosecutor v Momir Nikolic* (Case No. IT-02-60/1-S), Trial Chamber, Sentencing Judgment, 2 December 2003.
32. This provides: 'If an accused pleads guilty in accordance with Rule 62 (vi), or requests to change his or her plea to guilty and the Trial Chamber is satisfied that: (i) the guilty plea has been made voluntarily; (ii) the guilty plea is informed; (iii) the guilty plea is not equivocal; and (iv) there is a sufficient factual basis for the crime and the accused's participation in it, either on the basis of independent indicia or on lack of any material disagreement between the parties about the facts of the case the Trial Chamber may enter a finding of guilt and instruct the Registrar to set a date for the sentencing hearing.'
33. This extends to the possibility of adducing evidence on any factual aspect of the agreed facts which form the basis of the guilty plea, such as that of a witness for the purposes of sentencing; *Prosecutor v Simic* (Case No. IT-95-9), Sentencing Judgment, 17 October 2002, '[I]t would be wrong to allow evidence in the sentencing proceedings which in any way put in issue the agreed facts, and that witness statements or testimony that address agreed facts and an accused's person's responsibility for crimes already pled guilty to should not be allowed' (para. 26).
34. *Prosecutor v Deronjic* (Case No IT-02-61-S), Sentencing Judgment, 30 March 2004.
35. *Prosecutor v Deronjic* (Case No. IT-02-61-S), Dissenting Opinion of Judge Wolfgang Schomburg, 30 March 2004.
36. It is also important to note the deleterious effect that disproportionate sentences for such grave and aggravated crimes as genocide might have on sentences for murder cases in national jurisdictions such as the UK (van Zyl Smit, 2002).
37. Bush and Folger (1994: 84-5), for example, would argue that practices such as mediation have the potential to transform conflict through empowerment and recognition by citizens of the need to acknowledge and be responsive to the needs of others.
38. For example, the ICTY Appeals Chamber in *Delalic*, whilst acknowledging its significance, reaffirmed that rehabilitation could not 'play a *predominant* role' in the decision-making process, stating that it was clearly subordinate to deterrence and retribution as the main purposes of sentencing in the ad hoc tribunals; *Prosecutor v Delalic* (Case No. IT-96-21), Appeals Judgment, 20 February 2001, para. 806.
39. Seen in this light, the notion of 'instrumentality' means inclusion and participation for a purpose.
40. See further, Findlay and Henham (2005: chapter 8) for a consideration of the different dimensions of trial transformation.
41. Hogarth (1971) has demonstrated that the process of information selection and its significance in sentence decision-making is influenced by sentencers' prior attitudes, beliefs and penal philosophies.
42. We argue that this dynamic continues to predominate despite the alleged procedural 'drift' from adversarialism and the more blended normative paradigm of the ICC. See Vogler (forthcoming).
43. For useful commentary on the ICC's procedural norms, see Kress (2003) and Ambos (2003).
44. Vogler (forthcoming) notes that the trial phase has undergone a significant shift away from orality. However, it is important to point out that the terms 'adversarialism' and 'inquisitorialism' are used here to denote paradigms of trial justice, rather than in the narrow, positivistic sense of adversarial vs. inquisitorial modalities of international criminal procedure. Indeed, some commentators employ

these concepts as analytical categories against which to argue for a fair trial, taking elements from both; see, for example, Ambos (2003).

45. For writings which seek to elaborate the concept and context of legal culture, see Nelken (1997) and Nelken and Feest (2001).
46. Arguably, the impact of pre-existing legal and social influences on judicial discretionary decision-making will gradually diminish as a new legal culture is forged *de novo*.
47. Articles 353, 427 and 536 of the French Code of Criminal Procedure (1958); see further, Spencer (2002: 601).
48. Notwithstanding, the amount of discretion and the accountability of those exercising it should be made explicit and enforced. Schabas (2007: 295) suggests that ICC trial judges will increasingly use their powers to call evidence on their own initiative in the interests of finding the 'truth', rather than restrict admissibility to the strictures of adversarial contest.
49. Article 64(9)(a), ICC Statute.
50. Article 69(4), ICC Statute.
51. Invoking the civil law concept of liability as fixing interpersonal rights, duties and responsibilities emphasises the importance of consequential adjustment and reparation rather than maintaining the primary focus on blame and its penality.
52. 'A person who commits a crime within the jurisdiction of the Court shall be individually responsible and liable for punishment in accordance with this Statute.'
53. Article 25.3, ICC Statute.
54. For an interesting study, see Kiza and Rohne (2005).
55. Damaska (2008: 332) argues that the current emphasis towards individualisation tends to militate against notions of collective responsibility and creates an uneasy tension within the trial. However, Drumbl (2007) counters this limitation by arguing for a broader, community-based form of liability. The validity of both arguments is tested in chapter 8 against the theoretical and practical suggestions we propose in this volume.
56. This burden would be discharged by the Prosecutor during the deliberations to fix the *trial programme* in the pre-Trial Conference (see chapter 7). This innovation would transcend the remit of current status conferences because it would operate to fulfil the normative imperatives of the transformed trial.
57. A civil law model might be appropriate for the preliminary gathering and testing of evidence. See further de Hemptinne (2007).
58. By the RPE and supported by practice directions.
59. As Findlay (2008b: 210) points out, the duty to facilitate the merging of retributive and restorative forms of justice imposed on the Chinese judiciary under Article 172 of the Chinese Criminal Procedure Law has significant resonance for shaping the future direction of ICJ, especially that proposed by trial transformation.
60. Rule 98 *bis* ICTY RPE (adopted 10 July 1998, amended 17 November 1999, amended 8 December 2004): 'At the close of the Prosecutor's case, the Trial Chamber shall, by oral decision and after hearing the oral submissions of the parties, enter a judgement of acquittal on any count if there is no evidence capable of supporting a conviction.' Unfortunately, as Vogler (forthcoming) suggests, there has been a fairly rapid move away from orality by the ICTY towards the increased use of affidavit evidence since the introduction of Rule 92 *bis*. This has been especially marked since the *Milosevic* trial which pre-empted the introduction of Rules 92 *ter* and *quater* allowing affidavit evidence from persons present in court or from

those who were unavailable due to death, disappearance or medical condition to be admitted as evidence of material facts. See further Gordon (2007).

61. *Prosecutor v Oric* (Case No. IT-03-68-T), Oral Decision Pursuant to Rule 98 *bis*, 8 June 2005.
62. *Prosecutor v Tadic* (Case No. IT-94-I-T), Opinion and Judgment, 7 May 1997.
63. Not applicable to the ICC. See Rule 63(4), ICC RPE.
64. Schabas (2007: 294) suggests that there is no general rule excluding hearsay or indirect evidence as concerns the ICC.
65. This difficult judgment would be the responsibility of the judges whose duty would be to guard against any adverse consequences of admitting such evidence on the rights of all parties to due process and impartiality.
66. Article 78:
    'Determination of the sentence
    1. In determining the sentence, the Court shall, in accordance with the Rules of Procedure and Evidence, take into account such factors as the gravity of the crime and the individual circumstances of the convicted person.
    2. In imposing a sentence of imprisonment, the Court shall deduct the time, if any, previously spent in detention in accordance with an order of the Court. The Court may deduct any time otherwise spent in detention in connection with conduct underlying the crime.
    3. When a person has been convicted of more than one crime, the Court shall pronounce a sentence for each crime and a joint sentence specifying the total period of imprisonment. This period shall be no less than the highest individual sentence pronounced and shall not exceed 30 years' imprisonment or a sentence of life imprisonment in conformity with article 77, paragraph 1(b).'
67. Of course, we take the point that reparative justice is but one possible aspect of restorative justice, but it is the broader issues of compatibility raised by Zedner which are relevant to our argument.
68. She suggests that arguments for incorporating reparative elements into the criminal justice process are mainly pragmatic and economic.
69. Environmental and corporate crimes become relevant within this broader formulation.
70. For an excellent overview of this and other approaches to the relationship between law and legitimacy, see Cotterrell (1992: chapter 5).
71. For arguments against, see Raz (1979).
72. Note the limited participative role for victims in the English criminal trial process.
73. For a recent restatement, see von Hirsch and Ashworth (2005).
74. We would counter any suggestion based on Cohen's argument that such diversionary measures may perpetuate the hegemony of international trial justice by exposing those implicated in the transformed process to a greater degree of control and exposure to diversionary and interventionist strategies. On the contrary, our purpose is to diffuse the hegemony of the trial through rights protected measures to increase the legitimacy of its outcomes. See Cohen (1985).
75. For an assessment of the legal context, see Cote (2005).
76. Articles 53.1(c) and 53.2(c). For a comprehensive review of the legal debates surrounding the meaning of this phrase and its implications, see Ambos (2007). Ambos acknowledges: 'Clearly, whether one likes it or not, there is no other clause in the ICC Statute allowing so explicitly for policy considerations' (para. 52) and further: 'justice does not focus only on the case itself or is limited to criminal justice but encompasses alternative forms of justice and entails an overall assessment

of the situation taking into account peace and reconciliation as the ultimate goals of every process of transition' (para. 53, references omitted). Therefore, although the consensus view confirms that the autonomy of this concept remains firmly tied to its legal foundations, a liberal constructive interpretation of its capacity would permit the ICC Prosecutor to pursue broad justice interests within this normative framework. As we advocate, a transformation in the ideology and norms of the trial would be necessary to ensure the kind of victim inclusion and processual changes envisaged in this book. See Findlay and Henham (2005).

77. Recognition by the ICC OTP of the need to engage with victims and communities has been evident through the development of the ICC Outreach Programme (2006), and in urging greater victim and community input for ascertaining the interests of victims for the purposes of Article 53 of the ICC Statute (ICC OTP, 2007).
78. The Prosecutor may, *inter alia*, '[R]equest the presence of and question persons being investigated, victims and witnesses' (Article 54.3). Note that victims may make representations to the pre-Trial Chamber under Article 15(3) according to the RPE if the Prosecutor requests it to authorise an investigation *ex proprio moto*, or by virtue of Article 19(3) when the admissibility of a case is in issue. See further Baumgartner (2008).
79. What we envisage goes far beyond the development of case-management strategies. See further Langer (2005).
80. Possibly following on from Article 61.7.
81. This could be through mediation or other restorative form of justice.
82. Condorelli (2002) makes the important point that the hybridisation of criminal processes also reflects a wider trend towards the internationalisation of domestic judicial functions even in purely national contexts involving not just formal institutional processes, but also the growth of comparative judicial methodology by judicial actors.
83. For arguments supporting this approach in the broader context of international law, see Buchanan (2004).
84. This has been consistently reinforced in decisions of the ICTY. For example, in *Prosecutor v Krnojelac* (Case No. IT-97-25-T), Judgment, 15 March 2002: 'the overriding sentencing obligation considered by the Trial Chamber has been that of fitting the penalty to the individual circumstances of the Accused and to the gravity of the offences for which he has been found responsible' (para. 507); or, as in *Prosecutor v Sikirica* (Case No. IT-95-8-S), Sentencing Judgment, 13 November 2001 (citing the *Celebici* Appeal Judgement, para. 717): 'the overriding of the Trial Chamber in determining sentence is to individualise a penalty to fit the individual circumstances of the accused and the gravity of the crime' (para. 231).

6
Accountability Frameworks

Introduction

Our analysis of accountability is put at two levels: the internal and the external. Internal accountability considerations focus on access to justice for victim communities. A rights protection outcome as evidence of internal accountability is measured against access, inclusivity and integration for the key stakeholders in communities of justice. Our discussion of external accountability, on the other hand, is more concerned with exploring the place of ICJ as a form of global governance. Beyond ensuring the interests of trial participants, we argue that the trial as a key endorsement of ICJ should be capable of advancing the accountability of global governance. We have suggested (Findlay, 2008b) a reinvigoration of the justice component in a 'separation of powers' model for global governance. Problematic as this may be, it moves the motivation for current global governance away from satisfying the obligations of sectarian political hegemony. Consistent with a wider concern for humanity, ICJ may require of global governance a more pluralist regulation strategy which complements the cultural diversity implicit in communities of justice.

Internal accountability

The governance for ICJ provided by judicial discretion in its broader sense must be tempered by frameworks of accountability which are developed in tandem with its enhancement for justice transformation. However, this is not simply about the specific accountability of individuals for decisions made about the scope of procedural norms or the conformity of procedural norms to particular systems or paradigms of rights protection. Our conceptualisation of accountability reflects something more fundamental, which we regard as integral to determining the legitimacy of ICJ: namely, a broader notion of accountability which relates directly to the institutions of ICJ themselves. Consequently, we argue that the institutions of international penality should conform to the principles of humanitarian justice elaborated in chapter 1, especially the importance of inclusivity as extending beyond the individual to the collective, and the significance of this for establishing the legitimacy of ICJ. Hence, this is not a mere provincial issue of whether or not the practice of international trials offers access to justice. It extends to the global question regarding the meaning of accountability for the institutions charged to deliver ICJ, and its significance for governance.

The meaning of accountability

Norms of access and rights tend to be conceptualised within a narrow paradigm which relates to the conventional concentration of ICJ process on individual culpability and harm. Consequently, norms of access are seen as relevant to procedural and processual rules (legal, bureaucratic and administrative) which may or may not be deemed as compatible with the achievement of certain principled goals.[1] Rights, on the other hand, are portrayed as the corollary to access, as procedural rules designed to ensure that the aspirations/values embodied in the norms of access are actually achieved.[2]

However, we suggest a reconceptualisation of these notions of access and rights, particularly through promoting the idea of access to justice within the transformed trial as intimately connected to the instrumental capacity of judicial decision-making. We argue that the notions of access and reciprocal rights should extend beyond their present restricted conceptual boundaries and be related more directly to ideas of justice within victim communities. We therefore focus on establishing connections, dialogues and representations of justice from within victim communities, so that the idea of access to justice is unequivocally associated with the more holistic and representative justice we have described as the essence of the transformed trial.

Consequently, the notion of rights should be broadened and interpreted within a democratised framework for accountability, so that rights themselves are conceived as an essential component in maintaining the dialogue of justice with victim communities. In this way accountability moves beyond its conventional role of ensuring the principled enforcement of penal norms by enabling rights to become something that is more socially responsive, acting as a regulator of social justice whose purpose is to ensure that the pluralistic demands of transitional justice in post-conflict societies are met through sensitive interpretation and dialogue. All this is consistent with the pursuit of ICJ as a socialising rather than a coercive institution. It also reflects a purposeful mission for ICJ, providing a context where the ideological and philosophical rationales that inform policy and structure are negotiated in ways that reflect meaningful connections between the institutions of punishment and those individuals and communities affected by them.

We regard judicial discretion as a key variable for changing this notion of accountability to one that engages with significant justice demands and supports rights consistent with their achievement. Our belief that ICJ should be viewed as instrumental and transformative is evidenced by our equation of access to justice with a distinct conceptualisation of victim participation which suggests that victims and communities of justice should participate fully and have a significant input into discretionary decision-making processes occurring throughout the criminal trial.

This appreciation of discretionary decision-making is crucial for connecting with notions of restorative justice that resonate with the concerns of victims and communities of justice. It encourages insight into factors that promote the relative differentiation between notions of 'truth' and justice for victims and 'significant others' within their respective communities. The importance of this observation lies in the fact that the moral legitimacy of ICJ as currently conceptualised is equated with the nature and function of the process rather than what it actually signifies. Justice transformation is concerned with facilitating some conceptual linkage between the moral justifications for ICJ process and how these may be transformed processually to connect with notions of legitimacy for victims and communities of justice. Consequently, the framework for accountability must both mirror conceptually and facilitate the ideological plurality of ICJ and its representation as a set of moral prescriptions based on humanitarian principles; its embodiment as substantive and procedural norms in the foundation instruments of international courts and tribunals; and, most importantly, its transformation into normative imperatives that are regarded as legitimate by victims and victim communities.

The framework for accountability within an inclusive and transformative ICJ must therefore ensure that victims and the interests of communities of justice are recognised and enforced within the context of the transformed trial, and that procedural norms providing for victim participation are supported by enforceable rights for victims. Consequently, since judicial discretion is to become the key to changing the presently restricted notion of accountability, there is an increased need to direct this instrumental power by constantly reflecting it back to victim community interests. Therefore, the legitimacy for extending judicial authority in this way becomes a communitarian concern of inclusivity and integration, rather than a parochial reflection of retributive penality. For justice transformation, accountability where access is denied and rights are unenforced should facilitate the enhancement of judicial discretionary power to confront and reconcile competing interests more effectively.

These observations are portrayed in Figure 6.1 below. More particularly, it emphasises accountability as a vital corrective influence on justice delivery within the context of the transformed trial. Accountability as a function of process remains bound by its ideology and structure, so where access and

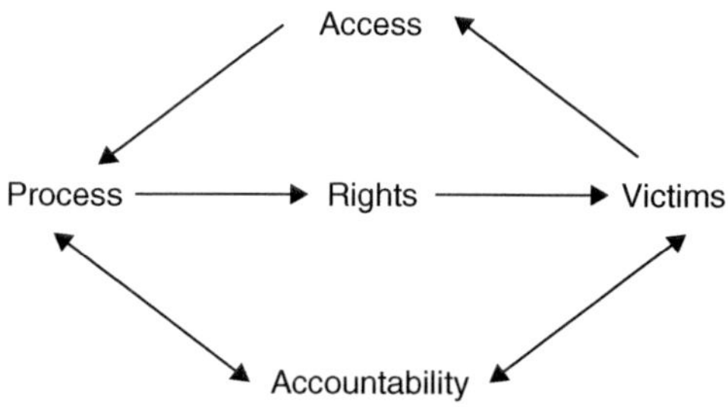

Figure 6.1 Accountability and justice transformation

rights are denied, or substantive and processual outcomes otherwise fail to satisfy the justice demands of victims and communities, the ideology and practice of accountability must be capable of responding to the corrective challenge by delineating the effective parameters and working principles necessary for transformative justice to function effectively.

The structure of accountability must also be sensitive to its own deficiencies as a controlling mechanism in the sense that it has to retain the flexibility to modify and respond to the knowledge of its own inadequacies where these are revealed. As we shall argue later, there may be occasions where the challenge faced is its own incapacity to rectify the problem with which it is faced. This may result from something much more fundamental than a technical or mechanistic failure, namely, the inability of the process itself to fulfil its mandate for justice transformation. This reflection back from structure to process and, more particularly, its implicitly legitimate extension of judicial discretionary power in such circumstances, is potentially catastrophic to the quest for impartial and representative justice.

Justice as presently conceptualised within international criminal trials serves a hegemonic model of accountability, exposing the failure of ICJ to engage with substantive and procedural rights beyond mere rhetoric. We have argued strongly that judicial discretionary power is a key variable for changing this notion of accountability to one that engages with significant justice demands and supports notions of access and rights grounded in humanitarian values which are consistent with their achievement. We argue that the context of justice delivery must be changed to one where the judge becomes central to determining the parameters of accountability within the transformed trial and for ensuring their sensitive interpretation and development during the course of the trial. Thus, the actual parameters of access and rights will reflect the compromise of relevant interests and demands derived from an ongoing process of dialogue and representation with all interested parties, especially victims and communities of justice. Within this supportive framework the wider relationship between the relative autonomy of the judiciary and notions of accountability within the transformed trial will develop.

Accountability and negotiated justice

To illustrate the significance of these arguments we begin by describing how the notion of negotiated justice currently relates to an enhanced role for judicial discretion within the transformed trial. The implications for the legitimacy of international penality and the governance of criminal justice resulting from the dangers posed to access and rights by institutionalised forms of negotiated justice are significant, driven as they are by a punitive dynamic and developing outside any foundational structures of accountability. For example, the effects of negotiated justice on proportionality in sentencing and the extent to which victims are able to participate in sentence decision-making are two key areas where institutional accountability is lacking. As presently conceived, the conceptual boundaries of proportionality are circumscribed by the partiality of retributive justifications for punishment, and it is this narrow vision which also dictates the philosophical remit and normativity of victim participation in trial decision-making. Satisfactory resolution of both these issues in the context of the transformed trial is therefore vital for the development of a more inclusive and rights-oriented form of international justice.

Furthermore, since norms of access and rights at the local and regional levels increasingly reflect their international development (and vice versa), questions of governance and accountability have inevitably become more acute. Consequently, the extent of the influence and control exercised by national and regional jurisdictions over the development of procedural norms at the international level is becoming increasingly significant, as is the reciprocal influence of international processes on local and regional forms of justice delivery. Although international humanitarian law and its institutionalisation clearly recognise the need for guarantees to protect access and rights to ICJ, the balance between due process and crime control considerations is currently weighted heavily in favour of punitive justice. Crucially for the transformation of trial justice, the relevant structures of accountability will need to ensure that this balance more accurately reflects the differing demands of retributive and restorative justice and the various constituencies requesting satisfaction. The capacity for justice administered by international courts and tribunals to reflect the plurality of the demands for justice made by victims and communities impacted by social conflict and war will be fundamental to achieving success in this respect.[3]

Access to trial justice and its reciprocal rights have been usefully conceptualised by Findlay (2002) in terms of:

- *access to the trial,* including diversionary mechanisms and the ability of victims to participate in pre-trial decision-making;
- *access by those within the trial,* including the ability of significant parties to influence discretionary decisions through, for example, allocution and/or impact statements; and
- *access to the community by the trial,* for example, the extent of community involvement in verdict delivery and sentencing, and the significance of trial outcomes.

All three notions have significance for pre-trial, trial and post-trial outcomes and suggest paradigmatic approaches against which to explore and evaluate norms of access and rights (Henham, 2004b).

However, the boundaries of accountability within which these paradigmatic principles operate will still be determined by whichever ideological constituency predominates, as resolved through the exercise of hegemonic power. ICJ based on new moralities argues otherwise. Within this inclusive context, it is possible to conceive of discrete issues, such as the nature and extent of victim participation, at each level of engagement in the trial. However, achieving the reality of justice transformation for ICJ involves changing its ideological context, and requires ongoing dialogue, recognition and assimilation of community expectations for the process. This is as true for conceptualising the scope and significance of accountability as it is for any other aspect of the transformation project.

Furthermore, the capacity for judicial discretionary power to deliver justice outcomes which resonate more effectively with a broader constituency of interests not only requires the social and cultural transformation of accountability as a conceptual tool within the changed ideology, but also the development of a reflexive structure for operationalising this new morality of justice.

Reconciling expediency and fair trial

A major obstacle to trial transformation is the culture of plea bargaining and its insidious effects on notions of due process. As so far developed and encouraged by the ICTY in particular, the concept of some kind of sentence discount being given in return for a guilty plea by the accused has been largely justified on the basis that it can make a significant contribution to truth-telling and thereby aid the process of peace and reconciliation in post-conflict societies. However, it is certainly arguable that a major underlying rationale for the encouragement of guilty pleas and the increasing use of plea agreements in the ICTY is the simple administrative expedient of speeding up the trial process with a consequent saving of resources, especially when faced with an increasing workload and deadline for case completion.

The dissenting judgment of Presiding Judge Wolfgang Schomburg in the *Deronjic* case[4] (see chapter 5) represents a significant attack on the use of plea agreements by the ICTY on the basis that they diminish the quality of justice by undermining the principle of proportionality. This argument hinges on the capacity for plea negotiations to distort truth in that the factual situations included in them are not only tailored to suit particular negotiated circumstances, but they are also selective in terms of the truths that offenders are willing to reveal. Plea agreements and guilty pleas produce sanitised and censored versions of the truth which tend to obfuscate the real extent of individual responsibility for international crimes, alienate victims and communities of interest and exclude the possibilities for restorative forms of justice.

Retribution and denunciation are the predominant penal rationales which sustain the penality of international criminal trials and which, therefore, provide the ideological framework for rationalising the practice of plea bargaining. The retributive balancing of moral claims to justice is crucially undermined by procedural devices like plea agreements,[5] because these impact directly on how harm and culpability are assessed for the purposes of determining the seriousness of the crime in specific cases. If guilty pleas were to be regarded intrinsically as mitigating factors, plea agreements could be conceptualised as particular examples of distributive justice, but this is hardly convincing where such techniques are used to support avowedly systemic interests under the guise of individualised sentencing. Furthermore, when the measure of retribution is itself highly questionable, as with all crimes where death ensues, sentence reduction in such circumstances may be seen as morally indefensible to many.[6] It may well be pertinent, therefore, to question how such self-serving devices as plea agreements can be morally justified in the case of those indicted for the 'crime of crimes'.[7]

To change the retributive context of plea bargaining in international trials requires an ideological shift towards trial transformation and a move towards the idea that procedural norms should promote moral reasons for punishment that reflect communitarian values.[8] Consequently, procedural norms should not be restricted by retributive considerations of proportionality and desert to the extent that their ability to serve social ends such as reconciliation and reparation for victims in post-conflict societies is nullified. Individualised punishment must therefore be able to embrace consequentialist themes so that procedural mechanisms such as plea agreements are informed by a rationality that promotes restorative as well as retributive forms of justice.

Within the current retributive context, the issue of consistency in sentencing practice is likely to become a significant one for the ICC as the throughput of cases increases. Inconsistency is likely to be exacerbated through the irrational use of plea agreements and guilty plea discounts because these mechanisms curtail the development of a coherent sentencing jurisprudence through the elaboration of general principles for sentencing. As such, it can be argued that these arrangements may pose a real threat to the rights of trial participants, especially victims. Furthermore, It will be difficult to challenge any plea agreement before the ICC which produces a disproportionate sentence on the basis that it prevents a trial on charges which reflect the accused's true criminality,[9] because the possibility of an appeal for an unjust and disproportionate sentence is effectively confined to allegations of disproportionality as regards the actual crimes charged and sentenced, rather than any negotiated way.[10] This is clearly deficient in establishing the necessary kind of accountability based on a fuller reflective account of what took place and its impact on victims and communities of justice. It simply reflects a notion of accountability where 'truth' is constrained and fashioned by retributive justice.

The problem of inconsistency is also exacerbated by the failure of the ICC Statute to create a hierarchy of offence categories which might inform the development of meaningful sentencing principles by the courts.[11] In addition, the only individual circumstances[12] specifically referred to as relevant to the Court on a review concerning reduction of sentence relate to the accused's willingness to cooperate with the Prosecutor, assistance in locating assets and the enforcement of the Court's judgments and orders in other cases.[13]

The scope of existing procedural norms

In terms of trial procedure, Article 65 of the ICC Statute provides that, where the accused admits guilt under Article 64.8(a), the Trial Chamber must satisfy itself that the admission was voluntary, that the accused understands the consequences and that the admission is supported by the charges and factual evidence then available to it.[14] Article 65.3 states that, if the Trial Chamber is not satisfied that that these conditions are established, it may deem the guilty plea as not having been made and proceed to trial. The presumption of innocence is enshrined in Article 66, which also confirms that the onus is on the Prosecution to prove to the satisfaction of the Court that the accused is guilty beyond all reasonable doubt.[15]

However, the ICC Statute and RPE are largely silent regarding the impact of a guilty plea on sentence. For instance, Article 76.1 refers only to the Trial Chamber's obligation to 'take into account the evidence presented and the submissions made', whilst Article 78.1 points vaguely to offence gravity and individual circumstances as being relevant to the determination of sentence. Rule 145 of the RPE does little more than explicitly mention the relevance of particular aggravating and mitigating circumstances, rather than providing guidance on how the Court might weigh such information. Rule 145.1(b) merely refers to the need to 'balance all the relevant factors', further examples of which are provided in Rule 145.1(c). Two examples of mitigating circumstances are listed in Rule 145.2(a) (i) and (ii), and six references are made to specific aggravating factors in Rule 145.2(b). Nowhere is there any explicit recognition or explanation of:

- whether a guilty plea counts as a mitigating factor; and if it does,
- what conditions, circumstances or principles should govern the impact the guilty plea has on the final sentence determination.

The absence of any discussion of these matters or their elaboration in the ICC Statute or RPE is a matter of considerable concern.

There is a need for entrenched rights of consultation and participation by victims in plea agreements and sentence discount decisions following a guilty plea before the ICC. At present, Article 65.4(a) of the ICC Statute contains a general injunction to the Trial Chamber in connection with proceedings where an admission of guilt has been made, whereby it may request the Prosecutor to present additional evidence, including witness testimony, if it 'is of the opinion that a more complete presentation of the facts of the case is required *in the interests of justice,*[16] in particular in the interests of victims' (emphasis added). Schabas (2007: 329) suggests that this provision appears to be aimed at situations where some kind of plea bargain is made between the Prosecutor and the Defence such that the rights and interests of victims may not otherwise be fully taken into account.[17] Another general injunction appears in Article 68.3, which is designed to ensure that the Court permits the 'views and concerns' of victims to be presented and considered at any stage in the proceedings where the 'personal interests of the victims' are affected, provided these are not inconsistent with notions of fair trial.

No doubt the sentiments embodied in these Articles are laudable, but scepticism regarding the extent to which crime control considerations will override any perceived need to obtain additional evidence in the interests of justice for victims remains. After all, the primary rationale of crime control is clearly evident in the sentencing judgments of the ad hoc tribunals where plea bargaining has taken place. Therefore, it cannot be stated with any conviction that victims' rights in the ICC are likely to be a paramount consideration. A more realistic assessment suggests that the *interests of justice* are more likely to be equated with notions of retributive justice[18] than victims' rights and reparation. The merging of retributive and restorative forms of justice in the context of trial transformation will provide the opportunity for the interests of trial participants and wider communities of interest to be identified and balanced. Within this framework it will be possible for personal autonomy to be maximised in a situation where the criminal process is being used to work towards integrated outcomes which promote peace and reconciliation in post-conflict states, because the rights and interests of individuals and groups and their relative demands for justice have been recognised.

The negotiations which preceded the formulation of the rules for the acceptance of guilty pleas in the ICC Statute were notable for the apparent misperception and suspicion on the part of civil law countries regarding the nature, effect and consequences of a guilty plea as commonly understood in common law jurisdictions (Behrens, 1998). However, as Behrens (1998: 439) points out, whilst the original ILC Draft[19] was treated with circumspection as it failed to specify the consequences of a guilty plea, detailed comparisons of the criteria used by judges in both trial styles in the sessions of the Preparatory Committee revealed remarkable similarities – particularly as regards judicial checks on whether the plea was made voluntarily and in full knowledge of the consequences. Thus the debate as to whether the procedure should be termed 'a guilty plea', 'confession of guilt' or 'admission of guilt' became superfluous, as is the provision eventually added to the ICC Statute, Article 65(5), which states:

> Any discussions between the Prosecutor and the Defence regarding modification of the charges, the admission of guilt or the penalty to be imposed shall not be binding on the Court.[20]

More important is the significance of the negotiating procedure in its broader sociological context. Clearly, a common theoretical assumption is the consensual nature of negotiation and presumed equality between the parties, yet the evidence tends to suggest that the impact of legal rules and procedures is merely to reinforce existing structural arrangements in society. As Tulkens (2002: 678) puts it:

> During proceedings, all the inequalities of the parties are reproduced – inequalities of condition (social origin, socio-economic level and cultural group), but also … inequalities of position.

Particularly significant in the present context is the potential reinforcement of social divisions and exclusion in the wider context of culture, be it transitional cultures or cultures fragmented by conflict, or the recognition of cultural pluralism. As such, negotiating procedures are potentially counterproductive for rationales promoting peace and reconciliation. The following aspects may be listed:

- the relative weakness of the accused's negotiating position as citizen of a subjugated state.;
- the absence of clear guidelines concerning the appropriateness of plea negotiations for the most serious crimes;
- cultural misunderstandings regarding the procedure and its effects;
- the extent to which victim communities should engage in negotiations;

- the fact that the procedure is conducted within the constraints of a retributive ideology;
- whether procedures based on expediency can engage with issues of social justice;
- obfuscation and lack of transparency regarding the nature of the process and its effects on the calculation of sentence

Our discussion of negotiated justice illustrates how procedural norms are context-specific to the extent that their legitimacy can only be assessed within the ideological framework in which they operate. Recent attempts by the ICTY to redefine or reposition plea agreements have simply served to compound the obfuscation already apparent in the model for justice delivery underwritten by existing international criminal institutions, as personified by the trial and the ideology of trial justice.

As we have argued, the moral legitimacy of the international trial form and its ideological justification, although symbolised as non-partisan through its universal appeal to humanitarian principles, is largely grounded in the penality of retributivism. Particularising ownership of this universal morality requires a paradigm shift in trial ideology through recognition that the legitimacy of trial justice must have concrete (i.e. contextual) significance and that this legitimacy is largely communitarian.

Our scenario

Plea bargaining provides an important example of how access to the trial itself may be restricted. We have noted how reliance on negotiated forms of justice by the ad hoc tribunals tends to compromise due process because of the retributive and adversarial context in which it takes place. Negotiated justice encourages disproportionate sentencing and obfuscation, but most importantly, as currently practised, it distorts 'truth' by excluding victims and communities from participating in the decision-making process.

Our scenario gives rise to a number of possibilities for negotiated justice, for example, the government's offer to cooperate with the ICC Prosecutor against General Lutobu in return for amnesty for the Minister of Information,[21] countered by the general's offer to cooperate in a prosecution against the government and the mining company in return for a (implied) reduction n the severity of the charges he might face, or a sentence reduction based on the defence of acting under superior orders.

Should the context for justice delivery retain its current retributive and adversarial dynamic, there is no doubt that acceptance of either negotiating position on the part of the ICC Prosecutor will produce a distorted trial outcome lacking moral legitimacy. The factual basis for the crimes eventually charged will be incomplete since the evidential 'truth' necessary for negotiated justice will be restricted to the minimum necessary for achieving retributive/adversarial goals. Not only will any negotiated outcome deny the possibility of testing the 'evidence' in open court, the acceptance of a charge as reflecting the totality of the accused's criminal conduct effectively denies the Court the opportunity to give full expression to the totality of that criminality through the imposition of a penal sanction which adequately reflects the seriousness of the crime(s) and the culpability of the offender. This may well prove to be the case should the ICC Prosecutor choose to deal with the general. There is no doubt that the effectiveness of international trial justice as a symbolic public expression and denunciation of past breaches of international criminal law will be seriously compromised if the totality of the punishment is not seen to be proportionate to the totality of the defendant's criminal conduct. There is also the very significant point that negotiated forms of justice are inappropriate where prosecutions for such grave crimes as genocide and crimes against humanity are contemplated.[22]

However, the more important issue of whether negotiated 'truth' is capable of contributing to justice depends on the capacity of the truth-finding body to deliver justice. We have argued for transformative trial justice on the basis that the legitimacy of the truth currently available in international trials is conditioned by retributive ideology and its effects on normative practice. Our argument acknowledges that for this kind of communicative theory to work, the ideology and norms of trial justice must relate to the moral contexts of action so criminalised. In addition, the outcomes of the trial should be conceived as forming part of a broader framework of transitional justice objectives. This can only be achieved if the Prosecutor engages with the issues of victimisation and community from the outset so that negotiations about charges and sentence are settled within the normative context of transformative justice. This means inclusion for victims and communities of justice in relevant decision-making, and recognition of the plurality of the 'truth' produced by the trial in determining the legitimacy attached to trial outcomes.

The Prosecutor's pre-trial obligations in delivering transformative justice (see chapter 5) will be concerned primarily with exploring ways for the trial programme to establish the collective 'truth' of what took place. This means that the facts to emerge through the adversarial and mediated stages of the trial should be accepted by all the relevant participants as a fair reflection of where collective liability lies, as well as providing a clear account of the role of particular individuals alleged to have taken part. Liability and accountability will reflect this communitarian and holistic approach. Reducing the ability of the trial to determine the parameters of collective liability for alleged acts of genocide would frustrate its capacity to promote compromise through mediated outcomes at later stages of the process, where mutually agreed in the trial programme as a beneficial way forward to achieve the objectives set for the trial and its participants.

Conceptualising accountability in the context of the transformed trial

This section identifies and elaborates some fundamental requirements for accountability within the context of justice transformation. It is essentially thematic, where appropriate using the phenomenon of negotiated justice to illustrate the need for change and the principles that should be established to inform the suggestions for transformation that follow. However, these themes and their elaboration should be considered as essential aspects of the rationality of justice transformation as generally conceived. Above all, they emphasise values of community, such as inclusivity and integration.

Identifying values

Evaluations of ICJ and systems of accountability for justice transformation must ensure that the values implicit in the following notions should underpin international trial justice.

Democracy

Notions of accountability in ICJ should ensure that relevant interests are identified, understood and given voice. This is not the mere rhetoric or tokenism typical of neoliberal polity, but rather affirmation of the essence of humanitarian justice; that is, to create new moralities which favour the legitimate interests of victim communities.

In the context of negotiated justice, as we have seen, there are significant deficiencies in victim engagement, this being primarily circumscribed by the foundation instruments of the international courts and tribunals. The ideology of retributive justice currently militates against representative forms of justice delivery, since it is in essence an ideology of control, one that facilitates agendas of social exclusion, alienation and suppression by political elites. Where states are subjugated, the relative weakness of its citizens is accentuated in proceedings that deliver a form of justice which fails to engage with their legitimate interests.

The true interests of victims, whether individual or collective, actual or potential, are also distorted by the adversarial nature of retributive justice delivery. In addition, norms promoting expediency, bureaucratisation and administrative efficiency do not engender social justice, but promote discrimination and social control. As Blad (2006: 108) suggests, a high level of institutionalisation, division of labour and bureaucracy is crucial in sustaining punitive and repressive criminal justice ideologies.[23]

The underlying absence of representation and participation inevitably corrupts the outcomes of negotiated justice, so that it is facile to suggest that the acceptance of responsibility which a plea of guilty implies can necessarily be associated with anything other than institutionally prescribed modes of defining crime and punishment. Further, as McCoy and Henham (2002) suggest, the true nature of the transaction being undertaken is inherently subjective and cannot be answered by the knowledge that remorse is sometimes real, or that consequentialist objectives may sometimes be achieved.

Justice is compromised rather than negotiated where law and structure fail to provide representative forms of accountability. For example, allegations of undue leniency in sentencing before the ICTY would be determined according to legalistic criteria, rather than being forged through balancing the objective exigencies of legal form against the subjective emotionality of individual and collective responses to the criminality as identified and processed. In such circumstances, the normativity of law is distorted, and its authority and internal integrity flawed by the ideological straitjacket within which it is forced to operate. This failure to infuse ICJ with the possibilities for achieving representative and humanitarian justice devalues current structures of accountability and renders them partial in their scope and effect.

Honesty

Accountability in ICJ is concerned with sustaining the foundations for trust and credibility. As argued earlier, transformed ICJ should reflect access to a more holistic and representative form of justice, with rights grounded in dialogues of justice with victim communities. Consequently, rights should be socially responsive regulators of social justice developed from humanitarian values, and imbued with an instrumental capacity to promote peace and reconstruction through sensitive interpretation and dialogue. Thus, we argue that the ideology of 'truth' should inform the policy and structures of ICJ in contextually insightful ways.

The nexus between 'truth' and accountability is absolutely crucial to the notion of trial transformation and the credibility of merging retributive and restorative forms of trial justice. We regard the conceptual dichotomy between 'truth' and 'justice' in terms of relativity as being counterproductive to the advancement of world peace and future human coexistence (Findlay, 2007). The unifying principles of humanitarianism in our conception of justice argue against such a divisive and fundamentally negative approach by promoting the morality of 'truth'. This morality is essential to the continued peaceful coexistence of humanity because it recognises that the principles of 'truth' are universal.[24]

Speaking in the context of the South African Truth and Reconciliation Commission, Wilson (2001: 13) argues that it is necessary to move beyond the ideological discourse of humanity to engage with cultural, ethnic or other social dimensions, as well as recognising the pragmatic reality of justice as a fluid and recursive concept (Wilson, 2001: 199). In concurring with this general conclusion, we maintain that trial transformation bridges the conceptual gap between ideology and relative reality by embracing and operationalising the notion of legitimacy within the context of international criminal trials. Thus, as Balint (2001: 148) suggests, effecting institutional and structural change by restoring the justice interests of victim and victim communities in post-conflict states will tend to promote political reconciliation.

Consequently, our interpretation of the relationship between accountability and honesty within the context of trial transformation is firmly aligned to the notion that *legitimacy* itself is a recursive and contingent affair. The role of accountability is to ensure that the integrity of rights and interests is consistently recognised and given effect through trial transformation.

Transparency

Accountability should promote truth-telling by making certain that the justice demands of victims and communities of interest are not obfuscated by the very processes that are designed to protect them, either in their recognition (initial and continuing), transmission or implementation. Similarly, the rationalisation and delivery of trial outcomes must be opaque and strategically effective. As such, judicial reasoning and the exercise of discretionary power must be continually scrutinised to maximise its instrumental capacity for delivering outcomes which promote the values and norms of trial transformation.

Mediation

Structures of accountability should facilitate the reconciliation of conflicting interests (see generally Beardsley et al., 2006). Viewed in this context accountability should be concerned with supporting a forum where restorative themes have the capacity for equal influence, together with those associated with punitive forms of justice. Hence, justice interventions should be directed towards establishing whatever normative structures will bring about healing (whether restorative or retributive or blended paradigms) by breaking the cycle of brutality that characterises the egregious crimes with which perpetrators are charged. The emphasis here is therefore to move beyond destructiveness, which may not necessarily mean moving beyond a need to satisfy the desire for punitive justice. Accountability here must ensure that pathways of diversion and mediation, and the institutionalised structures that support them, are not characterised by punitive labelling, allowing conflicts of interests to be centred, as O'Malley (2006: 229) suggests, rather than operating from an assumption that one party is necessarily in the wrong and the other in the right.

Peacemaking

Accountability in ICJ should promote outcomes which engage with the promotion of peace and reconciliation. The argument that international crimes should be tried in domestic courts to provide their outcomes with contextual significance actually *supports* the notion that retributive and restorative forms of justice should merge internationally, and that the form of international process should be flexible and responsive to the demands of victims and communities of justice in post-conflict societies.

This book is concerned with the reality of international penality, recognising the fact that international trial structures, like the ICC, already exist and are destined to function within a fragmented moral universe, dominated by the hegemonic aspirations of powerful states rather than united through the desire to achieve some cosmopolitan vision of justice grounded in humanitarian principles. Whilst certainly not dismissing arguments about the relative merits of international, national, regional or hybrid processes for dealing with breaches of international humanitarian law, we envisage trial transformation as a sanguine and pragmatic approach to institutional reform which reflects our fervent belief in the merging of restorative and retributive forms of justice delivery for international trials. Given this reality, and our clear endorsement of the importance of context (Findlay and Henham, 2005), our approach to trial transformation and the consequent development of discrete trial programmes (as suggested in chapter 5) suggests a partial transplantation of context, namely, the context of penality that exists within a specific domestic jurisdiction where war and social conflict have occurred. As such, it may be viewed conceptually as a way of shaping or giving coherence to the disparate contexts of ICJ, of disengaging structure, but transplanting it within a more coherent and inclusive moral universe driven by the rationality of humanitarian justice.

This notion is no different from that which sustains other structures of international governance. However, structures of ICJ need to engage with the human mind and will in ways which mere regulatory bodies do not because the perceived legitimacy of their outcomes actually validates them. In other words, their very existence as credible and effective structures for conflict resolution depends on the nature of the recursive relationship that exists between structure and human agency; so that for peacemaking to take place, there must be substance and reliability in that relationship.

Clearly, since international justice cannot by definition be justice delivered *in the locus of conflict*, it can never be equivalent or act as a substitute for the latter as a matter of objective fact. However, perceptions of justice are relative, so the subjectivity of penal outcomes, and their manifestation in physical (so objective) terms, has no temporal or spatial dimensions beyond those that are fixed through process. For this reason, international justice is in a sense transcendental; it particularises the human experience of conflict and locates it within a normative bubble which floats above conventional localised forms of accountability. Therefore, justice can only be grounded through its direct engagement with humanity, which is why we argue in chapter 1 for humanitarian foundations for justice which can direct the moral power of law for resolving conflict.

The normative context of justice delivers accountability without necessarily delivering responsibility beyond the narrow context of retributive stigmatisation. Accountability must promote understandings of events which engage with *real* attitudes, perceptions and understandings of *what actually took place*, thereby linking humanity in its resolution of the resulting pain of conflict. Hence, the setting for humanitarian justice must be capable of delivering something that moves beyond the sheer destructiveness of crime itself.

As Roche (2003: chapter 2) suggests, informal structures of accountability are as important as formal ones in promoting restorative outcomes and enhancing legitimacy through its instrumental effect on the quality of process. However, levels of accountability, moving through informality to formality, mean nothing if they are not rooted in foundations where restorative and retributive justice forms are given equal prominence, so that the regulatory function accountability performs is not simply regarded as an adjunct to conventional retributive, tariff-based sentencing prescriptions, but something that maintains the space and instrumental capacity for deliberation (Roche, 2003: 234–9), which judicial discretionary power requires.

Reconstruction

The capacity for building structures of accountability which foster peace and reconciliation ultimately depends on identifying ways of operationalising outcomes. This can be conceptualised within the following frameworks of accountability:

- *Reactive accountability* – ensuring that punishment reflects pluralistic justice demands.
- *Outcome accountability* – ensuring outcomes reflect perceptions held about the legitimacy of international trials within each community of interest and the purposes which those communities would like to see achieved by the trial process.
- *Processual accountability* – ensuring the nature and form of the process thought appropriate to facilitate the purposes described.
- *Purposeful accountability* – ensuring the kinds of outcome regarded as likely to contribute to the desired purposes.

In addition to their apparent linkage and interdependence, the above notions of accountability are all tied to the same objective: delivering perceptions of justice which resonate with the expectations of individuals or groups having a legitimate interest in ICJ more broadly, and those specific conflict situations which give rise to proceedings in particular. Superficially, at the theoretical and humanitarian level, each citizen of the world has a nominal interest in accountability for international crimes simply by virtue of belonging to the human race, as do all individuals, groups and communities specifically implicated by international courts and tribunals through the exercise of their jurisdictional functions.

As elaborated in chapter 1, we envisage conflict resolution through the transformed trial as a methodological imperative so that judicial discretion is regarded as a key variable for changing this notion of accountability to one that engages with significant justice demands and supports rights consistent with their achievement. Our belief that ICJ should be viewed as instrumental and transformative is evidenced by our equation of access to justice with a distinct conceptualisation of victim participation, which suggests that victims and communities of justice should participate fully and have a significant input into discretionary decision-making processes occurring throughout the criminal trial.

To achieve this level of accountability suggests that justice delivery through trial transformation must engage with the hegemonic realities of international and domestic power relations and how these impact on the role of ICJ as a context for effective governance. As Findlay (2008b) argues, however, the certainty of any productive engagement with relevant interests is by no means assured where competing moral frameworks inhabit the contextual terrain for rebuilding social cohesion. More particularly, the prospect for establishing any constructive dialogue within a supportive milieu presupposes a context for governance and accountability which will nurture a shared desire for restoring cultural and social cohesion. Herein rests the potential for ICJ as a form of governance to move beyond its conventional paradigmatic status as hegemony.[25] By converting its rhetoric of humanitarian justice into a coherent moral platform for delivering justice in localised contexts, ICJ can provide the necessary social impetus for understanding, fairness and consistency as the necessary foundations to repairing trust and healing broken communities.

Nevertheless, it is important not to attribute to ICJ a role in the governance of civil society which transcends its ideological and practical capabilities. As Braithwaite (2002: 207) suggests, institutional renewal is a precondition for engaging restorative justice in the battle to transform peace and build a society which actually enforces international humanitarian and human rights law. Where ICJ becomes crucial is in its exposure of 'truth' and its capacity to redefine the structures which regulate the behaviour of individual citizens in civil society. Its power lies in its ability to substitute the domestic politics of alienation, exclusivity and social control with a response based on humanitarian values which grounds individual autonomy within communities of interest. These foundations for social morality are, as we argue in chapter 1, essential preconditions for human life.

Globalisation continually redefines the 'contexts of control' and thus the contexts of accountability, 'leaving international criminal justice to offer a more accessible, heuristic and normatively convincing role in global governance and conflict resolution'.

Our scenario

On peacemaking

Two issues are crucial in terms of our scenario. The first is the contention that informal structures of accountability are as important as formal ones in promoting restorative outcomes and enhancing legitimacy. It is clear that in the rural communities of Cornucopia there is widespread suspicion on both sides of the legitimacy of urban and centralised criminal justice governance. For accountability to engage with context in this scenario there should be an invitation to explore indigenous forms of justice and the significance of these structures and their outcomes for the cultures of each tribal grouping.

It will be important from the outset, and certainly in terms of nominating interests and agreeing the trial programme, for there to be some recognition of how these indigenous forms of justice sit with the common law colonial system. As Guest (1999) identifies in Canada, there are three justice system models in operation:

1. the main criminal justice system that uses raw coercive force as its power base;
2. a criminal justice system that is attempting to augment itself with restorative justice processes and reconstitute its image after years of oppressing Aboriginal peoples;
3. Aboriginal justice systems within communities that use respect and teaching as the basis of knowledge for living together.

Model 2 does not feature in our scenario. However, Cornucopia certainly appears to reflect the coercive, retributive, adversarial, hegemonic model 1. Notwithstanding, we do not know whether either, or both, indigenous cultures have structures that focus primarily on restorative or retributive justice. Yet, as Guest (1999) points out, in the Navajo Justice and Harmony Ceremony, the Peacemaker does not ask if an existing relationship is bad or good. The evaluation of what is good and bad is not present. There exists only the constant flux of the movement of relationships within the community in the direction of discord or harmony. How harmony is attained when there is discord is a primary goal of the community. Re-establishing harmony may involve actions which would be labelled retributive by Western justice commentators, but this would be to miss the point that the rationale for the action is completely different. In fact, it derives from a fundamentally different vision of humanity and the nature of the human condition. As discussed in chapter 1, this vision has a holistic view of the individual constituted through the community.

The idea of individuals or groups coming into conflict and restoring harmony is, of course, restorative. The seizure of land, killing of livestock and dishonour of rape described in the second event of the so-called 'reign of terror' in our scenario can all add to discord and precipitate victimisation on a greater and more violent scale. However, as Henderson (1995) argues, to focus on these effects alone would be to ignore the hegemony of colonialism and the current partisan political hegemony which conceals and reinforces the systemic domination of indigenous peoples.

Such observations underline the need for the intervention of the ICC in our scenario to form part of a wider coordinated re-evaluation of indigenous justice culture on the island within the broader context of how to develop future governance structures and their normative foundations.

The second issue for our scenario derives from the proposition that restorative and retributive forms of justice must be given equal prominence so that the regulatory function accountability performs is not simply regarded as an adjunct to retributive justice. There are some important lessons to be learned from hybrid or internationalised trial forms when thinking about this issue in the context of the relationship of international criminal trials with indigenous or local structures of accountability. For example, Cockayne (2005) analyses the apparent paradox of why the combination of international resources and localised forms of justice so often fails to deliver the kind of justice which commands the moral authority of either the 'international community' or the relevant national community. He draws attention to the problems of Prosecutors having to denounce criminality in the name of both communities to diffuse tension; the fact that outcomes tend to criminalise behaviours often regarded as normal in transitional societies; and the failure of international criminal law and its agents to comprehend local social practices, regardless of their compatibility with international norms.

This last observation is particularly poignant in terms of our scenario because, as Cockayne (2005: 464) suggests, the result is exclusion from the trial of the voice of the local community and therefore the 'truth' it purports to establish. This tends to undermine the moral mission of international criminal law as presently conceived, namely, to punish and deter the perpetrators of international crimes (Cockayne, 2005: 466). There is no denying that local and traditional practices are relevant. However, it is not just a question of hybridisation. What Cockayne argues is also relevant to scenarios such as ours, where indigenous forms of justice and domestic forms coexist, albeit dysfunctionally, and intervention on the part of the ICC is proposed.

The key point is that the effectiveness of any attempt to regulate through retributive or restorative justice, and the appropriate balance, will depend on the extent to which local forms of justice are regarded as legitimate, as having moral authority, and the reasons why this is so. Crucially, the answers to these questions will depend on the moral basis on which these judgments are made and accepted by those who have been victimised by the conflict.[26] In other words, the issue is essentially one of understanding what constitutes the different contexts of justice at the local and international levels, and making a reasoned assessment of how different structures can work together in achieving the transition from conflict to peace, before intervention takes place.

This is precisely the kind of comparative contextual analysis that we advocate in chapter 7 in our discussion of the steps that need to be taken before setting up a trial programme. The difference our approach and that described by Cockayne (2005), where existing divisions are magnified through intervention because of a manifest failure to engage with context, is that the moral authority of the process, and therefore its findings and outcomes, are agreed before trial intervention begins because they are informed by the ideology and norms of transformative justice.

On reconstruction

The influence of transformative trial justice on institutional renewal is important in our scenario since the domestic courts and legislative foundations which support them are dysfunctional. There is also doubt about the capacity of local criminal courts to deal with any prosecutions that the ICC decides to proceed with, and a lack of confidence on both sides in the government's compromise of a truth and reconciliation commission.

Contrary to Braithwaite's bottom-up, restorative-led approach, trial transformation would form part of a coordinated multi-agency approach towards achieving transitional justice. It would form part of greater scheme of state regeneration. Herein lies transformative justice's potential to influence the governance framework of our island state. The trial's potential contribution to this would be resolved in the pre-trial status conference and would clearly depend on compromises on both sides. For example, there would need to be acceptance of the capacity of transformed trials to deliver impartial outcomes, whose findings are perceived by both sides as based on 'truth', as well as a willingness by both factions to see the trial as a restorative mechanism designed to make a significant contribution to the foundations of governance. This means parties seeing beyond past conflict, looking towards the road to peace and acknowledging the trial as one means for achieving this through outcomes promoting mutual understanding and reconciliation. Such a concept embraces the idea of collective accountability by emphasising the importance of bringing about a symbolic coming together of the conflict groups and engendering a unity of purpose in building a holistic future for both.

Developing principles for accountability in the transformed trial

We identify the following as areas requiring the development of principles for accountability in the transformed trial:

Norms – The development of substantive and conduct norms of accountability consistent with the ideology necessary to sustain justice transformation.

Communication structures – Principles concerned with ensuring the reliability and predictability of communication structures consistent with exploiting trial pathways that maximise the opportunities for outcomes promoting peace and reconstruction within post-conflict societies.

Responsibility – Establishing understandings of legal, institutional and operational responsibility for ensuring conformity to norms and their effective enforcement, which are consistent with the objectives of trial transformation.

Transparency – Democratising the decision-making process by removing normative and processual impediments to understanding within trial decision-making. This then establishes an interactive context which encourages forms of discourse directed towards the promotion of conciliatory and reconstructive outcomes for international trials.

Legitimacy – Making certain that the ideology and process of international criminal trials is inclusive, integrated and directed towards recognising and balancing conflicting demands for justice; and ensuring consistency of approach within this context.

We elaborate these headings in what follows, utilising by way of illustration (where appropriate) our example of the role of negotiated justice within the context of international criminal trials.

Establishing normativity

We suggest that the establishment of effective normative regulation requires adherence to the following principles:

- Ensuring the principled development of substantive and procedural norms – this means ensuring that such norms are interpreted in accordance with the ideology and purposes of the transformed trial.
- Establishing the boundaries of processual activity, including relationships – this extends particularly to making certain that, where the trial context admits, participants are not coerced or discourses constrained by unduly restrictive conduct norms, such as those designed to support a framework for retributive justice delivery.

- Enabling and clarifying norms of access and rights – these being dependent on an agreed formula for the balancing of public and private interests and outcomes guaranteed as freely negotiated and unfettered (Braithwaite and Strang, 2000).
- Ensuring transparency in decision-making – this extending to input and linkage, and feedback following on from decisions and outcomes.
- Ensuring responsibility for violations and failure to fulfil obligations is identified and remedied – 'responsibility' here being interpreted as coextensive with consequentialist aspirations for reintegration and the reconstruction of damaged relationships within communities.
- Ethical surveillance – this extends the strictures of accountability to the establishment of norms for the conduct of trial professionals, experts and victim/community representatives operating within a context of transformed justice delivery.

Ensuring accountability

Delivery of accountability for the transformed trial will be driven by objectives which emphasise the core principles for effective regulation described above. This suggests two main areas of accountability.

Discrete function

- Evaluating process outcomes.
- Comparing objectives and outcomes (ensuring restorative and punitive justice address similar constituencies).
- Suggesting immediate solutions.

One of the most difficult tasks in developing forms of accountability for the transformed trial will be maintaining an appropriate balance between retributive and restorative forms of justice. Despite the fact that trial transformation envisages structures which facilitate the merging of retributive and restorative justice consistent with the ideology of humanitarianism described in chapter 1, it would be naive to ignore the tensions for ICJ penality that this will produce. These tensions will be trial-specific in terms of establishing the contested terrain for justice requiring resolution. In addition, trial transformation will pose serious questions regarding the operational parameters for accountability when applying principles of humanitarian justice across cases.

The encroachment of criteria for accountability based on proportionality, fairness and restraint are not simply the concerns of retributive ideology. They will, of course, be integral to the achievement of justice within and across the transformed context for delivery. In this, the balance between restorative and retributive outcomes will not depend on a predetermined hierarchical penal status, as typified by some current hybridised manifestations (see Roberts and Roach, 2003). Instead, the proper context for reconciliation of retributive and restorative concerns will be developed from understandings of their relationship within relevant communities of justice.

Equating the concept of balance with that of proportionality within the context of trial transformation will not therefore be concerned with placing notional limits on the appropriateness of particular penal responses depending on whether or not they are restorative or retributive in character. Excessive leniency, harshness, discrimination or oppression where perceived as matters for concern will be countered through the provision of a strong framework of rights. Accountability will be delivered by ensuring that judicial and prosecutorial discretionary power is exercised within the holistic justice context of humanitarianism. Accepting the utilitarian maximising principle (see chapter 1) as a guide to instrumental decision-making within the trial will ensure that all claims for legitimacy are argued effectively and acted on appropriately.

Remedial functions

- Access to structures.
- Potential for policy changes (the need to bypass structures of formal accountability associated with punitive justice).
- Potential for ideological change (addressing the ideological 'power imbalance').

With regard to structures of access and governance there are several deficiencies in existing forms of accountability. For example, the extent to which breaches of human rights norms associated with the operation of procedural devices such as the guilty plea and plea agreements in international criminal trials might provide grounds for appeal or review is currently problematic. The position is uncertain since there are no specific provisions contained in the foundation instruments of any international criminal trial institution which deal with what is likely to happen when the sentence it imposes infringes human rights norms falling outside the ambit of its rules as presently interpreted.[27]

In addition to representing a manifest failure in accountability, this situation clearly has significant implications for the legitimacy of international punishment and criminal justice governance more generally. These derive from the dangers posed to human rights by institutionalised forms of negotiated justice produced by supranational organisations such as the ICC, driven as they are by a punitive dynamic and developing outside any institutionalised mechanisms of accountability. For example, the effects of negotiated justice on proportionality in sentencing and the extent to which victims are able to participate in sentence decision-making are key areas where institutional accountability is lacking. It is therefore vital to address both issues for the development of a more inclusive and rights-oriented form of ICJ.

Furthermore, since human rights norms at the local and regional levels are increasingly likely to reflect their international development (and vice versa), questions of governance and accountability will inevitably become more acute. Consequently, the extent of the influence and control exercised by national and regional jurisdictions over the development of procedural norms will become increasingly significant for human rights, as will the reciprocal influence of international processes on local and regional forms of justice delivery. Since international humanitarian law clearly recognises that guarantees should exist to protect individual rights, it is imperative that courts exercising international criminal jurisdiction provide a balance between maintaining the presumption of innocence through due process and the justification of punishment in its nature and extent. The capacity for justice administered by international courts and tribunals to reflect the plurality of the demands for justice made by victims and communities impacted by social conflict and war will be fundamental in achieving success in this respect.

There are further areas of difficulty for accountability in the sphere of appeals and review. Although, as Zappala (2003: 173) observes, the broader approach adopted in drafting the ICC appeals provisions, as compared with the ICTY and ICTR, probably reflects a move towards the civil law paradigm, the ICC Appeals Chamber is currently unable to develop a coherent sentencing jurisprudence informed by a rational statement of aims.[28] Additionally, the scope for constructive dissent may be radically circumscribed, since separate and dissenting opinions are normally restricted to points of law.[29] Since appeals by the Prosecutor are likely to focus on the question of undue leniency in sentences determined by the Trial Chamber, the Appeals Chamber will inevitably be limited in its ability to use such appeals to affirm parameters for sentencing practice. An important additional problem for the ICC Appeals Chamber in restricting its ability to develop a coherent sentencing practice will be the basis on which the issue of undue leniency is to be determined.[30] This decision will reflect significantly on whether the broad discretionary power of ICC judges can be harnessed to engage in any relational sense with particular aims or purposes for sentencing so that the penal aspirations and the desires of victims and communities for justice are deployed to safeguard the integrity of its legal norms and their interpretation through everyday procedural process.

Our scenario

In terms of *discrete accountability*, there are problems in our scenario relating to what the appropriate balance between retributive and restorative forms of justice should be. These will involve different perceptions of what may be proportionate and fair on both sides. Discrimination will be countered through the provision of a strong framework of rights.

As for *remedial accountability*, since particular outcomes will be sanctioned only if victims and communities of justice on both sides deem it appropriate, accountability will be predominantly localised and contextual. However, effective accountability can only be achieved if the outcomes are perceived to diffuse the perceived risk of victimisation on both sides. Working towards such an integrated and holistic outcome for the whole island will require a profound understanding of how transformed trial outcomes can contribute towards rebuilding the frameworks of governance. This will involve access to structures of transitional justice and an inclusive vision for the role of transformed trial outcomes.

Performing the remedial functions of monitoring ideology and policy requires different structures of formal accountability from those associated with punitive justice. These merely serve to sustain the hegemony of existing power relations and prevent the development of ICJ as a truly legitimate force for global governance. Increasing community control over justice delivery will ensure that it responds to local demands, thus precipitating the demise of purely or predominantly retributive solutions. Since particular outcomes will be sanctioned only if victims and communities of justice deem it appropriate, accountability will be predominantly localised and contextual, so encouraging a profound understanding of the relationship between harm and victimisation through developing contact and cooperation between conflict groups. Accountability will correspondingly focus on addressing the tensions that exist between risk and victimisation. By emphasising the relational context of responses to harm, democratic accountability and the protection of individual rights and civil liberties will become integral elements of ICJ. Thus, frameworks of accountability for ICJ will cease to be remote from their normative foundations, thereby encouraging vertical as well as horizontal contexts of integration (Henham, 2005: chapter 7).

External accountability

Our discussion of internal accountability has focused largely on the accountability of the judge (justicial personality) and how best to ensure access as we see it in humanitarian justice and the rights which are thereby endorsed. In addition, we have empowered the Prosecutor to determine contested victim interests and manage their access to later sites of trial decision-making. With victim communities central to our re-envisaged constituency for ICJ, the judge and Prosecutor are key players in ensuring the accountability of access, inclusivity and integration from a victim perspective.

However, consistent with the governance considerations which conclude this book, we suggest that there is another, equally important, level of external accountability where the transformed trial (and the justicial personality) will ensure ICJ its place in a separation-of-powers global governance model (Findlay, 2008b). In such a model, ICJ makes the other central interests in global governance accountable to humanitarian principles and communitarian rights rather than to sectarian political hegemony and discriminatory rights (Findlay, 2008b: chapter 7). ICJ in this model is crucial in requiring accountability from a more pluralist and culturally sensitive regulatory framework, with humanity (the global community) as the governance beneficiary.

In advancing a separation-of-powers paradigm for global governance, with ICJ an essential part of the judicial pillar, we acknowledge the model nature of this position and its limitations. Experience shows us that where a separation-of-powers model is invoked in liberal democracies, it is almost impossible for the judiciary to remain entirely outside and independent of the workings of the legislature and the executive. Having said that, the enunciation of global governance in the sense of a constitutional legality is relatively recent. In the context of global governance, the three pillars are at an early stage of development, and there is a clear and expressed reliance on ICJ as essential in the governance regulatory framework (Findlay, 2008b: chapter 2). In these circumstances confidence in the potential of ICJ and its justicial professionals to police communitarian rights and responsibilities as influences by the other two pillars, we suggest, is both actual and attainable. With the transformed trial, its humanitarian normative framework and its commitment to legitimate victim interests, both truth and fact, become tools in ensuring the accountability of global governance beyond sectarian political hegemony (Findlay, 2008b: chapter 1).

ICJ and its formal dedication to individualised liability and punishment have produced a narrow, partisan conceptualisation of human rights protection which excludes communitarian cultures. Furthermore, the tension between the narrow, formal regulation of ICJ and the considerably more pluralist regulatory opportunities offered by *alternative* ICJ paradigms has confounded the development of more effective resolutions for victim communities. As argued elsewhere (Findlay, 2008b), injecting a more communitarian focus through the transformation of ICJ will necessarily stimulate a reconsideration of pluralism in regulatory choices, along with a new normative framework to foster diversity in the protection of humanity.

Along with pluralism and an opening up to the wider possibilities of victim access to regulatory processes and outcomes, the challenges for accountability in terms of victim interests are made all the greater. By situating the dynamics of the transformed trial, as we have, in the enhanced discretion of the justicial professional (see chapter 5), it could fairly be argued that the governance capacity for ICJ is even more open to the preferences and prejudices of key decision-makers. We argue, therefore, that none of these developments towards plurality in regulation and their discretionary implications can wisely advance in a governance sense without a keen eye on the consequential accountability conditions.

Once the internal preconditions for transformed ICJ are declared accountable (internal accountability) the access, inclusivity and integration offered to legitimate victim interests has the capacity to enhance global governance by making it responsible to the communities over which it holds sway. The ability of ICJ to take on a role in effectively delivering accountability frameworks (something approaching the independent judicial review in a separation of powers paradigm) for global governance, necessitates the excision from political patronage and the selective citizenship it affords. A move away from the service of the dominant political alliance towards communities of justice is how this will be achieved. Preceding this repositioning, and for it to take hold in the long term, the normative location of ICJ within the service of humanity needs to be declared as both the crucial incentive for ICJ and the measure of world order in global governance.

As we argue in chapter 1, although appearing committed to the security of humanity, retributive justice institutions and individual liability processes (the international trial as it currently is) are failing to engage more than extraneously with legitimate victim community interests. This moral paradox presents a normative challenge for the development of communities of justice, when these communities as we indicate later are the structural domain in which ICJ will give its effect to accountable global governance. Hence, the task for governance (including ICJ) remains one of asserting acceptable forms of moral dominion over resistant as well as compliant communities (Findlay, 2008), and thereby applying wider citizenship and standing on which access, inclusivity and integration will rest. If there is ever to be an achievable world order that is more consensual than compelled, then an integrated, inclusive and accessible criminal justice will be essential to maintain it. These features of transformed ICJ can then represent wider measures of accountability for global governance dedicated to humanity and not simply hegemony.

We have indicated how the theory and practice of communitarian justice may be injected into the structures and formal procedures of ICJ by engaging with procedural traditions which have to date largely remained outside international trial practice. As this features in formal ICJ, a more pluralist community engagement will follow. Global governance will in turn need to move away from military intervention, civil sanction and criminal justice models of regulation, including other flexible pluralist regulatory forms. Such a development will mean that ICJ, along with other important regulatory frames, can embrace more diverse cultural influences and contextual deliberations than those narrowly prescribed through the present hegemony/governance nexus.

The influence of the dominant political culture over the development of ICJ thereby will be lessened. For these reasons, we are convinced that ICJ has a powerful opportunity to impose on global governance a transformed and transforming normative influence, and a victim sensitivity which will determine the measure of world order and good governance. This suggests that if legitimacy is re-grounded in victim communities through a normative and practical humanitarian focus (Findlay, 2008b), global governance can move its risk/security regulatory fixation away from politicised terror towards violence against the global community.

These links between the ideals of humanitarian justice and a greater role for ICJ as a form of governance are set out in Figure 6.2.

Humanitarianism – values and norms
What we define as fundamental values of humanity provide the moral foundations for transformative trial justice and its delivery (elaborated in chapter 1).

Communitarianism – obligations and rights
The delivery of humanitarian justice principles through the transformed trial depends on identifying the interests of victims and communities of justice, and giving effect to them (explained and justified in chapter 2).

Pluralism – structures and practices
Recognising that pluralism and diversity rather than hegemony and conflict will infuse other structures and practices of ICJ with the morality and norms of transformative justice (expanded in Findlay, 2008b, and located in transformed trial justice in chapter 7).

Governance – (re)conciliation and peace
Infusing global governance with ICJ's values and norms will promote peace.

Figure 6.2 Dimensions of international criminal justice as governance

Figure 6.2 envisages four key dimensions to our argument for ICJ's enhanced role in global governance. As we argue in chapter 1, our vision of transformative trial justice is based on the values and principles of humanitarianism. In order give effect to these and provide greater 'legitimacy' for trial outcomes (see chapters 2 and 4), we propose structures and practices which are developed from a communitarian perspective of justice, one that recognises that these competing views, especially those of victims and victim communities, must be identified and accommodated within transformed modes of justice delivery. However, such notions of relational justice can only contribute to governance if the choices are directed towards recognising pluralism and diversity rather than informed by hegemony and conflict. In the simplest sense, if citizenship and standing continue to be predetermined against victor's justice, then access to the transformed trial will remain unjustly and inevitably constricted (Findlay, 2008b: chapter 5).

What we are suggesting is that the infusion of other institutions and practices of global governance with the ideological and normative dimensions of transformative ICJ can provide a significant stimulus towards repositioning the focus of global governance. As Tamanaha (2007) argues, taking governance frameworks away from the risk/security nexus (Findlay, 2008b) and moving them towards a practical engagement with other, more pluralist regulatory concerns, such as economic market freedom, environmental rehabilitation, educational emancipation and labour equity, will democratise and broadcast interests and structures of global governance. This potential for infusing global governance with values and norms of (re)conciliation and compromise, rather than hegemony and conflict, has considerable significance for promoting world order in a humanitarian deviee.

The relationship between humanitarian transformative justice and ICJ as a moral and normative foundation for global governance is reciprocal. By this we mean that the extent to which the values and norms of transformed ICJ can infuse other aspects of global governance will be proportionate to its acceptance as an exemplar of best practice. In this sense good governance arises out of, and hence ensures, the communitarian and cultural integrity essential for the emancipation of human rights generically. Criminal sanctions and trial-focused truth and responsibility are regulatory mechanisms, but not the only regulators of an accountable governance commitment which enables the victims of global violence to receive rights protections indicative of governance best practice.

The purpose of this book is to invite the reader to engage with such ideas as practical possibilities. To support our argument for the rights potential of ICJ, we argue for a governance model of accountability beyond that for ensuring transformative justice. Here we suggest how the values and norms of transformative justice can infuse ICJ with imperatives for global governance which recognise pluralism and diversity. Chapter 8 includes a deeper discussion of how to develop the potential of ICJ for global conflict resolution and so release governance from partisan political domination.

At this point, however, it is useful to flag up the crucial location of ICJ accountability within dynamic communities of justice. Chapter 2 details the nature, composition, location and integration of these communities. In essence they are a meeting of principal stakeholders in ICJ. But they are more than just a place for negotiating particular or mutual interests. As true communities they coalesce with an eventual common purpose: the achievement of humanitarian justice. It would be naive not to identify the very different starting points for stakeholders on the road to a justice communion. In addition, a sophisticated understanding of actual communities of justice wrestling with the sort of contentions apparent in our scenario demands close attention to important decision sites on the way to a shared justice resolution. These decision-sites directed towards the trial process are detailed throughout the analysis in this book. They will be crucial to the type of communitarian justice which results from the various regulatory mechanisms chosen by any community of justice to solve its justice requirements. A detailed contextual interrogation of how any particular community of justice reaches consensus will also require getting to know the parties and relationships which form pathways of influence to crucial decisions.

How then does a community of justice promote ICJ as an accountability pillar in global governance?

- As with all communities, it provides 'boundaries of permission' within which discretion can be exercised and decisions have their acceptable reach.
- These boundaries are qualified by the same normative framework as that which confirms the justice for which the community strives.
- For this justice to be confirmed and to continue it must have legitimacy within the community.
- That legitimacy is crucially dependent on peace and order, which global governance is charged to ensure.
- The capacity of global governance to achieve peace and good order and to maintain their benefits relies on the widest support of the cultures and interests which contest in a community of justice.
- Therefore, good governance is achieved only when the instrumentalities and processes of governance are accountable to the legitimate interests within communities of justice.

We set out below those essential characteristics of transformative justice which we regard as crucial to its external accountability. In other words, they are fundamental to infusing the structures and practices of global governance with values and norms directed at peacemaking, rather than confrontation and exploitation. As chapter 8 explains, transformed ICJ can play a pivotal role in defining and regulating the morality and practice of what is acceptable practice by the institutions and structures of global governance. Equally important is the perceived legitimacy which this approach will bestow on governance outcomes.

In summary, we suggest the following core imperatives for a governance model of accountability for ICJ:

Ideological – Humanitarian
Normative – Non-partisan, tolerant, non-discriminatory, engaging, representative;
Conciliatory – Reconstructive
Practical – Participative, efficient, regulatory, transparent

These imperatives are clearly prescriptive and depend for their realisation on repositioning the norms and practice of ICJ with the transformative values described in chapter 1.

The pluralist regulatory framework adopted and employed by good global governance will be accountable to communities of justice as they have access to, are included within and are integrated into ICJ.

Notes

1. Naturally, these are developed from particular political ideologies.
2. The limitations of this approach are discussed in chapter 1 and in Henham (2005: chapter 6).
3. The humanitarian foundations for this instrumentality, and how the balance between competing interests is reconciled through utilitarian ethics, are discussed in chapter 1.
4. *Prosecutor v Deronjic* (Case No. IT-02-61-S), Dissenting Opinion of Judge Wolfgang Schomburg, 30 March 2004.
5. As does the use of parole or other mechanisms (judicial or administrative) which carry the potential for sentence modification.
6. See, for example, in England and Wales, the Home Affairs Select Committee's comments when discussing the Sentencing Guidelines Council's (2004) proposed guidance regarding the use of guilty plea discounts and their impact in murder cases.
7. In terms of truth-finding, arguably this is bargained away along with claims of genocide, and the chance of establishing that what happened elsewhere also amounted to genocide. See Henham and Drumbl (2005).
8. Essentially derived from the humanitarianism we discuss in chapter 1.
9. The extent of this 'truth' and whether what took place amounted to 'criminality' in broader sociological terms are likely to be contested.
10. Article 81.2(a) of the ICC Statute provides: 'A sentence may be appealed, in accordance with the Rules of Procedure and Evidence, by the Prosecutor or the convicted person on the ground of disproportion between the crime and the sentence.'
11. More particularly, by facilitating the ascription of weights to significant factors. Restrictions on the use of penalties beyond imprisonment and lack of clarity regarding the appropriate use of alternatives merely exacerbate this problem.
12. These may be raised during the trial, at a pre-sentence hearing or during the appeal process.
13. Article110.4(a) and (b) of the ICC Statute.
14. For further detail, see Behrens (1998). Schabas (2007: 293) supports the view that the ICC Statute achieves an acceptable pragmatic compromise in reconciling the opposing philosophical approaches to the concept of the guilty plea characteristic of common law and civil law jurisdictions.

    It is worth noting that in England and Wales, when the offender pleads guilty, the judge does not hear the evidence, only the Prosecution's statement of facts. Disagreements relating to the factual basis for sentencing may be resolved by a 'Newton hearing'. For further discussion, see Ashworth (2005: 354). The ICC Statute, Article 65.4 goes further in providing that the Trial Chamber may request the Prosecutor to present additional evidence, including witness testimony, in order to satisfy itself that a more complete presentation is made in the interests of justice.
15. Although the concept of the guilty plea is not generally recognised in civil law jurisdictions, an increasing number have more recently made procedural changes which effectively introduce plea bargaining practices in certain types of case. For further analysis, see Jung (1997), Tulkens (2002) and Langer (2004).

16. This condition has also been emphasised in more recent judgments of the ICTY. See *Prosecutor v Momir Nikolic* (Case No. IT-02-60/1-A), Judgment on Sentencing Appeal, 8 March 2006, para. 77, n. 191.
17. More generally, as Findlay (2002) suggests, access to justice at the international level fails to reflect that accorded to victims in several common and civil law jurisdictions, where direct access is given to the sentencing process. Certainly, in the case of the ICC, it does not extend much beyond protection for victim witnesses and victim compensation. See Articles 43(6), 68(2), (3) and (4), 75, 79 of the ICC Statute.
18. And possibly serving hegemonic interests, rather than the more balanced notions of penality invoked by the normative framework for the trial.
19. ILC Draft, Article 38, para. 1 lit.d) (UN-Document A/49/10, pp. 110ff.). As Behrens (1998: 459) observes, the Appeals Chamber in *Erdemovic* (decided during this phase of the negotiations) were forced to reopen the proceedings following the revelation by the accused that his guilty plea had been entered under duress and he had not been informed precisely about the nature of his plea.
20. Schabas (2007: 293) suggests that this provision was forced because of a general misconception on the part of certain civil law countries that undertakings between the Prosecutor and the judge were binding at common law.
21. The question of whether amnesty is an acceptable jurisdictional response under the ICC's doctrine of complementarity is contested. See Cryer et al. (2007: 131).
22. In many jurisdictions negotiated justice is completely rejected in cases alleging first degree murder.
23. Unlike Blad (2006: 114), however, we do not favour the creation of separate structural space for institutionalising restorative justice.
24. See further our discussion of the indigenous African ideology of *ubuntu* in chapter 1.
25. As Braithwaite (2002: 194) suggests, imposed solutions too readily follow on from 'elite mediation'. In essence, Braithwaite envisages the route to peace and reconciliation as a bottom-up process, beginning with restorative techniques, with criminal justice interventions as secondary elements to holistic restoration.
26. This is not to underestimate the complexity of the task where, as in Uganda, there are more than 50 ethnic groups and a multiplicity of indigenous structures of accountability. See further Fisher (2007).
27. As Zappala (2003: 171) points out, some protection is provided by Article 14, para. 5 of ICCPR, which provides that everyone convicted of a crime shall have the right of review of his or her conviction and sentence by a higher tribunal. However, disagreement persists on narrow doctrinal issues such as whether the right to appeal is limited to matters of law or mixed law and fact. Although Zappala (2003: 193) concludes that the ICC provisions dealing with rights of appeal and revision are 'far more balanced and in conformity with human rights standards than the provisions governing these proceedings before *ad hoc* tribunals', there seems to be no alternative available where the operation of an institution's procedural norms breaches the human rights of the defendant. One possibility canvassed by Cockayne (2001: 20) might be for recourse to the UN Human Rights Committee.
28. The general approach of the ICTY is to be found in the *Celebici* Appeals Judgment of 20 February 2001.
29. The views of the minority must be recorded where there is no unanimity (Article 83(4)).

30. The conventional view would be for the Appeals Chamber to apply an objective test, determining the basis on which a sentence might be considered as unduly lenient according to whether the Trial Chamber had committed an error of principle. In essence, this is a finding suggesting that a decision was reached which no judge could reasonably consider appropriate in the circumstances having applied his or her mind to all the relevant factors and considered the possible range of sentences.

7
Justice as Decision-Making: Principal Pathways of Influence

Introduction

This chapter considers how judicial discretionary power may best be mobilised in order to achieve a more inclusive and restorative form of justice for international trials. The changes we propose recognise that giving effect to the interests of victims and communities of justice will be a holistic exercise in which the development of appropriate relationships between trial professionals will be critical to their realisation. Professional actors in the trial will therefore be instrumental in recognising and protecting the interests of victims and communities, so reducing formalism and promoting inclusivity. The move will necessarily be away from an adversarial towards a collaborative commitment. This does not mean that the legitimate aspirations for retribution will be rejected. Rather, these will be required to coexist with other important aspirations of victims and communities, which the judge and the legal professionals will be called on to balance and recognise. The capacity of the trial to identify and facilitate victim interests will therefore require a judge-directed collaborative approach committed to a truth-finding process that is balanced rather than confrontational. Hence, the trial will be directed towards outcomes which can be retributive, restorative or degrees of both depending, on what is considered appropriate and achievable in giving effect to the legitimate interests of victim communities.

This chapter therefore identifies particular pathways of influence within the trial where the discretionary power of international judges and their ability to identify and address the interests of victims and communities of justice have the maximum potential for their realisation. Accordingly, it proposes a new procedural approach designed to realise the objectives of trial transformation by developing a *trial programme* for each specific trial, and suggests how this might function for the ICC by implementing procedural changes. The chapter goes on to elaborate how trial relationships might be reconfigured in order to deliver transformed justice most effectively for victims, again making suggestions for procedural changes to ICC rules and practice.

This novel approach is illustrated through a case study example. Finally, the chapter seeks to counter possible arguments against the use of mediated resolutions within the framework of transformed trial justice and considers their broader potential as elements of transitional justice.

Developing the trial programme

As argued in chapter 5, we believe that comparative contextual analyses can provide vital information about the justice demands of post-conflict societies. We propose a pivotal role for such analyses in providing the kind of information which could be utilised as the foundation for *trial programmes* developed for specific trials. The essence of each trial programme will reflect a consideration of the following:

- the attitudes towards punishment of the region or state where the alleged international crimes occurred (individual, societal and judicial);
- the perceptions held about the legitimacy of international trials within each community of interest and the purposes which those communities would like to see achieved by the trial process;
- the nature and form of the process thought appropriate to facilitate the purposes described;
- the kinds of outcome regarded as likely to contribute to the desired purposes.

Within this broad framework, particular emphasis will be given to:

- the extent to which the process should concentrate on the offender's individual criminal responsibility for what took place;
- how the trial can best be formalised to take account of perceived opportunities for alternative forms of reconciliatory process;
- the extent to which particular parties should be empowered to control any aspect of that process and for what purpose;
- whether to recommend any particular form of diversionary mechanism and at what stage;
- whether in-house or independent specialists need to be instructed.[1]

The management and direction of these principles for accountability will be particularised for each trial through their elaboration in the *trial programme*.[2]

In order to operationalise these principles as a context of accountability for the ICC will require a fundamental restatement of its regulatory framework. Taking plea agreements and guilty pleas as an example, this will require the ICC to develop a broad test of eligibility to operate within the changed purposes for the trial. We suggest that the test should be framed in conventional legalistic terms with regard to the determination of such matters as the voluntary and unequivocal nature of the plea, but designed to facilitate the admission of relevant contextual information relating to the perception and impact of any plea agreement or guilty plea on the justice demands of victims and victim communities, as effected through the participation of these groups of interest in the decision-making process.[3] Accordingly, the test itself would be applied by the Prosecutor, Defence, Trial Chamber judges, victims and community representatives in special pre-trial status conferences and feed into the determination of the trial programme.

Essentially, the test would combine objective and subjective components. In the context of plea bargaining this might take the following form:

- The first stage would involve identifying factors[4] having a possible mitigating effect and balancing the objective evidence against the subjective accounts of the accused. These factors would include evidence of remorse, repentance, contrition, seeking forgiveness, desire to establish the 'truth' and promoting healing through peace and reconciliation. Particularly important in this context would be the offender's genuine acknowledgement of his or her guilt and a desire to assume responsibility for his or her acts.[5] Encouraging others to come forward, a willingness to identify and testify against others or otherwise assist the Prosecutor to identify others and help bring them to trial would be considered, as would system advantages such as the timing of the plea, saving the time and expense of trial and witnesses attendance, and therefore reducing their distress.
- The second stage would examine the subjective impact of a guilty plea on victims and communities of interest by hearing evidence from those involved, or their representatives, rather than relying solely on expert reports.[6] Crucially, it would mandate those parties to the decision-making process[7] to initiate a broader consideration of how negotiated justice could contribute towards achieving a process outcome that gave due recognition to local demands for justice within the broader context of ICJ. In this respect, the hearing would consider the results of contextual analyses designed to produce in-depth and non-partisan evaluations of the needs of relevant stakeholders within the framework of a principled assessment of the role of the trial as contributing to the post-conflict and transitional justice phases of societal reconstruction.

  This vital second stage in establishing the trial programme suggests that this hearing will become the most significant aspect of the international criminal process, since it will determine the *modus operandi* for the subsequent process consistent with the ideology and norms of the transformed trial. In the context of negotiated justice, for example, particularly difficult issues will need to be addressed and resolved at this early stage in the proceedings.

A specific illustration of these difficulties arises in cases where the defendant pleads guilty to crimes such as genocide or crimes against humanity and the evidence against them is overwhelming and incontestable. In these circumstances, there may be a sharp division of opinion as to whether any form of sentence discount is appropriate, given the heinous nature of such crimes.[8] Certainly, as Zappala (2003: 89) suggests, based on the ICTR Appeals Chamber's unwillingness to entertain a sentence discount in *Kambanda*, it may not be appropriate to allow plea bargaining and plea agreements for crimes of extreme gravity.[9] In terms of the existing jurisprudence of the ICTY and ICTR, it is clear that the parameters and balance between crime seriousness and expediency have yet to be drawn. Furthermore, the apparent absence of any willingness on the part of the ad hoc tribunals to preclude such practices for the gravest crimes or lay down guidelines for sentencing practice confirms their tacit acceptance of negotiated forms of justice.

The ICTY case of *Dragan Nikolic* is typical in endorsing the legitimacy of discounting sentences in return for guilty pleas to indictments for the most serious breaches of international humanitarian law such as genocide by linking its discussion of them with the potential for reconciliation (paras. 243–52). The Trial Chamber explicitly accepted that acceptance of responsibility by admitting guilt is an important factor in the process of reconciliation, particularly the notion that it could lead to a more widespread acceptance of responsibility on the part of others involved in breaching the norms of international criminal law during social conflicts. Significantly, the Trial Chamber stated:

> This Tribunal is not the final arbiter of historical facts. That is for historians. For the judiciary focusing on core issues of a criminal case before this International Tribunal, it is important that justice be done and be seen to be done.
>
> (para. 122)

However, the significant issue is whether justice 'seen to be done' in the terms described actually *is* justice. This returns us to the issue of legitimacy, the question of whose 'truth' is being constructed and for whose consumption. The important differences in the measures and perceptions of punitiveness noted in the Balkans by Kiza and Rohne (2005) is testimony to the need for the sensitivities of communities of justice to be taken into account at the point where a decision is taken as to how the 'truth' in question is to be reconstructed and the purposes to be served by it (see chapter 5).

There is no doubt that, for restorative purposes, the linkage between a guilty plea, the 'acceptance of responsibility' and its perceived impact on peace and reconciliation is critical. For example, in the ICTY case of *Plavsic*[10] the defendant filed a statement in support of her motion for a change of plea[11] at the same time as a written factual basis describing the crime to which she pleaded guilty and her involvement in it. In the former, she accepted responsibility and expressed remorse and invited others to 'examine themselves and their own conduct'.[12] Significantly, she accepted responsibility as a leader for the grave crimes committed by others, whatever might have been their allegiance during the conflict:

> To achieve any reconciliation or lasting peace in BH, serious violations of humanitarian law during the war must be acknowledged by those who bear responsibility – regardless of their ethnic group. This acknowledgement is an essential first step.
>
> (para. 19)

The Trial Chamber took particular note of expert testimony from Dr Alex Borraine,[13] who suggested that, given Mrs Plavsic's prominence and symbolism as a Serb nationalist and political leader, her apology and apparently full, genuine and voluntary expressions of remorse were highly significant indicators for reconciliation. Recognition of the pain and suffering experienced was particularly significant in providing a degree of closure for victims and their families. The Trial Chamber concluded (para. 81) that the accused's guilty plea and acknowledgement of responsibility should carry significant weight in mitigation as a 'positive impact on the reconciliatory process'. It therefore accepted that the guilty plea and other expressions of remorse contributed towards establishing the 'truth' of what took place.

Clearly, both the context in which this decision was made and the fact that the implications drawn by the Trial Chamber relied heavily on expert testimony is less than satisfactory. No victims were questioned directly on the issue, nor were they, or any representatives from relevant communities of justice, represented in any decision-making which touched on the acceptance of the guilty plea, its significance as an indicator of 'acceptance of responsibility' or its broader implications as contributing towards the establishment of peace and reconciliation in the Balkan region. As we have argued, there are serious doubts about whether this kind of negotiated justice operating in the context of a (predominantly) adversarial trial paradigm is best placed to determine 'truth',[14] and indeed raises questions about the context in which this particular version of 'truth' is being produced, and for whom.

Although Article 65(4) of the Rome Statute[15] appears to offer the possibility of effective victim participation in decision-making relating to admissions of guilt, as argued earlier, the fact that the prescribed context for such participation remains firmly rooted in the extant retributive dynamic of ICJ renders this implausible.[16]

The two-stage development of a trial programme for the transformed trial will provide an appropriate context for exploring the extent to which an acknowledgement of guilt truly represents a step beyond symbolic acceptance of responsibility to form the basis for pursuing mediatory and integrative strategies whereby peace and reconciliation become realistic objectives for decision-making. Within this purposeful context, building on foundational values of trust, honesty and transparency, the 'negotiation' of justice can be regarded in a different light. Instead of the currency of 'truth' being assessed in terms of system gains, it is the currency of justice which becomes the measure of 'truth'. In consequence, the legitimacy of the accused's representations of 'truth' is determined within a shared context for justice based on communitarian concerns. These determine the relationship between 'truth' and punishment, and the role of punishment in the construction of justice leading to peace and reconciliation. For this reason, the place of suffering within individual communities and the social contexts for assessing the role of guilt in terms of its significance for individual and social responsibility differ from one such context to the next.[17] The important point for the trial programme is to establish the ideological and normative parameters for achieving justice within each context, and to provide the processual means for delivering outcomes best suited for their achievement.

Transforming relationships

Crucially, the delivery of the trial programme in each case will depend on the capacity of trial professionals to work together towards the common goal of transformative justice. To achieve this will require a fundamental change of approach in terms of how judges, Prosecutors and Defence lawyers perceive their role, together with ethical and procedural changes to facilitate this objective. Most important is the notion that the trial will no longer be conceived as predominantly adversarial where the primary aim is to produce a form of 'truth' which will satisfy the legal requirements of proving guilt or innocence. Rather, the concept of the 'trial' will itself change so that it is conceived as:

- a stage in a broad process of transformative justice;
- a mechanism designed to produce different forms of 'truth' and accountability;
- a processual context whose primary objective is resolving the contradictory demands for justice made in the aftermath of social conflict;
- a normative framework which allows trial justice to contribute to the satisfaction of communitarian concerns for peace and the reconstruction of civil society.

Consequently, this vision of compromise and integrative justice will mean that trial professionals see their roles in challenging and probing testimony, whether oral or written, as essentially working towards this common objective. As we have discussed, the delivery of this particularised form of justice may promote retributive as well as restorative outcomes, developed and refined as the trial progresses. Therefore, trial professionals should perceive the roles of offender, victim and community through the common lens of transformative justice, so that, for example, each has a similar view of the reasons governing the admissibility of evidence and the active participation of relevant stakeholders such as victims in specific decisions made by the Court.

However, within such a shared perception of the transformative goal of the trial, trial professionals will each have designated roles in facilitating this outcome as the process moves through phases of the trial programme as directed by the judge. As we have proposed (Findlay and Henham, 2005: 332), the judge, through advanced discretion and a more flexible normative framework, will be given the power to:

- direct diversion from one justice paradigm to another, within or beyond the trial;
- determine whether the production of truth through trial 'conversations' best suits the purpose of restorative or retributive outcomes;
- ensure that the access and inclusion of lay participants in particular are confirmed through the important stages of trial decision-making;
- adjudicate on motions by any participant in the trial to redirect the process from one justice paradigm to another;
- ensure that the service provided by trial professionals enhances access and inclusion for lay participants; and
- promote openness and accountability in the exercise of professional discretion.

It is by using discretionary power to change the nature of trial relationships that ICC judges will be able to give real meaning to victims' interests and rights. We now turn to consider how this can be achieved.

Transforming participation

At first sight, the powers already available to ICC judges to consider and permit victim participation appear to be a considerable advance on the ICTY and ICTR position.[18] Article 68 of the ICC Statute is especially significant.[19] It provides a far more detailed account of the nature of victim and witness protection[20] and their participation in the proceedings than does Article 22 of the ICTY Statute (Article 21 of the ICTR Statute). Article 68(1), for example, provides that the ICC 'shall take appropriate measures to protect the safety, physical and psychological well-being, dignity and privacy of victims and witnesses', and imposes obligations in this respect on the Prosecutor. Significantly, the provision goes on to state that the measures taken are not to be prejudicial to or inconsistent with the rights of the accused and a fair and impartial trial. This injunction is repeated in Article 68(3), which provides that the Court has the discretion to permit the views of victims and their concerns to be presented and considered at whatever stages in the proceedings it thinks fit, where the 'personal interests' of victims are affected.

The detailed implementation of these provisions is to be found in the ICC Rules of Procedure and Evidence (section III, subsection 3, Participation of victims in the proceedings, Rules 89–93) but, notwithstanding the detailed procedural injunctions contained therein, there is nothing that *obliges* the Court to admit relevant victim evidence. Read in conjunction with Rule 145, which deals with the determination of sentence, the ICC provisions concerned with victims do not provide for their unconditional participation in any stage of the proceedings.

Article 68 is conditional in several aspects. For example, the decision as to what constitutes 'the personal interests of the victims' is left to the Court's discretion, as is the decision whether to admit the victims' views and concerns at all. Article 68(3) simply mandates the Court to '*permit* their views to be presented and considered at stages of the proceedings *determined to be appropriate by the Court*' and then goes on to qualify that possibility further by adding that any such presentation and admission must be 'in a manner which is not prejudicial to or inconsistent with the rights of the accused and a fair and impartial trial'.[21] Rule 145(1)(C) merely obliges the Court to '*give consideration*' *inter alia* to the harm caused to victims and their families. There is no right for them to lodge a victim impact statement which *must* be taken into account in fixing the sentence.

In short, the ICC Trial Chamber's obligations do not extend beyond immediate victims within the jurisdiction of the Court and their families[22] to take on board the feelings and concerns of 'significant others' within victim communities. Although some attempt has been to provide mechanisms to address what these wider concerns might be, there has been limited progress in deciding how the Court might engage with them, or in considering whether what is proposed has any sort of moral legitimacy in terms of the wider victim community.[23]

Furthermore, there is no apparent indication, either in any rationale discernible from the foundation instruments or any procedural mechanisms, whether what victims are allowed to put forward and its admission subject to the Court's discretion might (or should) contain information along these lines. Again, the concerns of victims and victim communities appear to receive symbolic rather than actual attention.

Recent decisions of the Court on the procedural implications of victim participation have added to the sense in which emerging interpretations of the ICC's normative framework is forcing victims' interests to conform to the limitations of a process essentially focused on establishing individual responsibility for mass atrocity rather than one providing greater potential for conflict resolution through engagement with issues of collective liability.

Baumgartner (2008) discusses some of the procedural constraints on victim participation in the proceedings of the ICC. Several of these relate to the pre-trial stage and are therefore important in determining exactly when victims' interests may be considered and, crucially, the nature and scope of those interests, and the evidence required to substantiate them. Baumgartner (2008: 413) suggests that the ICC's victim participation regime appears to encourage a more objective approach because victim evidence on issues of jurisdiction and admissibility is more likely to be detached from the political interests of states and the individual interests of defendants. The term 'objective' in this context also suggests the normative detachment of victims from the pursuit of economic[24] as well as criminal justice, and so renders them more 'acceptable'[25] parties to the criminal process. Notwithstanding, the inherent difficulties of determining victims' interests remain, particularly assessing their credibility and in evaluating and collaborating information.

Some of the difficulties that may arise in the early stages of a case before the ICC revolve around the scope of the events in question and the bringing of specific indictments against identifiable individuals. For example, the pre-Trial Chamber and the Prosecutor have clashed over the issue of whether victims should be allowed to participate in the investigation stage of a 'situation' as defined by Article 13(b). This may include several incidents, perpetrators and potential indictments, whereas a 'case', as referred to in relation to the Prosecutor's *proprio motu* powers under Article 15(4), refers to a concrete incident with one or more specific suspects occurring within a situation under investigation.

The ICC pre-Trial Chamber considered whether participation by victims at the investigation stage might adversely affect the rights of the accused and the impartiality and independence of the investigation and the expeditiousness of the whole proceedings (de Hemptine and Rindi, 2006). Although the pre-Trial Chamber did not define the ambit of procedural rights for victims at such an early stage in the proceedings, in Baumgartner's opinion such victim involvement is adequately protected despite falling outside the general framework of the Article 68 regime.

Another important issue is the causal link under Rule 85[26] whereby victims must demonstrate that the harm they have suffered is a direct result of the commission of crimes falling within the ICC's jurisdiction. For 'situation' victims, the pre-Trial Chamber decided that it was not necessary at this early stage for the identity of those responsible to be determined, but that there should be some overlap between the circumstances surrounding the appearance of the harm and the occurrence of the incident. In relation to a specific case, the pre-Trial Chamber was of the view that there should be a direct causal link between the harm and the alleged crimes. However, when the case came before the Trial Chamber, it found that indirect in addition to direct harm should be included and that crimes need not necessarily be limited to those contained in the indictment. Instead, the Trial Chamber took the view that an evidential link could be established if the victim had been affected by an issue arising during the trial to the extent that their personal interests had 'in a real sense been engaged in it' (paras. 93-8).

Further elaboration of the appropriate parameters for victim participation was provided by the ICC Appeals Chamber,[27] which confirmed that the harm suffered by victims within the scope of Rule 85 must be personal, although it does not necessarily have to be direct. Significantly, the Prosecutor resisted the idea put forward by victims' representatives that they had a personal interest in the establishment of the charges on the basis that this served to confuse the victims' role with that of the Prosecutor (para. 52). The Appeals Chamber also determined that the harm and personal interests of victims in relation to their participation in the trial under Article 68(3) of the ICC Statute must be linked to the charges against the accused. Consequently, once recognised under Rule 85, pursuant to Article 68(3), victims will first need to establish their personal interest in the trial before they are permitted to express their views and concerns (subject to the Court's discretion), although this must not prejudice or be inconsistent with the rights of the accused and a fair and impartial trial (para. 61). Finally, the Appeals Chamber decided that victims may lead evidence pertaining to the guilt or innocence of the accused and to challenge the admissibility of evidence in so far as this fulfils the purposes of the trial, subject to a number of procedural safeguards. However, this must take place within the parameters set by the charges in the indictment, since these establish the issues to be determined and thereby limit the Trial Chamber's authority.

Nevertheless, the formal legal and procedural provisions promoting victims interests in the ICC have certainly been hailed as profound. As Zappala (2003: 232) points out in the following assessment of the advantages produced by the increased recognition for victims under the ICC regime:

> it is extremely important for international criminal justice that victims be involved in the proceedings. This increases the chances of achieving the objectives of reconciliation and the removal of injustice. Participation enables victims to feel that they are part of a mechanism designed to deliver justice. This may contribute to reducing a desire for vengeance and increasing the chances of a successful confidence-building process that may lead to national reconciliation and lasting peace.

Whilst we agree with Zappala (2003: 221) that 'in the ICC Statute an attempt has been made to increase the expansion of procedural rights for victims and expand them to the procedural dimension',[28] we would argue that this has been symbolic rather than concrete in its effects and has had little, if any, impact in addressing the fundamental philosophical and structural weaknesses affecting international criminal trials and sentencing. For these aspirations to become reality requires something more than an increased potential for change. In order to deliver trial process that contributes to reconciliation and the removal of injustice there must be a rationalisation of purpose favouring trial transformation and a normative model which ensures the proactive engagement of victims and other representatives of communities of interest.

In concrete terms, changes will need to be made to Rule 91 of ICC RPE (more particularly to Rule 91.2) in order to give the legal representatives of victims or particular groups of victims *rights* of participation in hearings, unless the Trial Chamber in a statement of written reasons shows good cause why such participation in any particular hearing of the Court might be prejudicial to the interests of any of the participants in the process. In other words, there should be a *legal presumption* giving rights of participation to representatives of all those who have been directly affected by what has taken place and whose 'legitimate' interests have been recognised by the Court in the pre-status conference, in addition to representatives of broader communities of interest who have otherwise satisfied the Registrar, through application under a modified Rule 89 ICC RPE, that their participation is appropriate.

In terms of sentencing, it is also recommended that Rule 93 of ICC RPE be modified to ensure that the views of victims or their legal representatives (or other victims as appropriate) are sought by the Trial Chamber on the question of sentence determination under Rule 145 of ICC RPE, rather than the Trial Chamber merely being obliged to give consideration to such matters, as is presently the case under Rule 145.1(c).

Procedural justice and trial transformation – an illustration

This section describes how the principles for trial transformation might be evaluated through a detailed examination of a specific structural issue which impacts significantly on the capacity of the ICTY, ICTR and the ICC to deliver trial justice, namely, the function of the dichotomy between the verdict and sentencing stages of the trial process. The ICTY decision in *Krstic* is selected as the focus for this analysis because it illustrates how this core issue influences both the nature and context of admissible evidence for sentencing. However, our analysis of the relevant issues in this case is not constrained by the dynamics of retributive trial justice; rather, the purpose of the exercise is to set the issues raised against the normatively flexible context of trial transformation.

Accordingly, it is helpful to begin by summarising the principles utilised for operationalising trial transformation. As we have emphasised, trial transformation does not depend on the rationale of retributivism to establish credentials of fairness or consistency, so-called 'principled sentencing'; rather, it follows the rationale of producing 'truth' to satisfy identifiable demands for justice. The 'trial programme' determines the form of the process in each case. This is developed from the previously identified[29] 'justice' needs of 'relevant'[30] post-conflict societies; which means that the needs of *all* identifiable 'significant parties' with a legitimate interest claiming justice are included. It also requires the provision of prior 'expert' submissions as to the context of particular justice claims that feed into the determination of the trial programme.

The trial programme sets the objectives and suggests an agenda for the transformed trial process. The purpose of the trial is to achieve a principled outcome through a process which goes as far as possible in identifying, substantiating, accommodating and reconciling competing justice claims. This may include retributive and/or restorative justice considerations, and/or the achievement of other consequentialist aspirations. The outcome of transformed trial justice should be a significant contribution towards achieving the transition from war to peace and reconciliation in a post-conflict society.

For trial transformation, verdict and sentence remain as identifiable stages but have a different symbolic and operational significance within a merged process. Consequently, it is more appropriate to refer to them as *findings* and *outcome* stages. A mediated outcome may become possible at any point in the process and the trial programme will anticipate possible processual scenarios to facilitate this process. For this reason there is no set trajectory for findings and outcome. Their significance will be in the contribution they make to achieving the desired outcome rather than as signifying a stage in an adversarial contest. Thus, the driver is problem-solving, how to achieve the desired form of 'truth', so that the retributive focus on individual responsibility becomes dissolved into a collective search for justice. This is not the same as establishing collective guilt or responsibility; it means that the process is more open to evaluating the meaning and significance of collective forms of behaviour and its contribution to whatever atrocity took place.

Although the elements of substantive offences require 'proof', the concept of 'probative value' takes on a broader significance in the context of trial transformation. The standard remains one of proof 'beyond any reasonable doubt' where testimony has a bearing on the issue of whether a 'crime' was committed or not. However, the outcome that follows a transformed trial process should not be seen in terms of 'guilt' or 'innocence'. What is important is the significance of the finding for the broader outcome which is being worked towards, namely, the contribution that this particular process can make in facilitating the transition from conflict to peace. So the introduction of victim impact testimony, for example, before verdict or sentence should not automatically be regarded as 'prejudicial' to a 'fair' trial simply on the grounds that it rails against the predictability and consistency demanded by retributive justice and the rules of adversarial contest. Such a restricted and negative conceptualisation of the role of victim evidence is only relevant within the context of a purely adversarial process. We argue for more than symbolic inclusivity for victims as the foundation for achieving transformative justice.

Evidential issues

One of the most important issues to impact on sentence decision-making in international criminal trials is the structure of the process, particularly, whether there should be a distinction made between verdict and sentence and provision for a separate sentencing phase of the trial. This decision has fundamental evidential repercussions for the sentencing outcome. The current position is that both the ad hoc tribunals and the ICC have a predominantly unified structure.

In the case of the ad hoc tribunals, both the Defence and the Prosecution have the right to present evidence relating to sentence and argue for an appropriate sentence at the end of the trial phase once formal pleadings have closed:

> Rule 85: Presentation of Evidence
> (A) Each party is entitled to call witnesses and present evidence. Unless otherwise directed by the Trial Chamber in the interests of justice,[31] evidence at the trial shall be presented in the following sequence ...(vi) any relevant information that may assist the Trial Chamber in determining an appropriate sentence if the accused is found guilty on one or more of the charges in the indictment.[32]

However, this was not initially the case with the ad hoc tribunals, since the respective RPE for the ICTY and ICTR (Part 6, section 4) implicitly provided for a system where evidence relating to sentence could only be heard once the decision as to guilt or innocence had been made:

> Rule 100: Pre-sentencing Procedure
> If a Trial Chamber finds the accused guilty of a crime, the Prosecutor and the defence may submit any relevant information that may assist the Trial Chamber in determining an appropriate sentence.

As discussed in chapter 4, early cases such as *Tadic* (ICTY)[33] and *Akayesu* (ICTR)[34] even went as far as to hold separate sentence hearings, but the later amendment of their respective rules removed this possibility. The rationale for this was essentially the bureaucratic and administrative one of speed and efficiency. The new procedure ensured that the presentation of evidence and pleadings on sentencing matters occurred *before* the verdict was determined, with the result that both phases of the trial are now reflected in a single judgment based on the merits of the case.

Rule 86(C) of the ICTY/ICTR RPE effectively provides that after the presentation of all the evidence pertinent to the trial of the issues the closing arguments of the Prosecutor and the Defence must 'address matters of sentencing'.

Rule 86: Closing Arguments

(A) After the presentation of all the evidence, the Prosecutor may present a closing argument; whether or not the Prosecutor does so, the Defence may make a closing argument. The Prosecutor may present a rebuttal argument to which the Defence may present a rejoinder.

(B) Not later than five days prior to presenting a closing argument, a party shall file a final trial brief.

(C) The parties shall also address matters of sentencing in closing arguments.

The ICC Statute adopts a similar model. Article 76(1) provides that following a conviction the Trial Chamber should move on to sentencing, taking into account relevant evidence presented and submissions made during the trial.[35] Significantly, Article 76(2)[36] provides that (in contested cases only and before completion of the trial) the Trial Chamber may (or must, if requested by the Prosecutor or the accused) direct a further hearing to hear any additional evidence or submissions relevant to sentence.[37]

Schabas (2007: 305) suggests that this procedure creates a strong presumption in favour of a distinct sentencing hearing following conviction, but this has not been the experience of the ad hoc tribunals. However, Zappala (2003: 198) argues[38] that the position regarding the ICC remains unclear as to whether there should be one decision containing both verdict and sentence, or two separate decisions. More constructively, Van Zyl Smit (2002: 14) suggests that the provision for separate hearings and pronouncement of sentences under Article 76(2) may prove a fruitful avenue for the development of sentencing jurisprudence on the appropriateness of life imprisonment.[39]

Arguments in favour of holding a separate sentencing hearing after conviction are considerable. For instance, in a mono-phase hearing, the necessary omission of mitigation evidence may prove prejudicial to the Defence when it comes to sentencing because it restricts the information concerning the individual's personal role in the commission of the crime and its immediate aftermath (Keller, 2001: 68). According to Wald (2003: 467, n. 63) this probably contributed to the Defence's failure in *Krstic* to make any submission on sentence:

> the Tribunal Rules call for the verdict and sentence to be issued simultaneously, thus putting the defence counsel in the unenviable position of having to make any pleas for leniency at the same time as he is maintaining that his client should be acquitted.[40]

The introduction of such evidence may also impact adversely on the accused's right to remain silent and to protection against self-incrimination. In particular, the Defence may be induced to introduce more witnesses during the trial process in order to establish the accused's good character and personal circumstances.[41] Alternatively, from the Prosecutor's point of view, a second hearing is likely to permit the introduction of aggravating factors, such as the accused's criminal record, that might be considered inadmissible for reasons of irrelevance during the trial proper (Schabas, 2007: 306). In any event, the range of admissible material for sentencing purposes is potentially considerable.[42]

Potential difficulties

Clearly, *Krstic* does raise some difficult questions, and although at first sight these appear to concern purely procedural matters, it is evident on closer examination that they highlight some fundamental concerns about the future credibility of international criminal justice more generally, not just international sentencing. We begin by summarising the relevant points:

1. Judge Wald questions the basis on which the Defence can make a plea for leniency at the same time as maintaining that the accused should be acquitted. As Keller (2001: 68) suggests, it is surely illogical for the Defence to present evidence about what might be the appropriate sentence for crimes to which the accused has pleaded not guilty and has not yet been convicted.
2. The accused's right of silence and the right against self-incrimination are compromised. It is surely correct to argue that, if an accused chooses not to give evidence or, having been sworn, without good cause refuses to answer any question, the Court may not draw adverse inferences about individual criminal responsibility from this.[43]

Commentators (see Keller 2001: 69) agree that eliminating the possibility of a separate hearing, as has been the experience of the ICTY and ICTR, undoubtedly diminishes the accused's right to silence and causes problems for the Defence where it wishes to introduce evidence in mitigation concerning the accused's role as a possible accomplice rather than principal, or efforts that the accused might have made in trying to reduce the suffering of victims, either during or following the commission of the crime. It is difficult to envisage the introduction of such evidence without at least risking the possibility of self-incrimination. It is also arguable that evidence relevant to sentence introduced during the trial phase, such as that relating to victim impact, may adversely affect a judge's perception as to the guilt or innocence of the accused and therefore be unfairly prejudicial because it has the potential to compromise the accused's right to a fair trial.

We suggest that such restrictions and their effects should be exposed for what they really are: procedural devices which exist to facilitate the adversarial context of justice delivery. They are crucial for establishing the nature and credibility of a particularised form of evidence (or 'truth') which is conventionally validated by the test of whether or not it is of *probative value*.

Consequently, it is evidence conceived and manufactured to serve the ends of adversarial justice, in other words, to establish the guilt or innocence of the accused. As such, these norms not only represent procedural obstacles to achieving greater inclusivity for victims through trial transformation, they actively help to perpetuate the narrow focus on retributive and deterrent punishment so characteristic of international criminal trials.

In essence, those exclusory rules of evidence which arguably protect the accused from otherwise prejudicial testimony are designed to safeguard the presumption of innocence, which is the cornerstone of the adversarial trial. The merging of the verdict and sentence stages of the trial further threatens the protection of these basic rights, as we have discussed. Consequently, the mere separation of these two stages would not change our assessment of the rationale and value of the evidentiary rules as they currently exist because it would not deal with the fundamental failure of the present system of trial justice to deliver a more inclusive, victim-centred resolution to the problem of achieving justice following mass atrocity.

We therefore suggest that these specific evidential protections and artificial structural impediments to justice are replaced within the transformed trial by ethical rules for conduct developed from the foundational moral aspirations for achieving justice we describe in chapter 1. Clearly, nothing can prevent judges from drawing adverse inferences about the conduct of any participants (whether lay or professional, offender or victim) within the context of any trial process. The crucial issue is whether the rationale and structure of the process in question serves to achieve something more than merely facilitating retributive forms of justice within a predominantly adversarial trial framework.

Although the transformed trial will include a determination about whether or not the legal requirements of an offence have been established, the purpose of the process extends far beyond this aspiration, as we have described. In particular, the trial programme will be designed to encourage the maximum participation of all those claiming justice, especially through the possibility of mediated settlements which seek to promote a more inclusive and restorative resolution. Consequently, a broader framework of participative rights will be balanced by an equally robust set of norms designed to protect those who come forward with evidence which could lead to progress in achieving outcomes that promote peace and reconciliation.

The need for change is evident from *Krstic*. Let us first consider the fears voiced by Keller (2001: 71) about Judge Wald's remark made after the conclusion of Witness DD's testimony: '[it] will help us in making our decision'.[44] Such remarks might imply that victim impact testimony could be prejudicial to the accused because of its possible impact on a judge's perception of the evidence. However, the dangers of such unfair prejudice are relevant primarily to the issue of guilt or innocence as determined within the context of an adversarial trial, and are driven by the need to deliver retributive justice.

Hence, Keller's (2001: 69) assertion that the presentation of such evidence on sentencing during the trial phase could 'endanger the integrity of the judicial process' needs to be seen within that narrow context.

Certainly, the broader debate concerning the desirability and effect of victim impact statements within the adversarial context of the common law world persists. More recently, Ashworth (2000a: chapter 9; 2002) has repeated his reservations, also suggesting that the use of victim impact statements in the context of adversarial criminal justice tends to increase sentencing severity; that they are a cynical political ploy used to appease victims' concerns whilst, in reality, such statements tend to corrupt substantive and procedural justice goals. Erez (1994), on the other hand, has consistently championed the use of victim impact statements, stressing particularly their cathartic and therapeutic aspects, and suggesting that they empower victims and help them cope with victimisation and the criminal justice experience (Erez and Tontodonato, 1990; Erez and Rogers, 1995; Erez, 1999: 551; Erez and Rogers, 1999; Rogers and Erez, 1999).[45] Erez also suggests that the incorporation of victim statements tends to enhance proportionality rather than increase penal severity, as Ashworth maintains.

However, as Henham and Mannozzi (2003) suggest in their comparative contextual analysis of victim participation in sentencing in Italy, and England and Wales, the manipulation and redistribution of judicial discretion within process models operating in the adversarial context, and the apparent empowerment of lay actors, is merely a functional response rather than one indicative of any meaningful increased democratisation. This analysis is also consistent with a general willingness on the part of both civil and common law systems to institutionalise criminal processes which are unconstitutional or otherwise in breach of human rights norms on the grounds of managerial or bureaucratic efficiency. Such manifestations have little to do with notions of integration as models for penal change.

These observations are consistent with two important conclusions emerging from Henham and Mannozzi's (2003) research:

- That the normative content of any criminal justice model is not the main influence on the extent to which judicial discretionary power impacts on the level of victim participation.
- That changes in the structure and form of criminal process without a corresponding re-evaluation of the overall purpose of prosecution, trial and sentence, beyond the perceived need to remedy procedural deficiencies, produce penal structures whose philosophical justifications are not easily reconciled with the existing stated aims of punishment and the normative model which embodies them.

By way of contrast, within the more inclusive processual context of the transformed trial, victim impact testimony is seen as an essential constituent for delivering a representative and consensual version of the 'truth'. This kind of deep contextual knowledge cannot be derived simply by remodelling the current adversarial paradigm for international criminal trials. For instance, the proposal of commentators such as Keller and Zappala for re-establishing a clear, two-stage distinction between verdict and sentence has significant practical implications for victim integration, more especially because the separation of verdict and sentence does not necessarily obviate the need for evidence to be reconstructed to serve the purposes of the sentencing phase. In England, for example, the difficulties caused by the need to establish the factual basis for sentencing are a direct result of the division of the trial into two distinct phases. In particular, evidence relevant to sentence (such as provocation, duress or mental capacity) may not be sufficiently explored, even during a full trial.[46] Where the offender pleads guilty, these difficulties are exacerbated, since the Prosecution and Defence accounts of the facts may differ considerably.

The transformed trial paradigm imposes a different rationale for seeking facts which consequently renders meaningless the introduction of artificial procedural dichotomies such as separate verdict and sentencing phases that simply replicate those of the adversarial paradigm since this would detract from the primary objective of producing a more conciliated and potentially reconstructive outcome to the trial.

It is clearly difficult to speculate and differentiate between inferences *properly* drawn from the accused's attitude and behaviour as aggravating and mitigating circumstances during the trial and the wider significance of such observations should the process be transformed and detached from the normative boundaries normally associated with admissible evidence in adversarial trials. Within the adversarial context, as noted earlier, no obligation rests on the Defence to present mitigating evidence based exclusively on the assumption that the accused is guilty. Excluding the introduction of potentially mitigating evidence on these grounds serves to promote the adversarial goal of establishing the guilt or innocence of the accused.

Instead, the emergence of such evidence during the course of the trial should be facilitated by a more flexible normative structure which is directed towards assisting the court or tribunal to determine the relative merits of the case against the accused. Whilst this broader kind of approach does not realise the potential of such evidence for deconstructing relationships of individual and collective responsibility, or those between alleged perpetrators and the harm done to victims and communities, it does provide a normative framework which facilitates their further investigation within a context sympathetic to the transitional needs of victims and communities seeking justice.

In the context of trial transformation, there is no reason why the responses and observable characteristics of the accused in terms of behaviour and general demeanour during the trial cannot be exploited for their relevance to outcome. Furthermore, there is no reason why expert medical, psychiatric and personal circumstances reports should not be requested at any stage in the process if pertinent to the pursuit of a constructive outcome for the process. Not only would the focused inclusion of such evidence promote a deeper understanding of the causal relationships which impact on individual and collective action, it would also signal opportunities for exploiting conciliation and mediation and their healing potential as part of the function of the trial process.

So, for example, General Krstic's apparent lack of remorse during the trial regarding the role he played in the genocide at Srebrenica[47] could, within the context of the humanitarian and restorative focus of the transformed trial, be taken as an issue worthy of further exploration through some form of mediated process when directed as appropriate by the Trial Chamber. The processual context would then be refocused in order to confront this finding of fact with further detailed victim testimony. Processual energy, and that of all the participants, would be directed towards investigating the possibilities for obtaining forgiveness from families and their victims, and understanding what contribution this might make to building the kind of justice necessary for peace and reconciliation.

Pursuing the contextual reasons for individual behaviour is an important step towards establishing the boundaries of responsibility, and by preventing the collectivisation of guilt discourages further social division and alienation (Galabru, 2006: 152). In short, a significant characteristic of the transformed trial is its capacity to explore and exploit feelings of contrition and penitence in the service of achieving a more inclusive form of justice.

In the final two sections, we reflect on some of the broader considerations which impact on the ability of judicial discretionary power to deliver this more inclusive form of trial justice. To begin with, we consider the problem of how mediated outcomes reached within the context of the transformed trial may be perceived. We then move on to examine how transformative trial justice sits within wider imperatives for transitional justice.

Mediation and trial transformation

The issue of allowing some form of mediated settlement in the face of serious violations of human rights is a contentious one. Various human rights institutions allow the parties the possibility of reaching a so-called friendly settlement, the basis of which typically consists of an agreement on the part of the individual who has suffered alleged human rights violations that they will no longer pursue their claim against the state in question in return for which the latter promises to compensate the individual and/or otherwise amend relevant domestic law to prevent future abuse, as necessary. The process resembles a negotiated and legally validated form of state amnesty.

One obvious example is the European Court of Human Rights, which has jurisdiction over states parties to the European Convention on Human Rights and Fundamental Freedoms (ECHR) and issues decisions in response to individual petitions, Following a declaration of admissibility, the Registrar is obliged to contact the parties with a view to reaching an agreement to settle the dispute without further process, provided that the terms of any settlement shows due respect for human rights as defined in the ECHR and its various protocols.[48] On the same basis, all settlements have to be approved by the Chamber (Rule 69(3)).

Similarly, The Inter-American Commission on Human Rights is charged with applying the norms embodied in the American Declaration on the Rights and Duties of Man to the actions or omissions of all member states of the Organisation of American States (OAS), and also the standards embodied in the American Convention on Human Rights to states parties to that instrument. Many cases before the Commission involve human rights abuses, including torture, disappearances and destruction of property. A typical example of such a 'friendly settlement' was reached in the case of *Ragnar Erland Hagelin* and *Argentina*.[49] Mr Hagelin, the petitioner, brought an action against the state of Argentina seeking compensation for damages following that state's claim that it had no knowledge of the whereabouts of his daughter, Dagmar Ingrid Hagelin, who had disappeared in 1977 during the era of the dictatorship. He also sought damages for the suffering experienced by the immediate family resulting from the disappearance. In 1994 Mr Hagelin filed a petition with the Inter-American Commission on Human Rights against Argentina in which the Commission denounced the violation of the following rights under the American Convention on Human Rights: the right to humane treatment (Article 5) the right to a fair trial (Article 8) and the right to property (Article 21). In the friendly settlement which followed, the government of Argentina undertook to pay compensation for all losses relating to the unlawful imprisonment and subsequent disappearance of Dagmar Hagelin. In return, Mr Hagelin agreed that the Inter-American Commission on Human Rights would close his case, thereby expressly waiving any other claim for other loss(es) related to the same events, whether in judicial or administrative tribunals or in another international body. The Commission was at pains to stress that, by agreeing to carry out this procedure, a state indicated that it would use its best endeavours to comply with the provisions of the Convention pursuant to the principle of *pacta sunt servanda*, which binds states to honour their treaty obligations.

The relevance of such mediated settlements to our discussion of international trial justice is considerable. One important question raised is whether mediated outcomes can be regarded as an appropriate response where individuals have perpetrated gross violations of international humanitarian law. Indeed, it is arguable that mediations may actually serve to undermine the perceived gravity of the alleged crimes and thereby destabilise the processes of transitional justice. Furthermore, as Mallinder (2006) suggests, encouraging mediation for victims who are content with retributive justice this might serve as a re-victimisation of those victims. There are also more specific questions about what would happen should attempts at mediation fail within the context of the transformed trial, and what enforcement mechanisms exist to ensure compliance with mediated settlements.

These questions raise a number of interrelated issues. Dealing first with the re-victimisation and processual points, our emphasis is on intensive pre-trial discussions about the nature of the victimisation and victims' and communities' justice aspirations, based, as far as practicable, on detailed comparative contextual analysis and evaluation and the development from this of a customised trial programme. This is designed to minimise the likelihood of re-victimisation in the terms envisaged by Mallinder simply because such factors will already have been taken into account.[50]

Similarly, mediation will not be advanced by the Court as a possible processual phase unless the fallback possibilities, including failure, have been anticipated and their consequences thought through at the earlier trial programme developmental stage. Although it is clearly impossible to anticipate all eventualities – indeed, the process advances the creative use of judicial discretionary power to enhance flexibility – the transformative potential of the trial largely depends for its realisation on the provision of the kind of comprehensive and penetrating comparative contextual analysis about victimisation in post-conflict states which is currently lacking in deliberations about trial justice as a positive contributor to reconciliation and peace.

As for the suggestion that mediation may be an inappropriate response which undermines perceptions of gravity, again this should not become a threat to trial transformation because the perceived effects of mediation will have already been explored and tested against the expert contextual commentary which inputs into the earlier trial programme development stage of the process. In other words, the possibility of pursuing any kind of outcome which may fall significantly short of satisfying the justice aspirations of the main players in the conflict will prevent its inclusion as a possible avenue for resolving the problem of the trial's potential contribution to post-conflict resolution. The possibility that a justice outcome predominantly centred on local needs and aspirations will fail to live up to the rhetoric and symbolism of universalised justice instruments or their enforcement mechanisms must be accepted, but it should be remembered that it is the failure of trial processes, especially those of the ICTY and ICTR, to move beyond these that has pre-empted the present debate about trial transformation.

More generally, any discussion involving redefinition, whether resulting from trial justice, truth and reconciliation, lustration or any other means inevitably has significant implications for social control and governance during and beyond the transitional justice phase. This is because, as Cohen (1995), citing Spitzer, so aptly describes, any determination about the facts of what has happened in the past inevitably creates an artificial barrier, a breaking of the relationship between past and future, so that policing the past becomes more a question of making sure that the past remains closed. Social control becomes a process involving the selective control and manipulation of memory. In the postmodern era, the certainty of this discourse has been replaced by what Cohen (1995: 48) calls the 'centrifugal' falling away of information and memory. The relativity of values and its controlling ideologies become increasingly difficult to identify, let alone predict, making it harder to prevent the absolution of the human rights abuses carried out by totalitarian regimes such as that of Argentina in the 1970s. In other words, to a greater or lesser extent, we gradually come to accept degrees of denial without necessarily being aware of its insidious effects on our perceptions and actions towards present and future human rights abuses, especially those amounting to international crimes such as genocide and crimes against humanity.

Our vision for transformative justice tries to counter this dangerous and subversive tendency via its focus on achieving accountability by coming to terms with the relativity of justice and its pluralistic demands through the ideological repositioning of ICJ towards increased inclusivity and its processual accommodation, with its emphasis on conciliated outcomes. The most important aspect of justice denial to guard against in its implications for global governance remains the strategic impunity given to individuals or agents of state power by other hegemonic states which instigate, control and manipulate world conflicts for their own cynical ends. Here the selectivity of control set beyond state borders must be policed by robust, internationally accepted structures which have a greater ability to force compliance with universal humanitarian norms than those existing currently enjoy.

Transformed trials and transitional justice

Thinking about the contribution of transformed trial justice to transitional justice is problematic. The reason for this stems from the fact that evaluations of the role of trial justice, whether international, hybridised or domestic, in dealing with the perpetrators of international crimes are obfuscated by the pervading influence of the adversarial/retributive dynamic. Consequently, they have an extremely limited view of the potential for trial justice to achieve anything beyond the carrying out of these objectives. Even in this context, the capacity for trial justice to deter international criminality except in isolated instances is limited. Consequently, we are left with a notion of the international trial as an instrument of retribution, condemnation and oppression.

As we have argued, the retributive dynamic in international trial justice has acted as a conceptual and normative barrier to engaging with the idea that trial outcomes can be part of a more constructive and inclusive penality. As a result, trial justice is deemed to lack the capacity for truth-telling found in structures such as truth and reconciliation commissions, and the international trial structure is seen as an inappropriate venue for pursuing reconciliatory and reparative objectives. True, international trials may manufacture a form of 'truth' and provide legal closure, but many regard this kind of truth as distorted by the limited rationale and objectives set for international trial justice. An example of this compartmentalised thinking about the capacity of international trial justice can be seen in the way in which its relationship within transitional justice is normally conceived. This is illustrated in the following summary of the main features of transitional justice provided by Bickford (2004: 1045–7):

- *Prosecutions* – prosecution of perpetrators, whether on the domestic level, in a hybrid internationalised court (i.e. the Special Court for Sierra Leone) or in an international court, such as the ICC.
- *Truth-telling* – establishing the truth about the past through the creation of truth commissions or other national efforts, such as engaging in major historical research, compiling victims' testimonials or oral histories, supporting the work of forensic anthropologists in determining the exact nature of victims' deaths, or exhuming their bodies.
- *Reparations* – establishing reparations policies that take into account the requirements of, or moral obligations to, the victims. These policies can include financial compensation as well as a variety of health (physical and mental) and education benefits, and symbolic measures, such as a state apology.
- *Memorialising* – remembering and honouring victims through a series of measures, including consulting with victims to develop memorials and museums of memory, converting public spaces such as former detention camps into memorial parks and interpretive sites, and catalysing constructive social dialogue about the past.
- *Reconciliation* – developing reconciliation initiatives, such as working with victims to determine what they require in order to experience healing and closure, and forging peaceful coexistence among former adversaries without sacrificing justice and accountability for perpetrators.
- *Institutional reform* – reforming institutions that have a history of abusive behaviour, including, for example, security forces or the police, in order to prevent future patterns of abuse and establish state-society relationships based on functioning and fair institutions.

Similarly, Borraine (2004) envisages clear divisions of function when describing the problems of defining transitional justice:

> we need to embrace a notion of justice that is wider, deeper, and richer than retributive justice ... Truth commissions, unlike prosecutions, often

> pay attention to the political, economic and social context in which these violations happened ...Truth Commissions are complementary to prosecutions and should not be seen as a substitute for judicial accountability and prosecution.

These comments clearly foresee a limited contribution on the part of international trials to transitional justice. Both Bickford and Borraine reflect a narrow, one-dimensional view of the instrumental capacity of international trial justice that is tied firmly to its conventional retributive and deterrent role. Hence, in order to move forward, the various aspects of transitional justice must be balanced and coordinated, held 'in tension to one another', as Borraine puts it.

However, the concept of transformative justice for the trial we have elaborated in this and previous work does not endorse this emasculated role for trial justice. We have argued for a form of trial justice which is capable of producing 'truth' and outcomes that engage directly with the values and objectives of inclusion, healing and reconciliation. Furthermore, as we argue in chapter 5, its communitarian context of accountability, based on humanitarian values, not only provides a crucial new dimension for strengthening ICJ as a form of governance, it has the potential to infuse other frameworks of governance, especially institutional structures, with its rationale and ethics. Consequently, international trial justice can play a significant role in establishing new parameters for the separation of powers in international governance by strengthening their moral foundations.

Within this broader context set for transformative trial outcomes, we have argued that their contribution to transitional justice includes many of the functions of other practices and structures, such as truth-telling and reparations, which are currently treated as self-contained areas. In suggesting this fundamental change in the instrumental capacity of trial justice, our aim has not been to detract from other structures and practices of transitional justice. On the contrary, we envisage transformed trial justice as a more effective and constructive partner for other structures and practices, whether these take the form of truth and reconciliation, indigenous or hybridised forms of justice. We see transformed trial justice as seeking to push forward the agenda of particular transitional justice programmes in more inclusive and constructive directions. In other words, transformative justice will enlarge the instrumental capacity of international trials and their outcomes in directions which will have a beneficial effect on transitional programmes generally.

However, there are a number of important issues to be faced when evaluating the contribution of transformed trial justice to transitional justice. As explained earlier, trial programmes will be developed for each context and the Prosecutor's Office will be instrumental in their development and implementation. This process envisages a broader engagement of trial outcomes with transitional justice programmes. Consequently, the Prosecutor will play a crucial role in delivering those aspirations for trial outcomes identified by the trial programme. Achieving this will require outcomes to be evaluated against the objectives set for transitional justice and the development of measures of satisfaction which go beyond those which might impact directly on victims and communities of justice. For example, their perceptions might be influenced by such factors as:

- emotional experiences;
- feelings about procedural justice; and
- whether aspirations for trial justice were satisfied.

However, the broader implications of these responses will need to be evaluated within the context of transitional objectives. This will involve looking beyond the immediate feelings individuals might have about the trial and its outcome by seeking to capitalise on the extent to which those same feelings of forgiveness might be extended to groups or communities that collectively orchestrated the mass atrocities in question. So, for example, the trial's transitional objectives may have established that retribution and deterrence were regarded by certain parties as essential precursors to restoring harmony. In other cases, these purposes might be regarded as part of the mechanism for resolution and transition. In the context of the ICC, it is important to bear in mind that the Court has no enforcement arm, so that enforcement of retributive/deterrent outcomes is not an option. Under the present regime such outcomes could not become part of a transformative agenda. The idea of enforcement for transformative purposes is clearly different; it follows from the transformation of ideology and process. In this context, retributive/deterrent aspirations may be realised.

It is also difficult to assess the basis on which individuals or groups attribute greater satisfaction to one kind of process over another – for example, transformative over retributive/deterrent. Satisfaction may ensue because the process was inclusive and participatory, or because of feelings held about its intrinsic value in resolving conflict and aiding transition. Similarly, the locus and length of trial proceedings, separation of outcome from cause, drawing a distinction between high- and low-ranking perpetrators, and differences between hybridised, internationalised, international and indigenous forms of trial all affect perceptions of legitimacy. In terms of timing, for instance, the window of opportunity and impetus for reconciliatory motives to be exploited may quickly dissipate.

Consequently, effectively coordinating all the elements of transitional justice, including prosecution, truth-telling, reconciliation, reparation and institutional reform, is critical – not least because, as Borraine (2004) suggests, reconciliation may be triggered at different times in transitional states. Such triggers may range from the indictment and prosecution of particular perpetrators, to the release of political prisoners, whereas the reform of institutional structures to achieve economic justice may be seen as more pressing, or equally, significant to the goals of criminal justice.

In addition, the interrelationship of each element for transitional justice will depend on the relevant context and its transitional needs. It cannot be assumed that these will correspond to any preconceived notions of governance[51] or the role and structures needed to deliver criminal justice (Teitel 2000: 224). As discussed earlier, these contingencies and the transitional aspirations of victims and communities of justice will be fed into the trial programme by utilising the methodology of comparative contextual analysis. In deconstructing the contexts which inform the reasons for conflict and the phenomenology of justice, it will be possible to move more effectively towards reconciliation and peace. However, it is crucial to bear in mind the contingent nature of transitional structures. As Teitel (2000: 230) cautions:

> transitional practices have an ambivalent character, the resort to these practices in political flux is in the service of unity; yet, there is also a loss ... Transitional justice is partial and limited. The resort to such settlements implies compromise; their potential lies in their ability to reconstitute the community

Teitel's injunction for transitional practices to engage community is instructive, since we have argued this for international trial justice throughout this book (and also in Findlay and Henham, 2005). The inclusive and communitarian focus for transformative trial justice is grounded in foundational humanitarian values and the principles we derive from them (see chapter 1). This focus also has the broader potential to infuse governance through the transitional phase, and beyond, with an ideological coherence that will support structures and practices that are directly responsive to the needs of victims and communities of justice.

In the final chapter, we consider how transformative justice can be further developed to give ICJ a significant role in global governance.

Our scenario

The kinds of factors which ought to be taken into account in developing a trial programme for our scenario, should proceedings go before the ICC, will be dictated by a transformative rather than a retributive dynamic, as currently exists. We have already touched on the difficult negotiating stance taken by the government and the choice faced by the ICC Prosecutor as to whether the Court should proceed against it or the general.[52] Were the ICC to adopt our proposals for transformative justice, these matters would be resolved well before the question of trial proceedings arises as the initial engagement of the ICC will go far beyond anything contemplated in the remit of the ICC's current Outreach Programme (see ICC Monitoring and Outreach Programme, 2006).

With transformed trial justice, the emphasis will be firmly placed on understanding the social, historical and political causes of the conflict by utilising the methodology of comparative contextual analysis. This will be an urgent priority. One of the most important things that this early phase will want to investigate is the indigenous penal culture of each conflict group and how this has informed the feelings which each group has about what form punishment should take in the aftermath of the conflict.[53] Coupled with this will be the broader issue of where these aspirations for justice fit into the view each group has about whether the society can be rebuilt, and if it can, what form this should take and how it should be done. The ICC will need to know exactly what each group feels about the role of international trial justice in this transitional phase.

As it stands, we know very little from the facts of our scenario about the views of each victim community on the question of punishment, except that they all want the offenders 'brought to justice'. We do know, however, that neither group has confidence in the Truth and Reconciliation Commission set up by the government, and that they want a mechanism where, as each sees it, the 'real' truth will come out. In addition, reconciliation and compensation have been mentioned.

Therefore, in deciding what will influence the design of the trial programme and how the trial's objectives will be set, comparative contextual analysis will concentrate on improving our understanding of how the perceptions of individuals and communities are constructed and their interrelationship. It will be particularly concerned to investigate the extent to which subjective factors, such as feelings and emotions, relate to how structures and outcomes of criminal justice are perceived – in other words, their legitimacy. Clearly, this is a complex and difficult exercise.[54] We do not know, for example, how each community feels about the role of formal punishment rituals or whether retributive or restorative justice forms are used, either separately or in combination, or crucially, whether practices that appear to conform to definitions or understandings[55] derived from other cultures and traditions actually exist at all. In other words, we remain ignorant of whether actions taken by the community in order to restore harmony are thought of in retributive, deterrent or restorative terms, or indeed, whether the notion of punishment has any significant role in maintaining community coherence. More significantly, there is no indication of where the line is drawn between resolutions governed by so-called 'law' and those which regulate the infringement of social norms, which (if any) have priority and why.

Given the fact that both sides are keen to clarify what they perceive as the media's deliberate mystification of the 'truth', attention might well focus on the issues of landownership, killing of livestock and rape described in the 'reign of terror'. For example, the social stigma attached to rape and other forms of sexual violence demands close scrutiny. However, it is very clearly culturally specific. Commonplace assumptions about factors which determine the status of women are likely to prove incorrect. Conclusions in this respect drawn by the ICTY following the Balkans conflict provide a good example. As de Londras (2007) points out, the ICTY in *Krstic* regarded it as common knowledge that the Bosnian Muslims of eastern Bosnia constituted a patriarchal society. Consequently, women were required to have a clear marital status (i.e. married, widowed or divorced) in order to constitute part of that society, and a woman whose husband was missing did not fit into any of these categories. However, the ICTY ignored the relative impact of power in determining status: 'would a wealthy, independent, respected Muslim woman in Srebrenica have experienced the patriarchal community identified by the Tribunal in its envisaged manner given the contradictions between powerful and powerless?' (de Londras, 2007: 123).

Each community will need to be satisfied about the capacity of the transformed trial to deliver inclusive and participatory justice swiftly and impartially. Obvious difficulties in our scenario lie in the fact that corrupt practices and oppression by the ruling tribal group predominate, the criminal justice system is politically compromised and there is little evidence of democratic principles at work in the institutions of governance. Consequently, it will be necessary from the outset for the ICC to coordinate its activities with other structures as part of a transitional justice strategy. Yet, much of what needs to take place in order to move from a situation of confrontation to peace is beyond the capacity of transformed trial justice alone to deliver. The UN Security Council may therefore need to mandate peacekeepers whilst institutional reforms begin to take shape. This may involve introducing some form of democracy, but again, the critical issue, as Iraq has demonstrated, is for the institutions to reflect culturally acceptable aspirations for governance.

Notwithstanding all this, as we have argued, transformed trial justice can play a crucial role as part of the transitional phase, but there must be a perception on both sides that the structures established are impartial and are driven by common objectives set for a return to civil society. If not, the contribution that transformed trial justice will be able to make to the core objectives of prosecution, truth-telling, reconciliation and reparations will be diminished (Keller, 2007). However, as we have argued, transformative trial justice has governance implications that extend beyond criminal justice, since the humanitarian values which infuse its ideology and practice will have a corresponding influence on the formulation of transitional justice policy and the structures for achieving it, as well as on the substance of the trial itself. In the case of our scenario, this potential will be critical to ensuring a successful transition and setting in motion the processes of reconciliation.

Notes

1. Ideally, there should be permanent specialists attached to the Court.
2. Since there is to be no 'trial' in the adversarial sense of a contest, the trial programme will aim to resolve the best way of advancing the process of trial transformation.
3. The possibility for developing this already exists by virtue of Article 65(4) of the ICC Statute, which provides that where the Trial Chamber is of the opinion that a more complete presentation of the facts of the case is required *in the interests of justice*, in particular the interests of the victims, the Trial Chamber may:
   (a) request the Prosecutor to present additional evidence, including the testimony of witnesses; or
   (b) order that the trial be continued under the ordinary trial procedures provided by this Statute, in which case it shall consider the admission of guilt as not having been made and may remit the case to another Trial Chamber (emphasis added). The important difference between this provision and the trial transformation we advocate is that the current Article 65 is constrained by the present ideological and processual shortcomings of adversarialised and retributive justice.
4. In previous jurisprudence of the ICTY and ICTR until the ICC begins to establish its own doctrine *de novo*.
5. See *Prosecutor v Babic* (Case No. IT-03-72-S), Sentencing Judgment, 29 June 2004, para. 68. Babic's decision to plead guilty resulted in his self-incrimination. The ICTY Appeals Chamber agreed that (1) the Trial Chamber had erred in finding that the appellant's conduct subsequent to the crime of persecution could not be considered in mitigation solely because it did not include the alleviation of the suffering of victims; and (2) the Trial Chamber committed an error of law in not taking into account the appellant's attempts to promote peace as a mitigating circumstance. The Appeals Chamber found by majority, Judge Mumba dissenting, that on balance this error did not have an impact on the sentence; Appeals Judgment, 18 July 2005.
6. For example, in *Babic*, n. 5, para. 69, the ICTY Trial Chamber referred to the report of a Dr Mladen Loncar which addressed the positive effect of Babic's guilty plea on the victims in particular, and in general on the entire population in the former Yugoslavia, including the Serbs. Loncar's report stated in reference to the guilty plea: 'This is a step towards healing, towards forgetting the past and turning to the future. Admission of guilt and remorse alone cannot restore unity and friendship, but it helps victims overcome the greyness of their past.' He added that Babic's confession 'expresses the truth which so many victims have "silently" been saying for all these years'. On the basis of this assessment the Trial Chamber considered that Babic's guilty plea and account of the events contributed significantly to the reconciliation process in the territory of the former Yugoslavia, in particular in Croatia and Bosnia-Herzegovina.
7. As to whether or not to accept the plea and/or plea agreement.
8. For detailed examination of the use of guilty pleas in this context, see Symposium on the Guilty Plea (2004).
9. Zappala's reasons for supporting the practice are not wholly convincing. He appears to advocate the pragmatic use of guilty plea discounts and plea agreements on the basis of their advantages to the Prosecutor in shortening investigations, and that it may be in the public interest to shorten the trials of minor participants

on the basis of cost. It should be noted that in many jurisdictions sentence discounts for guilty pleas are generally excluded for cases of first degree murder; see further Sieber (2004) Country Reports, especially section 4.1.2.4; Expert Report, cited in *Prosecuto v Dragan Nikolic* (Case No. IT-94-2-S), Trial Chamber, Sentencing Judgment, 18 December 2003, paras. 227–31.

10. *Prosecutor v Plavsic* (Case No. IT-00-30 & 40/1-S), Trial Chamber, Judgment, 27 February 2003.
11. Mrs Plavsic, who was 72 years old at the date of her trial, had at one time been a distinguished academic. She entered politics in 1990, becoming acting co-president of the Serbian Republic of Bosnia Herzegovina and later was a member of the Presidencies of Republika Srpska. It was established that the Bosnian Serb leadership, including Mrs Plavsic, had 'disregarded reports of widespread ethnic cleansing and publicly rationalised and justified it'. The original indictment contained counts alleging genocide, complicity in genocide and the following crimes against humanity: persecutions, extermination and killing, deportation and inhumane acts. Although she had initially pleaded not guilty to all counts at her first appearance before the Trial Chamber in January 2001, she subsequently entered a guilty plea to count 3 (persecutions, a crime against humanity) in October 2002. This plea was contained in a plea agreement made in September 2002, whereby the Prosecutor agreed to move to dismiss the remaining counts on the indictment. Accordingly, such counts were dismissed in December 2002.
12. Statement by Biljana Plavsic in Support of her Motion for Change of Plea pursuant to Rule 62 *bis*, 30 September 2002, para. 19.
13. Former Deputy Chairperson of the South African Truth and Reconciliation Commission and founding President of the International Centre for Transnational Justice.
14. Zappala (2003: 89) makes the important point that the determination of 'truth' where a guilty plea is entered is neither judicial nor pedagogical, and, therefore, appears to contradict the mission of international criminal courts to take account of victims' interests.
15. Article 65.4 provides that where the Trial Chamber is of the opinion that a more complete presentation of the facts of the case is required in the interests of justice, in particular the interests of the victims, the Trial Chamber may request the Prosecutor to present more evidence, including the testimony of witnesses, or order that the trial be continued under the statute's ordinary trial procedures, in which case the Trial Chamber must consider the admission of guilt as not having been made and may remit the case to another Trial Chamber.
16. See Damaska (2005) for a view suggesting a limited role for plea bargaining in the ICC as currently conceived.
17. As shown by Wilson (2001: chapter 7) in his discussion of the centrality of retribution to community justice in South Africa.
18. For legal analysis of victims' pre-trial participatory rights, see Stahn, Olasolo and Gibson (2006).
19. Rule 86 of ICC RPE contains a general injunction to the Trial Chamber and other Court organs when performing their functions under the statute or rules to take into account the needs of all victims and witnesses as directed by Article 68, especially children, elderly persons, persons with disabilities and victims of sexual or gender violence.
20. See Rule 87 of ICC RPE for details of their procedural implementation.

21. This is a necessary discretion to maintain balance between the competing rights of the parties.
22. Principle 2 of the UN Victims Declaration makes clear that a person may be considered a victim, regardless of whether the perpetrator is identified, apprehended, prosecuted or convicted and regardless of the familial relationship between the perpetrator and the victim. This principle further clarifies that the concept of victim 'also includes, where appropriate, the immediate family or dependants of the direct victim and persons who have suffered harm in intervening to assist victims in distress or to prevent victimisation'. Unfortunately, such clarification was not included by the drafters of the ICC provisions. See further commentary by Amnesty International (1999). The fact that there were multiple victims may be taken into account as an aggravating factor in the determination of sentence (ICC RPE, Rule 145(2)(b)(iv)).
23. Recognition by the ICC OTP of the need to engage with victims and communities has been evident through the development of the ICC OTP (see ICC Monitoring and Outreach Programme, 2006) and in urging greater victim and community input for ascertaining the interests of victims for the purposes of Article 53 of the ICC Statute (ICC OTP, 2007).
24. Through being joined to the action as a civil party as is common practice in inquisitorial trials.
25. In the sense that their evidence is less likely to be perceived as tainted by an economic motive than in the pursuit of establishing the 'truth' of the events which constitute the facts alleged in the indictment. Despite the ICC Prosecutor's suggestion that witness evidence relating to reparations should be admitted during the course of the trial rather than at a separate reparations hearing once the accused has been found guilty, the Trial Chamber has been reluctant to go that far, suggesting instead that such evidence should be admitted only in the interests of expediency (Decision on Victims' Participation, Situation in the Democratic Republic of Congo, *Prosecutor v Thomas Lubanga Dylio* (Case No. ICC-01/04-01/06-1119), 18 January 2008).
26. Once qualified under Rule 85, the Court is obliged to ascertain whether the three requirements for victim participation contained in Article 68(3) are satisfied. Significantly, by virtue of Rule 91, only victims who are legally represented qualify for specific 'enhanced' procedural rights which go beyond the right to participate in hearings. These may include questioning witnesses, experts or the accused. This is of particular significance where the personal appearance of large numbers of victims is a possibility, so the timing of any decision about common legal representation is vital.
27. Judgment on the appeals of the Prosecutor and the Defence against Trial Chamber I's Decision on Victim Participation of 18 January 2008; Situation in the Democratic Republic of Congo, *Prosecutor v Thomas Lubanga Dylio* (Case No. ICC-01/04-01/06 OA 9 A 10), 11 July 2008.
28. Zappala (2003: 232) does acknowledge certain practical drawbacks pertaining to the greater procedural participation possible for victims under the ICC regime.
29. Through preliminary research and investigation such as that carried out by Kiza and Rohne (2005).
30. Use of the word 'relevant' should not be taken to imply any exclusion or failure to recognise the justice claims of particular social groups involved in a conflict.
31. Significantly, since the textual amendment of Rule 100, there is no implication that the Defence should present evidence pertinent to mitigation of sentence on

the basis of the accused's guilt, but that its emergence should be part of the normal course of the trial and, therefore, directed towards assisting the tribunal to determine the relative merits of the case against the accused:

Rule 100: Sentencing Procedure on a Guilty Plea

(A) If the Trial Chamber convicts the accused on a guilty plea, the Prosecutor and the defence may submit any relevant information that may assist the Trial Chamber in determining an appropriate sentence.

32. Since the Rules refer to the submission of 'all relevant information' there is some doubt regarding the exact nature of the evidential material permitted and whether it may be treated as equivalent to evidence submitted in accordance with the Rules. Similarly, whether trial rules on the submission and admissibility of evidence also apply to the Trial Chamber's deliberations during the sentencing phase is a matter for conjecture (Zappala, 2003: 197).

    More recent ICTR decisions have attempted to clarify what information relating to aggravation and mitigation is relevant to sentencing and the appropriate burden of proof. For example, in *Prosecutor v Niyitegeka* (Case No. ICTR-96-14-T), Judgment and Sentence, 16 May 2003, 'It has borne in mind that the principle according to which only matters proved beyond a reasonable doubt are to be considered at the sentencing stage extends to the assessment of any aggravating factors, while mitigating factors are to be taken into consideration if established on a balance of probabilities. This Chamber reiterates that a particular circumstance shall not be retained as aggravating if it is included as an element of the crime in consideration' (para. 488).
33. *Prosecutor v Tadic* (Case No. IT-94-1), Sentencing Judgment, 14 July 1997.
34. *Prosecutor v Akayesu* (Case No. IT-96-4), Trial Chamber Judgment, 2 September 1998
35. Article 76: Sentencing
    1. In the event of a conviction, the Trial Chamber shall consider the appropriate sentence to be imposed and shall take into account the evidence presented and submissions made during the trial that are relevant to the sentence.
36. See Rule 143 of the ICTY Rules of Evidence and Procedure.
37. Article 76(4) confirms that (wherever possible) the sentence must be pronounced in public in the accused's presence.
38. Zappala (2003: 198–9) concludes: 'It is nonetheless clear that presentation of evidence on sentencing *will occur* prior to the decision on guilt or innocence' (emphasis added). He goes on to argue in favour of a two-step procedure which would more effectively protect the rights of the accused and suggests that this view was implicitly accepted by the ICTY in *Tadic*, where the Trial Chamber maintained a distinct procedure for judgment and sentencing despite the fact that the ICTY's new merged procedure under Rule 86(C) had already entered into force.
39. This being currently hampered by the failure of the ad hoc tribunals to develop principles of cardinal and ordinal proportionality, which in turn reflects the absence of a hierarchy of offence seriousness for sentencing purposes. This would allow different degrees of culpability to be reflected in the imposition of penalties. See generally, Henham (2003a: 93, 98).
40. Keller (2001: 69) refers to *Krstic* to illustrate 'the negative impact that the presentation of sentencing evidence during the trial can have on the perception and possibly the reality of the fairness of the proceedings'. Keller (2001: 71) further suggests how remarks made by Judge Wald regarding the impact of certain

testimony relevant to sentencing could have easily been interpreted as influencing her decision on the verdict.

41. As Zappala (2003: 198) suggests, this is hardly likely to prove expeditious.
42. This includes the detailed consideration of expert medical, psychiatric and personal circumstances reports and witness testimony that are admitted and evaluated purely for sentencing purposes.
43. The ECHR decided in *Funke v France* 10828/84 [1993] ECHR 7 (25 February 1993) that the right to remain silent was implicit in the general right to a fair trial under Article 6(1) of the Convention. However, the ECHR does not expressly guarantee the precise constituents of the rights actually comprised in Article 6 of the Convention. The substantive content of the law of evidence has been left largely to domestic law, with the ECHR being concerned more with questions of procedural justice. Accordingly, in the UK it remains the case that the silence of an accused at trial cannot be commented on by the prosecution, although the reverse is true for a co-accused. Notwithstanding, the Human Rights Act 1998 does include the right to remain silent, not to testify during the proceedings and not to be compelled to give self-incriminating evidence as specific rights to be included within the general right to a fair trial. It is also worth noting that Article 14.3(g) of the International Convention on Civil and Political Rights provides that 'In the determination of any criminal charge against him, everyone shall be entitled ... not to be compelled to testify against himself or to confess guilt'.
44. We agree with Keller (2001: 71) that Judge Wald's remarks were almost certainly made out of politeness to the witness: 'I have no questions for the witness except to thank you for coming and sharing your very sad story with the Tribunal. I think it will help us in making our decision. Thank you' (*Krstic* trial transcript, 26 July 2000, p. 5768).
45. Erez (1999: 555) concludes: 'Comparativists encourage us to increase appropriate legal transplants and decrease inappropriate ones. There is sufficient evidence at this point to suggest that VIS (among other victim-oriented reforms) is an appropriate transplant.'
46. The nature and extent of the admissible evidence will be constrained by the constituent elements of the substantive offence(s) which need to be proved by the Prosecutor. Emphasis, context and relevance will necessarily be different for sentencing.
47. Refered to by Wald (2003: 467, n. 66).
48. Article 38(1)(b) and Rule 62(1) ECHR. See Emmerson and Ashworth (2001: 40).
49. IACHR, Report No. 33/00, Case 11.308, 13 April 2000; see also IACHR, Report No. 45/06, Petition 12.207, Friendly Settlement, *Lizandro Ramiro Montero Masache* and *Ecuador*, 15 March 2006.
50. The information obtained about each conflict and the participants' demands and aspirations for trial justice by utilising the methodology of comparative contextual analysis will go far beyond anything currently achievable through the ICC's OTP. See ICC Monitoring and Outreach Programme (2006).
51. For example, Seils and Wierda (2005) suggest that prosecutions can play a positive role in encouraging a commitment to 'democratic' values. However, these effects are attributed as beneficial outcomes of adhering to the rule of law. They are not based on achieving more inclusive justice for victims and communities in transitional states by enhancing the legitimacy of trial outcomes.

52. On the problematic legal status of amnesties and the ICC, see Robinson (2003) and Stahn (2005). For an alternative approach to the use of amnesties, see Roche (2005).
53. For a good example of contextualised research, see Liu Institute for Global Issues and Gulu District NGO Forum (2005).
54. In specific terms, the test of eligibility to be applied in the special pre-trial conference stage (described earlier) will draw on evidence at two stages. These are designed to provide a context where a preliminary assessment of the 'objective' evidence can be made which fully acknowledges the subjective accounts of all participants claiming a legitimate interest in the trial outcome. The range of factors considered will depend on the context of each conflict, but the exercise will normally deal with balancing feelings which may be classified as vengeful and retributive through to forgiveness and a desire for reconciliation.
55. Including the rationales which inform the practices in question as well as the factors which have shaped them.

8

Conclusion: Legitimacy, Justice and Governance

Introduction

The ideas and practical solutions offered in this book are controversial yet challenging and necessary if we are to forge a more inclusive and legitimate future for ICJ. As the first trial before the ICC has emphatically revealed, tribunal justice, whether from adversarial or inquisitorial procedural roots, is straining to cope with the conflicts of interest naturally generated from a wide array of purposes for ICJ (see chapter 4). We confirm trial justice will and should remain the symbolic heart of ICJ. However, if that central role is to prevail with potent rather than peripatetic location, the international criminal trial needs to maximise its utility, accountability and thereby legitimacy for crucial stakeholders (Findlay, 2008b; and see chapter 3). For victim communities in particular, international trial justice delivery is not merely a matter of refining operational and procedural integrity. Nor is it, as some suggest, better guaranteed through reading down the purposes of ICJ through the trial model (Damaska, 2008). Earlier chapter specify a process of trial transformation designed to address the tensions arising out of a largely adversarial trial tradition grappling with encompassing justice purposes and resultant conflicts of interest largely beyond the conventional adversarial experience. There is nothing surprising in this. The new trajectory for the victim voice within the ICC naturally demands a reconsidered trial delivery. This transformation is not achieved by tinkering with victim representation. It needs to tackle fundamental concerns such as trial discourse, the nature of liability, the expansion of responsibility and the emancipation of professional discretion (chapter 4). Changing these and other fundamental trial features necessitates a new trial style for ICJ, which radically restructures decision-making and reimagines available resolutions.

Our fundamental belief that international trial justice must be transformed has materialised in this book based on our argument for the merging of retributive and restorative paradigms (Findlay and Henham, 2005). We are convinced that international trial justice should be conceived primarily as a problem-solving device which seeks and, above all, contributes to repairing the harm following social conflict and war. The peacemaking governance potential is what makes ICJ so different from adversarial trials in the domestic setting and necessarily reshuffles the prioritisation of international justice stakeholders. We place victims and resultant communities of justice (chapter 3) as the hub of the ICJ endeavour. From there we position trial justice within a holistic vision of ICJ, one which lives out a crucial bond between criminal justice and governance on behalf of humanity (Findlay, 2008b).

In particular, the conflict resolution and victim restoration roles for the court rely on the fullest understanding of contextual historiography. Yet, trials are trials and the considerations for the Court may seem bound by the indictment before it and the construction of the prosecution case. How, then, will truth-telling insinuate itself where fact and evidence are the restricted trial discourse? Trial transformation intends that when, through prosecutorial initiative, defence application, victim representation or judicial intervention, the incapacity of the adversarial mode to satisfy key legitimate interests are identified, diversion to 'truth-telling' and restorative resolutions will be an option. Whether this comes about through suspension of prosecution and conciliatory diversion or transfer to a formal truth-telling mode within the trial is a matter to be determined by the judge. The Rome Statute would not require amendment to achieve these procedural alternatives.[1]

As with the developing jurisprudence of the international criminal tribunals, trial transformation will be evolutionary, not instantaneous. Legal professionals within the court would need to approach transformation with goodwill for it to work. The member states will have to accept that transformation better enhances the expressed purposes of the Court, and thereby increase its legitimacy in the eyes of essential stakeholders, so that the original authority of the Court is neither withdrawn nor challenged by disgruntled signatories.

Transformation should impact on all aspects of the formal international trial process, from pre-trial through to transitional justice[2] outcomes. More broadly, we see ICJ as a strategic tool for restoring harmony to broken communities through its impact on governance. ICJ has the potential to drive the new moralities we argue for (chapter 1) beyond the transitional phase to effect political change. Such change will accompany greater inclusivity, access and integration for principal trial stakeholders. This in turn will see enhanced accountability through the expansion and creative impact of juridical discretion. The wider legitimacy which accompanies the greater satisfaction of legitimate victim interests through more vital and versatile trial determinations will sharpen the normative and action-oriented influence of ICJ in global governance (Findlay, 2008b: chapter 9).

Governability inextricably relates to constituency. In its governance mode, ICJ and the international criminal trial in particular should break free from the patronage of sectarian political hegemonies to represent the interests of victim communities and humanity as the essential justice constituency (Findlay, 2008b: chapter 9). Driving this would be the recognition that the governance capacity of ICJ depends for its legitimacy on much more than a limited political interest. As ICJ moves more to consider the interests of victim communities, the potential for the international criminal trial to offer wider justice resolutions will necessitate national and regional political imperatives to become more accountable to humanity in increasingly diverse practical ways.

We see the future legitimacy of ICJ as crucial for a successful nexus with global governance. The international trial either encapsulates or exacerbates the legitimacy challenge. In chapter 1 we established why ICJ must initially be conceived more normatively as 'a good' so it can relate more convincingly to the justice demands of different and contesting victim communities in post-conflict situations. The resultant engagement essential in our preferred communitarian justice model (see chapter 3) will, it is argued, be enhanced through the procedural transformations required to facilitate victim participation. Further, by diversifying trial outcomes, the invigoration of legitimacy offered by the communitarian model is likely (chapter 4).

Such an approach requires a more creative conversation about the legitimacy of international trial justice and its capacity to act as a force for reconciliation and peace. The direction of this conversation and the impediments to its satisfactory progression is the concern of this chapter.

We are conscious of those critics who dogmatically assert that the international trial is an inappropriate paradigm for developing more restorative forms of conflict resolution. They largely argue from one of two perspectives. First, that the aims of ICJ, and the international trial in particular, must be constrained to reflect conventional retributive and declaratory aspirations (Damaska, 2008). Next, there is the position that the separation of retributive and restorative justice avoids the infection of the latter with the institutional limitations of the former. Proponents of what has come to be termed transitional justice usually take this segregationist position, and a massive NGO movement has grown up around this. From a theoretical perspective, Christodoulidis (2000), for instance, implicitly regards formal ICJ as somewhat of a blunt instrument. He questions the capacity of legal rules to bring about reconciliatory functions like 'mercy' through the criminal process, seeing law as over-deterministic and incapable of proceeding beyond the categories imposed by the reductive nature of legal rules. From this proceeds the renunciation that essentially complex reflexive ethical decisions cannot be reached solely within a legal context. We counter that the new normative framework for ICJ (discussed in chapter 1) and the resultant trial transformation address both procedural and ideological impediments.

In terms of justice delivery, Roche (2005) suggests that ICJ is more concerned with a victim's physical injuries and material loss than emotional or psychological damage, such as loss of dignity, happiness, confidence, security, personal power and sense of self-worth. Even a modified form of trial more mindful of victims' needs (as in the ICC) 'remains an inherently unsuitable forum for pursuing reparation'. Again, this criticism can be read as a call for trial transformation as much as it is an endorsement of continued segregation of international justice paradigms. If reparation is to remain outside the frame of trial deliberations, then its settlement will not benefit from judicial arbitration. In addition, reparation opportunities and the trial's failure to engage with these will, in the eyes of victims, practically endanger the legitimacy of the trial as a mechanism for peace-making and state restoration.

Parmentier (2003) is similarly circumspect about the future potential of the ICC, arguing that it is ill equipped to establish forms of collective 'truth' or any other type of responsibility for large numbers of perpetrators or provide any symbolic or more structural measures to the victims. Parmentier (2003: 213) also suggests that the ICC's role as a complementary institution is best seen through its capacity to link the primary loci for retributive justice (i.e. nation-states). He further envisages retributive and restorative forms of justice as generally deliverable by separate mechanisms, as complementary, each with its specific characteristics and contributions to situations of mass violence. The critique again rests on the limitations of the ICC as it is, untransformed. The problems facing the court when dealing with collective liability (see chapter 4), are sufficient in themselves to stimulate even conventional legal analysis to consider substantive and procedural change.

Finally, Fletcher and Weinstein (2002) make the important point that there are

> no mechanisms to respond to the ways in which bystanders are implicated in the establishment and maintenance of societal structures that facilitate the onset and implementation of mass violence.

In their view, trials single out particular authors and perpetrators, omitting broader initiatives on rule of law, humanitarian assistance, democracy-building and economic development. Consequently, Fletcher and Weinstein also advocate multiple interventions and envisage criminal trials as continuing to perform an essentially retributive punishment role. By responding to just one dimension of the abuse of power, they suggest, criminal trials fail to address the phenomenon of collective power and its influence on individuals. We are, through the trial therefore, unable to address the social and collective forces that lead to violence.[3] The contextualisation of international trial justice is currently tied to individualised criminal responsibility and the single legal personality (chapter 4). Power imbalances essential to crimes of aggression and the abuse of process on which they rest will never be adequately redressed through bipolar adversary trial process alone. This presents us with just another argument for radical trial transformation, certainly in terms of the crimes it can address, the perpetrators it confronts and the determinations on offer.

It could be said that the analysis in earlier chapters has taken the critique of the separatists as a foundation endorsement for trial transformation. We have employed the features of segregationalist arguments to challenge the elements of trial transformation mapped out in this book. These criticisms have formed the flashpoints on which we have built the normative and procedural features of transformation.

As noted in chapter 4, the dominant influence over international trial process and sentencing is its operation within a largely adversarial framework focusing on establishing individual responsibility for legally defined guilt. This is not essentially an exercise in the distillation of truth. Nor are international trial deliberations geared towards developing understandings of the relationship between individual and collective forms of responsibility, and what this might mean for reconciliation and peaceful coexistence. Tallgren (2002) rightly regards this tendency for ICJ to produce 'unambiguous notions of guilt or innocence' as dangerously misleading. It establishes patterns of causality which conveniently ignore the complexity and scale of multiple responsibilities that signify the social reality of collective violence and mass atrocity. Trial transformation, on the other hand, promotes and relies on communitarian justice through recognition of collective responsibility and the diverse obligations which both generate (see chapters 3 and 4).

More recently, Drumbl (2007) has suggested the need to resort to more flexible and alternative regulatory paradigms such as tort, contract and restitution, so that the universal norms of accountability are rendered relational within an international justice context. He posits that, whilst rejecting notions of collective guilt, notions of collective responsibility and collective sanction do not recognise the collective nature of mass atrocity. In this regard the limited recognition of a divergence from legal liability to more holistic responsibility constrains his critique, as it does the resolutionary potential of the current international trial model. Drumbl goes on to argue that structures of accountability in ICJ need to be more proactive, rather than simply reactive, by providing incentives for controlling the behaviour of those who promote conflict. We agree, but from the position that the transformed trial opens up juridical discretion to a realm of accountability which has more to say for good global governance than pleas for accountable justice in a procedurally non-located sense. Drumbl suggests that sanctioning the individual in a way that is proportionate to their involvement in the collective wrongdoing will more easily facilitate the pursuit of restorative approaches. We concur on this but see no reason why the achievement of collective responsibility for communitarian justice which is both restorative and retributive cannot benefit from the due process environment of the transformed trial. In addition, criminal sanctioning is presently tied to the determination of individual criminal liability. Without a transformed capacity to engage with broader determinations of regulatory responsibility the international criminal trial will remain constrained to employ legal fictions in a clumsy effort to match collective perpetration with victim communities.

Addressing the punishment purpose of trial justice Drumbl invokes cosmopolitan theory to develop a reading of punishment which reflects his vision of a shared moral response to mass atrocity. His foundations for a morality of justice are consistent with promoting the kind of relational justice advocated by Norrie (2000: 202, 221), with its focus on attentiveness to context, trust, responsiveness to needs and the cultivation of caring relations. These ideas are tremendously important for building constructive justice outcomes because they emphasise that repairing relationships, building trust and working towards reconciliation and peace through ICJ need not be paradoxically opposed to retributive justice resolve. However, this revelation can only arise once there exists more profound contextual knowledge about the relativity of justice which reflects the pluralistic values and methods for its achievement in different cultures and traditions, whether or not these happen to coincide with state boundaries and domestic legality (Findlay and Henham, 2005: chapter 1). Without an essential move to pluralist regulation through enhanced process and resolution options in trial transformation, the international criminal trial risks relegation to symbolic and declaratory legitimacy and significance alone. This book offers a route out of this.

Certainly, for ICJ, its structures and processes, the challenge is not simply one of appreciating the relativity and relational context of justice in the immediate locality of war and social conflict. It is much greater than this, since it seeks to reflect justice for the local and the global. As we have consistently argued, structures which more readily accommodate themes of restorative justice facilitate the reconciliation of opposing moralities and provide a forum for mediating relationships and encouraging reconstructive strategies are urgently needed. Certainly, those sympathetic to restorative forms of justice (Braithwaite, 2002) are more likely to regard international trial justice, and ICJ more generally, as an important element in a complex and unique jigsaw for moving forward from war to peace and beyond. Indeed, Braithwaite (2002: 207) argues for institutional renewal as a precondition for engaging restorative justice in the battle to transform peace and build a society which actually enforces international humanitarian and human rights law.

Viewed in this light, the role of ICJ to expose 'truth' and define the capacity of those structures which regulate the behaviour of individual citizens in civil society is crucial (see chapter 4). This potential lies in its ability to substitute the domestic politics of alienation, exclusivity and social control with a response based on humanitarian values grounded within communities of justice (see chapter 3). This book has sought to develop such a response for ICJ emerging out of a new morality that envisages international trial justice as key to establishing constructive and relevant structures of governance at both the global and local level.

The new morality we argue for in chapter 1 provides the foundation for changing the ideology of ICJ. It does so by suggesting that international trial ideology needs to be reconnected with its communitarian roots. This is argued, first of all, through aligning the delivery of trial justice with the broader transitional needs of victims and communities of justice in post-conflict states so that it is firmly tied to the idea of reintegrating communities and the restoration of harmony among their contesting interests. Secondly, in order to achieve this, it becomes essential to move away from the notion of the international criminal trial as a focus for the delivery of retributive and deterrent justice within a predominantly adversarial normative trial framework. If the morality of the trial is conceived as being driven by a broader agenda of intrinsically beneficial values for humanity, then it follows that this should enable the procedural transformations we propose.

However, whilst recognising how vital yet difficult change will be, we propose major normative innovations which are inspired by the values we identify as comprising the new morality. At the same time we do not rely on a wholesale change in penal ideology to underpin international criminal trials. As we have long argued (Findlay and Henham, 2005), it is possible for retributive and restorative justice norms to be integrated within a transformed trial process, if the operational context of such norms facilitates a pragmatic, problem-solving approach in post-conflict situations. In other words, we advocate the principled use of juridical discretionary power at various decision sites within the trial, relieved of the dominant influence of retributive concerns for consistency and proportionality, or the exigencies of the adversarial contest.

We emphasise the notion of 'principled' sentencing because we wish to refute possible accusations that we are in fact proposing a destabilisation rather than a reassertion of rights by inviting the trial to assuage interests that cannot be satisfied through trial justice. In fact, we are asserting the opposite. Our vision of inclusivity, as realised through the trial programme, provides a normative context which will allow the process to pursue a broader range of solutions, including both retributive and restorative forms of outcome. We argue that such a normative framework can, and does, protect the rights of all participants. This is not because the new normative direction approximates some vague notion of 'balance', as Ashworth (1994) criticises, but because it provides a context for accountability that recognises and protects the integrity of all those who are acknowledged as having a 'legitimate' interest in the trial outcome. These are not just rights which are necessary to facilitate a form of trial which protect rights in the context of retributive and adversarial concerns. From this position it is essential to confront the critics who deny the need, or indeed the probity, in merging retributive and restorative trial outcomes as aims for the trial manifestations of ICJ. We do this to employ their critique as a justification for trial transformation.

Debunking the detractors

We made the assertion earlier in this chapter that the critique of our transformation project within the trial provided in part the materialisation of our new trial framework in both procedural and normative levels. In doing so we skated over some of the contrary thinking which opposes retributive and restorative synthesis for the international criminal trial. To make this more convincing for the reader yet be convinced it is worthwhile interrogating one of the most telling recent contributions to the reductionist position on the future of international trial justice, Mirian Damaska (2008) asked: 'What is the Point of International Criminal Justice'? Despite the expansive appearance of this interrogatory his reflection largely turns on the international criminal trial. He commences by hosing down the human rights optimists whom see in the trial manifestations of ICC and cautions against a celebration of 'milk teeth' against internationally punishable conduct. To this he sharpens an attack against the international criminal courts, starting with 'goal-related problems'. We will take his anti-analysis one point at a time in order to conclude on the convictions of trial transformation against the most erudite of opposition and misunderstanding. The points below provide a checklist as to why trial transformation solves rather than salves the limitations associate with Damaska's representation of the new age of international trial justice.

'Ivy of court's aspirations' – reduced aspirations?

Damaska rightly concedes that, in the 'real world', the hegemony of international relations curtails the fulfilment of those aspirations for universal justice for international crimes which have been set by some commentators. Instead, he envisages a minimalist role for international criminal courts in advancing the 'rule of law' in this domain (2008: 320). Notwithstanding this, we argue that international trial justice is pivotal to the governance mission of ICJ. We also take issue with Damaska's rather diminished view of the capacity of international trials to engage realistically with the many and various expectations of the victims of social conflict (2008: 341). This is illustrated by his suggestion that international judges 'limit their inquiries into the larger context to the very minimum required by the definition of international crimes' (2008: 341), and his view that pandering to those who envisage an enlarged role for victims threatens the very essence of adversarial trial. Furthermore, while Damaska adverts to the inherent difficulties of integrating retributive and restorative forms of justice (2008: 343), he fails to address the issue, preferring instead to deflect the focus onto the participatory role of victims, and reverting the rest to beyond the trial.

We counter Damaska's argument for restricting victims' aspirations in international trials through our holistic and inclusive approach to victim participation. This is based on the perception that the legitimacy of ICJ depends on assimilating individual and collective interests through the development of specific trial programmes for each trial. Therefore, instead of proceeding from a perspective which sets narrow expectations for the trial, we begin from a reverse perspective which addresses the following questions:

1. *How can the trial context be designed to facilitate an outcome that has greater legitimacy for the majority of those who have been involved in the conflict?* This includes the extent to which trial justice can be seen as making a transitional contribution to peacemaking as much as penality.
2. *In designing such a trial, how can the integrity of the context be retained and meaning given to the process as a trial, especially where the flexibility of the trial programme allows it to move from a contested to a mediatory context for evidence?* The answer lies in an essential retention of the trial as a model of progressional decision-making governed through juridical discretion. We add to the mix new sources for decision-making, new contexts in which decisions are achieved, new narratives for those decisions and new outcomes.

Overabundance – primacy of didactic objective?

Damaska focuses on international criminal law theory and its consequences, but he is rather weak when it comes to exploring the relationship between context and power, and how this has shaped existing trial ideology and its structures. In addition, his critique of the lack of clarity in trial objectives and its pedagogical implications fails to reflect the critical distinction between the aims of punishment and those of the trial as a whole.

Although Damaska's apparent aim is to discuss 'the point' of ICJ, in fact, he equates it with international trial justice throughout his article. In so doing, he fails to grasp an issue which is of vital concern to our position regarding the viability of transformed trial justice, namely, the relationship between the 'justice' of the trial and its perceived legitimacy. By simply equating ICJ with trial justice, Damasaka does not distinguish adequately the different contexts, global and local, against which the legitimacy of trial outcomes is judged, and how these are implicated in the trial. In our opinion this is crucial for understanding the nature and didactic potential of trial justice. While notions of universal justice remains symbolic and expressive, trial justice, we have argued, cannot effectively engage with the aspirations and needs of specific individuals and communities. The trial conflates the universal and the local, which is reflected in the objectives set for the trial as a context for evidence and 'truth'.

Damaska's didactic approach has two dimensions: the realistic and practical one of what is deliverable within the existing adversarial context; and the pedagogical concern whether the trial can deliver anything more than symbolism, in the form of retribution, deterrence, restorative justice, or whatever. We argue that the mission of trial justice is not readily conceived by this dichotomy since its pedagogic mission is both global and local, and its moral underpinning should reflect this. Correspondingly, we see the transformed trial as essentially didactic, being informed by a morality that seeks to draw together facts and values for instrumental reasons. In order to be effective, therefore, the 'moral fundamentals' of universal and localised ICJ must converge in a practical sense. We argue for a new moral rationale to underpin international criminal trials, and suggest an instrumental role for juridical discretionary power in realising its objectives through transformed procedures.

Tensions – dilemma of the target audience?

Obviating the dangers to which Damaska alludes (2008: 348), we advocate a participatory role for collective victims and communities of justice in the formulation of the charges. The whole point of our procedural reforms is that they are designed to achieve maximum legitimacy for the outcomes of trial justice from the outset. Our recommendation for extensive expert commentary through comparative contextual analysis, and its consideration in the development of the trial programme, is evidence of this. The orchestrated adverse local reaction to the ICC's recent indictment of the Sudanese President, Omar al-Bashir, is a good example of how the legitimacy of ICJ's universal mission to prevent impunity for international crimes can be undermined even before it has begun, and makes our case for the need to effectively translate local justice aspirations into the trial from the outset. As experience with the ICTY has shown (Henham and Drumbl, 2005), such tensions are exacerbated where questionable procedural mechanisms, such as plea bargains, are reached without there having been adequate participation by victims in the decision-making process. We have outlined modified rules for victim participation and reconceptualised the role that plea bargaining might play within the transformed trial, to counter these negative tendencies.

Damaska's notion of 'thick acceptance' by taking more account of the social context of international criminality, and the potentially catastrophic effect on the coherence of international criminal law which he envisages, is obviated through the changes we propose for the juridical role. Judges and prosecutors will exercise their decision-making powers operating within the enhanced flexibility that our transformed normative framework provides. The reason for this is that the transformed normative framework will already be adapted and sensitive to the legitimate interests of the target audience, and therefore cognisant of the trial's capacity to fulfil these aspirations through intervention and mediation, as appropriate. Juridical discretion, therefore, will benefit from a more finely tuned morality as well as the prevailing procedural determinants, and the conventions of due process.

Institutional competence – problematic substantive doctrines?

Damaska questions the competence of international criminal courts to deliver what he terms a 'satisfactory judicial historiography' (2008: 336). In particular, he doubts the capacity of the judiciary empathetically and consistently to engage with relevant contextual issues and assimilate them into their discretionary decision-making processes, the difficulty judges invariably have in breaking free from the tendency to interpret factual information in ways that fit into their preconceived attitudes and beliefs. It is axiomatic that the perception, assimilation and integration of relevant information in decision-making depends on the decision-maker's pre-existing attitudes and beliefs and, as we have readily acknowledged, there will always be limits to what may be expected from 'truth' of the trial. However, the concept of trial transformation is based on our view that the legitimacy of the 'truth' the trial produces will be significantly enhanced if judicial capacity is harnessed within a flexible normative framework which sees the trial as integral to a broader social purpose defined therein.

It is probably unreasonable to expect trials or, for that matter, any kind of resolutory mechanism, to provide a context for delivering the kind of 'truth' that does not 'blur over moral distinctions shared by ordinary people' (2008: 353). It is also probable that complete moral accountability is unlikely to be reflected through satisfying those evidential requirements that are tied to the substantive definitions of international crimes or degrees of culpability taken as indicia of seriousness for sentencing purposes. Notwithstanding, in trial transformation we have advocated a move away from individual legal accountability towards a more inclusive, and therefore collective, context for the trial as a forum for establishing 'truths' which reflect the diverse moralities of conflict, and respect their social and historical roots. This ideology is mirrored in the concrete procedural changes we have described, which include new rules for the admissibility of evidence and a flexible approach to proof, as well as broadening the notion of responsibility and the corresponding parameters for accountability.

Absence of ranking order – selective enforcement?

Damaska suggests that the failure to rationalise ICJ and develop principles for the delivery of trial justice[4] based on them has accentuated the gap between the symbolism of ICJ and the reality of its partisan engagement with different situations around the globe where gross violations of international humanitarian law are perpetrated. This is really a governance issue, which depends on how the institutions of ICJ can be strengthened and set free from the hegemonic influences which force them into selectivity and discriminatory practices. Accordingly, we address the implications of this in the closing sections of this chapter. Suffice to say here that a failure of principle might be interpreted with the eye of the political pragmatist as enabling ICJ to be more responsive and subservient to sectarian, monocultural and geopolitical imperatives for partisan governance models. Trial transformation essentially works against these governance subjectivities by advocating a more apparent and grounded normative substance for achieving the humanitarian constituency. In this respect, the exercise of discretion in selective enforcement will not be personalised and politicised if it is ruled by a definitive and procedurally actionable normative framework.

Postscript – the inevitability of transformation?

We take issue with Damaska's *sui generis* characterisation of ICJ, especially the notion that the dilemma of integrating conflicting goals and aspirations for trial justice is somehow rendered less significant as a result (2008: 340). Clearly, such a perspective contributes to Damaska's overall pessimism about the moral reach of ICJ and the consequent minimal expectations he appears to set for it. We have argued that the realisation of 'interests' through the trial has to be equated with what victims perceive to be legitimate and achievable in terms of process and outcome. Thus, when we advocate the injection of humanitarian values into the ideology and normative framework for the trial, we do so in the belief that the trial *should* be able to serve those legitimate expectations/interests, whether they consist of retributive, restorative or other 'justice' aims.

In the normative framework of accountability to humanitarian justice values, the reality of procedural fairness depends on juridical capacity within the transformed trial. Our account of how this could be exercised within a transformed normative framework engages with this issue against the limitations of each new decision-making context. For instance, considering the scenario:

- In pre-trial mode the ICC, preferring the accused person's due process, must act on challenges to fairness in the form of trial delay and evidentiary inadequacy.
- On the other hand, the release of the accused as a consequence of procedural unfairness will challenge victim witness confidence and thereby undermine the vital future cooperation of witness testimony.
- Faced with this dilemma would it be better for the court to resile from the adversarial mode and proceed to consider some of the restorative justice methods recommended by the truth and reconciliation commission?

We have proposed a credible, applicable normative framework that is flexible enough to respond to each context in a way that provides realistic solutions. Such responses should recognise the limits of transformative justice so that trial outcomes contribute to the satisfaction of 'interests' by meeting aspirations for 'justice' as far possible, recognising that 'interests' can only be fully satisfied outside the arena of the trial. The trial's limited didactic input then acknowledges the possibility that the target audience's 'justice' demands may well be satisfied by other processes of resolution, accepting that other 'interests', such as political or economic justice, also will have to look elsewhere for satisfaction.

We have argued that the problems identified by Damaska will not go away simply by lowering the horizons for ICJ. On the contrary, such an approach would leave ICJ more exposed than ever. For this reason, we suggest that it is crucial to begin by establishing new moral parameters for ICJ, so that the normative transformation we advocate can work against the partisan selection of those interests it chooses to recognise. We are convinced that this will help to counter the kind of disillusionment likely to result from the unfulfilled expectations and inconsistencies of ICJ as currently conceived and to which Damaska refers (2008: 365).

Having interrogated a 'para-critique', the circumspect reader may still require some grounded theorising to substantiate the need for transformation in recent trial experience. At the time of writing there is little of that on which to rest empirical enquiry. But we do have some features of the first ICC trial which not only link to Damaska's concerns but project on the appropriateness of our trial project. With that in mind let's postulate that the quasi-adversarial ICC trial framework is open to profound tensions in achieving what Damaska criticises as gargantuan goals. Does transformation have the answers for this if we simply focus on the conflict of interests revealed through prosecutorial disclosure (or not, as the case may be)?

Case-study in conflict of interest: prosecutorial disclosure

The tensions inherent in the procedures of the ICC, particularly from the perspective of victim interests, are not solely due to what Damaska sees as mutually exclusive or overestimated purposes for ICJ through the Court. There are genuine procedural impediments and tensions which are generated through the hybrid trial model confronting a range of diverse justice and peacemaking aspirations, in a politicised context for prosecution where conflicts of interest are rife. More than being the natural product of a particular trial model or overambitious justice purpose, such tensions are exacerbated by the substantive and procedural developments where victim interests are sensitised, but without appropriate independent victim inclusion at crucial decision sites in the trial. The paradoxical purpose of victim witnesses and the incapacity of the Prosecutor to argue the exclusive representation of those interests is a case in point. The Prosecutor needs victim witnesses to give oral evidence. The very process of bearing witness exposes the witness to retributive dangers and may challenge their later opportunity to seek reparations and compensation. Therefore, independent victim representation may be seen as a way of managing the conflict of interests in the Prosecutor's role with regard to victim witnesses. Yet victim representation can in turn confound the bipolar parameters of adversarial argument. This leads further to trial transformation presenting a more flexible array of decision styles and outcomes, which might minimise conflicts of interests that adversarial argument perpetuates.

Associated with this, for the ICC's Prosecutor's Office is the paradox of apparent independence in the shadow of political hegemony through the UN Security Council and its referral power. Annexed to the issue of prosecutorial independence is the investigative reliance on 'intelligence from UN agencies on the ground, and the assistance of NGOs in the field to identify victim witnesses'.[5]

The non-disclosure dilemma which occurred in the early days of the *Lubanga* litigation necessitated conflict between the Prosecutor and the bench, which not only challenged the integrity and independence of the judicial arm, but exposed the assertion of prosecutorial independence to genuine questions of trial governance. Even if the Prosecutor is independent, in an atmosphere of limited investigatory independence and obligation to the providers of third-party 'intelligence', can the Court realistically maintain its authority if judges are prevented from considering essential exculpatory evidence from either case on trial?

The additional concern in *Lubanga* was the extent to which the Prosecutor could claim to represent victim interests in the face of prosecutorial self-interest in exploiting victim witnesses. The pre-Trial Chamber was circumspect about this claim and, as a result, awarded victims the right of independent representation in the appeal against releasing the accused and suspending prosecution as a consequence of procedural, fair trial deficiencies.

The conflict of interest emerging out of the disclosure/non-disclosure issue in the *Lubanga* pre-trial arguments and deliberations highlights:

- difficulties associated with prosecutorial disclosure requirements in an adversarial model against victim interests, particularly bearing in mind the role of the Prosecutor as investigator and the necessary limitations on his sources of evidence (i.e. second-hand experience from NGOs and the UN);
- the challenge that this poses to judicial authority;
- tensions associated with equating disclosure to fair trial;
- return to the strains posed by the presumption of innocence and the roles it requires for adversarial parties, in light of victim interests; and
- the tensions these issues present for the achievement of victim-related justice goals.

The Prosecutor's main objections to independent victim representation at the preliminary stages in *Lubanga* centred on the perception that 'external participation' adversely affected the integrity of the investigation and the safety of victims and witnesses. If so, this might precipitate a serious imbalance between victims' rights and those of the accused person claiming due process protections. Significantly, the Prosecutor resisted the idea put forward by the victims' representatives that they had a personal interest in the establishment of the charges on the basis that this served to confuse the victims' role with that of the Prosecutor, advancing the charges on their behalf and the global community at large.

The Appeals Chamber determined that the harm they had experienced and the consequent personal interests of victims in relation to their participation in the trial under Article 68(3) of the ICC Statute must be linked to the charges against the accused. This propelled their argument for independent representation against concerns that prosecutorial trial interests did not necessarily coincide with legitimate victim expectation and their exposition.

Once recognised as victims under Rule 85 of the ICC's RPE, pursuant to Article 68(3) of the Rome Statute, victims first need to establish their personal interest in the trial before they are permitted to express their views and concerns (subject to the Court's discretion), although this must not prejudice or be inconsistent with the rights of the accused to a fair and impartial trial. The Appeals Chamber in *Lubanga* decided that victims may lead evidence pertaining to the guilt or innocence of the accused and challenge the admissibility of evidence in so far as this fulfils the purposes of the trial, subject to a number of procedural safeguards. However, this must take place within the parameters set by the charges in the indictment, since these establish the issues to be determined and thereby limit the Trial Chamber's authority. Crucially, it would seem that the Prosecutor retains effective control over the formulation of the charges and what sources of evidence are used. Disclosure of exculpatory evidence to the Court but not the accused or victims clearly taints the process by which indictments are formulated and compromises fair trial, from a prosecutorial perspective.

The conflict of interest theme implicates the independence of the Prosecutor in an adversarial role beyond an impartial officer of the court suggesting the role as that of a champion of the prosecution cause. Were it possible under the RPE, the adoption of a more inquisitorial, 'quasi-judicial' role would facilitate prosecutorial interventions and even diversionary outcomes and allow greater engagement with principles at the heart of trial transformation. Placing the Prosecutor under a positive duty to ensure that the pre-trial and trial process respects victim participatory rights can be justified if we argue for a transformed role for the juridical professional.

On the issue of tensions evolving out of the need for victim witnesses' oral evidence at trial, the matter of the Prosecutor's independence against his or her reliance on second- and third-party evidence means that there are essential normative tensions before we even consider the procedural realities presented through the disclosure contest. What can be made of this against concerns for 'legal truth' or 'fact', and the issues of juridical discretion, where independence and accountability are always in tension? In addition, to what extent is the consent and volition of victim interests compromised by their road to the court littered with enticements of reparation?

These essential conflicts between independence, representativeness, autonomy and privilege resonate in any adversarial trial system since penal ideology has to be given shape through political hegemony and authority. There is no defence against the partisan influences through which 'community morality' is sustained by a sectarian 'rule of law'. If any, the 'truth' sought through case-to-case conflict in adversarial trial justice and beyond is so tainted by conflicts of interest with prosecutorial authority at the centre. In the transformed trial, on the other hand, the possibility exists that victim communities have the opportunity to establish publicly what they regard as 'their' own truth.

Trial transformation holds normative tensions at bay by juridical discretionary within the rights framework of fair trial. We propose greater transparency and a public space to challenge sectarian trial hegemony, exhibited in the advancement of prosecutorial self-interest under the guise of independence. The *Lubanga* disclosure débâcle strengthens the case for transforming the trial process, let alone the supportive ideology through new moralities for the advancement of a humanitarian constituency above debates concerning prosecutorial independence. *Lubanga* illustrates the moral bankruptcy of the ICC's retributive straitjacket and how this narrowly defines the reach of its justice capability

If our restorative proposals for the transformed trial are mainstreamed and accepted by changing the normative framework, the Prosecutor and legal professionals will be forced to promote our more victim-focused approach to trial justice. The most important point in the progress to a new professionalism is how the development of the trial programme ties local communities and their interests very specifically to the trial process. Aligning the process closely to transitional justice objectives will allow restorative initiatives a greater chance of fulfilment within a trial rights framework free from sectarian conflicts of interest. The setting out of clear objectives for trial decision-making beyond retribution and deterrence and linking these clearly to the way in which the delivery of justice will be pursued in a specific trial should ensure that the principles of distributive justice are more closely connected. From this, the social reality of conflict and its resolution become independent concerns for international criminal trial prosecution rather than those political interests and alliances which prompt initial prosecutorial intervention. Of course, this still does not overcome the hyper-selective and politicised issue of how conflicts are chosen for trial.

In *Lubanga* the establishment of victims' 'personal interests' was set against the rights of the accused and a fair and impartial trial. However, this juxtaposition assumes that the notion of a trial is somehow insulated from the penal ideology which sustains it and the consequential partisan influences of selective political hegemony to which it is indebted. The tension between the ICC's more 'objective' approach to victim participation on issues of jurisdiction and admissibility, and its more 'subjective' approach to participation as regards the trial proper highlighted by *Lubanga* cannot easily be resolved within its existing normative framework.

By effectively ignoring the broader social and economic contexts of victimisation from the outset, the ICC in *Lubanga* proceeded to narrow the potential ambit of its resolutory capacity further by tying participation firmly to the trial objective of establishing individual accountability. At the micro-level, this is reflected in the rationale used by the ICC Prosecutor in seeking to retain control over the charges and the evidence which could be drawn on to prove them. Such an approach would be countered if victims were not perceived as a threat to the the Prosecutor's role, as currently circumscribed, so that their evidence is less likely to be considered tainted by motives other than that of establishing the 'truth' of the events which constitute the facts alleged in the indictment.[6]

The need to abstract human behaviour from its social context and describe it in terms which satisfy possibly partisan accounts of the 'truth' of events, as defined by legal categorisations of harm and culpability, is obviated by trial transformation. The very willingness of the transformed trial to engage with the broader communal dimensions of social conflict from the outset mirrors very strongly its holistic approach to ICJ, one that envisages trial justice as contributing to transitional needs and governance, both local and global. In other words, trial transformation sees procedural norms and trial outcomes as serving interests beyond the immediate context of the trial, rather than the reverse.

Transformative justice values demonstrate coexistence, that is to say, asserting the rights of the individual *in* the community and balancing the interests of individual and collective hegemony through ICJ. Therefore, the transformed trial envisages ICJ as elemental to social solidarity, and fighting political partisanship, economic poverty, crime and other threats to humanity, rather than its current perception as an external force to be treated with suspicion, concerned with establishing and exploiting its own 'truth' for partisan reasons. Transformative justice emphasises humanity and coexistence over conflict, envisaging ICJ as providing the humanitarian structures to balance these opposing tendencies.

Now considering the resolution of tension exhibited in *Lubanga* and its revisionist roots in adversarial trial, we look forward to the enhancement of the ICJ's legitimacy and governance potential through a new trial style where conflicting interests, far from being denied, are celebrated. The transformed trial will mean a transformed influence for ICJ in global governance. How this can be materialised is set out in the following sections.

Designating trial justice as new global governance technology

It is now widely accepted that ICJ is a crucial tool in post-conflict global governance (Findlay, 2008b). However, the governance aspirations for ICJ have led to institutional and process distortions that compromise claims to justice, or at best create parallel 'para-justice' paradigms, which foster domination and can deny rather than complement democracy and civil society (see Findlay, 2008b: chapter 7).

The transformed trial process as described in this book offers a new way forward for the place of ICJ in global governance. This is not simply a consequence of trial transformation and the resultant enhancement of trial legitimacy in ICJ. As the next section shows, the struggle for legitimacy is advanced but hardly won through trial transformation alone. Communitarian justice models, supported by a transformed trial process, require a reconstructed normative framework for ICJ (see chapter 1). Out of this will emerge a shift in international penal ideology, which we see as victim-driven and harm-focused. Despite the problems associated with distinguishing victim status and recognising competing victim interests, victim focus remains essential for ICJ where the collectivity of harm and perpetration is what distinguishes its jurisdiction.

Along with the transformed trial project, the achievement of communities of justice through new trial decision-making paradigms holds out the real possibility for enhanced legitimacy and sharpened governance engagement without necessitating a new legislative framework for the ICC in particular.

Humanity as a focus for the injection of international criminal law into global conflict begets a strong recognition of legitimate victim interests. For the legitimacy of the justice/governance network, therefore, to be long-lasting, its aspirations must shift from conflict resolution compatible with hegemonic dominance to a much wider commitment to peacemaking for the benefit of civil society. The inherent plurality of conceptions of international criminal law and ICJ reflects the desire of victim communities for governance to confront the real and pressing harms of global crime. This is yet to be achieved through international trial justice. It is also missing from the imperatives of sectarian and hegemonic global governance.

If ICJ is part of a global governance model hell-bent on social and cultural exclusion, prospects for legitimacy are both short-term and short-lived. Here we return to the distinction between the valorised victim citizen and the alienated resistant community (Findlay, 2007; and chapter 3). Governance which services only the interests of the heroic victim or victim community will in fact exacerbate the divide between resistance and citizenship (see chapter 3). In the long term, if ICJ is reserved for 'valorised victim communities', as defined by a dominant global political hegemony, then the governance potential of ICJ will be compromised. Along with this, conceptions and applications of justice become the province of some against others and are not simply determined by the causes, direction, nature and consequences of harm. Uncoupling ICJ from harm in favour of sectarian political exclusion will not only call into question the reality of global justice and its institutions, but the integrity of ICJ as a governance tool when liberal democracy is the aspirational model.

Justice will not always align with political dominance and hegemony. ICJ has had little say in its inclusion in the global governance project, and therefore its formal institutions and processes may all too readily reflect post-military order maintenance and retributive concerns of 'victor's justice'. The international criminal tribunals, arising as they have out of the security blocs in the UN Security Council, have rarely demonstrated resolutions which challenge the post-conflict political order of dominant global hegemonies. General ascriptions to rule of law jurisprudence, or to a natural growth from principled domestic prosecutions, cannot invest ICJ with a constitutional legality sufficient to authorise and legitimate compromised global governance (Ellis, 2009). International prosecutions are not directed against the operatives and interests of the dominant alliance, nor do they expose or critique the geopolitical interests of that alliance. From the point of view of its constitutional foundations, the ICC cannot administer such 'lop-sided' justice or be so closely connected to military victory, in the manner it selects on behalf of an unrepresentative Security Council, and claim to execute its mandate on behalf of humanity.

Certain formal incarnations of ICJ portray more clearly than others anything but internationalism in their constitution, intention and stated or unstated purposes. The Hariri Tribunal, the Special Tribunal for Lebanon, created under the auspices of the United Nations to judge the assassins of Rafik Hariri, a former Lebanese prime minister who died in a truck bomb explosion in February 2005, and of several anti-Syrian politicians and journalists murdered subsequently, for instance, could never claim a cosmopolitan or even communitarian justice direction. Syria, which politically controlled Lebanon at the time of Hariri's death, remains the chief suspect when motivations for the murder are considered. An initial report by a UN commission, which began investigating Hariri's death in 2005, implicated several senior Syrian and Lebanese officials.

No other international tribunal has been established on the basis of one man's murder, thus making the Hariri Tribunal unique in ICJ and some say highly politicised and selective as a consequence. Amnesty International suggested that the tribunal was 'politically selective' and that it should address the enormous number of other serious crimes committed in Lebanon in recent decades, especially during the 1975–90 civil war. 'The mandate is by far the narrowest of any tribunal of an international nature,' Amnesty alleged.[7]

Claims of political bias have plagued the UN investigation of Hariri's killing since its inception. It is widely held that the UN tribunal owes its existence to the interests of the US, which saw it as a useful tool to put pressure on

Damascus to behave better in Iraq, cease meddling in Lebanese affairs and stop backing militant anti-Israel groups such as Lebanon's Shi'ite Hizballah. If this is the context in which the tribunal can be justified and its influence on regional order substantiated, then the sectarian and hegemonic directions for ICJ in global governance are blatant.

But a rapprochement for Syria with the West and the possibility of resumed peace talks with Israel could be derailed if the tribunal issues indictments for senior Syrian figures. Given the stakes, it is no surprise that suspicions have arisen of a deal being concocted in which the Syrian leadership is spared prosecution in exchange for progress on peace with Israel, loosening its close ties to Iran and an end to meddling in Lebanon.

At its inaugural session the Chief Prosecutor revealingly identified the unique work of the tribunal as the first court to try 'an act of terror'. References to 'justice' were replete throughout the opening remarks.

The UN has established a committee to monitor interference in the judicial process and insists that the tribunal will remain impartial. Even so the appearance of partiality and the blatant particularity of geopolitical focus will dog the tribunal's operations and suggest its legitimacy is too entwined with sectarian US/Israeli political endorsement. Such reservations have the potential to infect and challenge the governance potential of other, less apparently sectarian ICJ institutions.

Crimes of aggression and tensions for governance

As the Hariri Tribunal symbolises in the most politicised fashion, the governance dimension of ICJ, while problematic, is inevitable and to be encouraged. The increased application of ICJ within global governance has the potential to be more sectarian if crimes of aggression eventually find their way into the field of offences that can be prosecuted before the ICC and the tribunals. Through the possible fracturing and dislocation that could occur to the internationalism of global justice when crimes of aggression are more generally incorporated into state jurisdictions, ICJ may soon be exposed as an impotent governance force without radical transformation. More so, it could be argued that attempts to resolve crimes of aggression before international courts and tribunals will reveal how fragile are the international or cosmopolitan imperatives in ICJ.

Crimes of aggression are where most clearly domestic state interests contrast and conflict with global governance agendas, particularly where the states concerned may stand opposed to the current dominant political alliance. Add to this the contested evaluation of aggression where states are in transition, subject to internal warring or in post-conflict reconstruction, and the governance capacity through prosecuting aggression becomes divided and deeply problematic.

Despite the definitional difficulties and political self-interest surrounding the emancipation of crimes of aggression, we agree that these offences must be tried before the ICC. Another argument for trial transformation is that the need for what Naqvi (2009: 248) refers to as 'truth amnesties' might be a powerful inducement for political cooperation in the prosecution of crimes of aggression before the ICC. International criminal trials, therefore, would need to offer a transformed capacity to negotiate truth and from there mediate restorative outcomes in a context where truth achieves responsibility where fact and liability may not have been possible. Again, the 'relativity' of truth in contests over who is the aggressor will be a challenge for the mechanics of the criminal trial. This is where the transformed normative framework, focusing as it does on the interests of an identifiable humanity, will act as a levelling agent. Human dignity is a measure of truth and a locus for a 'right to truth', but:

> it may be argued that the 'right to truth' stands somewhere on the threshold of a legal norm and a narrative device ... lingering doubts about its (current) normative content and parameters leave it somewhere above a good argument and somewhere below a clear legal rule.
>
> (Naqvi, 2009: 273)

Trial transformation where truth-telling requires responsibility for crimes of aggression will have a powerful and positive influence on global governance, at least at a declaratory and didactic level. In this respect an expansion of trial aspirations to confront crimes of aggression, we would argue, will confirm the utility of transformation and its increased capacity for good global governance.

Again in this respect we are at odds with Damaska. Where he advocates judicial restraint, we encourage judicial discretion. Even so, Damaska does not deny that probing into matters beyond narrow concerns with specific crimes is a desirable undertaking:

> If criminal trials were the only instrument for placing international criminality into a broader context, then the abandonment by the judges of their aspiration to be historians might plausibly be criticised as foreshortening the horizons of those who have the advancement of human rights at heart.
>
> (2008: 342)

While Damaska is willing to consign this role and its positive influence over human rights to adjudicatory and resolutory frameworks beyond the trial, we say it is the due process commitments of the trial that can better provide real agency for achieving rights.

For the governance potential of ICJ to be sharp-edged through the trial process focus of the book, the challenge is to reconcile expansive justice aspirations with a transformed trial model. If trial transformation in particular is not embraced, the consequences will be increasingly negative for both global governance and ICJ legitimacy (Findlay, 2008b).

Trial transformation is just one essential step in the development of ICJ as a more vital and credible component of global governance. The argument goes that, rather than sealing off ICJ from global governance by denying its peacekeeping and conflict resolution roles, these should be given greater prominence and capacity as a result of a humanitarian normative framework and a communitarian procedural form. With these characteristics, ICJ can and will break free of sectarian dominion as the alternative argument for its governance role. For instance, against Damaska we assert that, given a 'truth-telling' role (see chapter 4), the international trial will further ground its accessibility and accountability with victim communities. The search for true stories as well as sharp punishment will enable ICJ to help heal community divisions in preference to denying their relevance through political dominion.

New building blocks for governance and ICJ

In a paper looking at recent shifts in criminal justice policies in domestic common law jurisdictions, Alan Norrie posits certain 'structural conditions, forces and developments which predicate [transitional criminal law's] shape and development' (Norrie, 2009: 13). While these are discussed in the context of the laws of nation-states, their application to 'liberal law' models which hold internationally are helpful for an appreciation of 'where to ICJ and global governance', indulging legal regulatory forms.

Norrie problematises the relationship between law and authoritarianism by suggesting that what is seen often as an opposition to liberal legal theory in fact involves a relation of 'mutual implication or co-entailment'. This, we agree, holds with the dysfunctional (in justice terms) contemporary connection between ICJ as the process for international criminal law and sectarian authoritarianism sponsoring its role in global governance. The multiple implications of global political hegemony for the application of ICJ are shaped – and are what shape – authoritarian global governance. Co-entailment between ICJ and sectarian political sponsorship challenges the place and potential of ICJ in making accountable and responsive a global governance model for a communitarian constituency.

Essential to the trajectory of ICJ within global governance is legal individualism and, as Norrie suggests, consequent forms of citizenship within a liberal democratic model of global society, pertaining to political, civil and social spheres. Norrie argues for a fusion of these spheres after the Second World

War until the end of the 1970s, in a period of consensus. What then followed was an unravelling and reconfiguration of these forms of citizenship.

> In their newly fissile condition, new possibilities, conflicts and contradictions for criminal law and justice emerged. In the process, the authoritarianism at the core of legal individualism becomes more evident. (Norrie; 2009: 14)

Norrie identifies an increase in retributive understandings of criminal behaviour, an increase in notions of dangerousness for a minority of criminals and the development of new styles of criminal justice and new mechanisms of control alongside traditional ideas of crime and punishment as developmental characteristics of criminal justice in eras of authoritarian crisis. Such a crisis, we allege, is central to the new globalisation and governance considerations which it spawns (Findlay, 2008b).

Let's test Norrie's indicia for change as they might apply to ICJ and global governance in transition. The post-war international military tribunals were clearly an attempt to create an atmosphere of constitutional legality wherein victor's justice would be distanced from armed violence to procedurally constructed retribution. Along with the authority mechanisms of the UN, the more recent international war crimes tribunals aspired to reconfigure victor's justice to become a jurisprudence of international criminal law and justice clearly directed to conflict resolution and state reconstruction in a more permanent sense. With the creation and commissioning of the ICC, a principal institution of global governance and authoritarian legitimacy, the UN Security Council, legislated for a more permanent nexus between ICJ, peacemaking and global order. The recognition of global crimes against humanity as profound challenges to good governance has justified the creation of an international criminal jurisdiction with at least a retributive procedural focus, as hegemonic authority and legitimacy are challenged (Findlay, 2007).

At the same time as international terrorism assumes risk/security prominence in globalisation and global governance (Findlay, 2008b), extraordinary ICJ institutions like the Lockerbie Special Court and the Hariri Tribunal coloured the governance aspirations of ICJ with sectarian politics. Further, the detention of suspected terrorists at Guantanamo Bay, flying in the face of Geneva Convention protections, was justified as an extraordinary response to a critical authoritarian and legitimacy challenge (Wilson, 2009). Para-justice excesses such as extraordinary rendition and even torture were tenuously incorporated into an ICJ governance agenda from similar crisis response perspectives (Jessberger, 2005). Dangerousness as a consequence of authoritarian and legitimacy crisis makes for the development of new and radical control forms in parallel with the retributive jurisdiction (Habermas, 1975; Garland, 2001).

Against these post-conflict, institutional ICJ responses, it could be argued that ICJ has been injected into global governance most commonly to address emergencies, and in the wake of radical military intervention. In this sense the ICJ/governance nexus is inextricably tied to crises of authority and legitimacy.

So far we have focused on the formal ICJ paradigms. Reflecting on the less formal or alternative justice institutions such as truth and reconciliation commissions the 'response to crisis' governance theme for ICJ also holds. There can be little doubt that the transition to a relatively peaceful post-apartheid state in South Africa depended significantly on the restorative governance capacity of its truth commission (Freeman, 2006: chapter 1). The crisis here was one of amnesty against impunity. Authoritarian reconstitution would not have been achieved unless victims' stories were told and acknowledged. Legitimacy rested heavily on the new state's capacity to move beyond retributive justice models while seeking that responsibility be directed to contrite perpetrators in an atmosphere of reconciliation rather than mass punishment.

As will often be the case with large-scale transitional justice experiments such as truth and reconciliation, it does not take long before victims create a new crisis of legitimacy and a challenge to authority if all their expectations are not addressed (Aertsen et al., 2008: Part 1). This is an important reason why we advocate trial transformation which seeks to incorporate retributive and restorative justice expectations recognising legitimate victim interests.

In conventional criminal justice terms, a central difficulty with restorative paradigms in ICJ is their fit with the law's individualism. As we discuss in relation to truth/fact, responsibility/liability considerations (see chapter 4), the individualised focus of retributive justice is counterintuitive to collective responsibility and community victimisation global crime realities. That said, individualised liability is central to a punishment-driven justice model and thereby comfortably connects with governance parameters celebrating exclusive notions of citizenship and victim valorisation (see chapter 3).

However, we are told that global governance is for a *global community*. Global crime is against cultures, collectives and communities. Perpetrators are militia, armies, organisations and even nation-states. In which case, where is the place for limited standing through sectarian citizenship and an individualised interpretation of liability, when global governance must recognise communitarian imperatives?

Ramsay (2006) suggests that interrogating recent historical conceptualisations of citizenship assists in understanding the place of legal individualism in any redirection of criminalisation and criminal law. For his analytical purpose, Ramsay identifies the following citizenship forms:

- *Civil citizenship* – rights necessary for individual, primarily economic, freedom. The rights and responsibilities of this citizen take on a universal category and the criminal law becomes based on the free, individual subject.

- *Political citizenship* – where the commitment is, in addition to individual rights and freedoms, to a universal order in which the individual has a right to participate in political decision-making.
- *Social citizenship* – introducing standards of social and economic welfare into penal measures across a range of aspects of life. This form generates forms of regulation not essentially aligned to subjectivist concerns, focusing more on control outcomes of harm, fault and blame.

In the context of liberal democratic notions of global governance, citizenship remains exclusive and intensely sectarian, influencing understandings of individualised liability, subjective penality and discriminatory imaginings of dangerousness and protection. We assert (see chapter 3) that victim valorisation from militarist to criminal regulatory paradigms is yet to be challenged in the global governance nexus with ICJ. Trial transformation will specifically confront and confound this citizenship form as it looks to serve a humanitarian constituency and to manage a more communitarian justice framework.

Against Ramsay's frame of citizenship, it is useful to plot some possible developments around the future standing and constituency of global governance, with transformed ICJ as an active component. This is possible because of our assertion that justice transformation will rest on a communitarian and more inclusive constituency for ICJ and global governance.

The aims of international criminal justice are said to foster civil citizenship. However, this we would argue presently depends on preferred sectarian standing or status as the valorised victim. Following on justice transformation, the victim within wider communities of justice will extend the notion of the 'civil'. Therefore, the rights protection offered through ICJ will collectivise. Political citizenship in contemporary global governance is now constrained. To address this, transformation is built on aspirations for access, inclusivity and integration. As a consequence, wider and richer political citizenship will be possible. The conflation of restorative and retributive paradigms and outcomes in justice transformation will enable social citizenship to become a proof of justice within global governance. For ICJ as a governance tool, control will remain as a focus, but removed as a response to emergency and embedded as a prerogative for humanity and its protection. Social and communitarian harm will be the measure of criminality rather than its challenge to political hegemony. Blame will be negotiated to achieve a range of legitimate victim interests, rather than focusing on individual liability alone to facilitate retributive penality. Fault will ground responsibility and may emerge from the stories of truth as much as the triumph of fact. Harm, fault and blame will proceed to peace more than to punishment.

Conclusion – governing for peace, not punishing resistance

Norrie (2009: 18) rightly identifies that the criminal law is not only just about moral relations between individuals. It is also the basis of a system of state control over individuals. As essential agents of governance and governability, criminal law and justice processes will incorporate into regulating world order in a similar fashion to their domestic governance influence (Simon, 2007). That said, state necessity may intervene to moderate the impact of individual rights and responsibility when criminal law and justice inform global governance. This can be seen in the control over due process justifications behind the detention regime in Guantanamo Bay.

The control potential of ICJ, we would suggest, has until now offered its most potent attractions for sectarian political governance globally. In so doing, the legitimacy of global governance has been strained by the sectarian application of control through justice strategies. The way forward for the nexus between ICJ and global governance, if it is to maximise rather than diminish mutual legitimacy, must recognise communitarian constituency, collective rights protections institutionally guaranteed and control through consensus and ascription, not military muscle or retributive fear.

Findlay (2008b) identified the relationship between the new globalisation, focused as it has been on a risk/security nexus, and the sectarian global governance priorities towards order and control. ICJ, Findlay suggests, has been co-opted into the global governance framework as a post-military intervention strategy addressing conflict resolution and therefrom, hegemonic legitimacy. This role for ICJ has not only undermined its wider legitimacy in delivering justice to the world, it has also failed to invest adequately in global governance the legitimacy anticipated to derive from victim community satisfaction. There are many reasons for this, not the least of which being that the international criminal trial as it currently operates exemplifies the partiality and cultural selectivity of victim status, consequential standing in ICJ and valid citizenship within a sectarian governance model. Parallel to this have been challenges to the fundamental legitimacy of ICJ in its limited or broader functions posed by the proliferation of para-justice aberrations denying the fundamental normative frameworks set for ICJ, formal and informal. Findlay concludes with a plea for communitarian justice models internationally. These should be directed towards a victim constituency, reliant on an interventionist and accountable juridical discretion, which will then enhance the wider legitimacy and accessibility of a liberal global governance.

The mission for the text, which this chapter concludes with, has been to materialise this foundation for transformed global governance, critically assisted by the presence and pertinence of a transformed international criminal trial. The transformed trial, we admit, will not on its own achieve the shift from sectarian to humanitarian global governance. However, as the critics and proponents of trial transformation agree, the didactic function of criminal trial justice will shore up the essential normative framework and enhance crucial stakeholder confidence on which a new age of global governance can rely.

Where does global governance go from here? Underpinning the aspiration for a more inclusive ICJ, more independent criminal justice influence on global governance and thereby a more accountable and legitimate global governance paradigm should be the search for justice procedures which serve humanity as the *global community* to be governed. This is not a vague aspiration, but a specific redirection away from sectarian political proscription towards a more just and inclusive coverage for international criminal justice and global governance. In turn, assuming that ICJ will retain its influence over global governance as globalisation moves from risk and security in the face of economic meltdown and environmental chaos, humanitarian focus will surpass sectarian sensibilities as governance embraces more pluralist regulatory forms.

The change in the nexus between ICJ and global governance as we see it commences with a realignment of normative considerations towards law and justice as 'good' (chapter 1). These should then, in the right discretionary climate, translate into decision-making sites which ensure rather than deny stakeholder access, inclusivity and integration (chapters 5-7). This procedural emancipation will only be comfortably and compatibly aligned with a governance paradigm which is more universal, democratic and accountable (chapter 3).[8] The legitimating consequence from this realignment will see the impact of legal and social responsibility accommodate legitimate communitarian interests which until now have failed to clear the hurdles of criminal liability and punitive resolution (chapter 4). Real conflict will be resolved in adversarial or mediatory contexts which benefit from a common rights/obligation framework (chapter 2).

As with our discussion of the mechanics behind a new ICJ relying on a transformed trial process, developed in the second half of this book, global governance will be transformed as it relies on the new ICJ as part of its pluralistic regulatory frame.[9] The foundations of ICJ and the governance influence it portends, having moved to a more communitarian authority and legitimacy framework, and the role of ICJ in collectivising and protecting the rights of humanity, will bring pressure to bear on justice and governance transformation.

The complex regulatory pressures attendant on global warming and generated by the recent world economic collapse require an international approach to global ordering not seen even in the risk/security phase of globalisation. This has meant an unexpected reconsideration of global governance in which pluralist regulation gains preference over military might and sectarian aggression. Governance globally is being transformed. We argue that ICJ will assist in this trend if its compatibility with pluralistic regulation strategies is enhanced

How is this transformational relationship to be achieved? The consequential influence of trial transformation, through to accessible and communitarian ICJ and on to an accountable and legitimated global governance is the answer.

Our final reflections concern how ICJ for global conflict resolution can separate governance from political domination and achieve a new reality for governability and criminal justice within cosmopolitan and internationalised contexts. While transformation is akin to continuous revolution, we need to identify the difference between images and reality, between the concealed and revealed. Transformation must be in action and confirmed through satisfaction. Transformation can advance a didactic mission, through (say) the 'show trials' of the ICC, but its product must be to resolve conflict as a consequence if the aspirations of ICJ are to amount to more than fine words. Transformation means not only change for institutions and processes but for the governance 'messages' broadcast to a new audience. In this respect, transformed ICJ and governance takes us back full circle to the normative aspirations proposed at the beginning of this book.

Recognising the paradox it represents, to some extent transformation is like the hand puppet 'Lamb Chop' and her 'Song that Doesn't End'.[10] The soft and loveable lamb has no voice without the ventriloquist, no expression without the moving fingers and no impact on an adoring child audience without the humanity behind the puppet. The image itself has no life, except in the minds of those so young as not to distinguish fact from fantasy. The message of the song has no influence, no authority, no reality without the voice concealed from view. The song has no end, only when the limp toy is transformed through the life of the voice, by the physical intervention and the personality behind the allegory. The song ends before it begins if the hand behind the mask remains removed. Only when Shari Lewis (the puppeteer) enlivens Lamb Chop will the song begin never to end. The puppeteer transforms the puppet. And the puppet image transforms the immediate audience experience through the song's promised permanence. The song never ends so long as the transformation 'goes on and on my friend'.

The analogy is important for imagining transformation. Global governance is the song and ICJ the puppet with the promise. In an age of risk/security globalisation the hand within and the voice without are sectarian, hegemonic and intent on influencing a gullible audience. Trial transformation offers a new puppet image and the opportunity for reconstructing the intent of the puppeteer. We are not so naïve as to suggest that political influence will be magically replaced by the hand and voice of humanity. Governance remains an intensely politicised process. What the transformation of ICJ can achieve is an interest to address a critical and informed audience, one not required to accept the unreality of the puppet play as a condition of enjoying the song. In a transformed trial, transformed ICJ and transformed governance progress, the audience of all ages and experience has the opportunity interrogate the singer and the song.

Despite our efforts to determine its conditions and plot its progress, trial transformation is a work in progress. Irrespective of the criticism that the aims of ICJ are too expansive, ICJ and global governance will continue to seek world order through peacemaking more than warmongering. This is not necessarily a result of political revision from neo-conservative to social democratic hegemony, even though there is evidence of this. More starkly it comes as a necessary by-product of the need for internationalism to confront the new challenges in the next phase of globalisation, one in which the nation-state or corporation cannot provide an adequate regulatory focus.

Crucial for the intersection of trial justice and conflict resolution is the confidence and capacity of victim communities (chapter 3). In all of this the cynic's reservations remain: How, or even why, should communitarian justice be achieved when hegemonic order celebrates punishment over peace? The answer, as with the limitations of individual rights and liability paradigms, rests in the recognition that the threat to world order is becoming vastly more encompassing. ICJ must accommodate and address an ever-expanding victim community base. Otherwise it will be demoted in the rush to find global regulatory models that shore up economic modernisation and salvage endangered environments. The climate for world order will no longer rely on brief periods of violent instability followed by enforced retributive or deterrent justice. Prevailing periods of peace will be essential if economic repositioning and environmental restitution can ever be achieved.

Three conditions are required, in our view, for the transformed trial to reposition ICJ in order that its peacemaking aims prevails in global governance, at least to the same extent as the contemporary quest for sectarian control and sequestered order.

1. *Collective perpetration and communal victimisation will be distilled and addressed through a new jurisprudence of ICJ.* This is more difficult than it seems. Take first the determination of victim status and the recognition of contested victim interest. This is not simply a matter of better emancipating those victims who have under the current age of globalisation been marginalised from global citizenship for risk/security considerations. In addition, the transformed trial will need to confront and adequately conciliate in conflict and post-conflict societies the reality that one community's victim is another community's perpetrator. And when it comes to perpetration, the criminal law has not conventionally addressed levels of responsibility. In fact, in some criminal law traditions association with the criminal conduct at any stage and to any degree may eventually receive equal punishment. Without the development of responsibility paradigms which recognise contribution or aggregation, the need to sophisticate and sensitise collective perpetration will be all the more difficult.

2. *International criminal trials will present an opportunity for restorative and retributive outcomes to be tailored to legitimate victim interests.* As indicated earlier, this is not merely a challenge for new procedural regimes. Admittedly, truth and fact will require reconciliation within trial narrative and discourse. Appropriate pre-trial and trial decision sites will need to be identified for the purposes of restorative rather than retributive deliberation. Above all, juridical discretion and legal/professional goodwill must be incorporated and encouraged so that what Hogg (1983) refers to as 'hierarchies of knowledge' do not become intractable impediments to achieving transformation without fragmentation. Hogg's 'superstructures of expertise and specialists' must be enlisted to the transformation project.[11]
3. *The nexus between international criminal justice and global governance will be redirected more instinctively towards conflict resolution rather than conflict authorisation.* This in turn will produce transformed governance as a consequence of improved access and accountability. We have emphasised the non-negotiable commitment to humanity – victim communities in particular – as the new constituency for ICJ, if trial transformation is to proceed. Humanity will, therefore, advance as the 'global community' towards which governance is directed. The global community will materialise in specific victim communities who should benefit from peacemaking and conflict resolution interpretations of justice and governance. Measures for achieving peace and reducing conflict will become empirical evaluators of good global governance.

Governing for peace and conflict resolution must move beyond narrow sectarian concerns for world ordering if justice is to endorse legitimacy. This means that the exclusionist propensity of ICJ must become the first victim of trial transformation. ICJ as an agency of repression for sectarian global hegemony will be revealed as incompatible with peace and conflict resolution imperatives. Retribution and deterrence as the motives for trial resolution will be forced into balance by legitimate victim community aspirations also for restoration (chapter 3).

In describing and analysing the legal response to ghetto riots and disorder in domestic contexts, Balbus (1977) suggested that the operation of legal regulation is the product of the dialectics of repression in the bourgeois liberal state. These are represented as:

- the maintenance of social order through the effective repression of resistance and rebellion;
- the reproduction of state legitimacy through adherence to formal rational (due process) procedures; and
- the organisational maintenance through efficient processing of defendants according to the internal bureaucratic processing of a court system.

ICJ to date has exhibited similar operational dialectics, replacing state interest with hegemonic and sectarian international alliance motivations. The place of transformed ICJ in a revised global governance perspective is to resolve these dialectics in a humanitarian pursuit for peacemaking over selective repression and conditional protection.

In this respect the place of ICJ in global governance is not as a certifier, authoriser or empowering agent. It is a peacemaker, employing a carrot-and-stick approach through trial resolutions. Conventional power structures advanced through legal regulatory forms recede when conflict resolution comes to the fore as the legitimate and legitimating purpose of ICJ.

> Law is neither the truth of power, nor its alibi. It is an instrumental power which is at once complex and partial. The form of the law with its effects of prohibition needs to be restituated among a number of other non juridical mechanisms.
>
> (Foucault, 1980: 141)

Trial transformation is the new regulatory form in so far as it declares the conditions for humanitarian justice resolutions. Its place within reconstituted ICJ is didactic and restorative, enabling victim communities to claim much more through the rich mix of non-juridical alternatives. Once transformed, global governance no longer needs an alibi. Peace is the consequence of responsibility claimed through truth-telling and maintained by restoration as well as penalty. Humanity is ordered through compliance and conflict becomes the indication of the ungoverned rather than the precursor to sectarian governance.

Notes

1. The Rules of Procedure and Evidence prevailing in pre-trial and trial proceedings would have to be adjusted to enable this discretion.
2. In this respect we are using transitional justice not as a new justice paradigm but rather as the integration of restorative with retributive outcomes.
3. This, of course, begs the question as to the extent to which any form of resolution or intervention, including trials, can avoid contamination and deliver justice irrespective of power.
4. RPE, 363 ('discrepancy between word and deed').
5. This raises additional challenges to independence and presents provocative conflicts of interest for the NGOs as well as for the Prosecutor.
6. Decision on Victims' Participation, Situation in the Democratic Republic of Congo, *Prosecutor v Thomas Lubanga Dylio* (Case No. ICC-01/04-01/06-1119), 18 January 2008.
7. See *Time Magazine* 1 March 2009, 'Lebanon on Edge as Hariri Tribunal Starts'.
8. We hold this view mindful that it does not reflect the contemporary reality of domestic political engagement, while drawing close to the ideological pretence

of state governance within the prominent political partners in the dominant international alliance.

9. The limitations of this text do not allow for a detailed argument regarding the inevitability of pluralistic global regulation. Suffice to say our confidence in this eventuality rests in charting the shift in globalisation priorities since the global economic collapse in 2008. Recovery strategies have witnessed a reaffirmation of modernisation and free market capitalism as the global economic frame. At the same time, uniform regulatory strategies have resorted to pluralist economic and social engagement, in which legality and criminalisation are playing a role in boundary setting.
10. http://www.youtube.com/watch?v=1_47KVJV8DU&feature=related
11. See Hogg (1983).

Bibliography

Aertsen, I., Arsovska, J., Rohne, H., Valinas, M. and Vanspauwen, K. (eds.) (2008) *Restoring Justice after Large Scale Violent Conflicts*, Cullompton: Willan Publishing

Albrecht, H. G., Simon, J., Rezaei, H., Rohne, H. C. and Kiza, E. (2006) *Conflict and Conflict Resolution in Middle Eastern Societies – Between Tradition and Modernity*, Berlin: Duncker & Humblot

Albrecht, H. J. and Kilchling, M. (2005) 'Victims of Terrorism – Policies and Legislation in Europe', Max Planck Institute for Foreign and International Criminal Law, European Committee on Crime Problems, Second Meeting, 18–20 May

Aldana-Pindell, R. (2002) 'In Vindication of Justiciable Victims' Rights to Truth and Justice for State-sponsored Crimes', *Vanderbilt Journal of Transnational Law* 35, 5: 1399

Amann D. M. (2000) 'Harmonic Convergence? Constitutional Criminal Procedure in an International Context' *Indiana Law Journal* 75: 809

Amann, D. M. (2002) 'Group Mentality, Expressivism and Genocide', *International Criminal Law Review* 2: 93

Amann, D. M. (2006) 'Impartiality Deficit and International Criminal Judging' (28 November 28). Available at SSRN: http://ssrn.com/abstract=955431

Ambos, K. (2003) 'International Criminal Procedure: "Adversarial", "Inquisitorial" or Mixed?' *International Criminal Law Review* 3: 1

Ambos, K. (2007a) 'Joint Criminal Enterprise and Command Responsibility', *Journal of International Criminal Justice* 5, 1: 159

Ambos, K. (2007b) 'Legal Framework of Transitional Justice'. http://www.peace-justice-conference.info/download/Ambos_NurembergStudy_070512.pdf 69–72.

Amnesty International (1999) *The International Criminal Court: Ensuring an Effective Role for Victims* (AI Index: IOR 40/10/99)

Andersen, A. M. (2003) 'Restorative Justice, the African Philosophy of *Ubuntu* and the Diversion of Criminal Prosecution'. Paper presented at the 17th International Conference of The International Society for the Reform of the Criminal Law, The Hague, Netherlands

Arendt, H. (1969) *On Violence*. London: Allen Lane

Ashworth, A. (1989) 'Criminal Justice and Deserved Sentences', *Criminal Law Review* 340

Ashworth, A. (1983) *Sentencing and Penal Policy*. London: Weidenfeld & Nicolson

Ashworth, A. (1994) *The Criminal Process: An Evaluative Study*. Oxford: Oxford University Press, 1st edition.

Ashworth, A. (1996) 'Crime, Community and Creeping Consequentialism', *Criminal Law Review*: 220

Ashworth, A. (2000a) 'Victims' Rights, Defendants' Rights and Criminal Procedure'. In A. Crawford and J. Goodey (eds.) *Integrating a Victim Perspective within Criminal Justice*. Aldershot: Ashgate

Ashworth, A. (2000b) 'Testing Fidelity to Legal Values: Official Involvement and Criminal Justice', *Modern Law Review* 63, 5: 633

Ashworth, A. (2000c) *Sentencing and Criminal Justice*. London: Butterworths, 3rd edition

Ashworth, A. (2002) 'Responsibilities, Rights and Restorative Justice', *British Journal of Criminology* 42: 578

Ashworth, A. (2005) *Sentencing and Criminal Justice.* Cambridge: Cambridge University Press, 4th edition

Ashworth, A. (2006) *Principles of Criminal Law.* Oxford: Oxford University Press, 5th edition

Balbus, I. (1977) *The Dialectics of Legal Reference,* New York: Sage

Balint, J. (2001) 'Law's Constitutive Possibilities: Reconstruction and Reconciliation in the Wake of Genocide'. In E. Christodoulidis and S. Veitch (eds.) *Lethe's Law: Justice, Law and Ethics in Reconciliation.* Oxford: Hart

Bankowski, Z. (1988) 'The Jury and Reality', in M. Findlay and P. Duff (eds.) *The Jury Under Attack,* Sydney and London: Butterworths

Barton, C. (2003) *Restorative Justice: The Empowerment Model.* Sydney: Hawkins Press

Bauman, Z. (1998) *Globalisation: The Human Consequences.* Cambridge: Polity Press

Baumgartner, E. (2008) 'Aspects of Victim Participation in the Proceedings of the International Criminal Court', *International Review of the Red Cross* 90, 870: 408

Beardsley K. C. et al. (2006) 'Mediation Style and Crisis Outcomes', *Journal of Conflict Resolution* 50: 58

Beccaria, C. (1764) *Of Crimes and Punishments and Other Writings* [*Dei Delitti e delle Pene*], ed. R. Bellamy, trans. R. Davies with V. Cox and R. Bellamy. Cambridge: Cambridge University Press (1995)

Becker, H. (1973) *Outsiders.* New York: Free Press, 2nd edition.

Behrens, H-J. (1998) 'Investigation, Trial and Appeal in the International Criminal Court Statute (Parts V, VI, VIII)', *European Journal of Crime, Criminal Law and Criminal Justice* 6: 429

Bell, J. (2001) *French Legal Cultures.* London: Butterworths

Benjamin, W. (1978) *Critique of Violence, Reflections: Essays, Aphorisms, Autobiographical Writings.* Ed. P. Demetz. New York: Harcourt, Brace Jovanovich

Bickford, L. (2004) *The Encyclopedia of Genocide and Crimes Against Humanity.* New York: Macmillan Reference, vol. 3

Bikundo, E. (forthcoming) 'International Criminal Law, Abusing Process and Criminal Aggression: Virtue's Homage to Vice'. PhD thesis, University of Sydney

Blad, J. (2006) 'Institutionalizing Restorative Justice? Transforming Criminal Justice? A Critical View of the Netherlands'. In I. Aertsen, T. Daems, and L. Robert (eds.) *Institutionalising Restorative Justice.* Cullompton: Willan Publishing

Blattmann, R. and Bowman, K. (2008) 'Achievements and Problems of the International Criminal Court: A View from Within', *Journal of International Criminal Justice* 6: 711

Borraine, A. (2004) 'Transitional Justice as an Emerging Field'. Paper presented at the Repairing the Past: Reparations and Transitions to Democracy symposium, Ottawa, Canada, 11 March

Bottoms, A. E. and Brownsword, R. (1982) 'The Dangerousness Debate after the Floud Report', *British Journal of Criminology* 22: 229

Braithwaite, J. (1989) *Crime, Shame and Reintegration.* Cambridge: Cambridge University Press

Braithwaite, J. (2002) *Restorative Justice and Responsive Regulation.* Oxford: Oxford University Press

Braithwaite, J. and Fisse, B. (1993) *Corporations, Crime and Accountability.* Cambridge: Cambridge University Press

Braithwaite, J. and Strang, H. (eds.) (2000) *Restorative Justice: Philosophy to Practice.* Aldershot: Ashgate

Broomhall, B. (2003) *International Justice and the International Criminal Court: Between Sovereignty and the Rule of Law.* Oxford: Oxford University Press

Buchanan, A. (2004) *Justice, Legitimacy and Self-Determination: Moral Foundations for International Law.* New York: Oxford University Press

Bush, R. and Fogler, J. (1994) *The Promise of Mediation: Responding to Conflict through Empowerment and Recognition.* San Francisco: Jossey-Bass

Carcano, A. (2002) 'Sentencing and the Gravity of the Offence in International Criminal Law', *International and Comparative Law Quarterly* 51: 583

Casanovas, P. (1999) 'Pragmatic Legal Contexts'. Paper presented at the International Pragmatics Conference on Pragmatics and Negotiation, Tel Aviv University/ Hebrew University of Jerusalem, 13–16 June

Cassese, A. (1998) 'Reflections on International Criminal Justice', *Modern Law Review* 61, 1: 1

Cassese, A. (2007) 'The Proper Limits of Individual Responsibility under the Doctrine of Joint Criminal Enterprise', *Journal of International Criminal Justice* 5: 109

Chadwick, E. (2003) 'It's War Jim, but not as We Know it: A Reality Check for International Laws of War?' *Crime Law and Social Change* 39, 3: 239

Chambliss, W., Michalowski, R. and Kramer, R. (forthcoming) *State Crime in a Global Age.* Cullompton: Willan Publishing

Chapman, A. (2004) 'The Complexity of International Criminal Law: Looking beyond Individual Responsibility to the Responsibility of Organisations, Corporations and States'. In R. Thakur and P. Malcontent (eds.) *From Sovereign Impunity to International Accountability: The Search for Justice in a World of States.* Tokyo: United Nations Press

Cherif Bassiounii, M. (2003) 'Truth, Justice and Amnesty'. In L. Chand Vorah et al. *Man's Inhumanity to Man: Essays on International Law in Honour of Antonio Cassese.* Leiden: Martinus Nijhoff

Christodoulidis, E. A. (2000) 'Truth and Reconciliation as Risks', *Social and Legal Studies* 9: 179

Cockayne, J. (2001) *From a Culture of Immunity to a Culture of Accountability: International Criminal Tribunals.* The International Criminal Court and Human Rights Protections Report on the International Conference, University of Utrecht, Netherlands, December

Cockayne, J. (2005) 'Hybrids or Mongrels? Internationalized War Crimes Trials as Unsuccessful Degradation Ceremonies', *Journal of Human Rights* 4: 455

Cohen, S. (1985) *Visions of Social Control.* Cambridge: Polity Press

Cohen, S. (1995) 'State Crimes of Previous Regimes: Knowledge, Accountability, and the Policing of the Past', *Law and Social Inquiry* 20: 7

Condorelli, L. (2002) 'Is There a Need for Internationalised Courts and Tribunals?' Paper presented at the Internationalised Criminal Courts and Tribunals: Practice and Prospects conference, Universiteit van Amsterdam, The Netherlands, 25–26 January

Cornell, M. Rosenfeld and Gray Carlson, D. (eds.) (1992) *Deconstruction and the Possibility of Justice.* New York and London: Routledge.

Cote, L. (2005) 'Reflections on the Exercise of Prosecutorial Discretion in International Criminal Law', *Journal of International Criminal Justice* 3: 162

Cotterrell, R. B. M. (1989) *The Politics of Jurisprudence: A Critical Introduction to Legal Philosophy.* London: Butterworths, 1st edition

Cotterrell, R. B. M. (1992) *The Sociology of Law: An Introduction.* London: Butterworths, 2nd edition

Cryer, R., Friman, H., Robinson, D. and Wilmshurst, E. (2007) *An Introduction to International Criminal Law and Procedure.* Cambridge: Cambridge University Press

Daamgard, C. (2008) *Individual Criminal Responsibility for Core International Crimes.* Heidelberg: Springer Berlin

Daly, E. (2002) "Between Punitive and Reconstructive Justice: The Gacaca Courts in Rwanda', *NYU Journal of International Law and Politics* 34: 355

Damaska, M. (2005) 'Negotiated Justice in International Criminal Courts', *Journal of International Criminal Justice* 3: 3

Damaska, M. (2008) 'What is the Point of International Criminal Justice?' *Chicago Kent Law Review* 83, 1: 329

Danner, A. M. (2003) 'Enhancing the Legitimacy and Accountability of Prosecutorial Discretion in the International Criminal Court', *American Journal of International Law* 97: 510

Danner, A. M. and Martinez, J. (2005) 'Guilty Associations: Joint Criminal Enterprise, Command Responsibility, and the Development of International Criminal Law', *California Law Review* 93, 75: 77

de Hemptinne, J .(2007) 'The Creation of Investigating Chambers at the International Criminal Court: An Option Worth Pursuing?' *Journal of International Criminal Justice* 5: 402

de Hemptinne, J. and Rindi, F. (2006) 'ICC Pre-Trial Chamber allows Victims to Participate in the Investigation Phase of Proceedings', *Journal of International Criminal Justice* 4: 342

de Londras, F. (2007) 'Telling Stories and Hearing Truths: Providing an Effective Remedy to Genocidal Sexual Violence against Women'. In R. Henham and P. Behrens (eds.) *The Criminal Law of Genocide: International, Comparative and Contextual Aspects.* Aldershot: Ashgate

Derrida, J. (1990) 'Force de Loi: la "Fondement Mystique de l'Autorité"'/Force of Law: the "Mystical Origin of Authority"', *Cardozo Law Review* 11: 919

Derrida, J. (1992) 'Force of Law: The "Mystical Foundation of Authority"', in D. Cornell, M. Rosenfeld and D. Gray Carlson (eds.) *Deconstruction and the Possibility of Justice.* New York and London: Routledge

Derrida, J. and Anidjar, G. (eds.) (2001) *Acts of Religion.* London: Routledge

Dignan, J. and Cavadino, M. (1996) 'Towards a Framework for Conceptualising and Evaluating Models of Criminal Justice from a Victim's Perspective', *International Review of Victimology* 4: 153

Drumbl, M. (2000) 'Punishment, Postgenocide: From Guilt to Shame to *Civis* in Rwanda', *New York University Law Review* 75: 1221

Drumbl, M. (2005) 'Pluralising International Criminal Justice', *Michigan Law Review* 103: 1295

Drumbl, M. A. (2007) *Atrocity, Punishment, and International Law.* Cambridge: Cambridge University Press

Duff, A., Farmer, A., Marshall, S. and Tadros, V. (2004, 2006, 2007) *The Trial on Trial,* three volumes. Oxford: Hart

Edwards, I. (2003) 'Victim Participation in Sentencing: The Problem of Incoherence', *Howard Journal of Criminal Justice* 40, 1: 39

Ellis, M. (2009) 'International Justice and the Rule of Law: Strengthening the ICC through Domestic Prosecutions', *Hague Journal on the Rule of Law* 1: 79

Emmerson, B. and Ashworth, A. (2001) A *Human Rights and Criminal Justice.* London: Sweet & Maxwell, 1st edition

Erez, E. (1994) 'Victim Participation in Sentencing: And the Debate Goes On', *International Review of Victimology* 3: 17
Erez, E. (1999) 'Who's Afraid of the Big Bad Victim? Victim Impact Statements as Victim Empowerment *and* Enhancement of Justice', *Criminal Law Review* 545
Erez, E. and Rogers, L. (1995) Crime Impact v. Victim Impact: Victim Impact Statements in South Australia', *Criminology Australia* 6: 3
Erez, E. and Rogers, L. (1999) 'Victim Impact Statements and Sentencing Outcomes and Processes: The Perspectives of Legal Professionals', *British Journal of Criminology* 39, 2: 216–39
Erez, E. and Tontodonato, P. (1990) 'The Effect of Victim Participation in Sentencing on Sentence Outcome', *Criminology* 28: 451
Eser, A. (2002) 'Individual Criminal Responsibility'. In A. Cassese, P. Gaeta and J. Jones (eds.) The Rome Statute of the International Criminal Court: A Commentary. Oxford: Oxford University Press
Findlay, M. (1994a) The Ambiguity of Accountability: Deaths in Custody and Regulation of Police Power', *Current Issues in Criminal Justice* 6, 2: 234
Findlay, M (1994b) *Jury Management in NSW.* Melbourne: AIJA
Findlay M (1999) *The Globalisation of Crime.* Cambridge: Cambridge University Press
Findlay M (2001) 'Synthesis in Trial Procedures? The Experience of International Criminal Tribunals', *International and Comparative Law Quarterly* 50: 26
Findlay, M. (2002) 'Internationalised Criminal Trial and Access to Justice', *International Criminal Law Review* 2: 237
Findlay, M. (2006) *Criminal Law: Problems in Context.* Melbourne: Oxford University Press.
Findlay, M. (2007) 'Terrorism and Relative Justice', *Crime Law and Social Change* 47: 57
Findlay, M. (2008a) 'Juror Comprehension and the Hard Case – Making Forensic Evidence Simpler', *International Journal of Law, Crime and Justice* 36: 15
Findlay, M. (2008b) *Governing through Globalised Crime: Futures for International Criminal Justice.* Cullompton: Willan Publishing
Findlay, M. and Henham, R. (2005) *Transforming International Criminal Justice: Retributive and Restorative Justice in the Trial Process.* Cullompton: Willan Publishing
Findlay, M. and McLean, C. (2007)'Emerging International Criminal Justice', *Current Issues in Criminal Justice*, 18, 3: 457–80.
Finnis, J. (1980) *Natural Law and Natural Rights.* Oxford: Oxford University Press
Fisher, K. J. (2007) *Demanding Accountability: Judgement, Punishment and Forgiveness in Ugandan Traditional Processes of Justice.* Vancouver: Canadian Consortium on Human Security Policy Brief
Fletcher, G. (1995) *With Justice for Some: Victims' Rights in Criminal Trials.* New York: Addison-Wesley
Fletcher, G. P. (2005) 'Parochial versus Universal Criminal Law', *Journal of International Criminal Justice* 3: 20–34
Fletcher, G. P. and Ohlin, J. D. (2005) 'Reclaiming Fundamental Principles of Criminal Law in the Darfur Case', *Journal of International Criminal Justice* 3, 3: 539
Fletcher, L. E. and Weinstein, H. M. (2002) 'Violence and Social Repair: Rethinking the Contribution of Justice to Reconciliation', *Human Rights Quarterly* 24: 573
Fogarty, G. (2005) 'Is Guantanamo Bay Undermining the Global War on Terror?' *Parameters* 35, 3: 59
Foucault, M. (1977) *Discipline and Punish; The Birth of the Prison.* Harmondsworth: Penguin
Foucault, M. (1980) *Knowledge/Power* London: Harvester Press

Freeman, M. (1999) 'Obligations, Institutions and International Justice'. Paper presented at the workshop on International Distributive Justice: Cosmopolitanism and its Critics'. European Consortium for Political Research, 27th Joint Sessions of Workshops, Mannheim Centre for European Social Research, University of Mannheim, Germany, 26–31 March

Freeman, M. (2006) *Truth Commissions and Procedural Fairness*. New York: Cambridge University Press

Friedrichs, J. (2005) 'Global Governance and the Hegemonic Project of Transatlantic Civil Society'. In M. Lederer and P. Muller (eds.) *Criticising Global Governance*. New York: Palgrave Macmillan

Galabru, K. (2006) 'Reconciliation in International Criminal Justice: Lessons from Other Tribunals', *Open Society Justice Initiative*: 151

Garcia-Sanche, M. et al. (2008) *Evaluation of the Victims' Advocate Scheme Pilots*. London: Ministry of Justice, Research Series 17/08, October

Garland, D. (1996) 'The Limits of the Sovereign State: Strategies of Crime Control in Contemporary Society', *British Journal of Criminology* 36: 445

Garland, D. (2001) *The Culture of Control*. Oxford: Oxford University Press

Goldstein, A. (ed.) (2006) *Forensic Psychology: Emerging Topics and Expanding Roles*. New York: John Wiley & Sons

Gordon, G. S. (2007) 'Toward an International Criminal Procedure: Due Process Aspirations and Limitations', *Columbia Journal of Transnational Law* 45: 635

Guest, J. (1999) 'Aboriginal Legal Theory and Restorative Justice, Parts 1 and 2', *Justice as Healing*. Native Law Center of Canada http://www.usask.ca/nativelaw/publications/jah

Haack, S. (2004) 'Epistemology Legalised: Or Truth Justice and the American Way', *American Journal of Jurisprudence* 49: 43

Haan, V. (2005) 'The Development of the Concept of Joint Criminal Enterprise at the International Criminal Tribunal for the Former Yugoslavia', *International Criminal Law Review* 5: 167

Habermas, J. (1975) *Legitimation Crisis*. Boston, MA: Beacon Press

Hall, K. (2004) 'The Power and the Role of the Prosecutor of the International Criminal Court in the Fight against Impunity', *Leiden Journal of International Law* 17: 121

Held, D. (1997) 'Democracy and Globalisation'. MPIfG Lecture Series Economic Globalisation and National Democracy, MPIfG Working Paper 97/5, May

Held, V. (2004) 'Care and Justice in the Global Context', *Ratio Juris* 17: 141

Henderson, J. Y. (1995) 'Exploring Justice as Healing', *Justice as Healing*. Native Law Center of Canada, http://www.usask.ca/nativelaw/publications/jah

Henham, R. (2001) 'Theory and Contextual Analysis in Sentencing', *International Journal of the Sociology of Law* 29, 3: 253

Henham, R. (2003a) 'Some Issues for Sentencing in the International Criminal Court', *International and Comparative Law Quarterly* 52, 1: 81

Henham, R. (2003b) 'The Philosophical Foundations of International Sentencing', *Journal of International Criminal Justice* 1: 64

Henham, R. (2004a) 'Some Reflections on the Role of Victims in the International Criminal Trial Process', *International Review of Victimology* 11: 1

Henham, R. (2004b) 'Conceptualising Access to Justice and Victims' Rights in International Sentencing', *Social and Legal Studies* 13, 1: 27

Henham, R. (2005) *Punishment and Process in International Criminal Trials*. Aldershot: Ashgate

Henham, R. (forthcoming a) 'International Penality as a Force for Achieving Peace through Justice'. In M. Findlay and R. Henham (eds.) *Exploring the Boundaries of International Criminal Justice*. Alsdershot: Ashgate

Henham R. (forthcoming b) *Sentencing and the Legitimacy of Trial Justice*. Cullompton: Willan Publishing

Henham, R. and Drumbl, M. (2005) 'Plea Bargaining at the International Criminal Tribunal for the former Yugoslavia', *Criminal Law Forum* 16: 49

Henham, R. and Mannozzi, G. (2003) 'Victim Participation and Sentencing in England and Italy: A Legal and Policy Analysis', *European Journal of Crime, Criminal Law and Criminal Justice* 11: 278

Hogarth, J. (1971) *Sentencing as a Human Process*. Toronto: University of Toronto Press

Hogg, R. (1983) 'Perspectives on the Criminal Justice System'. In M. Findlay, S. Eggar and J. Sutton (eds.) *Issues in Criminal Justice Administration*. Sydney: George Allen & Unwin

Hudson, B. A. (1998) 'Doing Justice to Difference'. In A. Ashworth and M. Wasik (eds.) *Fundamentals of Sentencing Theory*. Oxford: Clarendon Press

Hudson, B. (2003) *Understanding Justice: An Introduction to Ideas, Perspectives and Controversies in Modern Penal Theory*. Buckingham: Open University Press, 2nd edition

Hutton, N. (2008) 'Institutional Mechanisms for Incorporating the Public'. In A. Freiberg and K. Gelb (eds.) *Penal Populism, Sentencing Councils and Sentencing Policy* Cullompton: Willan Publishing

Indemaur, D. (2008) 'Dealing the Public in Challenges for a Transparent and Accountable Sentencing Policy'. In A. Freiberg and K. Gelb (eds.) *Penal Populism, Sentencing Councils and Sentencing Policy*. Cullompton: Willan Publishing

ICC Monitoring and Outreach Programme (2006) First Outreach Report, International Bar Association and Human Rights Institute, June http://www.ibanet.org/images/downloads/ICC/06_2006_June_ICC_First_Outreach_Report_Final.pdf

ICC OTP (2007) Policy Paper on the Interests of Justice http://www.icc-cpi.int/library/organs/otp/ICC-OTP-InterestsOfJustice.pdf

International Law Commission (1994) *Sentencing Yearbook*, Vol. II, Part 2. Report of the Commission to the General Assembly on the Work of its 46th Session Draft Code of Crimes against the Peace and Security of Mankind, UN Doc. A/49/10

Jessberger, F. (2005) 'Bad Torture Good Torture: What International Criminal Lawyers May Learn from Recent Trials of Police Officers in Germany', *Journal of International Criminal Justice* 3: 1059

Joseph, S. (2004) *Corporations and Transnational Human Rights Litigation*. Oxford: Hart

Judah, E. and Bryant, M. (eds.) (2003) *Criminal Justice: Retribution v. Restoration*, New York: Hayworth Social Work Press

Jung, H. (1997) 'Plea Bargaining and its Repercussions on the Theory of Criminal Procedure', *European Journal of Crime, Criminal Law and Criminal Justice* 5: 112

Kay, J. (2004) 'Redefining the Terrorist', *The National Interest* 7: 87

Keller, A. (2001) 'Punishment for Violations of International Criminal Law: An Analysis of Sentencing at the ICTY and ICTR', *Indiana International and Comparative Law Review* 52

Keller, L. M. (2007) 'Seeking Justice at the International Criminal Court: Victims' Reparations', *Thomas Jefferson Law Review* 29: 189

King, M. (1978) 'A Status Passage Analysis of the Defendant's Progress through the Magistrates' Court', *Law and Human Behaviour* 2: 187

Kirchengast, T. (2006) *The Victim in Criminal Justice*. Basingstoke: Palgrave Macmillan

Kittichaisaree, K. (2001) *International Criminal Law*. Oxford: Oxford University Press

Kiza, E. and Rohne, R. (2005) *Victims' Expectations: The International War-Victim Survey.* Freiburg, Germany: Max Planck Institute for Foreign and International Criminal Law

Kiza, E. and Rohne, R. (2008) 'Victim Expectations Towards Justice in Post-Conflict Societies: A Bottom-up Approach'. Unpublished conference paper.

Kress, C. (2003) 'The Procedural Law of the International Criminal Court in Outline: Anatomy of a Unique Compromise', *Journal of International Criminal Justice* 1: 603

Kyriakakis, J. (2007) 'Australian Prosecution of Corporations for International Crimes: The Potential of the Commonwealth Criminal Code', *Journal of International Criminal Justice* 5: 809

Lacey, N. (1988) *State Punishment.* London: Routledge

Langer, M. (2004) 'From Legal Transplants to Legal Translations: The Globalization of Plea Bargaining and the Americanization Thesis in Criminal Procedure', *Harvard International Law Journal* 45: 1

Langer, M. (2005) 'The Rise of Managerial Judging in International Criminal Law', *The American Journal of International Law* 53: 835

Lederer, M. and Muller, P. (2005) (eds.) *Criticising Global Governance.* New York: Palgrave Macmillan

Levi, M. (1997) *Consent and Dissent in Patriotism.* Cambridge: Cambridge University Press

Lipscomb, R. (2006) 'Restructuring the ICC Framework to Advance Transitional Justice: A Search for a Permanent Solution in Sudan', *Columbia Law Review* 106: 182

Liu Institute for Global Issues and Gulu District NGO Forum (2005) 'Roco Wati Acoli: Restoring Relations in Acholi-land: Traditional Approaches to Reintegration and Justice', September http://www.ligi.ubc.ca/sites/liu/files/Publications/JRP/15Sept2005_Roco_Wat_I_Acoli.pdf

Logan, W. (2008) 'Confronting Evil: Victims' Rights in an Age of Terror', *Georgetown Law Journal* 96, 3: 721

Louw, D. J. (1998) 'Ubuntu: An African Assessment of the Religious Other'. Paper delivered at the 20th World Congress of Philosophy, Boston. http://www.bu.edu/wcp/Papers/Afri/AfriLouw.htm

Maher, G. (1988) 'The Verdict of the Jury'. In M. Findlay and P. Duff (eds.) *The Jury under Attack,* Sydney and London: Butterworths

Mallinder, L. (2006) 'Transforming International Criminal Justice – Review', *British Journal of Criminology* 46, 1: 155

Mansoor, F. Z. (2005) 'Reassessing Packer in the Light of International Human Rights Norms', *Connecticut Public International Law Journal* 4: 262

Mathiesen, T. (1990) *Prison on Trial.* London: Sage

McCorquodale, R. and Simons, P. (2007) 'Responsibility beyond Borders: State Responsibility for Extraterritorial Violations by Corporations of International Human Rights Law', *Modern Law Review* 70, 4: 598

McCoy, C. and Henham, R. (2002) 'Is the Trial Penalty Inevitable? Guilty Plea Discounts in American and British Courts'. Unpublished paper

Mekjian, G. J. and Varughese, M. C. (2005) 'Hearing the Victim's Voice: Analysis of Victims' Advocate Participation in the Trial Proceeding of the International Criminal Court', *Pace International Law Review* 17/1: 1

Michaelson, C. (2003) 'International Human Rights on Trial: The United Kingdom's and Australia's Response', *Sydney Law Review* 21, 3: 275

Milanovic, M. (2007) 'State Responsibility for Genocide: A Follow-Up', *European Journal of International Law* 18, 4: 669

Mills, A. and Stephens, T. (2005) 'Challenging the Role of Judges in Slaughter's Liberal Theory of International Law', *Leiden Journal of International Law* 18: 1

Naqvi, Y. (2006) 'The Right to the Truth in International Law: Fact or Fiction', *International Review of the Red Cross*, 88, 862: 245–73

Nelken, D. (ed.) (1997) *Comparing Legal Cultures.* Aldershot: Dartmouth

Nelken, D. and Feest, J. (eds.) (2001) *Adapting Legal Cultures.* Oxford: Hart

Norrie, A. (2000) *Punishment, Responsibility and Justice.* Oxford: Oxford University Press

Norrie, A. (2001) *Crime, Reason and History.* London: Butterworths

Norrie, A. (2009) 'Citizenship, Authoritarianism and the Changing Shape of the Criminal Law'. In B. McSherry, A. Norrie and S. Bronitt (eds.) *Regulating Deviance: The Redirection of Criminalisation and the Futures of the Criminal Law.* Oxford: Hart

Ocampo, L. M. (2006) 'Opening Remarks', *Fifth Session of the Assembly of State Parties.* Hague: ICC.

Ocampo, L. M. (2007) Address to the University of Sydney Law School, Sydney, Australia, 8 August

OECD (2000) *Guidelines for Multinational Enterprises.* http://www.oecd.org/document/28/0,3343,en_2649_34889_2397532_1_1_1_1,00.html

Ohlin, J. (2007) 'Three Conceptual Problems with the Doctrine of Joint Criminal Enterprise', Journal of International Criminal Justice 5: 69

O'Malley, P. (2006) 'Risk and Restorative Justice: Governing through the Democratic Minimization of Harms'. In I. Aertsen, T. Daems and L. Robert (eds.) *Institutionalising Restorative Justice.* Cullompton: Willan Publishing

Osiel, M. (2005) 'Modes of Participation in Mass Atrocity', *Cornell International Law Journal* 38: 793

Packer, H. (1968) *The Limits of the Criminal Sanction.* Stanford, CA: Stanford University Press

Pakes, F. (2004) *Comparative Criminal Justice.* Cullumpton: Willan Publishing

Parmentier, S. (2003) 'Global Justice in the Aftermath of Mass Violence: The Role of the International Criminal Court in Dealing with Political Crimes', *International Annals of Criminology* 41: 203

Pratt, J. (1998) 'Towards the 'Decivilizing of Punishment', *Social and Legal Studies* 7: 487

Rachlinski, J. (2007) 'A Positive Psychological Theory of Judging in Hindsight', *University of Chicago Law Review* 65: 571

Radzinowicz, L. (1966) *Ideology and Crime.* London: Heinemann

Ramsay, P. (2006) 'The Responsible Subject as Citizen: Criminal Law, Democracy and the Authoritarian State', *Modern Law Review* 64: 29

Raz, J. (1979) *The Authority of Law: Essays on Law and Morality.* Oxford: Oxford University Press

Roberts, J. V. and Roach, K. (2003) 'Restorative Justice in Canada: From Sentencing Circles to Sentencing Principles'. In A. von Hirsch et al. *Restorative Justice and Criminal Justice: Competing or Reconcilable Paradigms?* Oxford: Hart

Roberts, P. (2006) 'Theorising Procedural Traditions: Subjects, Objects and Values in Criminal Adjudication'. In A. Duff et al. *The Trial on Trial*, Vol. 2. Oxford: Hart

Robinson, D. (2003) 'Serving the Interests of Justice: Amnesties, Truth Commissions and the International Criminal Court', *European Journal of International Law* 14: 481

Roche, D. (2003) *Accountability in Restorative Justice.* Oxford: Oxford University Press

Roche, D. (2005) 'Truth Commission Amnesties and the International Criminal Court', *British Journal of Criminology* 45: 565

Rock, P. (2009) 'Hearing Victims of Crime: The Delivery of Impact Statements as Ritual Behaviour in London Trials for Murder and Manslaughter'. In A. E. Bottoms and J. Roberts (eds.) *Victims in the Criminal Justice System*. Cullompton: Willan Publishing

Rohne, H. C. (2003) *The Victims and Witnesses Section at the ICTY*. Freiburg: Max Planck Institute for Foreign and International Criminal Law

Rogers, L. J. and Erez, E. (1999) 'The Contextuality of Objectivity in Sentencing among Legal Professionals in South Australia', *International Journal of the Sociology of Law* 27: 267

Romano, C. (2002) 'Procedures for Establishment'. Paper presented at the Internationalised Criminal Courts and Tribunals: Practice and Prospects conference. Universiteit van Amsterdam, The Netherlands, 25–26 January

Schabas, W. (1997) 'Sentencing by the International Tribunals: For a Human Rights Approach', *Duke Journal of Comparative and International Law* 7: 461

Schabas, W. A. (2001) 'International Humanitarian Law: Catching the Accomplices', *International Review of the Red Cross* 83: 439

Schabas, W. A. (2007) *An Introduction to the International Criminal Court*. Cambridge: Cambridge University Press, 3rd edition

Schunemann, B. (1999) 'The Role of the Victim within the Criminal Justice System: A Three-tiered Concept', *Buffalo Law Journal* 3: 33

Seils, P. and Wierda, M. (2005) *The International Criminal Court and Conflict Mediation*. International Center for Transitional Justice, Occasional Paper Series, June

Sentencing Guidelines Council (2004) *Draft Guideline-1: Reduction in Sentence for a Guilty Plea*, London, August.

Shearing, C. (2003) 'Punishment and the Changing Face of Governance', *Punishment and Society* 3: 203

Sieber, U. (2003) *The Punishment of Serious Crimes: A Comparative Analysis of Sentencing Law and Practice*. Vol. 1: *Expert Report*; Vol. 2: *Country Reports*. Freiburg, Germany: Max Planck Institute for Foreign and International Criminal Law

Simon, J. (2007) *Governing through Crime: How the War on Crime Transformed American Democracy and Created a Culture of Fear*. New York: Oxford University Press

Spencer, J. R. (2002) 'Evidence'. In M. Delmas-Marty and J. R. Spencer (eds.) *European Criminal Procedures* Cambridge: Cambridge University Press

Stahn, C. (2005) 'Complementarity, Amnesties and Alternative Forms of Justice: Some Interpretative Guidelines for the International Criminal Court', *Journal of International Criminal Justice* 3: 695

Stahn, A., Olasolo, H. and Gibson, K. (2006) 'Participation of Victims in the Pre-trial Proceedings of the ICC', *Journal of International Criminal Justice* 4, 2: 219

Sudnow, D. (1965) 'Normal Crimes: Sociological Features of the Penal Code in a Public Defender Office', *Social Problems* 12: 255

Sweeting A., Owen, R., Turley, C. et al. (2008) *Evaluation of the Victims' Advocate Scheme Pilots*. Ministry of Justice Research Series 17/08 London: Ministry of Justice

'Symposium on the Guilty Plea (2004) Part I: Theoretical Background', *Journal of International Criminal Justice* 2: 1018

Tallgren, I. (2002) 'The Sensibility and Sense of International Criminal Law', *European Journal of International Law* 13: 561

Tamanaha, B. Z. (1979) *Realistic Socio-legal Theory: Pragmatism and a Social Theory of Law*, Oxford: Clarendon Press

Tamanaha, B. Z. (2007) 'Understanding Legal Pluralism: Past to Present, Local to Global', *Sydney Law Review* 29

Teitel, R. G. (2000) *Transitional Justice*. New York: Oxford University Press

Thomas, D. A. (1979) *Principles of Sentencing*. London: Heinemann, 2nd edition

Time Magazine (2009) 'Lebanon on Edge as Hariri Tribunal Starts', 1 March

Trankle, S. (2007) 'In the Shadow of Penal Law: Victim Offender Mediation in Germany and France', *Punishment and Society* 9: 395

Tschudi, F. (2008) 'Dealing with Violent Conflict and Mass Victimisation: A Human Dignity Approach'. In I. Aertsen, J. Arsovska, H. Rohne, M. Valinas and K. Vanspauwen (eds.) *Restoring Justice after Large Scale Violent Conflicts*. Cullompton: Willan Publishing

Tulkens, F. (2002) 'Negotiated Justice'. In M. Delmas-Marty and J. Spencer (eds.) *European Criminal Procedures*. Cambridge: Cambridge University Press

Twining, W. (1992) *Evidence and Proof*. Aldershot: Dartmouth

Twining, W. (2005) *Rethinking Evidence: Exploratory Essays*. London: Butterworths

Tyler, T. T. (ed.) (2008) *Legitimacy and Criminal Justice*. New York: Russell Sage Foundation

van Zyl Smit, D. (2002) 'Punishment and Human Rights in International Criminal Justice'. Inaugural lecture as Professor of Comparative and Penal Law, University of Nottingham, 30 January

Vogler, R. (2005) *A World View of Criminal Justice*. Aldershot: Ashgate

Vogler, R. (forthcoming) 'Making International Criminal Procedure Work: From Theory to Practice'. In M. Findlay and R. Henham (eds.) *Exploring the Boundaries of International Criminal Justice*. Aldershot: Ashgate

von Hirsch, A. and Ashworth, A. (2005) *Proportionate Sentencing: Exploring the Principles*. Oxford: Oxford University Press

von Hirsch, A., Ashworth, A. and Shearing, C. (2003) 'Specifying Aims and Limits for Restorative Justice; A "Making Amends" Model?' In A. von Hirsch et al. (eds.) *Restorative Justice and Criminal Justice: Competing or Reconcilable Paradigms?* Oxford: Hart

Wald, P. M. (2003) 'General Radislav Krstic: A War Crimes Case Study', *Georgetown Journal of Legal Ethics* 16: 445

Weitekamp, G., Parmentier, S., Vanspauwen, K., Valinas, M. and Gerits, R. (2006) 'How to Deal with Mass Victimisation and Gross Human Rights Violations: A Restorative Justice Approach', in Uwe Ewald and Ksenija Turkovic (eds.) *Security in Post-Conflict Societies*. Nato Security through Science series. Amsterdam: IOS Press, vol. 13: 217–41.

Wilson, R. A. (2001) *The Politics of Truth and Reconciliation in South Africa: Legitimizing the Post-Apartheid State*. Cambridge: Cambridge University Press

Wilson, R. (2009) 'A Long, Strange Trip: Guantanamo and the Scarcity of International Law'

http://hq.ssrn.com/Journals/RedirectClick.cfm?url=http://papers.ssrn.com/sol3/cf_dev/AbsByAuth.cfm?per_id=29638&partid=258190&did=44041&eid=60369212>

Zahar, A. and Sluiter, G. (2007) *International Criminal Law: A Critical Restatement*, Oxford: Oxford University Press

Zappala, S. (2003) *Human Rights in International Criminal Proceedings*. Oxford: Oxford University Press

Zedner, L. (1994) 'Reparation and Retribution: Are they Reconcilable?' *Modern Law Review* 57: 226

Zedner, L. and Hoyle, C. (2007) 'Victims, Victimization, and the Criminal Process'. In M. Maguire, R. Morgan and R. Reiner (eds.), *The Oxford Handbook of Criminology*. Oxford: Oxford University Press

Author Index

Subject Index